Here Comes the Night

JOEL SELVIN

Here Comes the Night

THE DARK SOUL OF **BERT BERNS** AND THE DIRTY BUSINESS OF **RHYTHM & BLUES**

COUNTERPOINT

BERKELEY

Library of Congress Cataloging-in-Publication Data

Selvin, Joel.
 Here Comes The Night : the dark soul of Bert Berns and the dirty business of rhythm & blues / Joel Selvin.
    pages cm
 ISBN 978-1-61902-302-4
1. Berns, Bert. 2. Sound recording executives and producers--United States--Biography. 3. Rhythm and blues music--New York (State)--New York--History and criticism. I. Title.

 ML429.B357S45 2014
 782.421643092--dc23
 [B]

2013043961

ISBN 978-1-61902-302-4

Cover design by Jeff Miller, Faceout Studios
Interior Design by meganjonesdesign.com

Photo Credits: Getty Images; 24, 40, 80, 134, 338, 422, William "PoPsie" Randolph; title page, 274.,Broadcast Music Inc.; 154, 196, 226.,Carmine DeNoia; 318., Author; 117. George Schowerer; 174. All others courtesy the Berns family.

COUNTERPOINT
1919 Fifth Street
Berkeley, CA 94710
www.counterpointpress.com

Printed in the United States of America
Distributed by Publishers Group West

10 9 8 7 6 5 4 3 2 1

contents

To Brett and Cassie
You made it possible

Bert Berns (center) with Jerry Wexler, Tom Dowd

Starring
Bert Berns—songwriter, record producer, Bang Records
Ahmet Ertegun, Jerry Wexler—Atlantic Records
Jerry Leiber, Mike Stoller—songwriters, record producers, Red Bird Records
Jeff Barry, Ellie Greenwich—songwriters, record producers

The Producers
George Goldner—record producer, Red Bird Records
Phil Spector—record producer, Philles Records
Luther Dixon—songwriter, record producer, Scepter Records
Jerry Ragovoy—songwriter, record producer

The Songwriters
Burt Bacharach—songwriter
Carole King, Gerry Goffin—songwriters
Doc Pomus, Mort Shuman—songwriters
Bob Feldman, Richard Gottehrer, Jerry Goldstein—songwriters
Wes Farrell—songwriter

Music Publishers
Don Kirshner—music publisher, Aldon Music
Jean and Julian Aberbach, music publishers, Hill & Range Music
Bobby Mellin—music publisher, Mellin Music

The Engineers
Tom Dowd—Engineer
Brooks Arthur—Engineer
Phil Ramone—Engineer

Label Owners
Morris Levy—Roulette Records
Florence Greenberg—Scepter Records

With
Carmine De Noia ("Wassel")—artist manager
Tommy Eboli—acting capo, Genovese family
Patsy Pagano—union official, Genovese family
Sonny Franzese—Colombo family

And Musical Appearances by
Van Morrison
Neil Diamond
Solomon Burke
Freddie Scott
The Drifters
The Beatles
And many more . . .

Berns with the Goya guitar at his penthouse

INTRODUCTION

B ERT BERNS WAS one of the great originals of the golden age of rhythm and blues. He prospered and thrived under the auspices of Atlantic Records, a company devoted to authentic, vibrantly musical rhythm and blues records at the forefront of the art form. Under the beneficent encouragement of Atlantic's Jerry Wexler, Berns developed into one of the leading record men of his day. His records with Solomon Burke established Burke as one of the most formidable figures of the rhythm and blues world, shoulder to shoulder with peers such as Sam Cooke, James Brown, Jackie Wilson, and Ray Charles. He brought the heart of the mambo into rock and roll—not the supple Brazilian samba rhythms found in records by Jerry Leiber and Mike Stoller or Burt Bacharach, but fiery Afro-Cuban incantations that pulsed with sex and sin. Almost alone among his contemporaries on the New York scene, Berns traveled to England as his song "Twist and Shout" rose as an anthem to a new generation of British musicians, where he made key records in the country's pop transformation. As he devoted more time to running his own record label, Bang Records, Berns started the careers of future giants Van Morrison and Neil Diamond.

All the time Berns was making records, he was in a hurry. After falling ill with rheumatic fever as a teenager, Berns was told he wouldn't live to see twenty-one. He didn't even start in the record business until he was thirty-one years old, and once he started, success couldn't come quick enough for him. He devoured his career. He vaulted from the ranks of the amateur into the highest realms of the music world in less than two years, and his ambition never flagged. The ever-present damaged heart drove him relentlessly, as it filled his waking hours with the terror of death, fears he masked with a carefree, happy-go-lucky façade. *Tick . . . tick . . . tick.* Only a few intimates knew that Berns was standing on a trapdoor. It leaked into his songwriting. Other writers could employ the songwriting clichés around hearts without irony, but for Berns, these similes and metaphors were his life. The cries by his singers came from deep within Berns. He was a man with a bum ticker and he carried his doom like a cloak around his shoulders. For Berns to write *take it . . . take another little piece of my heart* was a plea straight from his life. When his own dark tragedy combined with the pathos of his music, his life took on epic dimensions.

At the end of his life, as the stakes rose sharply and events spiraled out of his control, Berns associated with big-time operators in organized crime, both personally and professionally. It caused a fissure in his world, but Berns was comfortable with these men and what they represented. He was a man who needed to take shortcuts. Threatened by a fatal catastrophe, surrounded by a world where moral boundaries blurred easily, Berns broke some eggs making omelets. In the end, his inflexible fate collided with his greatest aspirations and their frustration, a cataclysmic denouement of almost operatic grandeur.

As long ago as 1976, Ben Fong-Torres in *Rolling Stone* called Berns "one of the great untold stories of rock and roll," but there are a number of reasons why the story of Bert Berns has never been told before.

The performers rather than the creators of this music have been traditionally celebrated. Berns died more than forty years ago and never hired a press agent. Also he made powerful enemies during his lifetime who worked hard to erase his memory and diminish his accomplishments. When I first called Jerry Wexler, the man everybody most associates with Berns's career, and told him I planned to work on this book, Wexler's affable tone disappeared. "I'll tell you this," he said. "I don't know where he's buried, but if I did, I would piss on his grave."

On the other hand, when I told Wexler some time later that I had completed some initial chapters, he asked to read them and phoned back almost immediately. "Mesmerizing," he said. That didn't mean he changed his mind about helping with the book. "Hell, no," he said. His own recollection of Berns captured in his published memoirs appears to have been largely cribbed from Charlie Gillett's book on Atlantic Records, *Making Tracks*.

The first time I asked him about Berns some twenty years earlier—when I first wrote a small article about Berns in the "Records" page of the *San Francisco Chronicle*, about the same time Ben Fong-Torres wondered in *Rolling Stone* about the story—he felt more sentimental. "He was my son," Wexler said.

In 1960, Berns entered an enchanted village inhabited by a tribe of crazy geniuses. They made records and had no idea they were developing an entire school of art. They worked alongside each other. They collaborated. They competed. They copied each other. They stole from one another. They ate and drank together and used the same arrangers and musicians on their records, which they made at the same studios. They kept offices in the same buildings and rode the elevators together.

Almost the entire music business at the time was housed in two Midtown Manhattan office buildings. The Brill Building contained the established music business dating back to the swing era. Dozens of publishers, songwriters, and assorted ancillaries to the bustling music business kept offices there, from Duke Ellington to Johnny Marks, the Jewish Christmas song specialist who wrote "Rudolph, the Red-Nosed Reindeer." Two blocks away, busy warrens in 1650 Broadway teemed with scrappy comers who were practicing the dark arts of rock and roll, would-be usurpers with their eyes on big bucks and the hit parade. The two spheres blended into one seamy mass as rock and roll took over the charts and Berns stepped on the scene.

The story of Bert Berns lies buried under layers of history. Much of his music has gone unheard since its original release. Many of the details of the process have been lost to time. The participants themselves have difficulty recalling long-ago events that did not seem noteworthy to them at the time. "It's like trying to remember wallpaper you hung forty years ago," said Artie Butler, the arranger who made so many of these great records.

The rhythm and blues world in New York was a small pond full of big fish—"We were all characters," said Morris Levy of Roulette Records—and the life and work of Bert Berns was intricately entwined in the inner workings of that little village. Along with Leiber and Stoller, Atlantic Records, Burt Bacharach, Hill & Range, George Goldner, and all the others, Berns made music history.

In a few short years, a handful of hustlers and obsessed visionaries watched the music they made move from tiny dark corners of society into the full glare of the mainstream pop arena, a staggering shift in the culture fed by converging forces of history. It was the richest gold strike in music business history, and the men who made it happen were tough, unscrupulous bastards who made up the rules as they went along.

In the end, Berns's career almost perfectly encapsulated the height of the New York independent record scene and the fierce world of rhythm and blues. He walked onstage in those days after the emergence of rock and roll where the New York music business utterly dominated the pop music universe. When he died seven turbulent years later, the day was done. Corporations were buying up the last independents standing. New songwriters and new songs stocked the hit parade. The pop music world had turned a page.

These songwriters wrote all these songs expecting them to go up the charts, down the charts, and never be heard again. Shakespeare probably felt the same way. But their music never disappeared. It was embedded in the sounds of the Beatles and the Rolling Stones and all who came after. These songs became the new standards, publishing bonanzas that turned out to pay dividends long after the initial recordings' lives on the charts ended. That was never part of the original grift.

Berns wasn't the greatest of the era, although his best work was as good as anybody's. But his unique voice as a songwriter, producer, and record man is so deeply ingrained in the vocabulary of pop music it has become common parlance. Songs of his such as "Twist and Shout," "My Girl Sloopy," or "Piece of My Heart" have been covered, quoted, cannibalized, used as salvage parts, and recycled so many times, his touch has just dissolved into the literature. His name may be lost, but his music is everywhere.

Like Burt Bacharach and Phil Spector, Berns was a disciple of Leiber and Stoller. They all studied at the feet of the masters. Bacharach turned Leiber and Stoller's *baion* rhythms into gorgeous, baroque pop. He brought to the rhythm and blues world an uncommon and unexpected continental touch of high-art chamber pop he knew firsthand from conducting Marlene Dietrich's cabaret act in all the European capitals.

Spector matched the majesty of Leiber and Stoller's symphonic rhythm and blues with cacophonous mulch he borrowed from producer Frank Guida of Norfolk, Virginia, where Guida presided over clattering, blurry, throbbing productions on records by Gary "U.S." Bonds and others he released on his own Legrand Records. Guida was an authentic barbaric primitive, and Spector took the basic Leiber and Stoller blueprint and filtered it through that gauzy sensibility to create a truly thunderous sound on his productions with the Crystals, the Ronettes, and other Philles Records acts.

Berns specialized in three-minute r&b grand operas, all emotional drama and gospel fury, always with Arsenio Rodriguez's *ritmo diablo* insinuating itself between the lines. He transformed the Leiber and Stoller archetypes into yet another deeply personal scenario.

Drawing from the same rich talent pool of songwriters, arrangers, session musicians, engineers, and artists, these men made almost entirely different records with the same resources. Berns was the funky one, the street cat, the producer who spoke the musicians' language. He was not a schooled musician like Bacharach, but he could read and write music. He played piano well enough to get his point across and could wring a galloping, signature sound out of his nylon-stringed guitar that stitches its way through a number of his productions, Berns working both sides of the glass.

Like most of his contemporaries, Berns depended on arrangers such as Garry Sherman or Teacho Wiltshire to pencil out his vision, but his records with the same arrangers and sidemen sound distinctly like Bert Berns records and bear little relation to work by the same people with other producers. During his first year in the record business, Berns fumbled around for his voice, but once he cemented his spiritual link to the mambo and rhythm and blues, he instinctively grew into an auteur, an artist who used personal themes to fashion universal messages.

Berns made fifty-one pop chart singles in seven years; nineteen in 1964, his first year as Atlantic Records staff producer, the same year the Beatles and other British rock acts swept America. He made a lot of records that didn't hit the pop charts but sold r&b, almost took off regionally, bubbled under, and otherwise showed signs of life not indicated by the pop charts. He did records that never charted with important artists such as Tammy Montgomery, Wilson Pickett, and Patti LaBelle and the Bluebelles that rank among the best of their careers. He wrote or cowrote almost everything he recorded.

Berns worked with every major figure in his field at the time. He was closest to Wexler, but Atlantic founding partner Ahmet Ertegun also encouraged Berns. He wrote songs with Leiber and Stoller, one of the few outsiders the pair ever admitted to their songwriting circle. Burt Bacharach and Berns shared two sides of a crucial Gene Pitney single early in their careers, and Berns later reworked Bacharach productions with session vocalist Jimmy Radcliffe. Bacharach could be seen playing the piano at parties at Berns's penthouse. Berns and Luther Dixon, one of the vastly underrated producers of the era, created "Twist and Shout" by the Isley Brothers. Phil Spector not only produced the previous, little-known first version of Berns's most famous song but also produced Berns himself as a vocalist named Russell Byrd.

With the great Aldon Music songwriting teams—Barry Mann and Cynthia Weil, Carole King and Gerry Goffin—Berns cut important records on their songs. Carole King does not recall meeting Berns—she well remembers his work—but she arranged and played piano on a hit single Berns sang, so they worked in the studio together. Jeff Barry and Ellie Greenwich were not only close friends with Berns, and pitched in making records on many of his sessions, but they also brought him their discovery, Neil Diamond, for Berns's record label.

His touch suffused all his collaborations. His enthusiasm could not be contained. He was never a passive cowriter. Even on songs substantially written by Berns's cowriter Jerry Ragovoy, Berns stamped his hallmarks all over the numbers, preserving at the same time Ragovoy's voice—funky little touches like the "C'mon, c'mon, c'mon" part in Garnet Mimms's "Cry Baby."

Unlike other characters on the scene, Berns could also write songs by himself. Some of his collaborators, in fact, almost appear invisible in the final mix, as if they served as little more than sounding boards Berns rewarded with half the copyright.

He kept at the ready a collection of musical phrases, chord changes, and lyric ideas that he switched around willfully, shamelessly, resorting to familiar motifs that he could often open up in surprising and powerful new ways. He took an almost incidental guitar lick from a record he did with r&b vocalist Marv Johnson and turned it into the dramatic, glistening guitar part that anchors his record with British rock group Them, "Here Comes the Night," played by twenty-year-old British session musician Jimmy Page. He rewrote the chord changes to "La Bamba" and the unofficial Cuban anthem, "Guantanamera," over and over again, coming up with remarkably fresh approaches to the same basic song structure.

His songs entered the literature even during his lifetime. "Twist and Shout" reverberated around the world. His "My Girl Sloopy," recast as "Hang On Sloopy," was a number one hit in 1965 by the McCoys on his Bang Records, in addition to more than fifteen other versions recorded the same year. Janis Joplin did "Piece of My Heart" with Big Brother and the Holding Company less than a year after Berns made the Erma Franklin original. The British Invasion groups all cut Berns songs—Beatles, Rolling Stones, Animals, Yardbirds, many others. When guitarist Jimmy Page recorded the debut album with his new band, the one track the group didn't release from the sessions was a cover of Berns's "Baby Come On Home," which went by the working title "Tribute to Bert Berns" during those first Led Zeppelin sessions. Although they never met, John Lennon knew who Bert Berns was.

The career of Bert Berns played a huge part in the story of Atlantic Records, the landmark label that pioneered the spread of rhythm and blues. His critical role is largely missing from accounts of the company's illustrious history, at least in part, because of who was left to tell the story. History belongs to those who write it, and Atlantic partners Ertegun and Wexler spent many years buffing their reputations, painting a picture of their contributions often at odds with the facts. Their appealing personal styles and undeniable feeling for the music allowed then to operate with impunity in the relative moral universe of the rhythm and blues world. "They were a better class of thieves," said Ben E. King fondly.

Virtually alone among the independent rhythm and blues record labels, Atlantic managed the transition into the corporate era of the record industry. How the label survived may be more a matter of hustle and pluck than vision and strategy, but it is also true that once the company was sold and folded into a corporate conglomerate, Atlantic ceased to be a force in the culture. However, the company's legacy is a rich vein of American music, a multitude of voices, songs, and records that shaped music around the world.

Songwriter Ellie Greenwich laughed at the idea that they wrote about their own lives. "We wouldn't do that," she said. These song-writers were not self-conscious artists exploring their inner lives. They operated under an industrial mandate. Their music's appeal was designed to sell records; any self-serving "artistic" motives were point-less. Under such strictures, however, these men and women made magnificent music, these glorious records, filled with imagination, wonder and beauty.

Of course, artists have no other experience to draw from but their own and inevitably even songwriters and producers operating within the most commercial parameters will reflect on their own lives. Themes emerge over the course of a body of work. While lyricist Jerry Leiber etched brainy, smart-aleck social commentaries and Gerry Goffin con-tinually returned to dreamy aspirations and wish fulfillment, Berns kept reaching for tears. He wanted his singers crying. He pushed vocal-ists on his records to the brink, trapped in desperation and fraught with urgency. Why all the tears? Jeff Barry said that if he kept coming back to it, it probably was something more than a professional decision.

ELLIE GREENWICH MAY have allowed herself the luxury of distancing herself emotionally from the teen dramas she and her husband Jeff Barry created, such as "Leader of the Pack" or "Chapel of Love," but Berns couldn't. His looming mortality magnified every event, every song, every week's chart positions. This wasn't just music to Berns. This wasn't some high-stakes con game for the hip, witty, and clever. This was life and death to Berns. To write his desperate songs, to make these singers sing the songs the way he needed them to be sung, to con-struct these gothic records as temples of sound, to reach deep into his mad Russian heart and wrench loose the pain and fear, Berns peered into his own dark soul for his music. Every song took another piece of his heart.

Berns in the Bronx

I.

Bronx [1950] + Havana [1958]

S ID BERNSTEIN MANAGED the Tremont Terrace, a mambo parlor about ten blocks from where he lived, while he went to Columbia, hoping to be a writer. The club was housed in a former Con Ed regional office in the Bronx and owned by a middle-aged couple who made a living renting it out for weddings, bar mitzvahs, any catered event. Bernstein started out publicizing their Friday night dances at twenty-five dollars a week. With the South Bronx becoming home to a substantial Puerto Rican population and the growing interest in Latin music around town in 1949, Bernstein and his employers decided to change the name of the place to the Trocadero and began presenting a series of Latin dances.

But it wasn't only Puerto Ricans with their long-limbed elegant ladies who attended. Mambo fever shot through the town that year and the catering hall was thronged with blacks from Uptown and Jews from the Bronx, a rare, almost unprecedented microcosm of the city's melting pot in a nightclub. One night Bernstein saw a young man dancing the mambo who he thought must be a movie star. The lithe young fellow not only danced with a remarkable fluid grace but also dressed beautifully. Bernstein stopped working to watch him dance. He started to notice the handsome, attractive dancer returning night after night and was eventually introduced to him by a fellow patron.

He had a wiry, coiled body and a practiced waterfall curl that landed perfectly in the middle of his forehead. His parents owned a prosperous dress shop on the Grand Concourse in Fordham, the most affluent end of the Bronx, and they dressed him well. His name was Bert Berns.

He was twenty years old, but he still played stickball in the streets. He didn't go to school and he didn't have a job, but he nursed vague show business ambitions. Bernstein was immediately taken with this amiable hustler. They became best of friends. They double-dated. They cruised out to Coney Island for hot dogs in the car Berns borrowed from his mother. He dazzled Bernstein playing the piano. Bernstein was even more impressed to learn that the strong, supple melodies Berns was playing he had also written. The two of them shared an eager enthusiasm for Latin music, enthralled to be working even the peripheries of this blossoming scene.

Like many young Jews in New York, Berns was smitten with the mambo. The Latin beat had only recently exploded on the New York nightlife scene, spreading out since Machito and his Afro-Cubans started playing downtown three years earlier in 1946. Cuban émigré Frank Grillo—Machito—and his brother-in-law Mario Bauza, the band's arranger who had roomed with Dizzy Gillespie during their tenure in the brass section of the Cab Calloway Orchestra, introduced their trademark blend of Latin jazz to New York in 1940.

Bauza left Calloway, and he and his brother-in-law, who had become a regulation *rumbalero* singing with Xavier Cugat and Noro Morales, among others, finally started the band they had long been planning. Machito and his Afro-Cubans were ground zero of the Latin jazz movement in the United States. Pulling together the cream of Cuban musicians living in New York, they erected their dream orchestra that combined the daring sweep of big band jazz with the fire of Cuban rhythms. The band made its debut December 1940 at the Park Palace, a dance hall uptown in Spanish Harlem.

While Machito served out his military duty during the war, Bauza imported Machito's foster sister, Graciela Perez, from Cuba to sing with the band. After the war, the group became the center of a gathering storm of Afro-Cuban music in New York. In 1946, Machito's orchestra made its first appearance downtown at the Manhattan Center around the same time the Alma Dance Studio at the corner of Fifty-Third Street and Broadway in Midtown started a weekly Latin night that would become headquarters to the rapidly growing scene once the hall changed its name to the Palladium Ballroom.

The bebop revolt was in full bloom on the New York nightlife circuit, and young Turk jazzmen like Charlie Parker, Dexter Gordon, and others flocked to the rhythmic riches of Machito's bandstand, jamming with the orchestra or using the band on recording dates. Pundits called the resulting hybrid Cubop. Bandleader Stan Kenton borrowed Machito's Cuban percussion section to record his version of "The Peanut Vendor," the song that introduced Cuban music to America sixteen years before, and the two bands played a signal double bill downtown at Town Hall in 1947.

Gillespie had formed his own big band, and his friend Bauza introduced him to *conguero* Chano Pozo, a wild-eyed, dark-skinned Afro-Cuban who brought Latin rhythms to the world of jazz. Pozo was killed the following year in 1948—shot in a fight with a drug dealer who sold him some bad dope, believing Yoruban spirits would protect him from the bullets—but he left an indelible imprint on the rhythmic blueprint of jazz.

The Palladium Ballroom was the hip place to be. Jazz musicians like Dizzy Gillespie and George Shearing hung out at the club, around the corner from the busy Fifty-Second Street jazz clubs, and a modern, young white crowd packed the dance floor, drinking in the tropical rhythms and carefree, sensual atmosphere. Marlon Brando, a struggling actor at the time, attended frequently. The Latins in the crowd used to refer to the abundant Jewish girls on the scene as "Bagel Babies." Like

the rock and roll music that emerged a few years later from the subterranean depths of urban black music, this ethnic exotica offered a colorful, pulse-quickening alternative to the soporific sounds of the day's
puerile, lily-white hit parade. Compared to prevalent pseudo-operatic
pop such as Vaughn Monroe's "Ghost Riders in the Sky," this music
smoldered with open sensuality, not to mention the wanton forbidden
thrill of the mixing of races, heady stuff for knowing youth in a country
just waking from its postwar stupor.

Two other key Latin bandleaders also emerged. Tito Puente, the
brilliant young timbales master who played briefly with Machito before
entering the navy during the war, attended Juilliard School of Music
on the G.I. Bill after the service and joined the prominent band led by
former Xavier Cugat sideman Cuban pianist Jose Curbelo. In 1947, he
left Curbelo and started his own *conjunto*, the Piccadilly Boys. The following year, his recording of "Abaniquito" became one of the first hits
of the new New York mambo record label, Tico Records.

Also recording for Tico was the Mambo Devils, another new
mambo band put together by bongo player and vocalist Tito Rodriguez,
who spent five years with the great Noro Morales before playing alongside Puente in Curbelo's group. Rodriguez had Latin lover matinee idol
good looks and a warm way with a romantic ballad. His band brought
together some of the top Latin players in town and was soon a regular
attraction, almost the house band, at the weekly Palladium dances.

The founder of Tico Records, a handsome young Jew from Queens
named George Goldner, was one of the regular dancers at the Palladium,
a mambo-mad children's clothing salesman from the Garment District
in a lucky suede hat. Goldner would also become a central figure in
the emergence of rock and roll and the entire independent record business. Goldner spoke Spanish, danced a fabulous mambo, and married
a saucy Latin American girl. He was such a prominent fixture on the
scene that musicians started to come to him for business advice and
he knew them all. He borrowed money from his parents and took a

bath presenting mambo dances in Newark, New Jersey, a province the Latin music craze hadn't yet reached. Still, he was convinced by the manager of the big Broadway record retailer, Colony Records, to start a mambo label. He borrowed more money from friends in the Garment District and, at age twenty-nine, launched Tico Records in 1949, a label that proved to be crucial in the spreading of the mambo in America. Goldner busily began to record all the emerging titans in the field, starting with Puente and Rodriguez.

The fifties was a renaissance age of Afro-Cuban music. New York's thriving market for the music echoed the exciting, exuberant sounds coming from Havana, a destination Caribbean gambling resort and tourist trap whose rich, decadent nightlife throbbed to a tropical beat, drawn from the island's wealth of musical folklore.

Perez Prado was a young Cuban arranger and pianist with the Havana musical institution Casino de la Playa Orchestra in 1943 when he first cautiously tried incorporating mambo rhythms into his music. It was not especially well received. He was somewhat more successful on his first road trip, playing Buenos Aires in 1947. But when he hit Mexico City the following year, the town went mambo mad. Signed to RCA Victor International, Prado relocated to Mexico City and began recording. He cut "Que Rico el Mambo" in December 1949, and, rushed to the market before Christmas, the record was an instant smash. All through Latin America, the demand for Prado records went through the roof. He released more than twenty-five singles the next year.

Prado was all shimmering brass, blasting trumpets, belching trombones, groaning saxophones, carefully layered against the tangy Cuban rhythms. There were no improvisational sections for soloists. Prado formalized the mambo, giving the rough edges a glossy sheen. He was a gaudy vulgarian who framed the sensuous essence of the mambo with a glamorous, even somewhat baroque, setting. His mambo-for-the-masses may not have earned Prado respect in the more sanctimonious quarters of the Broadway Latin jazz crowd, but he was definitely the king of the mambo.

He played the part. Prado was quite the showman. Conducting his band with a baton, often wearing gold lamé tails and jeweled gloves, he would dance, clown, do midair leg kicks. There was no jazz in his shows. The goateed Prado would punctuate passages with his peculiar signature dog bark—the indecipherable exhortation "*Dilo!*" or "Say it!"

His success did not come so quickly in the United States. He took only his maracas player and vocalist with him to California in 1951. Armed with a book full of complicated charts, Prado threw a band together in Los Angeles, including a few players who worked with his hero, Stan Kenton, such as key trumpeter Pete Candoli, master of those piercing high notes. He rehearsed their asses off for three days and did a string of dates on the West Coast that knocked everybody dead. He drew a sold-out crowd of twenty-five hundred to Los Angeles' Zenda Ballroom and thirty-five hundred a week later at Sweet's Ballroom in Oakland. His Waldorf Astoria Starlight Room engagement may not have been so successful, but New York jazz snobs always wrote off Prado as not authentic. But Prado was the man who took the mambo worldwide and, in 1955, to number one on the American charts with "Cherry Pink and Apple Blossom White." A cornerstone of cotillion dances for the next generation, the million-selling song was actually recorded as the theme song to a latter-era Jane Russell movie called *Underwater!* And on the record label, it said clearly—"Mambo."

Mambo had entered the pop lexicon. Perry Como sang "Papa Loves Mambo." Vaughn Monroe did "They Were Doin' the Mambo." Rosemary Clooney went so far as to try "Mambo Italiano." Rhythm and blues records capitalized on the mambo craze, too. Ruth Brown recorded "Mambo Baby" for Ahmet Ertegun's fledgling Atlantic Records, and on the West Coast, a pair of young white r&b songwriters, Jerry Leiber and Mike Stoller, outfitted their vocal group the Robins with "Loop de Loop Mambo." Even television's favorite couple included real-life

Cuban bandleader Desi Arnaz, who first clicked in 1946 with "Babalu." He played, well, a Cuban bandleader with his real-life wife Lucille Ball on the TV comedy *I Love Lucy*.

Arsenio Rodriguez, the great blind Cuban musician who invented the mambo in 1939—he called it *ritmo diablo*, the devil's rhythm—himself first turned up in New York in 1947, drawn by word of a miracle operation that could restore his sight. It took the doctor an examination no longer than five minutes to tell the thirty-six-year-old Cuban bandleader that he would never see again. His optical nerves were damaged beyond repair. Later that day, after a short nap, Rodriguez summoned his brother to write down the words of a song that came to him in his sleep, and the remarkable man dictated the lyrics to his classic "La Vida Es un Sueno (Life Is but a Dream)." He may not have gotten his sight back, but he did get his first taste of this rather amazing Cuban music scene growing in America and he returned to settle in New York in 1953.

In the early fifties, the major labels basically ignored the mambo craze. The records didn't sell in large numbers and the phenomenon appeared limited to the five New York City boroughs. That left the field open to small-time hustlers and innocent enthusiasts like George Goldner. At the Tremont Terrace, Sid Bernstein was booking all the working Latin bands into the former Con Edison building with the little balcony and the bustling kitchen in the heart of the Bronx—Machito, Puente, Rodriguez.

When Bernstein brought in rumba king Noro Morales, he met the bandleader's younger brother, Esy Morales, who was playing flute in his brother's band. Esy Morales had scored a hit, "Jungle Fantasy," the year before in 1949 in a Hollywood movie and Bernstein was surprised to find him working in his brother's outfit. Within days, he clinched a deal to manage Esy Morales, and his friend Bert Berns talked Bernstein into going into the record business. They called their company Magic Records. No kidding. It may not have been much, but they were in the record business.

Berns found a girl singer fresh out of Taft High School in the West Bronx named Edith Gormezano who called herself Eydie Gorme. She was working as a Spanish interpreter for a theatrical supply export company during the day and taking classes in the evening at City College in foreign trade and economics. In high school, she had been the featured vocalist of the school band and star of many school musicals, but she was not planning on a career in show business. She started working on weekends in a band led by former City College classmate Ken Greenglass, a trumpeter who also acted as her manager. Berns took Bernstein to a ballroom near his home in Fordham to hear the pretty young girl singer. Bernstein agreed she had talent and looks.

They each put up $700 and set up a session. Berns knew a drummer named Herb Wasserman who wrote songs, and he supplied a pair of novelty numbers. "M & X" made "Mairzy Doats" sound like Cole Porter. The chorus was a garbled, nonsense run at "If you have any ham"—"F-U-N-E-M"—to which the answer went "O-S-I-F-S-M"—"Oh, yes, I have some ham" . . . "F-U-N-E-X O-S-I-F-S-X." Ham and eggs. M & X. They paired their girl singer, Eydie Gorme, with a big band singer born Manny Levin who went by the gentile-sounding name Bob Manning. They hired a band led by Les Elgart, a trumpeter who had knocked around the big band scene before forming his own dance band only a few years earlier. Bernstein also brought in Esy Morales on the same session to record "African Voodoo," a vague remake of his hit from the previous year.

They took an office downtown in 1650 Broadway, a Theater District office building filled with fly-by-night music publishers and record labels, pressed up a few hundred copies of both records, and waited for the money to come rolling in. Berns wrote and copyrighted a batch of songs for their music publishing division, Magic Music, with titles like cheap paperback novels: "Kiss of Love," "Roulette Wheel," "Then It's Goodbye to You," and "High Heels Clicking on a Lonely Street." The songs he wrote were never recorded. The records they released disappeared without a trace. Berns and Bernstein quietly folded their tent and slipped back into the Bronx. Within months, both were out of show business. Bernstein had left the club business to manage Esy Morales full-time, only to have Morales, a diabetic who didn't take care of himself, keel over dead from a drug-related heart attack at age thirty-four a few months later in 1950. Berns also needed to find a new scheme, but it would be many years before anything turned up.

THE WINTER OF 1957 in Cuba had a fairy-tale quality. Meyer Lansky opened his Hotel Riviera in December 1957, a glittering twenty-one-story, 440-room edifice rising up by the sea from the Malecón, decorated in turquoise mosaic. Rooms at the Riviera were booked solid into the next year. The money rolled in. Big shots who thought nothing of writing a check for $30,000 or $40,000 at the end of an evening gambled in the formal elegance of Lansky's casino. Tourists flooded Havana. The town was crawling with sharpies looking for a piece of the action.

The sandy beaches looked like snow, and the ocean and the sky were both so much the same deep blue, you couldn't tell where one ended and the other began. It was a city of promise, allure, cheap come-ons, and fast grifts. It was a city with its skirts raised. The trade winds blew riffraff and high rollers alike into town. The casinos brought the wiseguys and showfolks, the musicians and the dancers, the boozers and the dreamers, the chiselers and the schemers. It may have been Cuba, but Broadway types packed the cafes and strolled the sidewalks of the Prado in the long hours of the afternoon. People who knew each other from Manhattan would run into each other on the streets of Havana and think nothing of it. To a select crowd, Havana was like an extension of New York. They crowded around over mojitos at El Floridita, where Hemingway drank. The place was lousy with the same cheap hustlers and con artists you could find anytime on Fifty-Second Street. Havana was their kind of town.

Everywhere in Havana there was music. Under the balmy skies of this Paris of the Caribbean, life was good. And everywhere there was the mambo, sophisticated languor that just hung in the air, a vital pulse to this sinful city. Since Meyer Lansky opened his new hotel, with Ginger Rogers christening the Copa Room, there had been plenty of work in town with a cast of thousands playing lounges and shows all over the place. The casino flew in Hollywood sorts by planeloads for the opening. Alfred Hitchcock and Bill Holden could be seen playing roulette in the egg-shaped Gold Leaf Casino. Lansky didn't care much for Ginger Rogers's act. "She can wiggle her ass," he said, "but she can't sing a goddamned note."

The casinos operated on the shady side. The boys in Havana knew they were dealing with suckers, not real gamblers. They maintained a speedy check-cashing routine worked out where they would fly checks overnight to Inter-American Check Service Inc. in Miami, who worked to secure the transfer of funds before recalcitrant gamblers could act on any nagging second thoughts. Smart money steered a wide berth around Havana's crooked casinos.

From the rarified enclosures of the Havana Yacht Club or the lush estates of Vedado, the panoramic heights immediately outside downtown Havana, the ruling classes could avert their eyes from the utter degeneracy that was their city's stock-in-trade. Some of the more adventuresome might even travel down to see the famed nightclub performer named Superman, who measured his manhood with twelve silver dollars and would demonstrate the exact source of his stage name several times nightly in one of the more well-known prurient attractions of Havana nightlife.

The town oozed sex—the sultry nights, the flimsy clothes, the abundant prostitution. A languid sensuality blew into town with the sea wind. The whole place was a teeming cauldron of sex, sin, and idolatry—set to a rumba beat.

The rhythms came directly from pagan rites. Unlike the American slaves, whose wary slave owners forbade them drums because they feared they could carry a language used to foment revolt, Cuban slaves kept their drums, and more. They kept their language and they kept their religion, simply disguising it to suit the Catholic colonialists. Nearly two dozen deities survived the voyage from western Africa in this religion that came to be called Santeria in Cuba and Voodoo in Haiti. The Santeria priests simply gave their Yoruban gods the names of Catholic saints. Chango, the Yoruban god of thunder, became Santa Barbara. Babalu Aye, *orisha* of infectious diseases, turned into San Lazaro. And so on.

This typifies the singular approach to assimilation that built the Cuban culture. They easily blended the practices of Santeria and Catholicism. It was this very mixture of Spain and Africa that made Cuba. In this accommodating spirit, the slaves were able to keep Africa alive in Cuba. In the early eighteenth century, the Spanish Catholic Church allowed the creation of *cabildos*, societies where Africans of shared heritage could get together, speak their language, conduct their rites. And play their drums.

The drums were holy. They spoke in the language of the gods. Whenever the Cubans wanted to evoke a link to the spirit, there was drumming and there was chanting. Specific rhythms were associated with specific deities, specific drums to specific rituals. In Nigeria, the *bata* were said to belong to Chango, the most graceful dancer of the *orishas*. While the rumba was said to have been invented on the docks of Havana by men beating on codfish boxes, the *bata* was always the spiritual heart of the music. Rumba comes from *guaguanco*, music that goes back hundreds of years to when the Spanish brought flamenco to Cuba. These two musics, the rhythms of Africa and this Spanish style, mixed together and led to early versions of the rumba.

The histories of Cuban music and American music are like parallel universes. The busy trade route between Havana and New Orleans may have provided some piquant cross-pollination long ago. Early New Orleans jazzmen sometimes played in a habanera style from Cuba, and

Jelly Roll Morton always spoke of what he called "the Spanish tinge" as an essential ingredient to his early jazz. In fact, some of the earliest recordings of anything remotely resembling jazz does not come from the white Americans imitating the black New Orleanians, as commonly presumed, but a racially mixed orchestra recorded in Havana almost ten years earlier. But New Orleans is more Caribbean than American in many ways, and once jazz moved up the river, this Cuban element was lost from its story for decades.

No doubt it was the music that drew Bert Berns to Cuba during the winter season of 1957–58, no matter what vague ideas he had or stories he told people before he left. The snaking *guajiro* rhythms drew him like a beacon to Havana. He and his pal Mickey Raygor, another ne'er-do-well from the Bronx, may have talked about putting together a comedy act for Havana nightclubs. Berns goofed around on such an act with Howard Storm a couple of years earlier. Storm was a young up-and-coming comic struggling to make it when he met Berns at Hansen's, the Broadway drugstore where show business types without offices of their own congregated. Berns sweet-talked Storm into coming out to the Bronx to rehearse a two-man act with Berns as the piano-playing straight man. Storm took a couple of subway rides out to some Bronx catering hall where Berns had managed to commandeer a stage with a piano during the afternoons. But nothing ever came of it.

Nothing ever came of any of Berns's schemes to get into show business. He held down a few nothing jobs, but none that ever lasted. He wrote a few songs with some other writers, especially Al Rubin, who managed to place their calypso-flavored song, "Way Down by the Cherry Tree," with vocalist Micki Marlo on Capitol Records. He tried touting singers. He knew all the Broadway characters. His brother-in-law and sister, when they went on their honeymoon cruise, were surprised to discover when he saw them off that Berns knew the ship's entertainer, former child star Bobby Breen. He knew the players. He knew some of the moves. He knew how to look and he knew the phone booths at

Hansen's. But, at age twenty-nine, Bert Berns had nothing going on and nothing coming up. He lived in a dump in the West Village he couldn't afford and sneaked out to the Bronx every so often, where his soft touch mother would slip him money behind his disapproving father's back.

In Havana, Berns drank too much rum, smoked reefer, and slept on the beach. He and Raygor got involved in some half-baked plans to buy a nightclub, only to back out when they discovered they were actually negotiating the purchase of a whorehouse. He soaked up the atmosphere, hanging out in clubs by night, making the scene, and taking it all in. The rhythm of the *orishas* began to surround Berns.

Berns and Raygor ran out of money after a couple of months and headed home long before the good times in Havana crashed to a close. Over the years, Berns would tell many different stories about his stay in Cuba. He told people he ran guns and drugs. His brief stay in Cuba became a touchstone in his life—a physical connection to his spiritual roots in the rhythm of the *orishas*, a pilgrimage to the home of the mambo, a moment where he was a part of all the madness, romance, and glamour swirling in the Havana night air. It may even have served as a galvanizing, cathartic event that provoked him out of his indolence and gave him his greatest artistic vision, his blending of the mambo and rock and roll. And it was always the source of stories, even though nobody at home knew the names of fabled musicians like Beny Moré or Arsenio Rodriguez, who had drawn him to Havana in the first place. But when he got home, he did tell his sister he met Fidel Castro.

Ahmet Ertegun, Nesuhi Ertegun, 1947

II.

Washington, DC [1947]

A HMET ERTEGUN WENT into the recording studio the first time without any idea of what he was going to do. Smitten with American jazz, the young son of a distinguished Turkish diplomat took a raunchy blues singer who called herself Little Miss Cornshucks into a rented Washington, DC, studio in 1942 with a piano and a tenor and recorded her singing a few songs just for the hell of it.

Already balding, not yet twenty years old, the bespectacled young man wore crisp blazers and alligator shoes with a gleaming polish. He grew up ritzy in the luxury and privilege of embassy life. His father was the most trusted advisor to Mustafa Kemal Ataturk, the inspirational father of modern Turkey, who posted Munir Ertegun in the great capitals of Europe—Paris and London—before dispatching him to Washington, DC, where the brilliant, cultured diplomat became a personal favorite of President Roosevelt.

His older brother Nesuhi had taken nine-year-old Ahmet to see Cab Calloway and his Orchestra in London and, shortly after that, the Duke Ellington band. By the time the two young men landed in Washington with their family in 1934, they were thoroughly indoctrinated, with visions dancing in their heads of black men in tuxedos and their bright, shiny, brassy music. They combed black neighborhoods door-to-door looking for old 78 rpm records. They hosted Sunday brunch jam sessions at the Turkish embassy, and a procession of jazz greats such as Lester Young and Sidney Bechet, highly amused at the invitation, waltzed through the elegant quarters when the Ertegun boys lived there. They presented jazz concerts outside the embassy—their first featured bluesman Leadbelly at the Washington Press Club.

When the Erteguns' father died in 1944, he was initially buried in Arlington National Cemetery, and after the war, his body was shipped home with great pomp and ceremony by President Truman on the USS *Missouri*, only months after the Japanese signed the surrender on her decks. Their mother and sister went with their father. Nesuhi had married a gal who owned a record store and was working for a jazz record company in Los Angeles. Ahmet moved to more humble surroundings in DC—no more limousines, servants, or cooks—and continued to study for a master's degree in philosophy in the evenings. He sold the massive record collection he and his brother accumulated to plump up the small allowance his family could afford. During the day, he spent a lot of time sitting around Waxie Maxie's, a record store around the corner from the Howard Theatre in the black section of town.

These were Ahmet's wilderness years, absorbing the business through osmosis while lounging around listening to records and doing nothing. Owner Max Silverman was a philosopher king who held forth on a wide array of topics. Ahmet took a second trip to the recording studio after Little Miss Cornshucks, upon meeting a potential partner in Maxie's store, a square who put up the dough. Ahmet cut several sides with orchestra leader Boyd Raeburn, who ran a progressive big band working sort of a Stravinsky-meets-Kenton wrinkle. Again Ahmet had no plans for the recordings—he thought he might play them for his friend John Hammond, running artists and repertoire (a&r) at Mercury Records with Mitch Miller—but his partner made off with the masters.

Ahmet talked Waxie Maxie Silverman into bankrolling his next recording venture, but this time Ahmet brought along somebody who had actually made records before, Herb Abramson, a record collector

Ahmet had known since the embassy jam sessions. Abramson, working in A&R at National Records while studying dentistry at New York University under a grant from the army, was also a fashionable, handsome man-about-town. He had the added attraction of having made genuine records with Billy Eckstine, the Ravens, and Big Joe Turner, among others. Ertegun and Abramson were going to start two labels, Quality and Jubilee, one for jazz and the other for gospel, but didn't get much further than cutting a couple of records that went nowhere. Abramson soldiered on with a new partner in Jubilee, bandleader Jerry Blaine, who wanted to make Jewish comedy records, but soon sold out.

Ahmet still wanted to start a label and make records. He buttonholed bandleader Lionel Hampton about raising money for a label, and the jazzman agreed, only to have his wife scotch the deal. Instead, Ahmet approached an Ertegun family friend, their dentist, Dr. Vahdi Sabit, who mortgaged his house and came up with $10,000 to back the play. Ahmet moved to New York and slept on the Abramsons' living room couch. They changed the name of the company to Atlantic Records at the last minute after they discovered that the name Horizon Records had already been taken. They crossed out "Horizon" and wrote in "Atlantic" on the partnership papers. Abramson was named president; Ahmet vice president. Herb's wife Miriam, also named vice president, managed the office and handled the accounting. The first session was conducted November 21, 1947, by a quartet called the Harlemaires, a vocal group they found through arranger Jesse Stone. Ahmet thought the gambit might last a couple of years.

Ahmet could not have predicted the cataclysmic musical and social tides that were going to sweep the label's artists and records in only a few years into the foreground of American popular music. He didn't even know how to make records; that was what Abramson was around to do. He was a slick hipster trying to make his hustle work. He was smart, educated, cultured, but the independent record game was no place for pantywaists and Ahmet wasn't one of those either. Still, there is no way he could have envisioned for himself the kind of success he would experience in very short order. Although the label would come to define the rhythm and blues era and Ahmet's innate taste, elegance and sophistication never stood in the way of his deep appreciation of the funky blues—rather just the opposite—Atlantic did not start out with a program, a strategy, or even a specific kind of record the label intended to pursue.

In the first year, they made a variety of records. With ex–Lionel Hampton trumpeter Joe Morris, they cut "Lowe Groovin'," an instrumental named after a Washington, DC, disc jockey that did well, aided by considerable airplay from the deejay in question, Jackson Lowe, and Ahmet's old pal, Waxie Maxie Silverman, who played the record on the radio show he sponsored in exchange for free goods for his store. They recorded jazz pianist Erroll Garner. "Blue Harlem" by Tiny Grimes blared out of ghetto jukeboxes all over New York City. Ahmet learned well all those afternoons in Waxie Maxie's that customers didn't want fancy jazz; they wanted down and dirty blues records they could dance to. The company rented a $65-a-month ground-floor suite at the Hotel Jefferson on Fifty-Sixth Street between Broadway and Sixth Avenue. Ahmet shared the bedroom with a Turkish poet and cousin who hung out with the Greenwich Village crowd, while the record company operated out of the other room. The hotel switchboard answered the phone and took messages, so they didn't need to hire a secretary.

When their New Orleans distributor called looking for an obscure record he couldn't find by Stick McGhee, Ahmet decided to record a version of his own and found the only McGhee he knew—bluesman Brownie McGhee—at home in Brooklyn. As it happened, the Stick McGee in question was Brownie's brother, who was visiting him at the time. A session was arranged (brother Brownie played guitar and shouted along on the choruses), and the resulting record, "Drinking Wine Spo-Dee-O-Dee," was the label's first hit record when it was released in February 1949. It sold seven hundred thousand copies.

Ertegun and Abramson went south that year to search out more real blues talent. New York musicians looked down on the earthy music and it was always a problem getting the New York cats to cut the kind of sides Ahmet wanted. He usually had to compromise and let them do two or three jazz numbers for every blues. They recognized Blind Willie McTell playing on the streets of Atlanta from his old 78s. They found the epochal New Orleans pianist called Professor Longhair playing at some dump in New Orleans white people never ventured into, only to learn he had been signed just days before by Mercury Records. They recorded him anyway.

The next time they went south, they brought with them arranger Jesse Stone, who had been working on Atlantic sessions since the first one. Grandson of a slave, raised in a show business family, Stone started performing at age four in a vaudeville dog act in the Midwest. He made his first record, "Starvation Blues," in 1927 for Okeh Records. He knocked around Kansas City and came to New York in 1936, when Duke Ellington ran across the all-girl vocal group called the Rhythm Debs that Stone was leading in Detroit. Ellington landed the girls a job at the Cotton Club and laid his Harlem apartment on Stone rent-free.

Stone worked at the Apollo Theater, did arrangements for Jimmie Lunceford, Chick Webb, and others. He helped start Louis Jordan. He took songwriting lessons from Cole Porter. His song "Idaho" was a Top Five pop hit for Benny Goodman in 1942, and Jimmy Dorsey made a big record out of his "Sorghum Switch." He worked with Herb Abramson at National Records and was the only one of the Atlantic team who knew his way around sheet music.

Stone took notes on what he heard on that Southern trip and immediately applied what he learned to their New York recordings. When saxophonist Frank Culley showed up at Atlantic with a tune he called "Sergeant" that he claimed to have written, Stone immediately recognized it as his "Sorghum Switch" and gave it a spiffy new arrangement and title, "Cole Slaw." Culley's record didn't become a hit, but Louis Jordan took the tune Top Ten R&B in the summer of 1949.

Ertegun and Abramson signed a young singer named Ruth Brown, who was managed by Cab Calloway's sister, after catching her act in a Washington, DC, club. Ahmet was particularly impressed by the way she handled the old Little Miss Cornshucks number "So Long." On her way to New York City to make her debut at the Apollo and record for Atlantic, Brown was in a car crash that crushed both her legs. She spent months laid up in a Chester, Pennsylvania, hospital. Ahmet visited her on her twenty-first birthday to sign the contracts in her hospital bed. Atlantic paid her medical bills before she ever stepped into the studio. She was still on crutches and wearing leg braces when she finally did. Ahmet had her sing two songs on a four-song date with the Eddie Condon band. He held little commercial hope for Condon's traditional jazz, but he also saw the session as an opportunity to expose a new singer. Of course, they did the Little Miss Cornshucks number, and the damn thing made the *Billboard* R&B Top Ten in 1949, the label's second hit.

But it was the Jesse Stone arrangement for Ruth Brown's "Teardrops from My Eyes" that smoothly blended the robust raunch of the New Orleans r&b with the svelte sound of the New York big bands. The baritone sax belches and shimmering brass slide in behind the beat. Stone plants a throbbing bass figure in the foreground to encourage dancers. Brown gives the song a fierce, bold delivery, and saxophonist Frank "Cole Slaw" Culley honks his guts out on the bridge. "Teardrops from My Eyes" hit number one on the r&b charts and was one of the best-selling r&b records of 1950. Ruth Brown—and Atlantic Records— had arrived.

Ahmet was not a fan of the vocal group sound and Atlantic had recorded little of it, but after the massive success of the Orioles' "It's Too Soon to Know" in 1950, vocal groups were too popular for Atlantic to ignore. Through a fellow they knew who worked at an independent distributor in Washington, DC, the company signed the Clovers, a five-man group they auditioned in Waxie Maxie's store. Ahmet wrote "Don't You Know I Love You"—using the pen name Nugetre, or Ertegun spelled backward, to avoid possible embarrassment in the event he wound up pursuing a diplomatic career anytime in the future—and used Frank Culley's band to back the group on the record date. Saxophones were a new touch for vocal group records. Ertegun thought the performance was more white, more Ink Spots, than he intended when he wrote the piece but realized the group turned the record into something special. "Don't You Know I Love You" was another number one r&b hit for the label in 1951, followed immediately by another number one with "Fool, Fool, Fool," a song Ertegun insisted the Clovers record against their wishes. It sounded better to them as it went up the charts.

In 1950 and 1951, Atlantic recorded Mary Lou Williams, the Billy Taylor Quartet, Leadbelly, Al Hibbler, Lil Green, Sidney Bechet, Meade Lux Lewis, and Mabel Mercer, among others. In July 1951, Ahmet and Abramson went to Chicago and recorded ailing pianist Jimmy Yancey, whose left arm was partly paralyzed, and some other notable local talent. While in Chicago, Ahmet was knocked out walking down Maxwell Street to see black people dancing to his Clovers song on portable record players.

Ahmet knew Kansas City blues shouter Big Joe Turner from concerts at the embassy. Abramson had recorded him at National Records, and Jesse Stone first met him as a teenager in Kansas City. When Ahmet heard Big Joe was subbing for an ailing Jimmy Rushing with the Count Basie Orchestra at the Apollo, he went to the show. Big Joe Turner was a force of nature, not a jazz singer. Turner didn't know the material and kept coming in late and the band ended choruses before Big Joe did. The set was a train wreck. When Ahmet finally found the singer after the show, he was up the street already nursing a drink at Braddock's Bar, miserable and dejected. Ahmet talked Turner into going with Atlantic and wrote him a song, "Chains of Love," a rewrite of the old Albert

Ammons number, "Mecca Flat Blues" (Nugetre strikes again), that landed the roly-poly baritone at number two on the r&b charts in 1951.*

Ruth Brown had the biggest rhythm and blues record of the year in 1953 for Atlantic with "Mama He Treats Your Daughter Mean," a song that took considerable cajoling on Ahmet's part to get her to record. They ran the session at a stage studio on Fifth Avenue at Fifty-Seventh Street, and along with arranger Jesse Stone, they brought in engineer Tom Dowd, a recording engineer they had come increasingly to rely on since the boyish Dowd first showed up as the unexpected substitute at an early Atlantic session at Apex Sound.

Dowd was a remarkable young man, a classically trained pianist who as a teen worked during the war on the secret Manhattan Project that developed the A-bomb. When he went back to college and found that the nuclear physics he learned making the bomb was still classified top secret and the professors were living in the Dark Ages, he decided to become involved in the new science of tape recording. He cut his first hit in 1949 when he recorded vocalist Eileen Barton singing the insipid "If I Knew You Were Comin' I'd've Baked a Cake," a number one hit for National Records, not only one of the biggest-selling records by any independent label at the time, but also one of the records that made rock and roll necessary. Dowd was bringing uncommon audio clarity and balance to Atlantic's records, the kind of care and attention to detail almost entirely unknown elsewhere in the rhythm and blues world.

In February 1953, Uncle Sam called Abramson. After the Army had paid for his dental education, he was drafted and sent to Germany. On his way out of the country, the last thing he did for the label was rehearse bandleader Joe Morris in Montgomery, Alabama, working up a song with the band's female vocalist, Faye Adams, called "Shake a Hand." When nobody else from Atlantic moved to bring the band into

---

*Ahmet liked to record his songwriting demos in the Make-a-Record booth at the Times Square subway station.

the studio, Morris took the record to Al Silver's Herald label and had the biggest r&b hit of 1954.

The most obvious candidate to replace Abramson was Jerry Wexler, the thirty-seven-year-old former *Billboard* magazine reporter who changed the name of the magazine's charts from "Race Records" to "Rhythm and Blues" in 1949, literally naming the music. They were already all friends and spent weekends together at Fire Island. The Atlantic guys had offered him a job the year before running their publishing company, but without any participation in artists and repertoire, record production, or a piece of the action, Wexler demurred. This time they offered him $350 a week and a 13 percent share of Atlantic for a $2,000 investment. Ahmet spent the money on a new green Cadillac convertible for Wexler.

Wexler had grown up insolent and conniving in the streets of Washington Heights. A street-smart wiseacre who spent more time in Artie's Poolroom than any classroom, Wexler had read just enough books to be dangerous. His father was a Polish immigrant who worked his entire life as a window washer. His mother was a real character, a card-carrying Communist and modern woman with grand designs for her reprobate son. When he flunked out of college in New York, she sent him packing to Kansas State University, thinking he couldn't get into trouble in the middle of all those cornfields, only to have her derelict, jazz-mad boy spend his time in gin mills in Kansas City, where he saw Big Joe Turner working as a singing bartender. He didn't last the second year. He came home to a dismal life, ennobled solely by the grace of jazz. By day, he washed windows alongside his father. By night, he haunted the music emporiums of Fifty-Second Street and Harlem, far removed from the daylight drudgery as he shared a joint with his hipster friends in the basement of Jimmy Ryan's.

He was drafted during the war but served only in Florida and Texas. He completed his journalism degree at Kansas State after his discharge and moved back home to Washington Heights. He was thirty years old, married, living with his in-laws, yet to find his first real job. When he finally found work at the weekly music industry trade magazine *Billboard*, Wexler felt perfectly at home among the pluggers and cleffers on Broadway, the rack jobbers on Eleventh Avenue, hanging out at the bar at Birdland. He tipped Patti Page's manager to a country song, "Tennessee Waltz," that would make the girl thrush a major star. After he left *Billboard* for old-line publishers Robbins, Feist, Miller, Wexler introduced Columbia Records a&r director Mitch Miller to a couple of big numbers in 1951—"Cry" by Johnny Ray and "Cold, Cold Heart" by Tony Bennett, which took country songwriter Hank Williams into the pop charts for the first time. But Wexler hated his job, playing stooge to some old-time Alley sleazebag. He thought the Atlantic guys were the cognoscenti of the cognoscenti and he aspired to their level of cool.

Wexler came to work in 1953 at the Atlantic offices at 234 Fifty-Sixth Street, above Patsy's restaurant. It had been a speakeasy during Prohibition called the 23456 Club, and the creaky, excruciatingly slow elevator belonged to that bygone era. Most visitors preferred the rickety wooden staircase. Atlantic occupied the top floor. A stockroom took up the back. In front was one big room with several desks and a grand piano. Wexler and Ahmet sat side by side, although Wexler arrived early in the morning and Ertegun never showed up before noon, sometimes not until hours after that.

When they held recording sessions, they stacked one desk on top of the other and pushed them to the side of the room and rolled the chairs into the stairwell. Tom Dowd, whom the company hired exclusively to make their recordings, made some modest improvements on the recording equipment. The floor sagged and creaked. There was a skylight in the middle of the sloped ceiling. The company sometimes still rented time at outside recording studios, but mainly this was where Atlantic operated at the time Big Joe Turner came into the makeshift studio for a historic February 1953 session to record "Shake, Rattle, and Roll."

Atlantic had made a record the previous year with Turner in New Orleans, but the principals weren't even on the scene—they just sent Turner into the studio with a bunch of local New Orleans players (who included pianist Fats Domino) and he came back with "Crawdad Hole" and "Honey Hush." Ertegun and Wexler did meet up with him in Chicago in October 1952 and recorded "TV Mama" with Chicago guitarist Elmore James, and they cut "Midnight Cannonball" with him in December in New York.

Jesse Stone wrote "Shake, Rattle, and Roll" under his pen name Charles Calhoun. They pushed the desks to the walls and brought the camp chairs out. Ahmet, Wexler, and Stone barked the background vocals. Pianist Harry Van Walls rippled little boogie-woogie triplets under the song's rhythm and Turner croaked Jesse Stone's vivid eroticism: "You wear those dresses the sun comes shinin' through / I can't believe my eyes all that mess belongs to you."

"Shake, Rattle, and Roll" was one of those mythical convergences of personalities, history, and music, frozen in time through the majesty and mystery of magnetic tape recording. It is an entirely unselfconscious record that does not recognize or acknowledge the rapidly changing audience for the music; it is the epitome of the classic unfettered rhythm and blues record, a great, roaring blast of lust and boogie-woogie that echoes through the years. When Bill Haley and His Comets recorded "Shake, Rattle, and Roll" the following year, the lyrics were cleaned up, the arrangements pepped up, and the foreboding, ominous mood of the original dissipated, but the song's irresistible beat remained. The Haley record cracked the pop Top Ten, sold more than a million copies, and was one of the key records in the emergence of rock and roll.

At some point, Herb and Miriam Abramson had given Ahmet a copy of the 1951 record "Baby Let Me Hold Your Hand," on a small West Coast label called Swing Time by an artist named Ray Charles. Ahmet couldn't stop playing it. Sixteen-year-old Ray Charles

Robinson, who went blind as a child shortly after watching his brother drown, left blind school in 1946 in Florida an orphan and took a bus to Seattle because that was as far away as he could get from Florida. He gigged around the Seattle area, polishing his Charles Brown imitation, and was working as piano player and musical director for bluesman Lowell Fulson when Atlantic bought his Swing Time contract for $2,500 in 1952.

At the first Atlantic session with Ray Charles in New York, the strong-willed pianist tangled with arranger Jesse Stone over musical ideas, but when he returned for a second date in May 1953, Stone stayed out of Charles's way, sensing someone who needed to express himself. Ahmet warmed up Charles at rehearsal the night before, enthusiastically singing with Charles, accompanying him on a song Ertegun had written called "Mess Around."

"Hold your baby tight as you can," Ertegun half sang, half shouted, "spread yourself like a fan and do the mess around."

While his new partner Jerry Wexler watched goggle-eyed from the other side of the glass, Ahmet leaned over the piano and walked Charles through the wiseacre blues, "It Should Have Been Me." Charles sprayed little bursts of Bud Powell bop and Jimmy Yancey boogie-woogie between takes. On the tape of the evening, he sounds like nothing so much as someone searching for his voice. The next day's session yielded his first chart hit for Atlantic, "It Should Have Been Me," the talking blues Ahmet had deftly demonstrated.

A month after the Ray Charles session, Ahmet was in the studio with a new group called Clyde McPhatter and the Drifters. He went to Birdland to see Billy Ward and the Dominoes, an oddball booking. Ahmet thought the world of Clyde McPhatter, the lead tenor of the Dominoes, best known for the raunchy 1951 hit "Sixty Minute Man," although McPhatter sang lead on the group's 1951 debut, "Do Something for Me." Ahmet felt McPhatter's voice had a magical, almost angelic quality. Ward was a tough cookie who ran a tight ship and levied harsh fines for perceived infractions. Ahmet immediately noticed that McPhatter was missing from the lineup at Birdland, went backstage at intermission, and learned that Ward fired McPhatter five days before. He rushed to a phone booth, looked in the book, and found several McPhatters listed. On his first call, he reached Clyde's father, who handed the phone to his son. McPhatter came to the Atlantic offices the next day and they cut a deal.

After the June 1953 session didn't yield any satisfying masters, McPhatter put together a second group of Drifters around a pair of brothers, Gerhart and Andrew "Bubba" Thrasher, whom he knew from singing in church. Jesse Stone rehearsed the group extensively and wrote a new song, "Money Honey," that would launch the group's historic career after they returned to the studio in August.

Atlantic never expected to sell records to whites. They made records for blacks and sometimes even tailored pop material for the rhythm and blues market. Wexler, in fact, was looking for an r&b group to cover the latest Patti Page record, "Cross Over the Bridge," when he stumbled across the label's first great pop hit.

He took a Bronx vocal group that called themselves the Chords into the studio in March 1954. For the afterthought B-side, the group offered a swinging, almost jazzy, largely indecipherable piece of inspired lunacy called "Sh-Boom." The B-side caught fire on the West Coast. The label stripped the Patti Page cover off the single—thinking to save it for later—rereleased the single, and quickly dumped off half the publishing for $6,000 to Hill & Range. The Chords version on the new Atlantic subsidiary label, Cat Records, hit the pop charts in June 1954. A week later, the cover version from the Canadian vocal group called the Crew Cuts charted. Although the Chords version made extraordinary inroads for an independent r&b record on the pop charts, winding up nicking the bottom of the Top Ten, the smooth, gleaming white version went all the way to number one and Atlantic, unfortunately, had kept only half the publishing. Best six grand Hill & Range spent all year.

While Atlantic was beginning to see some benefit from a subterranean shift in popular tastes as the market began to expand for rhythm and blues records, the company did not derive income from the sales of cover records. Neither did the artists. When r&b chart veteran LaVern Baker finally managed to land a record on the pop charts with "Tweedlee Dee" in January 1955, the plain white cover version by Georgia Gibbs that came out two weeks later outsold Baker's smoking record. Baker couldn't help holding a certain resentment toward Gibbs. She also couldn't resist her little joke. Always a nervous flyer and headed out on tour, Baker took out flight insurance at the airport, named Georgia Gibbs the beneficiary, and sent her the insurance papers.

Ray Charles summoned the Atlantic chiefs to Atlanta in November 1954. He had been tooling around the South building his own band, learning to play them like an instrument, finding his sound. They say the crowds dancing to his band in tobacco barns raised so much dust from between the floorboards, partners couldn't see one another. The Atlantic guys sent him material from time to time, but he liked little of it. Instead he was working on his own songs. The trumpet player in the band brought him a half-done piece based on an old gospel song and Charles put some finishing touches on the number and started playing it onstage, as he and his band continued a string of endless one-nighters with T-Bone Walker and Lowell Fulson. Since he didn't have any dates in the New York area, but he had four songs rehearsed and ready, he told Ahmet and Jerry to meet him in Atlanta, when he came into the Peacock Room for two weeks.

Ertegun and Wexler went straight to the club from the airport. Even though it was afternoon, Ray and the band were set up on the bandstand. When Ahmet and Jerry stepped foot in the club, Charles knew they were there and sent the band straight into "I Got a Woman." In a moment, they realized that Charles had coalesced all the elements they saw in him, pulled together the disparate forces within him, and found his voice. They booked time where they could find it—a local radio station where they had to stop recording at the top of the hour while an announcer came in and read the news—but they left town with four tracks in the can, including "I Got a Woman."

The single went number one R&B after it came out in January 1955, connecting Ray Charles for the first time across the country with black disc jockeys and audiences. They followed their best instincts with Ray Charles and left him alone. It was a novel a&r strategy, not widely practiced in the industry, and Atlantic was going to be rewarded, not with just another hit record, but also with an artist whose voice would reach multitudes. The records they were making were defining rhythm and blues, and rhythm and blues was spreading out on the nationwide record scene underneath them. With Ray Charles, they had the good sense to just let it happen.

Frankie Lymon, George Goldner

III.

New York City [1955]

THE FIVE TEENAGERS who called themselves the Coupe de Villes were accustomed to moving their impromptu rehearsals. They would sing in the hallways, the same songs over and over, until the neighbors complained. They often retreated to the hallway in bass vocalist Sherman Garnes's building across the street from Edward W. Stitt Junior High School at the corner of 165th Street and Edgecombe Avenue, the heart of Harlem's Sugar Hill neighborhood.

One of Sherman's neighbors, who used to stop and listen to the boys practice, brought them a stack of letters, love poems his girlfriend had written him. He suggested they work up some material of their own. The group roughed out a melody and the harmonies together. Herman Santiago and Jimmy Merchant punched the lyrics in shape, working around a line from one of the girl's poems: "Why do birds sing so gay."

Richie Barrett, who lived on 161st Street, was something of a neighborhood hero. He was not only the handsome lead vocalist of the Valentines whose record "Lily Maebelle" lit up New York radio that spring of 1955 (and was paying the bills at Rama Records), but he was also doing some artists and repertoire work downtown for George Goldner, the mambo man who also produced the Valentines' records and owned the Rama label, his venture into the world of rhythm and blues. The Coupe de Villes used to stand under Barrett's balcony and sing "Lily Maebelle." Barrett couldn't fail to notice the kids singing his hit with the crazy Puerto Rican lead vocalist, Herman Santiago.

Barrett finally agreed to listen to the group rehearse at the Stitt auditorium and was impressed enough with their new original song to take the group—now calling themselves the Premiers—downtown to meet Goldner. The always-natty Goldner wore an embroidered shirt and a mohair suit. His latest chart success, the Cleftones, a five-man vocal group from Queens, only a couple of years older than the Premiers and who had the hit "You Baby You," were also visiting the West Forty-First Street offices, discussing plans for another record, and stayed to watch the audition.

Goldner, who expected a Latin band, wondered where all the instruments were. Barrett had them sing anyway. Herman Santiago had a cold and couldn't sing well and Goldner asked the youngest member of the group, thirteen-year-old Frankie Lymon, to try singing the lead. The kid couldn't even get the words right, but Goldner loved the song and changed the title to "Why Do Fools Fall in Love."

Goldner squeezed the group into the dinner break during a recording session planned for a group called the Millionaires (vocalist Benny Nelson would later change his name to Ben E. King), backed by saxophonist Jimmy Wright and his band, Goldner's usual studio crew.* They quickly cut two songs and Wright gave the group their name on their way out of the studio—he called them the Teenagers. When the record was released in January 1956 on Goldner's new Gee label, the label read "The Teenagers featuring Frankie Lymon" and the songwriting credit read "Lymon-Santiago-Goldner."

"Why Do Fools Fall in Love" was not just another hit record. It was a coded signal to a young generation. The youthful exuberance of the record jumped out of the speakers; it was music that couldn't have

---

*Saxophonist Wright began his career in the late thirties playing around Harlem clubs in a trio with another young musician just starting out, pianist Thelonious Monk.

been made by grown-ups. In an instant, teenager Lymon and his fellow Teenagers became worldwide recording stars. Within a month of the record first hitting the charts, the Teenagers were topping the bill at sold-out Easter week concerts at the Brooklyn Paramount. By summer, they were costarring on a nationwide tour with Bill Haley and His Comets, whose number one hit the year before, "(We're Gonna) Rock Around the Clock," was the shot heard round the world.

Lymon stepped into the lead vocalist role clearly under considerable coaching from Richie Barrett, whose influence on Lymon's phrasing is obvious. But in Lymon's naïve bravura performance, he transformed the effervescent lead vocal into a stylistic tour de force, a defining moment for rock and roll. All over the country, young singers started taking cues from Lymon and would for years to come. But even more than the musical influence the record wielded, "Why Do Fools Fall in Love" was nothing less than a declaration of independence from the New York streets.

The Teenagers' hit tangled up in the Top Ten that April 1956 with Elvis Presley's "Heartbreak Hotel" and Carl Perkins's "Blue Suede Shoes" in those heady first few months of the year, as rock and roll broke wide open on the national scene. While Perkins and Presley represented the Southern side of the movement, Frankie Lymon and the Teenagers were the unmistakable product of New York City.

The men who made these rhythm and blues records were tough, desperate men. They were the bottom-feeders of the Midtown music world; hucksters and grifters working the far reaches of the established music business. Coarse and vulgar, they rubbed shoulders with all sorts of Broadway types, from the doubtful to the regal. They lived in a realm of their own design and they sometimes didn't return their phone calls. These men lived in a netherworld where fearsome gangsters were their business associates, although they were never mentioned aloud, and whores were routine business expenses. The rhythm and blues racket operated many levels beneath the carriage trade record industry represented by major labels such as Columbia, Decca, or RCA Victor. They played by different rules.

More than simply granting themselves writing credits on songs they had nothing to do with composing, they avoided paying royalties altogether. Of course, they maintained all the publishing rights. They treated performers anyway as interchangeable or disposable. Singers were like trolley cars—another one would be coming along any minute. But at the same time, all these men marveled at the magic sound of a hit record—the sound of beaver pelts slapping on the trading block—and held those associated with the feat in high regard. Stardust sparkled in their footsteps.

These men were largely unsentimental about music, but saw the record business as an opportunity. They wanted to break into a racket that had been controlled by a few major record companies since the war ended ten years before. They didn't have stockholders and boards of directors. What they did have was moxie, some muscle, and money. And they spread it around.

Payola was more than a way of life for independent record labels and rhythm and blues broadcasters; graft, corruption, and bribery were weapons that allowed the little guys to compete with the major labels, who were somewhat more parsimonious with the $50 bills. But payola is as old as the music business. Music publisher E.B. Marks remembered greasing downtown nightclub singers in the Gay Nineties to work the catalog. Gilbert and Sullivan paid payola. During the swing era, song pluggers would routinely slip ten bucks to the Mickey Mouse bandleaders to get a chorus played. The rhythm and blues crowd simply elevated the practice.

And payola never made a hit. The public makes the hits, and if a record doesn't have it in the grooves, it doesn't have it. Payola can buy a chance, the opportunity, a little exposure, but it can't turn a stiff into a hit. With the rhythm and blues field almost exclusively catering to the black audience, nobody outside their parochial little world would have ever noticed the systemic corruption if it hadn't been for rock and roll. And what was rock and roll anyway, other than rhythm and blues records that were sold to whites?

Rhythm and blues drove the New York independent record scene that had emerged in the years following World War II. The sleek, slinky sound of the city's streets was making its insidious way into the antiseptic lives of Eisenhower-era white American youth. Rhythm and blues radio stations were only a spin away down the dial. With pop music just another thread in the fabric of society, it was no coincidence that the Supreme Court handed down the *Brown* decision ordering the desegregation of public schools in 1954, the same year rock and roll emerged in force. Rock and roll was the desegregation of the hit parade.

As the robust vitality of the rhythm and blues records swamped the insipid cotton candy of "How Much Is That Doggie in the Window," opportunities opened up for small labels with ears on the street. Scattered around Tenth Avenue were dozens of such independent record companies along the Street of Hope. Every so often, someone got lucky. Larry Newton's Derby Records clicked with "Wheel of Fortune" by Eddie Wilcox and Sunny Gale in 1952. These were the kind of bottle-rocket records that kept the street humming.

Al Silver, who already ran a record pressing plant, started Herald Records in a Greenwich Village basement in 1952 and cut hit records with the Nutmegs, the Mello Kings, and the Five Satins, among others. Hy Weiss and his brother Sam started Old Town Records around the same time in a converted cloakroom at the old Triboro Theater on 125th Street and Third Avenue, taking the name from a defunct stationery company where Sam Weiss once worked so they didn't have to buy new letterhead. They made records with the Fiestas and the Solitaires and had the first record by Richie Barrett's Valentines a year before "Lily Maebelle."

Jerry Blaine was a moonfaced bandleader who made some sides for Brunswick Records in the late thirties but got into the record distribution business in the forties. His Cosnat Distributors handled most of the key independent lines in the New York City area. He worked with jazz and r&b record collector/producer Herb Abramson at National Records making Big Joe Turner records. In 1947, he bought out Abramson from their newly formed Jubilee Records. Blaine initially called his new label It's a Natural, but retreated the next year to Jubilee when the owner of National Records complained the name was too similar.

Blaine caught a little lightning when he signed the Orioles, after watching the vocal group lose to pianist George Shearing on television's *Arthur Godfrey's Talent Scouts*. Formed in 1947 as the Vibranaires in Baltimore, the group was managed by a young white lady, an amateur songwriter with no professional show business experience named Deborah Chessler. The group's 1948 recording on Blaine's It's A Natural label was Chessler's song, "It's Too Soon to Know," a monster hit that went number one on the rhythm and blues charts and even pierced the Top Twenty on the all-white pop charts.

The record made the group a phenomenon. Mobs greeted the group's Apollo Theater shows. By 1950, the Orioles were the most popular vocal group in the country and opened the door for the sound of the urban streets on the pop charts. Orioles vocalist Tommy Gaither died in a car crash when he fell asleep at the wheel on an endless road trip in 1950. The group was teetering on its last legs when the Orioles' glorious cover of a gospel song by country singer Darrell Glenn, "Crying in the Chapel," caught an updraft and sold a million as the vocal group sound swamped the charts in 1953.

George Goldner had still been doing brisk trade in Latin records on his Tico label—*timbalero* Tito Puente had become a major Latin music star under Goldner's direction—when he decided to move into the rapidly growing rhythm and blues field in 1953. When he did, he stumbled into the biggest success of his career.

Cliff Martinez, an agent Goldner knew from the local Latin scene, brought him the Crows, a quintet from Harlem formed in 1951 that

Martinez signed after the fellows won the amateur contest at the Apollo Theater. He put the five Crows together with another client, vocalist-pianist Viola Watkins, who needed a vocal group and guitarist for her act. The Crows needed a pianist and arranger. After the first Crows single on Rama came and went, a second was released the following month in June 1953, a slow ballad written by Crows baritone Bill Davis, "I Love You So," and "Gee," an odd, little nothing of a song Davis also wrote that went *da-duda-da-duda-da-duda-da—Gee, I love that girl.*

When the record was first released in June 1953, Goldner pushed the ballad as the A-side. The single received some scattered attention around the country, building to the point in September where *Billboard* noted the growing interest in the flip side. Then Huggy Boy had the fight with his girl.

Dick "Huggy Boy" Hugg, Los Angeles' top nighttime deejay, broadcast his KRKD show nightly from the front window of Dolphin's of Hollywood, a popular all-night record store in the middle of black Los Angeles, at the corner of Vernon and Central Avenues. He and his girlfriend had a fight and she left to drive home across town to North Hollywood. He put on her favorite record, "Gee," and kept playing it until she got home and called. She worried that he would be fired if he didn't stop playing the record and he said he wouldn't stop until she agreed to come back. She did, but the damage had been done.

The next Tuesday, Goldner called the disc jockey to tell him he had made "Gee" a smash. Within weeks, "Gee" sold more than fifty thousand records in Los Angeles alone and was rapidly spreading across the country. By January, Goldner had not only sold a lot of records, but also landed high on the pop charts, rarified air for rhythm and blues records. Using a patchwork network of independent distributors, tirelessly working the phones himself with disc jockeys and record retailers, Goldner proved it possible for a New York independent label to have a nationwide hit.

However, he was also losing so much at the racetrack, he sold the publishing on his hit song to Meridian Music for what the trades described as "a lot of money." Meridian Music was one of a number of publishing companies owned by Morris Levy.

For the rest of his life, Morris Levy would loom as an ominous figure over the Broadway music trade, a lifelong handmaiden to mobsters, a bully to anyone who did business with him, and the black-bag man behind the scenes of the record business. The FBI always figured Levy as the front man for the syndicate in the record business, and that was not without a certain basis in fact. At the same time, Levy was not a scary, threatening figure—he knew those people—but a wisecracking, avuncular *yiddishe macher*. He kept his finger in every part of the music business. He owned nightclubs. He promoted tours. He loaned money to musicians. He had music publishing.

Levy loved copyrights. They don't talk back, he liked to say. When he first started his publishing company, he commissioned blind pianist George Shearing to write "Lullaby of Birdland," named after the nightclub at Fifty-Second Street and Broadway that Levy operated, and the damn thing went on to become a standard, recorded a few hundred times.

Although he was only twenty-eight years old in 1955, Levy already had a colorful past. His father and a brother died when he was young, and after his other brother, Irving, joined the Navy, he grew up poor, living alone with his mother in the Bronx, running around the neighborhood since they were children with Vincent "The Chin" Gigante, fingered as the triggerman in the botched hit of mob boss Frank Costello in 1957. He dropped out of school in the sixth grade after assaulting a teacher. At age fourteen, working as a hatcheck boy at the Greenwich Village Inn, he came to know Thomas Eboli—called Tommy Ryan— an up-and-coming soldier in the Genovese family. At age sixteen, he went to work as a darkroom boy in the Ubangi Club, which was run by those guys. He wound up working his nightclub photography racket in a number of their clubs.

In 1945, after a year in the Navy, Morris, his brother Irving, disc jockey Symphony Sid, and nightclub impresario Monte Kay took over a fried chicken restaurant on Broadway and turned it into a jazz club. When they started booking bebop players such as Charlie Parker and Dexter Gordon on Monday nights, lines snaked out the front door. The Royal Roost was a big success, but Levy got screwed by his partners and the club sold out from under him.

In December 1949, Levy and Kay bought Birdland—named after Charlie Parker, known to all as Bird—from mobster Joseph (Joe the Wop) Cataldo and turned the Fifty-Second Street basement into the head-quarters of New York jazz—Dizzy, Bird, Miles, Monk, and all that. The full Count Basie Orchestra used to play three or four two-week stands every year, the sign outside the club reading simply BASIE'S BACK.

There was an unholy alliance between Morris Levy and George Goldner. A sharp guy who knew all the angles, Levy wasn't a record man. He could wheel and deal, con and connive, but George Goldner had the magic touch. He could scrape a bunch of kids off the street, throw them in the studio with a raggedy-ass band, and come out with gold. What Levy had was money, which Goldner always badly needed, hardly surprising given that he could lose $50,000 in a day at the track. Wherever Goldner operated, Levy was never far away.

The five fellows in the Cleftones took the subway train down from Jamaica in Queens to Goldner's office. In December 1955, their single "You Baby You" had been the first release on Goldner's new label, Gee Records, named after his Crows hit. The group and their manager—a white friend from Jamaica High School who sang poorly and decided instead to take a backstage role—were surprised to find two rough-looking gentlemen in the office with Goldner, who wasn't sitting at his desk. Instead, sitting at Goldner's desk was a man who introduced himself as Morris Levy and told the group these other two menacing fellows were their new managers. Informed that they already had a manager, Levy took the young man they identified out in the hall.

When they returned, the Cleftones had new managers, Tommy Vastola and Johnny Roberts.

Gaetano "Tommy" Vastola had a number of nicknames—Corky, the Big Guy, the Galoot. He was a physically imposing man about Levy's age who owned a nightclub in Coney Island near Nathan's called the Riptide and ran with the Colombo gang. His uncle, Dominick Ciaffone, was known as Swats Mulligan, a big-time gangster with the Genovese family. Vastola was credited as coauthor of the Valentines' hit "Lily Maebelle" and took a similar cowriting credit on "You Baby You." In between loan sharking, grand larceny, and labor racketeering, Vastola liked to keep his hand in the music business. Johnny Roberts worked for him.

Morris Levy and Tommy Vastola did a lot of business together. With Levy a largely unseen power behind Goldner's throne, he could hand off plums to his buddies like the Cleftones management or songwriting credits on Goldner productions (Vastola is doo-wop songwriting aristocracy, coauthor of the Wrens' vocal group classic "Hey Girl," the Valentines' "I Love You Darling," and another couple of dozen vintage-era pieces). Levy had his hooks into Goldner but good. Levy owned a piece of Gee Records. He owned outright the publishing to Goldner's biggest hit, the Frankie Lymon and the Teenagers' 1956 Top Ten hit "Why Do Fools Fall in Love." He made more money off the record than Goldner did. Way more.

ALL THE NEW York–based labels were well aware of a growing network of rhythm and blues disc jockeys with popular radio shows popping up in every city in the country. Especially well known to them was Cleveland disc jockey Alan Freed, who, under the name Moondog, had been blasting their records on the airwaves since 1952. While underground currents were already streaming across the country, immutable forces no doubt already in motion, no one thing probably boosted the rock and roll revolt more than Alan Freed coming to New York City

radio. Certainly no single event so empowered the men of the rough-
and-tumble world of the New York independent record business. In
greedy, arrogant, drunken Alan Freed, the father of rock and roll, they
found a willing coconspirator in their grandest plans and ambitions,
whom they treated like the patsy he was.

Freed's Cleveland radio show had already hit New York from
Newark, New Jersey radio station WNJR beginning in December 1953,
running taped copies of his original broadcasts with the local commer-
cials clumsily hacked off. Freed, who presented what was undoubtedly
the first rock and roll concert, Moondog's Coronation Ball, in Cleveland
in 1952 (the first rock and roll riot took place outside the same night),
brought a similar rhythm and blues program to the Newark National
Guard Armory in May 1954, featuring New York–based vocal group
the Harptones, the Clovers, Muddy Waters, Charles Brown, and others. More than eleven thousand screaming teens mobbed the place.
Thousands more were turned away.

"Hi, everybody," said Freed, opening his debut nighttime airshift
on New York's WINS in September 1954. "This is your old Moondog
here, with rhythm and blues records with the big beat in popular music
in America today, for everyone out there in the Moondog kingdom."

Freed hit the city like a fireball. In a minute, he was the town's
top deejay. Almost as quickly, he also found himself in court, losing a
lawsuit to a blind street singer who wore a Viking costume and called
himself Moondog. The court only awarded the singer chump change,
but Freed also lost the right to use the Moondog name. Welcome to
New York.

That night, drinking at his customary watering hole, P.J. Moriarty's
on Fifty-First Street, Freed dreamed up the cockamamie notion of copy-
righting the term "rock and roll." That way, Freed could protect his
radio show's new name, *Rock and Roll Party*, and extract tribute from
interlopers violating his trademarked term. "Rock and roll" was rapidly
gaining currency in the public tongue, replacing "rhythm and blues."

Freed was introduced to Morris Levy by Jack Hooke, a small-time operator on the fringe of the music business who knew Freed from Cleveland and had been instrumental in his moving to New York. Levy filed a copyright notice for "rock and roll" on behalf of Seig Music, a corporation comprised of Levy, Freed, one of Freed's Cleveland business partners, and radio station WINS. Freed pounded the phrase on the radio, insisted the station refer to him as a "rock and roll" disc jockey, and was a key instigator in spreading the term beyond the boundaries of any enforceable copyright. Within weeks, the phrase "rock and roll" became part of the national vocabulary. And the moneybags sprouted wings and flew away.

Freed's fingerprints were all over the music business. He managed the vocal group the Moonglows and was credited as coauthor on their hit "Sincerely." He was also given a writing share by Chess Records of the 1954 Chuck Berry hit "Maybellene." He owned a piece of a Cleveland record distributorship. He made a pile throwing concerts in Cleveland and, with Levy's backing, started doing concerts in New York. Levy, who produced a nationwide jazz tour, "Birdland Stars of 1955," featuring Sarah Vaughan, Erroll Garner, Lester Young, George Shearing, and the Count Basie Orchestra, put up the dough and split the action with Freed, who pumped the concert on the radio.

The "Rock 'n' Roll Jubilee Ball" sold out two shows at the six-thousand-seat St. Nicholas Arena, better known for boxing matches, featuring Clyde McPhatter and the Drifters, Fats Domino, Joe Turner, the Clovers, Ruth Brown, and others in January 1955. An Easter week run at the much larger Brooklyn Paramount blew out the house record with a whopping $107,000 gross. Freed was big business.

Before long, he was living in splendor in a sixteen-room, half-century-old stucco mansion called Grey Cliffe on a two-acre grassy knoll on the Connecticut shore. Freed remodeled the guesthouse into a remote studio where he would do his nightly broadcasts. He bought the place for a princely $75,000 and had two mortgages, one held by

Jerry Blaine of Jubilee Records and the other by Morris Levy. Atlantic Records paid to build a swimming pool.

A lot of labels kept Freed on a monthly dole. Atlantic Records partner Jerry Wexler would take $600 cash in a paper bag every month and give it to Freed's bagman in a cloakroom at the Brill Building. When Atlantic hit a terrifying cold streak, Wexler went to see Freed to ask if he could carry the label for a couple of months. "I'd love to, but I can't do it," Freed told Wexler. "That would be taking food out of my children's mouths."

Freed had no problem being a son of a bitch, but keeping him in line was his manager Tommy Vastola, most certainly put in place by Morris Levy. When Freed showed up bruised and battered at one point, it was widely assumed to be the result of a beating administered by Vastola, product of four reform schools. "This kid could tear another human being apart with his hands," the FBI overheard his gangster uncle Dominick Ciaffone (Swats Mulligan) tell another boss.

What Alan Freed did in New York City, Dick Clark would take across the land. The Philadelphia after-school TV teen dance party host went nationwide on the ABC-TV network in August 1957. After a four-week trial run, *American Bandstand* was being carried by sixty affiliates and watched by millions of viewers. ABC-TV added the show to its permanent daytime schedule.

Freed and Clark were a study in contrasts. Sunny, squeaky-clean gentile Clark took over the local afternoon show in July 1956, after the original host was arrested for drunk driving. The twenty-six-year-old broadcaster quickly began to extend his tendrils into the music business. A grateful local label gave Clark a piece of the copyright to "Butterfly," a hit by Philadelphia rock and roller Charlie Gracie, and introduced Clark to the publishing game. Gracie made twenty appearances on *Bandstand* before he sued his label for back royalties. He got a small settlement but never again appeared on *Bandstand*.

As with the New York independents and the Freed show, a thriving Philadelphia independent record scene, with ready access to the national exposure *Bandstand* afforded, grew up around the show—Cameo-Parkway, Swan, Jamie—and Clark had a piece of them all. He didn't play the Danny and the Juniors record "At the Hop" until he owned half the publishing. When he did, the record was an instant smash. Clark played "Sixteen Candles" by the Crests on the Coed label only four times in ten weeks. But after the publishing was assigned to January Music, another one of Clark's pubberys, he slammed the side twenty-seven times in thirteen weeks.

With Freed and the rest of New York radio leading a nationwide surge, rock and roll was paying off big-time for the New York independents. Levy sabotaged Goldner's Tico label when he advised his top record seller, Latin bandleader Tito Puente, to sign with RCA Victor in 1956 (where Puente would that year record his classic album *Dance Mania*). Levy decided to enter the record business and took George Goldner as a partner, along with two other shady characters, Joe Kolsky, who had a piece of Goldner's labels, and his brother Phil Kahl, who had been running Levy's publishing. Together they started Roulette Records.

Right out of the box in January 1957, they hit it big. Picking up a local master out of some oil blotch in Texas, Roulette released both sides of the original single separately and scored two huge rock and roll hits—"Party Doll" by Buddy Knox, which went all the way to number one, and "I'm Sticking with You" by Jimmy Bowen. By April 1957, trade magazines noted that Goldner had left the label and also sold his interests in the Gee, Rama, and Tico labels to Levy, failing to mention that Goldner was paying off gambling losses and that he was, at age thirty-nine, practically washed up.

Down but never out after leaving Roulette, Goldner moved across the street and opened up Gone and End Records in 1650 Broadway. He had not lost his knack for finding hit acts. Five girls calling themselves the Chantels, who grew up singing together at St. Anthony of Padua School in the Bronx, all dressed alike and, after days of rehearsing two songs written by lead vocalist Arlene Smith, went downtown and presented themselves at Goldner's office because he produced Frankie Lymon and the Teenagers. Although Goldner frequently auditioned groups who dropped by—there were often lines waiting in the hallway outside his door—he wasn't there that day.

The girls shifted strategy and, a week later, stood outside the back-stage door at the Brooklyn Paramount after one of the Alan Freed shows and performed an impromptu audition for the Valentines as they left the building. Richie Barrett immediately took the group under his wing and rehearsed them for weeks before presenting the group to Goldner. "He's Gone," the first Chantels release, did very well, and the second, the plaintive gospel call of "Maybe," broke the Top Twenty in December 1957.

Barrett, one of the secrets of Goldner's success, next brought Goldner a group called the Chesters, vocal group veterans with a single out on another New York independent. Goldner cut the group's two originals and, not satisfied with either, gave the group a song by Alley veteran Al Lewis, whose old chestnut "Blueberry Hill" Fats Domino had revived to great effect the previous year. Lewis had a new song, "Tears on My Pillow," that the group hated, but Goldner made them sing. After a handful of indifferent takes, Goldner told lead vocalist Anthony Gourdine to sing in the baby voice he used when he spoke. One of Goldner's guys changed the group's name to the Imperials and Alan Freed named the lead vocalist Little Anthony. The record was a Top Five hit on the End label in 1958.

Goldner was not musical in any practical way, but he knew what a record should sound like. By using the same basic group of musicians, Goldner had a sound he could trust, and he knocked out records by the dozens. He became a master of studio technology, such as it was, and his 1959 record with the Flamingos, his brilliant, shimmering "I Only Have Eyes for You," used the new electronic echo with as much as three seconds' delay. The vocals break the surface of the sound like the reflection of the moon rippling across a lake. The harmonies sound as if they are being piped in from some other planet. Lead vocalist Nate Nelson gives a flawless performance of the Harry Warren standard, and the record stands as one of the greatest achievements in the field, the acme of the entire era.

While most disc jockeys who took cash from the labels at least gave the records a spin for the money, Dick Clark conducted business from such regal heights, payola was paid him as a tribute, offered up so that he might even deign to pay attention. Cash was not enough. Even handing over the publishing might not be enough. A man like Goldner had to give up almost everything just so Dick Clark would think about helping him. This was a tough racket and nobody extracted their pound of flesh from the guys with any greater relish than Dick Clark.

When the payola scandal hit in late 1959, hot on the heels of quiz show champion Charles Van Doren testifying before the same congressional committee about rigging the TV show *Twenty-One*, Goldner, Freed, Clark, and all the others were dragged through the witness chair. With an election year looming and rock and roll blamed as one of the great social ills of the day, these congressmen bent to the task of cleaning up this cesspool of corruption, even though the practice of payola wasn't, strictly speaking, illegal.

Freed, who switched from WINS to WABC in 1958, refused to sign a statement saying he never accepted payola until he saw one signed by Dick Clark, who worked for the same corporation. WABC fired Freed. Although Levy warned Freed to keep quiet, he shot off his mouth in a quarrelsome, contentious interview with columnist Earl Wilson and the headlines on the *New York Post* front page were the same size as V-J Day ("Alan Freed Telling All"). Levy phoned Freed. "What the fuck did you do?" he said.

Dick Clark's labyrinthian holdings in the music business were so complex, committee investigators needed to prepare charts for the committee to lay out all seventeen different corporations Clark owned and the more than eighty different individuals with singular business associations with him. He even owned a record pressing plant. Of course, Clark had divested himself of all his music business interests by the time he appeared before the committee. But he was too valuable a property to ABC. He would keep his job. Clark was going to weather the same storm that sunk Freed.

A chastened, dour Goldner faced the congressmen, seated by his lawyer, and ratted out Clark to the subcommittee. He tried to explain himself ("I'm a traveling man and a recording man. I spend fourteen or fifteen hours rehearsing, recording, and traveling quite a bit . . . "). He described in detail how he transferred title to Clark's publishing companies to four copyrights (including the 1958 Top Twenty-Five hit "Could This Be Magic" by the Dubs) through Vera Hode, a former Morris Levy employee who was still working in Goldner's 1650 Broadway office when she went to work for Clark.

Mr. Lishman: "What benefit would you get out of this?"

Mr. Goldner: "Hoping that he would play my records."

Mr. Lishman: "And the only profit you would make would be on the sale of records?"

Mr. Goldner: "Yes, sir; that would be my profit."

Mr. Lishman: "You wouldn't receive anything at all, either from mechanical royalties—"

Mr. Goldner: "Not anything from the publishing end of the tunes."

Mr. Lishman: "Nothing."

Mr. Goldner: "Nothing."

Mr. Lishman: "The only profit you could expect would be from the sale of the records."

Mr. Goldner: "Yes, sir."

Mr. Lishman: "Did Dick Clark play all these songs on his show, the *American Bandstand* and the *Dick Clark Show*?"

Mr. Goldner: "I think three of the four were played; I don't think 'Beside My Love' was played."

Mr. Lishman: "And what happened to the three that were played? Did they—"

Mr. Goldner: "'Could This Be Magic' was a chart record; 'Every Night I Pray' was a chart record; 'So Much' was a chart record, too; three records hit the top 100 charts."

Mr. Lishman: "Did they hit the top before Dick Clark started plugging them?"

Mr. Goldner: "I don't think so."

Berns at the piano

IV.

1650 Broadway [1959]

I RVING BERLIN WOULD often find himself trapped in the elevator with these horrid young rock and rollers. He would scowl and look away as he went to his seventh-floor office. The sleazy songswipers of his own age were bad enough, but these hotshots, barely older than the teenagers who bought their songs, had found entirely new ways to be uncouth.

The twelve-story building at 1650 Broadway on the corner of West Fifty-First Street housed plenty of music business offices. A few were even distinguished tenants, like Berlin, the man who wrote "There's No Business like Show Business," "White Christmas," and "God Bless America." "St. Louis Blues" composer W.C. Handy also kept his office in the building. But, for the most part, 1650 was rock and roll.

There was nothing especially noteworthy about the building at a glance. A drugstore held down the corner on Broadway. The office building entrance was around the corner on Fifty-First Street, large chrome numerals "1650" above a revolving door. But nothing less than a tumultuous revolution was going on inside. From within these walls, insurgents were mounting an assault on the New York music business, an elite, time-honored industry established before the turn of the century.

In the four years since rock and roll first struck a chord in the national breast, this awful scourge had shown no signs whatsoever of crawling back into whatever gutter it came from in the first place. The haggard, jaundiced music business professionals had seen passing fancies come and go time and again over the years, but this earsore just kept coming, like some untoward swarm of insects sweeping out of the cracks in the sidewalk. To these old hands, rock and roll sounded like musical illiteracy, the undignified, untutored keenings of woebegone Negroes, hicks, and juvenile delinquents.

The major labels had lost control of the hit parade. In four years, the big labels—Columbia, RCA Victor, Decca—had gone from having four-fifths of the Top Ten hits to less than a third. The maverick independents with their rock and roll records had taken half the marketplace away from the big companies. But even more seriously, the old-line publishing companies were out of the picture. Only twenty years earlier, a mere twenty-two publishers, every single one based in New York City, owned the Top Ten. In 1959, sixty-nine publishers from eight states shared the take. What's more, only two of the publishers who had Top Ten records in 1939 lofted new entries in the Top Ten twenty years later.

These publishers suddenly out in the cold were not small potatoes, but esteemed Broadway institutions, some nearing a hundred years old. The unthinkable had occurred. The palace gates were open. The infidels were feasting at the table.

Upstairs at 1650 Broadway, Don Kirshner and his partner Al Nevins were running a tidy little success of a music publishing firm, Aldon Music, chiefly off two writers—Neil Sedaka and Bobby Darin, who were both starting to sell records under their own names. Sedaka started cutting his own songs at RCA Victor after Connie Francis took his "Stupid Cupid" Top Twenty in 1958. After many failed attempts, Bobby Darin finally landed on the hit parade in 1958 with "Splish Splash," a kind of calculated dance hit featuring characters from other rock and roll songs. Darin was so intensely neurotic about his success in the record business that he developed a savage case of psoriasis that disappeared the week his single hit the charts.

Mambo man George Goldner headed up several independent labels out of his offices in the building. He had long before abandoned the mambo in favor of rhythm and blues and rock and roll and kept losing everything he made at the racetrack. But he was still finding acts and turning out hits. Dick Clark of TV's *American Bandstand* maintained an office in the building for his Sea-Lark (C-Lark, get it?) Enterprises, a publishing company made rich by gifts of copyrights from record men seeking favor from the *Bandstand* broadcaster. Clark, the single most powerful disc jockey in the country, was way beyond the simple $50 handshake adequate for his less exalted colleagues. Instead of simple payola, Clark got royola, the gift that keeps on giving.

On another floor, songwriter and music publisher Aaron Schroeder was having a great year. He landed a couple of key Elvis Presley B-sides—"Anyway You Want Me" on the back of "Love Me Tender" and "I Was the One" behind "Heartbreak Hotel"—in the crucial year of 1956 when everything Presley sang sold by the millions. But this year, in 1959, not only did he have new singles by Presley ("A Big Hunk o' Love") and Sinatra ("French Foreign Legion"), but he also had records with Pat Boone, Cathy Carr, the Kalin Twins, Annette Funicello, and Conway Twitty. The royalty checks all came addressed to 1650 Broadway.

With the established forces in popular music unable to relate to this shift in popular taste, the game was up for grabs. People selling records out of car trunks only a few years before were emperors of the charts. Singers nobody ever heard of, singing songs by writers nobody knew, were outselling the bluest of the blue chips. Anybody who could sound like he knew what was going on could get a shot. Any shot could score. It was a field day for hucksters and con men, a breed always crowding the edges of show business on Broadway. It was also an opportunity for ambition, good luck, and even talent to pay off. Every day people heard tell at eateries along the strip like Jack Dempsey's or the Turf about the latest amateur songwriter riding the top of the *Billboard Hot 100*. Sooner, not later, anyone with thoughts along those lines found their way to 1650 Broadway.

Bert Berns was always a talker. With his lopsided grin and the eyes with the conspiratorial glint, he could be a smooth salesman. Every hustler needed a gift of gab and Berns came well supplied. Ed Feldman was an older, overweight, bald Jewish guy, a *schlub* who made a bundle in the building trades, but always had a yen to be in show business. Berns convinced him to pony up $10,000—big bucks—to start a record label. With Feldman's money in his pocket, Berns ran across the drummer he knew from the Eydie Gorme record, Herb Wasserman, who had a couple of songs and was thinking about branching out himself. With a friend of Wasserman's named Ray Passman, another comer songwriter, the three of them decided to take a sixth-floor office.

In some respects, he couldn't have found less likely business partners, since both Wasserman and Passman were professional jazzbeaux who looked down their noses at rock and roll. Only a couple of years older than Berns, Passman was a hipster and scenemaker who caught the bebop bug as a youth in Manhattan during the forties. He clerked at Broadway Music Store and followed Charlie Parker around town, eventually landing a job as a counter boy at George Paxton Music in 1951. Meanwhile he worked at writing songs. It took him five years, but he had his brush with success. Copping a melody from an old children's song, he came up with enough of a tune to attract the attention of seasoned Tin Pan Alley hand Sunny Skylar, best known for writing "Besame Mucho." Using his brother-in-law's name on the songwriting credit he now shared with Passman, Skylar got "I'm Gonna Love You" to the Ames Brothers, whose 1956 single of the song nicked the bottom of the charts for a couple of weeks. That was long enough to get Passman out from behind the counter, two thousand bucks in his kip.

Passman had pieces of records on Jaye P. Morgan and the DeJohn Sisters, although neither ended up doing much. He and Herbie Wasserman wrote this doofus number, "Don't Promise Me (The Can Can Song)," that Mitch Miller did with the DeJohn Sisters, who had "(My Baby Don't Love Me) No More" in the Top Ten the year before. The song's publisher, Goldie Goldmark, a suspect character, always claimed he left the sheet music lying around, which is how this dame Robbin Hood ended up getting her hands on it and recording it, too. Still, when Miller got pissed off, Goldmark coughed up a thousand bucks to help him cool down. Nothing much happened with both records, so it didn't matter to Passman and Wasserman either way.

Herbie Wasserman was a tall, spindly drummer who worked with pianist-vocalist Barbara Carroll. He and bassist Joe Shulman backed the doll who played like Bud Powell in a long-run engagement at the Embers, where the society crowd discovered her. They played in the cast of *Me and Juliet*, a Broadway musical in 1953 that also featured a young Shirley MacLaine. Carroll married Shulman the following year and, when he died only three years later, Herbie, out of a job, hooked up with Ray Passman. They cut an album with a big mama pianist and singer named Patti Bown, but got sharked out of the tape by someone faster and wiser upstairs at Columbia Records, and were both looking for a setup when they went into business with Berns.

Berns grew up around people like Passman and Wasserman, since all three of them were raised in the Bronx. The Bronx of Berns's youth was a wondrous place, a happy haven on the slopes overlooking Manhattan where an old Italian gentleman used to take a merry-go-round door-to-door selling rides to kids in the neighbor-hoods. The fountain in Crotona Park behind the Borough Hall was surrounded by formal flower plantings and still called Victory Park from World War I days. Open-air trolleys and horse-drawn laundry wagons were common sights on the streets. And although the Bronx Borough Day parades down the Grand Concourse every year in June ended in the thirties, there were still massive veterans' parades down the broad, European-style boulevard every Memorial Day.

Landscaped by Frederick Law Olmsted, the man who built Central Park, the Grand Concourse was a tree-lined boulevard six lanes wide that ran through the heart of the Bronx. The lower end was lined with art deco doorman apartment buildings built in the twenties, after the New York subway system made living in the Bronx fashionable. But it was Babe Ruth who put the Bronx on the map. Yankee Stadium opened for business in 1923 and during baseball season the Yankee home run hitter daily drew thousands of fans who had never before been to the Bronx.

The Concourse Plaza Hotel, across the street from the Bronx County Hall at 161st Street and Grand Concourse, was the social center of the borough, and while there were large Irish and Italian neighborhoods in the Bronx, the upscale Grand Concourse was Jewish. At 169th Street, in fact, three synagogues stood shoulder to shoulder. At 188th Street, just below Fordham Road, Loew's Paradise Theater was a four-thousand-seat movie palace with a statue of St. George slaying the dragon above the clock on its impressive façade. The mahogany-paneled lobby featured an ornate marble fountain with goldfish swimming in the basin. The Italian baroque interior was a forest of columns and imitation Michelangelo statuary with a ceiling painted like the night sky with stars fashioned out of pinpoints of light. The Bronx was a world unto itself, a world in which children growing up need not dream beyond.

Bert Berns's father, Charlie Berns, came by himself to the United States from Russia in 1912 at age twenty-one under the name Kisiel Berezovsky. He found work as a salesman in the Garment District, lugging huge bolts of cloth around all day on his shoulders. His future wife had arrived in New York at the age of two in 1901. Her older sister carried her in a basket. Charlie and Sadie were married Christmas Day 1924 at Grossinger's, the Catskills resort where they met and would vacation every August for the rest of their lives. Owner Jennie

Grossinger gave them a silver samovar as a wedding present. Shortly thereafter, they started a little dress shop on Prospect Avenue in the East Bronx. That enterprise prospered, Depression or not, and in 1932, they opened Berns Dress Shop, next door to the sumptuous Loew's Paradise on the Grand Concourse.

IF IT'S DIFFERENT, IT'S BERNS read the store's motto across the front window. They ran the finest dress shop in the Bronx. Doctors' wives and builders' wives from Yonkers and above shopped at Berns. Sid, as Sadie was known, was a hardworking iron woman, a self-taught seamstress and a tireless shop owner, good-looking enough to have worked as a model before her marriage. Charlie Berns was a man full of big ideas, a bit of a character. When his first son was born on November 8, 1929, he named him after the pacifist freethinker, the epitome of libertarian thought at the time, Bertrand Russell Berns.

Charlie and Sid worked day and night, from seven in the morning past midnight. They moved the family, which, two years after Bert was born, came to include a younger sister, Sylvia, to an apartment building around the corner from the shop. Like much of the Bronx, Creston Avenue was a canyon of boxy, five-story apartment buildings, although the Bernses lived in a building slightly more elegant with both an elevator and a doorman. The bare brick wall of the backside of Lowe's took up much of the vista across the street. But the Bernses weren't home much. Their life centered around the thriving store. The children were tended by nannies and, as soon as they were old enough, sent away to school. During summer, they went to camp. Their parents visited every Sunday. From the first of August through Labor Day every year, the dress shop would close and the family would spend the month at Grossinger's.

Baseball loomed large for all young boys in the Bronx before World War II and Berns was good enough to dream about the major leagues while playing stickball in the streets. He also showed an artistic bent. He began by copying photographs out of the newspaper, and his draftsmanship impressed his father enough, Charlie bought the young boy a full set of paints and charcoals. He and his sister would go down to Manhattan's Museum of Natural History and Bert would set up his easel. A crowd would cluster watching him draw.

At camp, he was the designated sign painter, as well as camp bugler, blowing "Reveille" every morning and "Taps" every night. He also owned a pair of drumsticks and sat in the window playing them on the sill. If he and his sister led something of a lonely childhood, they came to depend on each other and never thought of their life as unhappy. Bert would sometimes wait at the front post of the camp on Sundays, eagerly anticipating their parents' weekly visit and he would sometimes sneak out of the Creston Avenue apartment and check the shop, as if making sure his parents were still there, without letting them know. He once caught cold checking on them continually in a rainstorm.

During the war, the Bronx belonged to the women left behind. Men in khaki uniforms could be seen visiting before they shipped out. But the only ones who stayed were schoolchildren, old men, rejects, and those whose work had been deemed vital to the war effort. Windows on every street were filled with blue star cards signifying sons away at war. A gold star meant the son had been killed in action. There were shortages and rationing and air raid drills with sirens blasting in the night.

Bert was fourteen years old when he got sick in 1945. It started as a sore throat, but it didn't go away. His fever soared. He went to the hospital, where strep throat was diagnosed. He went home. He went back to the hospital. He went home. He went back to the hospital several times. He was a very sick young man. He had contracted rheumatic fever, a bacterial inflammation that can severely damage the valves. It scarred his heart. For a teenager in the forties, when open-heart surgery was as much science fiction as flying to the moon, it meant a death sentence.

His parents sent Bert and Sylvia to boarding school in Florida. A doctor had recommended the warm weather for Bert's health, but the weather was terrible the whole time they were there. Neither of them liked the school outside Miami. They ran off to cousin Bertha, who used to work at the dress store, but who had married and moved to Miami. Bert got sick again. They went home and Bert never went back to school. He spent most of a year in bed, and once he got back on his feet, his attitude changed. He read it somewhere in a book or something and it became his creed—live fast, die young, and leave a good-looking corpse.

They bought a baby grand piano from the family upstairs and Bert took lessons. His father liked to think his son might pursue a career as a concert pianist and Bert did show promise at the piano. Neighbors would open their windows to hear young Bert play. Charlie used to like to stand at the window and sing bits of opera. He fancied himself a lover of serious music and thought a career in the fine arts would make an excellent choice for his sickly son. Bert learned quickly on the piano, but he still hit the streets. Over his parents' vocal objections, he would play baseball. He went mambo dancing. He took out girls. He did what he wanted, when he wanted. Right away, he made it clear he was not going to live in fear of this time bomb ticking in his chest.

Bert also knew the angles. The guys he hung out with were attracted to his kind of crazy vitality. Whether they were roaring around drunk in someone's car or trolling for dates at dances, Bert was the center of attention. He cultivated a practiced look—he fussed endlessly over his hair. He landed a job as an emcee at a small nightclub off Arthur Avenue. It was a place where people came to learn the mambo, and mostly he gave dance exhibitions. But he talked his way into a shot at the mike and loved messing with the crowd. "This week, as we do every week," he said, "we bring you our annual show." Nobody paid him any attention, but he didn't care.

He was popular with the girls. He looked good, dressed well, danced great. His younger cousin Burt Gordon was astonished one night to see Bert having an argument with a pretty blonde at a dance.

Bert, it seems, wanted to hand her off to cousin Burt, but the girl was not having any of it. She was embarrassed in front of her friends about Bert's cousin being a couple of years younger, but Bert managed to convince her. His cousin was dumbfounded to see this work, but he and the girl had a fine time, while Bert went after some other, more desirable prey.

Summers always meant Grossinger's. Jennie Grossinger took what had been a seven-room farmhouse in 1914 and, ten years later, turned it into a hotel for five hundred. With his family spending every August at the *hamische* resort outside Liberty, New York, Bert practically grew up at Grossinger's. The Catskills resort catered to the show business crowd, and people like Sophie Tucker and the Ritz Brothers were frequent guests. Other acts got their start in the hotel's showroom, most notably Eddie Fisher, who was "discovered" by comic Eddie Cantor singing at the Terrace Room during the 1946 season. It was all a setup arranged by his manager, Milton Blackstone, a theatrical agent who ran the entertainment program at the hotel since day one. It may have been a ruse, but it worked. Fisher went straight from Grossinger's into the Copacabana that fall and springboarded into stardom. Bert, who was less than a year younger than the singer, got to know Fisher that summer and watched the whole deal at Grossinger's from the sidelines.

Bert knew his way around the resort. He would entertain the other guests after dinner playing "Moonlight Sonata" on the piano. He won a bottle of champagne for taking first place in a dance contest and he could follow the mambo all over that neck of the woods. Tito Puente's band worked at the Swan Lake Resort and Tito Rodriguez played the Stevensville. Machito and the Afro-Cuban All-Stars were at the Concord, the biggest, fanciest place in the so-called Jewish Alps. Bert came to look forward to his family's vacation as a time when he could operate without the constraints of the city, but stay on the inside track. So he was more than a little surprised to find himself falling in love. It was nothing more than a summer romance with a big-city girl, but that had never happened before, and when the girl broke it off, Bert was devastated. It was his first taste of heartbreak.

There were tensions at home, too. Charlie was openly critical of Bert. He wanted his son to play classical music, but his son didn't know what he wanted to do. The two men clashed and Bert decided to skip town. He had a car and he drove to Florida, where cousin Bertha arranged a job for him playing background music in the balcony overlooking a seaside hotel lobby. By the time he returned to New York, he was determined to live on his own. He rented a dump downtown in the West Village and got a square job working for Diner's Club, which didn't last long. He could always count on a handout from his mother when he went home for dinner on Sundays to get his weekly share of abuse from Charlie about how he was wasting his life.

He took a brief fling at marriage, a short-lived union with a good-looking brunette named Betty from Philadelphia. The woman quickly concluded that Bert, already in his midtwenties, clearly had little hope of assuming anything remotely resembling adult responsibilities in the immediate, or perhaps even intermediate, future. She went home and, again, he was crushed. In fact, he was still carrying something of a torch when he met Rita Constance.

A voluptuous, redheaded knockout, a few years older than Berns, Rita Constance played a little piano, sang like Sarah Vaughan, and looked like a million bucks. She grew up in Philadelphia and hit New York at twenty, ready to be a star. She got an $8-a-week apartment with Eddie Fisher's girlfriend from the chorus line at the Copa and put together an act. Without realizing her loftiest aspirations, she did get work. She did some TV and played a lot of clubs. She spent seven years living with comic Len Maxwell, whom Berns also knew, although she kept other boyfriends stashed in various cities around the country. She and Berns struck up a romance and took over a crappy little walkup on Bethune Street in the West Village.

Greenwich Village in the late fifties was a burbling cauldron of social unrest and creative ferment. The goatee and leotard set were digging poetry, cool jazz, and folk music in the cafes and bars that dotted the avenues and side streets. Thelonious Monk played the Village Vanguard, a tiny cellar on Seventh Avenue. Jack Kerouac and Allen Ginsberg were reading poetry in coffeehouses. "Tom Dooley" by the Kingston Trio hit the top of the charts in October 1958 and the smell of cappuccino leaked out onto MacDougal Street from the Commons, the Gaslight, the Cafe Wha?, the Folklore Center, and elsewhere. Camus and Sartre were literary watchwords. Self-styled sick comedians like Lenny Bruce and Mort Sahl made fun of the conformists. *San Francisco Chronicle* columnist Herb Caen coined the term for these disaffected youth, beatniks, and they wore it proudly. Like crazy, man, crazy. But the Village had long been a stronghold of bohemianism. Years before, Welsh poet Dylan Thomas drank himself to death on a corner stool at the White Horse Tavern on Hudson Street in the West Village, just around the corner from where Bert and Rita lived.

Although he may have worn a beard, Bert was not himself a beatnik. He did look close enough to pass for one on a TV program. His father called him a bum. He sat around their apartment, listened to albums of bullfight music, and constantly strummed his guitar, a nylon-stringed Goya that he likely mistook for an authentic Spanish guitar with that genuine Cuban *guajiro* sound. Most people did. The inexpensive guitar was actually manufactured by the Swedish company Hagström, better known for accordions, a confusion they undoubtedly intended when they named the guitar model the Goya. Flamenco guitar was very popular and it wasn't going to hurt sales to have people think it was Spanish.

Bert didn't have many clothes and never wore a necktie. He did comb his hair scrupulously, carefully trying to disguise the receding hairline. Sometimes he simply clunked a tweed hat on his head and didn't take it off. He played piano and guitar and listened to Cuban records for hours. He didn't bathe often and when Rita bitched about that, he told her he had a rheumatic heart and the doctors told him to avoid the shock of the water. She never believed that malarkey about his heart. The guy was too good-natured and happy-go-lucky to be facing death.

He was fascinated with bullfights, something that must have appeared extravagantly exotic to a kid from the Bronx. He pecked away at a novel, a gritty urban coming-of-age story about a young classical pianist and his conflicts with his father. He wrote short scripts and talked big about dreams of success, travel to Europe, the good life up ahead. Rita brought in some money playing club dates and Bert would run up to the Bronx every so often to have his mother slip him some more dough. He still owned a junky car, although he would occasionally borrow his mother's white Thunderbird, and he could always hustle up a dollar for gas somewhere. The couple would often grab a spaghetti dinner at Luigi's, where two people could eat and drink a glass of wine for five bucks. He was scuffling, although he was careful to keep telling Rita how great everything was going to be.

He was always on the lookout for a score, a quick knockdown like this dunce Ed Feldman, the investor. Once Bert, Passman, and Wasserman set up shop at 1650, they let Feldman answer the phones. After all, he wanted to be in show business. They arranged the office with Herb and Ray stationed in the front room and Bert holding down the back room, all their names on the door. Herb talked his girlfriend, Joan Wile, into playing secretary, although she was more showgirl than typist, even if she had graduated from college. Berns knew the first thing he had to do with Feldman's money—put out a record with Rita. He selected a piece of material from the hit second album by Harry Belafonte, "Troubles," a cool, finger-snapping blues written by Belafonte himself.

The New York–born, Jamaica-raised vocalist Belafonte was a pop phenomenon at the time along the lines of Elvis himself. He abandoned a career as a conventional nightclub pop vocalist to sing folk and was drawn to the calypso songs he heard growing up in Kingston, Jamaica, where he spent eight years as a boy with his Jamaican mother. In 1951, he introduced his new act at the Village Vanguard and slowly began to build acceptance for his mixture of traditional American folk and Caribbean calypso. With the explosive success of "The Banana Boat Song" in 1957, Belafonte graduated to phenomenon status, as many pop prognosticators predicted calypso would wipe the upstart rock and roll off the map that first year after Elvis. Such was not to be the case, but Belafonte did hold down center stage in the pop panorama for a moment. The selection of his urbane blues for Rita's record seemed calculated to bridge the gulf between her jazzy inclinations and the pop appetite of the public. They pressed up a few hundred copies on the Performance label, a big treble clef next to the name on the label.

This was a common routine for the hustlers of 1650, press up a handful of records under some insignia, send them around to radio stations, and see if something starts happening somewhere. If a record caught fire, say, in Pittsburgh, it was easy to cut a deal with another more legit record company a rung or two up the ladder. Deals like this took place every day. Of course, for every deal that happened, there were another ninety-nine that didn't.

But Bert, flush with Feldman's money, didn't leave it there. He grabbed Rita and took her and a pile of records down to Florida to visit some radio stations where the sun was shining. Nice trip, but no soap. Rita's record sank like a stone in a lake.

Bert had bigger plans for the next outing. He teamed with a big teddy bear of a singer who called himself Bill Giant, although his name was Ethan Goldstein. He was a hardworking family man with a sweet voice and designs as a songwriter. He sang some jingles and fronted a club band that did weddings, bar mitzvahs, what have you. With a friend of his who called herself Anna Shaw, an old Tin Pan Alley hand who specialized in Spanish songs, Giant fashioned a corny tribute to the disaffected youth of Greenwich Village. Bert saw a possible quick buck in the idea. Downstairs at the recording studio in the 1650 basement, Allegro Studio, Bert and Bill put their voices together on the choruses, while Bill handled the lead on the verses to the song "Beat Generation." They called themselves the Beatniks.

The similarity with the jokey rhythm and blues records songwriters Jerry Leiber and Mike Stoller were making with the Coasters was only enhanced by the presence of saxophonist King Curtis on the track (Herb Wasserman handled the drums). But the record fell considerably short of the sly parody and social commentary of the Leiber-Stoller songs for the Coasters. The Beatniks were patently a one-shot novelty offering and, even as such, not all that noteworthy. Even Edd (Kookie) Byrnes of TV's *77 Sunset Strip* sounded more authentic on his beatnik parody record. But Berns was savvy enough to keep the publishing for both "Beat Generation" and the flip side.

If that idea wasn't goofy enough, Bill Giant's next one was even better. He wanted to do a rock and roll version of the Gettysburg Address. Giant was sure this would be the big breakthrough. American history was hot on the hit parade at the moment with Johnny Horton taking "The Battle of New Orleans" to the top of the charts. With a little rat-ta-tat martial drumming mixed in behind the rock and roll beat, these two wacky guys half sang, half recited "Four score and seven years ago . . . " They even managed to convince Bob Thiele, a big shot at Decca Records who had resurrected his old Signature label, to put the thing out.

Thiele might have known better. He was a record producer who had started a label as a teenager living in Forest Hills, recording classic jazz by veterans such as Coleman Hawkins and James P. Johnson. He folded the company in the midfifties when he went to Decca, where he hit it big with a string of square pop hits by Teresa Brewer, the McGuire Sisters, and Debbie Reynolds' "Tammy." He started to dabble in rock and roll, signing Buddy Holly and Jackie Wilson. He resurrected his Signature label in 1959 with records by TV host Steve Allen, but even Thiele, hot as he was, didn't have a clue.

In short order, Thiele pumped out records on his label aimed at the pop field from every imaginable direction. Among the more than two dozen records he released that year were numbers by Lawrence Welk's musical director George Cates (with whom Thiele had a huge 1956 hit for Decca on "Moonglow and the Theme from 'Picnic'"), Steve Allen and his wife Jayne Meadows, r&b singer Jimmy Ricks of the Ravens, monologist Eddie ("The Old Philosopher") Lawrence, and rock and roller Arch Hall Jr., whose storied B-movie career was preceded by "Monkey in My Hatband" on Signature. Thiele hadn't found the mark with any of the singles he put out on Signature the first year back in business. "The Gettysburg Address" by Bert and Bill Giant was no exception, just another idiotic crack at breaking into the hit single field that went nowhere, cooked up at 1650 Broadway.*

The place was crummy with characters. Mickey Lee Lane was born Sholom Schreiber, an eighteen-year-old kid with *chutzpah* who wandered the halls of 1650, knocking on doors. Berns liked the little motor-mouth Jew rock and roller whose father was a cantor and traveling salesman. Rock and roll crazy, Lane used to take the train from Long Island with his sister Shonnie into Manhattan and dance on the Alan Freed rock and roll TV show. Tired of the home recordings he made on his father's Webcor tape deck, he pawned his elaborate electric train set to pay for a full-fledged session downtown. He and his sister released a single, "Toasted Love," on the Brunswick subsidiary of Decca in 1958, and Lane had been haunting the hallways of Broadway music business office buildings ever since, when he wandered into Berns's lair and played him some of his home recordings.

---

*On the other hand, Thiele did score on the hit parade by the end of the year with an incredibly stupid number, "Uh! Oh!" by the Nutty Squirrels, which sold damn near a million records and was nothing more than a couple of old jazz duffers speeding up their vocals until they sound like chipmunks scat-singing. Maybe "The Gettysburg Address" wasn't such a bad idea after all.

Lane hung out at Berns's office every time he came to the city. He played piano on demo sessions for Berns. Sometimes he supplied handclaps and sometimes he just watched. He wound up writing a song called "Don't Stop" with Bert and Ray Passman, which Passman published, although the song was never recorded. They did make a demo of Lane's own "All I Want to Do Is Dance," and when Lane showed Bert another song he had written, Bert switched a few lines around, tossed off a couple of new lyrics, and added his name as cowriter to the song, "I Want to Be Loved," not that there was any stampede to record that either.

Ersel Hickey, another Broadway character whom Berns wrote a couple of songs with, was somewhat better known. His 1959 hit "Bluebirds over the Mountain" may not have climbed that far up the national charts, but New York radio treated it like a number one smash. Hickey kept an office a couple of blocks down the street in the Brill Building at 1619 Broadway, the big music business office building at West Forty-Ninth Street and Broadway.

The twenty-five-year-old rocker came from upstate New York, near Rochester, where a photographer took a crackerjack shot of Hickey, leg cocked sideways, his guitar pointing ahead like a lance, and put him in touch with Mike Corda, a sometime songwriter and personal manager who handled Italian pop singer Enzo Stuarti. They cut a demo version of "Bluebirds" that wobbled along on a quirky, awkward rhythm and lasted only a minute and a half. But they knew they had something special, something that in its own tiny way was perfect. They leased the master to Epic Records, where Corda had previously placed Stuarti.

In 1958, however, the stripped-down rock and roll sound was on the way out, and although "Bluebirds" struggled up the charts, fighting its way to number seventy-five, it was a battle to go that far. Hickey was in the hands of New York–based major label executives, not Memphis good ole boys who might have understood his down-to-earth rock and roll sound better. By the time Hickey was set to record his third single for the label, a subsidiary of stodgy Columbia Records, he was given the choice of two songs written by Alley old-timer Al Lewis, who cowrote "Blueberry Hill" in 1940. Lewis had also recently scored with "Tears on My Pillow" by Little Anthony and the Imperials and formed a publishing venture with up-and-coming music publisher Don Kirshner. Both demos were sung by Kirshner's songwriting partner, Bobby Darin. Hickey picked "You Never Can Tell" and went nowhere. Fats Domino, who had done so well with his version of "Blueberry Hill," took "I'm Ready" and sailed into the Top Twenty.

Like Lane, Hickey wrote a couple of songs with Berns that did nothing. But Berns loved knowing Ersel. A jubilant Berns burst into Hickey's Brill Building office one morning, waving the album just released by Mexican American rocker Ritchie Valens, who had died that February 1959 in the same plane crash that killed the Big Bopper and Buddy Holly. The Valens hit "La Bamba," with its familiar C-F-G-F progression rooted deeply in the Latin sound that fascinated Berns, was his current favorite song. "Look," he told Hickey, "you're right next to 'La Bamba.'" And, yes, Valens's version of "Bluebirds" was the second cut on the album, immediately following "La Bamba."

But Berns was getting nowhere. He ran through Ed Feldman's money. His girlfriend grew tired of his mouthful of promises. When they were threatened with eviction, his cousin Burt Gordon, by now a practicing attorney in Manhattan, made a couple of convincing phone calls to stall the landlord. But when the rent was still not forthcoming, Rita and Bert went sneaking out in the middle of the night from the dump with the fake fireplace and the kitchen in the hallway, carrying what few possessions they had. For Rita, it was the end. Exasperated at his endless stream of schemes and plans for the future, she no longer believed Bert. She never really liked his music, another jazz snob looking down her nose at rock and roll. She decided he would never make it and split for Florida without him.

Bert was disconsolate. He pleaded his case over the long-distance wires, promising changes, asking her to marry him. But Rita stayed in Florida. Losing his girlfriend and the apartment was one thing, but he also couldn't pay the rent on his office at 1650. Herbie Wasserman liked Bert—everybody did—but he also thought he was a semitalented know-nothing who was never going to amount to anything. But then Wasserman also thought of rock and roll as children's music. He wasn't above putting something together called "Rebel Yell" with trumpet and tympani and grown men going "Whoop! Whoop!" He would do that (and even managed to sell it to a label), but he didn't have to like it. Berns actually liked the stuff.

Berns managed to ingratiate himself with Russ Miller, who worked next door as office manager for Robert Mellin Music. Bobby Mellin was an old-time music publisher who wrote some pretty big records for the Ames Brothers and ran his own publishing company. He spent most of his time conducting the operation from England. Berns wanted to write songs, but it wasn't clear he knew how. Miller knew Berns would make a great song plugger. It didn't matter how the songwriting turned out. Berns had the perfect enthusiasm for a pitchman to represent the firm's songs to other music business characters. He gave Berns a job at $50 a week (and $50 in expenses) and signed him to a contract on February 12, 1960. It was now official; Bert Berns was in the music business. His career had begun.

In moving into the Broadway music world, Berns was stepping into a fierce game already underway. At the advanced age of thirty, he would be little more than a novice among men who had invented the game he was going to play. These were unscrupulous pirates who had already made off with much of the hit parade, once thought impregnable, from big, established companies with far greater resources. They did this through ingenuity, perspicacity, hard work, and sheer ruthlessness that the more genteel, polite ends of the music business couldn't match. These were hard men, playing tough, as Berns was about to learn. It was the dirty business of rhythm and blues.

Jerry Wexler, Ahmet Ertegun, Miriam Abramson, 1955

V.

Atlantic Records [1955–60]

H ERB ABRAMSON CAME back from the Army to a different Atlantic
Records in April 1955. Wexler now worked side by side with
Ahmet, in the desk where Abramson used to sit. Jerry was opinion-
ated, pushy, temperamental, a perfect partner for passive-aggressive
Ahmet, and they were on fire on the charts. "Flip Flop and Fly" by Big
Joe Turner was number two R&B and "I Got a Woman" by Ray Charles
was racing up the r&b charts to number one. Ahmet and Jerry were the
team now and Jerry didn't particularly like Abramson.

Abramson's wife, Miriam, ran the business end of the operation.
She was a caustic hard-boiled dame with a mouth on her, who shared
Wexler's zeal for protecting the Atlantic bank account. To complicate
matters further, Abramson turned up with his pregnant German girlfriend, whom he wanted to marry.

Miriam Abramson took the Atlantic stock in their divorce settlement. She and Herb had a three-year-old son together and the split was
bitter. They still worked at Atlantic, Herb in an office on one side of the
main room and Ahmet and Jerry in an office off the opposite side of the
room. In August 1955, Atlantic bowed a new label, Atco Records, and
placed Herb in charge. Abramson was increasingly being marginalized
in the company he founded.

Ahmet also wanted to bring his brother Nesuhi into the company. Nesuhi was still living in Los Angeles—although no longer married to the lady who owned the record store—and he had been offered a post with one of Atlantic's chief competitors, Hollywood-based Imperial Records, recording home of Fats Domino and other New Orleans rhythm and blues artists. The Atlantic partners could not allow Ahmet's brother to go to work for the other side, especially Imperial owner Lew Chudd, who was a favorite target of inveterate practical joker Ahmet. He delighted in torturing the largely humorless Chudd, for instance, phoning him and pretending to be one "Chester" Domino, uncle of Fats, asking about royalties and suggesting he stop by the office for "a little taste."

Nesuhi was impressive—fluent in several languages yet thoroughly conversant in slangy jazz talk, he had studied at the Sorbonne, lived in the same building as Sartre, broken bread with Camus. He had launched a nationwide traditional jazz revival when, at the request of coast-to-coast radio show host Orson Welles, he threw together a bunch of the old New Orleans men around trombonist Kid Ory. He taught the first university course on the history of jazz at UCLA.

They all kicked in stock to bring Nesuhi into the partnership, even though Abramson and Nesuhi didn't really like each other. The cultured, suave Nesuhi Ertegun joined his younger brother's growing concern at a propitious time. Under Nesuhi's supervision, Atlantic developed a strong jazz program that, right from the start, spanned the traditional Dixieland jazz of Wilbur De Paris to fresh, contemporary fare such as the Modern Jazz Quartet. He moved Atlantic strongly into the rapidly growing market for long-playing albums. Atlantic albums were quality products that came in sturdy cardboard with glossy covers, with intelligent liner notes and discographical recording details, nicer pieces than even the majors were turning out.

It was Nesuhi who found Leiber and Stoller, the songwriters who would lead Atlantic into new vistas. When Jerry Wexler heard the regional hit by the Colts, Los Angeles City College students who were handled by the Platters' manager, Buck Ram, he immediately recognized the song, "Adorable," as perfect fodder for the new lineup of the Drifters. Lead vocalist Clyde McPhatter had been drafted in May 1954 and the once-productive franchise had been lying fallow for more than a year. In a rush to beat the smaller label to the national market, Wexler asked Nesuhi Ertegun to conduct a session with the Drifters in Los Angeles, where the group was touring and Nesuhi had been living for ten years. Wexler told him to record "Adorable" and whatever the hell else he wanted.

Nesuhi first met songwriter Jerry Leiber shooting pool in the basement at USC law student Jimmy Tolbert's house. Tolbert was a nephew of Lester Young, and the jazz crowd hung out at his parties. Leiber and Stoller spent a lot of time at Jimmy Tolbert's, where they both met their black girlfriends. Leiber and his songwriting partner Mike Stoller were semicelebrated in South Central at the time as the white cats who wrote r&b songs for Charles Brown, Jimmy Witherspoon, and Amos Milburn. Their song "Hound Dog" had been one of the biggest r&b records of 1953 for Big Mama Thornton. They were currently operating their own record label, Spark Records, out of a Melrose Avenue storefront, writing and producing brilliant records, such as the comic blues "Riot in Cell Block Number Nine" by the Robins. Nesuhi knew Leiber and invited him to join him as a tennis partner on his forthcoming honeymoon, as he was getting married for the second time. Leiber went along and played tennis with Nesuhi every day, while his bride sat by the pool.

Not only did Nesuhi include Leiber and Stoller's "Ruby Baby" among the five songs he recorded with the Drifters during his three-hour session at Los Angeles' Modern Records, but he convinced them to fold their label and come to work for Atlantic Records. The Spark label never had any distribution outside the West Coast, and although some of the records made a little noise, none ever sold truly well. The label was an uneasy partnership between the songwriters, a music business professional named Lester Sill, and Stoller's nervous investor father.

(Wexler proved astute in his judgment about "Adorable." The record was a Top Five *Billboard* R&B hit for the Drifters, the crucial first single by the group after the departure of the popular lead vocalist McPhatter, introducing lead tenor Johnny Moore, who was to have an illustrious career with the band. In fact, three of the five songs produced by Nesuhi Ertegun in the September 19, 1955, session made the charts.)

In November 1955, Leiber and Stoller signed a deal with Atlantic Records to sell the Spark masters and continue to produce records for Atlantic, the first independent production deal in the business. The Atco rerelease of "Smokey Joe's Cafe," the final Spark record by the Robins, sold 250,000 copies, instead of 90,000. Leiber and Stoller were so jazzed, they hung a sign in their office reading WEST COAST DIVISION, ATLANTIC, ATCO AND CAT RECORDS.

With "Smokey Joe's Cafe" Leiber and Stoller had come into their own as the preeminent composers of rhythm and blues. They were inventing the language and sound of the music, the basic vocabulary, the artistic palette. These two twenty-two-year-olds were in full bloom as a creative team and they were about to be swept to the top of their world by forces beyond their imagination.

"Smokey Joe's Cafe" introduced what Leiber liked to call "audio playlets," although "Riot in Cell Block Number Nine" the previous year already owed as much to the radio drama *Gang Busters* as it did Muddy Waters. With Leiber's ear for dialect and the expert comic timing of the experienced vocal group, enforced by scrupulous rehearsals conducted by Leiber and Stoller, the record captured a rich cartoonish atmosphere in vivid sound pictures, tied together by a ribbon of piano from Mike Stoller, a kind of street talk mini-opera told in three acts and nine couplets.

Leiber's widowed mother had run stores in black neighborhoods, first in Baltimore, then Los Angeles. Leiber had grown up at ease around that culture. He was short, stocky, and extravagantly verbal and had one brown eye and one blue eye. Stoller's mother was a former model and Broadway actress who dated George Gershwin and descended into a lifetime of melancholia as a housewife in Queens. Stoller took stride piano lessons from James P. Johnson, Fats Waller's teacher, and ran around the jazz clubs of Manhattan before his family moved to Los Angeles when he was sixteen. He was attending Los Angeles City College in 1950 when Leiber contacted him about writing songs after getting his number from a mutual acquaintance. Stoller was not impressed until Leiber showed up at his house with notebooks full of lyrics. Stoller saw all the ditto marks and realized this crazy kid, three weeks his junior, was writing blues.

In April 1956, Mike Stoller took the first sizable royalty check he ever received, moved out of the apartment he shared with his wife of one year, Meryl, and put their belongings in storage, and they headed off to Europe for a three-month tour. One of the highlights was hearing the great Edith Piaf in her concert at the Olympia in Paris introduce their "Black Denim Trousers and Motorcycle Boots"—the big hit Stateside by a tight, bright, white vocal group on Capitol Records called the Cheers that paid for the European trip.

On the return home, they booked passage on the *Andrea Doria*, an Italian ocean liner that sank in the dark seas off Nantucket on July 25, 1956, the night before it was supposed to dock in New York City, after ramming an outbound Scandinavian ship. More than sixteen hundred passengers and crew were rescued and forty-six people died. The Stollers' lifeboat was picked up by a United Fruit steamer. Lester Sill and Jerry Leiber took a cab to the pier where the boat was docking. Leiber brought a silk suit, assuming Stoller would be wet and need dry clothes. But Leiber was excited about news that couldn't wait—he blurted out they had a big hit record. The old Big Mama Thornton hit, "Hound Dog," had been recorded by Elvis Presley, he told Stoller.

"Elvis who?" said Stoller.

So rapid had been the ascension of Elvis Presley that Stoller had missed it in its entirety during his three months tooling around Europe.

Presley's first RCA Victor single, "Heartbreak Hotel," hit number one only a month before. "Hound Dog," the second single, was streaking up the charts as they were fishing Stoller out of the drink.*

They had two records looming high on the charts—"Hound Dog" and "Down in Mexico," the first Leiber-Stoller record with the Coasters, the new edition of the Robins, who split in two after Leiber and Stoller went to Atlantic. One set of members stayed with the group's manager and kept the name, the Robins. Lead vocalist Carl Gardner and bass vocalist Bobby Nunn put together a new group, managed by Lester Sill, and called themselves the Coasters, to underline the group's association with the West Coast. "Down in Mexico" was another satiric set piece, a comedic travelogue loping along a slinky Latin beat Stoller copped from playing with *pachuco* bands when he first hit L.A.

With two records on the charts, the boys decided to cool their heels in New York. They moved out of the Algonquin into an apartment on Seventy-First Street between Fifth and Madison Avenues. They briefly took a job as heads of East Coast r&b a&r for RCA Victor but quit after Leiber couldn't tell his office cubicle from the others coming back from lunch. They whipped up some songs for Atlantic artists—"Fools Fall in Love" for the Drifters, "Lucky Lips" for Ruth Brown—caught some plays, had drinks, dinners, and more drinks with the Erteguns and Wexler. After a couple of months, Leiber split for Hollywood and Stoller remained behind.

After "Hound Dog," Jean Aberbach of Hill & Range, the Elvis Presley music publishers, had wanted more songs, and Leiber had the nutty idea to send over "Love Me," a corny country music takeoff they originally did for the Spark label with a duo from Oakland called Willie and Ruth. Presley, who apparently went through life entirely without any sense of irony, loved the dopey song, sang it straight, and made it

---

*Atlantic made a $25,000 offer to sign Elvis—that was all the label could afford—but Colonel Parker held out for a $40,000 guarantee from RCA Victor, the largest advance ever given any recording artist at that point.

one of the most popular records of 1956. Aberbach bought an interest in Leiber and Stoller's publishing company, making Hill & Range their partners.

Stoller returned to Los Angeles in early 1957 and he and Leiber started working on the next Coasters record. The song "Young Blood" had been born earlier in New York when Wexler challenged Leiber to write lyrics for a title dreamed up by songwriter Doc Pomus, a burly bear of a blues singer on crutches, owing to a childhood bout of polio. Leiber finished the song in the car on the way to dinner at Wexler's house in Great Neck. They were listening to playbacks at Atlantic's new Fifty-Seventh Street offices the next day and Leiber recited the lyrics to Stoller, who went to the piano and put them to music on the spot.

Back together on the West Coast, they made four songs with the Coasters in February 1957 at Hollywood Recorders and were surprised to see the "Young Blood" A-side eclipsed a couple of weeks after its May release by the flip, "Searchin,'" a song riddled with references to the radio detective shows of Leiber's youth—*Charlie Chan, Sergeant Friday, Boston Blackie*. The record, which showcased the increasingly formidable artistic command of the songwriting/record production team, became Atlantic's first million-seller.

Before Leiber and Stoller, the Atlantic chiefs had to rely on intermediaries such as Jesse Stone for the creation of the music. They dabbled in songwriting but almost always in collaboration with another more musically skilled coauthor. Wexler had a lot of song credits but never wrote a song by himself in his life. The music of Leiber and Stoller was their vision from beginning to end. Leiber demonstrated the vocals to the performers, showed them the exact timing and intonations he wanted. Stoller played the piano and together they rehearsed the group until the Coasters became their voices. Sometimes Leiber even sang with the group on the sessions. The Coasters, skillful performers, were just the singers; Leiber and Stoller were the artists. They didn't write songs—they wrote records.

Jean Aberbach then summoned the pair to New York to cook up numbers for the new Presley movie, *Jailhouse Rock*. They caught Miles at the Village Vanguard, Basie at Birdland, Monk at the Five Spot. They checked out some museums. They saw a couple of Broadway shows. Eventually Aberbach showed up at their room in the Gorham Hotel and planted himself on their couch until the boys got off the dime. They finished off four songs in that one afternoon (the last one they wrote, "I Want to Be Free," may have had some unspoken subtext). A month later, back in Los Angeles, they dined with Colonel Parker, Presley's controlling manager, at the Beverly Hills Hotel, having him check them out before meeting Presley later that week at the recording session at Radio Recorders, where Big Mama Thornton had recorded "Hound Dog."

Presley surprised Leiber and Stoller with his knowledge of r&b records in general and their work in specific (he knew their early, pre-Atlantic Ray Charles cover, "The Snow Is Falling"). They cut Leiber and Stoller's title track to the film, Presley's bassist and drummer swiping the intro from a swing version they remembered of "The Anvil Chorus." The next day, they returned to work out proper arrangements for their songs "Treat Me Nice" and "I Want to Be Free." Stoller took over the piano bench for the second song, and after they were done with that, with Leiber virtually running the session from the studio floor, they decided to throw in "(You're So Square) Baby I Don't Care," leftover from the New York writing session.

Leiber and Stoller returned to Presley recording sessions in September at Radio Recorders, where Elvis was finishing a Christmas album. At the studio, Jerry and Mike knocked off a blues riff about Christmas (*Santa Claus is coming down your chimney tonight*) that Presley loved and instantly recorded, along with all the old Bing Crosby crap they were making him sing that afternoon. They also slipped in the plaintive ballad "Don't" that they wrote specifically at Elvis's request and had already sent along some months earlier. When

Colonel Parker got hold of Jean Aberbach and finished chewing him out about songwriters taking material directly to Elvis, bypassing the music publishers and management, Leiber and Stoller never set foot in the studio again with Elvis.

They took the Coasters to Chicago and recorded in the Chess Records studios in July 1957 with bassist Willie Dixon and the other Chess sidemen, but neither "Idol with the Golden Head" nor "What Is the Secret of Your Success" were destined for charts success despite the sophistication of the material and the confidence of the performance and production. A December session in New York yielded an indifferent pair of masters, and before the end of their first million-selling year, the Coasters had slipped off the charts entirely.

Atlantic Records wasn't doing much better. Sales had slowed from a fairly good year in 1956, when the label lofted hits by Big Joe Turner ("Corrine Corrina"), Ray Charles ("Lonely Avenue"), and newly signed artists Ivory Joe Hunter ("Since I Met You Baby") and Chuck Willis ("It's Too Late"), both r&b veterans other labels let slide. Clyde McPhatter, back from the army, scored with "Treasure of Love." LaVern Baker's "Jim Dandy" did pretty well, after Wexler kept it in the can for almost a year. But the label went cold the next year.

The one light in the leaden release schedule was "Mr. Lee" by the Bobbettes, a group of teenaged girls from Harlem's P.S. 109 who charmed Ahmet with a mean-spirited little song about a teacher they especially despised. Ahmet had them clean up the lyrics, and the girls' youthful exuberance carried the record into the Top Ten in July 1957. "I'm going to *shul* for y'all," their Atlanta distributor said. Wexler was very amused at Jews speaking in Southern accents, but he was beginning to wonder how long this could last.

Two records recorded and released within weeks of each other in spring 1958 reversed Atlantic's failing fortunes. Leiber and Stoller banged out the song "Yakety Yak" in about fifteen minutes one afternoon at Leiber's Washington Square duplex. Stoller sat down at the piano and started playing what he thought was a Coasters-like rhythm. Leiber, in the kitchen boiling water for tea, shouted out, "Take out the papers and the trash." Stoller shouted back, "Or you don't get no spending cash." They had never worked in Atlantic's new studios before (the record company offices had been moved and Tom Dowd converted the fifth floor on Fifty-Sixth Street to full-time recording). Leiber wanted to back his bet on "Yakety Yak" with a Coasterized version of "Zing Went the Strings of My Heart." Two other songs were also recorded at the session—"Three Cool Cats" and "Stewball"—but Leiber need not have worried. "Yakety Yak" exploded when it was released in June 1958, racing to number one on the Pop and R&B charts. Three weeks later, the second record, "Splish Splash" hit the charts.

Wexler signed Bobby Darin to Atco after he bought a handful of demos the Bronx-born singer, fresh from a hitless stint as a Decca Records artist, recorded by himself in Nashville. Wexler picked up the recordings as masters and assigned him to Atco and Herb Abramson. The rock-and-rolled "I Found a Million Dollar Baby (In a Five and Ten Cent Store)," the old Billy Rose warhorse, did a little something, but not much. Two subsequent singles did less and Abramson told Ahmet he was going to drop Darin from the label. Ahmet had grown fond of the kid, who used to play piano in the Atlantic waiting room, wailing away on Ray Charles numbers. Ahmet had a feeling for him. He booked Darin into half of a session he planned the next week for jazz vocalist Morgana King.

They cut three songs in their half of the three-hour session— "Queen of the Hop," "Judy Don't Be Moody," and "Splish Splash." Darin dashed off the song "Splish Splash" at the apartment of disc jockey Murray "The K" Kaufman, whose mother fancied herself a songwriter and came up with the title. She got half the copyright. It never hurt to have a famous disc jockey (or his mother) holding a financial interest in a song. The arrangements were done in the studio and the two Morgana King numbers cut in the split session were never even released. "Splish Splash" took off and streaked up the charts behind "Yakety Yak."

This April 10, 1958, session was also the first time engineer Tom Dowd used his new eight-track recorder. He ordered the equipment nine months earlier, one of the first production models to come from Ampex, and put it to work as soon as he unpacked the crates and wired it up, making Atlantic Records the first company to routinely record in stereo.

Afraid the label was going to drop him as Abramson threatened, Darin had gone into the studio and cut another one of his songs, "Early in the Morning." Murray "The K" Kaufman sold the master to Brunswick Records, who released the record under the name the Ding Dongs. Atlantic's lawyers quickly took the record back from Brunswick and Ahmet released it by the Rinky Dinks. Brunswick countered by having the song covered by one of their artists, Buddy Holly, and the two versions battled it out on the charts (the Rinky Dinks record topped out at twenty-four and Buddy Holly's finished at thirty-two). Ahmet forgave Darin; he was suddenly the label's best-selling artist. Abramson, however, was through. The remaining partners scraped together $300,000 and bought him out of the company he started. His ex-wife never spoke to him again.

With Leiber and Stoller turning out these exceptional Coasters records, Ahmet and Wexler handed over the Drifters, an almost bankrupt enterprise, to Leiber and Stoller. The group was managed by former trumpet player George Treadwell, husband and manager of Sarah Vaughan, and somewhere along the line, he copyrighted the name and so, in effect, owned the group. Members were paid a small salary and did not share in either record royalties or performance fees. As a result, there was always an undercurrent of dissatisfaction in the group and members came and went with some frequency. When Leiber and Stoller took a transitory lineup into the studio with lead tenor Bobby Hendricks on his only session with the group and cut their song "Drip

Drop" in April 1958, it had been more than a year since the group had been in the studio.

Treadwell had a contract with the Apollo Theater for two performances a year by a group called the Drifters. Wexler also saw juice in that tomato. Treadwell fired the entire existing set of Drifters and hired another vocal group called the Five Crowns to be the new Drifters. The Crowns had been around the scene even longer than the original Drifters, with various members, under various names. Their latest record was on some nothing label called R&B Records distributed by Atlantic. The twenty-year-old lead vocalist Benny Nelson—now calling himself Ben E. King—had the bones of a song that Leiber thought might do the trick. During rehearsal, Stoller started playing a fancy little countermelody and Leiber got the idea to use strings.

They ended up with twenty-six pieces on the date, far too many for the Atlantic studios. The sessions moved to a studio called Coastal on Forty-Second Street, which was built in a ditch. The booth was in the third balcony and the studio was in the orchestra—deep, narrow, high. Sound bounced all over the place and nobody could see each other. They rented some tympani that quickly went out of tune. Arranger Stan Applebaum copped a string line from Tchaikovsky's *1812 Overture.* Leiber's recent enthusiasm for Brazilian music, inspired by the recordings of Italian actress Silvana Mangano, led them to experiment with the slow samba rhythm called *baion.* Vocalist Charles Thomas, who was supposed to do the lead vocals and did sing the other two songs recorded that day, choked, and baritone Ben E. King stepped up, even though he was supposed to sing the bass part. The other Drifters were floating off in some key all their own. It should have been a fiasco, but there was something about the record that sounded intriguing. Stoller thought it sounded like two different radio stations tuned to the same frequency. They took it to play for Wexler, who was eating a tuna fish sandwich at his desk. He sprayed tuna all over. "That's the worst piece of shit I've ever heard in my life," he said.

"There Goes My Baby" not only hit the top of both Pop and R&B charts, sold more than a million copies, and started a second act for the Drifters that would prove even greater than the first act, but also opened up the whole idea of symphonic r&b. Leiber and Stoller had taken rhythm and blues into a new realm. While most of the record men in the r&b field held the music in veiled contempt, Leiber and Stoller loved the music they made. They shared that with Ahmet and Jerry. These were passionate men pursuing their own destiny, borrowing from everything, making it up as they went along, loving what they were doing.

Leiber and Stoller stumbled slightly on the "Yakety Yak" follow-up—another radio drama story song from Leiber's childhood, "The Shadow Knows," that didn't click—but they were back on track with consecutive Top Tens in 1959 with "Charlie Brown," "Along Came Jones" and "Poison Ivy," each one a gem, little masterpieces of comic timing. LaVern Baker scored with "I Cried a Tear" in late 1958, but mainly, the established Atlantic acts—Ruth Brown, Big Joe Turner, the Clovers, Ivory Joe Hunter—were done. The label lost Clyde McPhatter in a bidding war that MGM won for $50,000. But Leiber and Stoller had brought the Drifters back from the dead, Bobby Darin was the label's first teen star, and Ray Charles finally produced the breakthrough record Atlantic always knew was in him.

"What'd I Say" was an elongated riff and series of nonsense couplets Ray and his Raelettes invented one night on the bandstand. It worked so well, they tried it again the next night, and the next, slowly polishing this gospel abstraction. When they rolled into Atlantic studios to record the piece in February 1959, it was more than seven minutes long and nobody knew what to do with it. After some judicious edits, Tom Dowd turned the piece into two heart-stopping three-minute cuts. A two-part minisuite for r&b orchestra and gospel quartet. This was something everybody knew what to do with. Wexler ordered the two-sided single held for release until summer when teens hit the beaches with their transistor radios. The piece entered the literature as a bandstand standard almost as soon as it was released. "What'd I Say" single-handedly elevated the level of expression in the r&b idiom.

In May, Nesuhi Ertegun brought together the entire Count Basie band and seven key members of the Duke Ellington orchestra to back Ray Charles on big band sessions arranged by a young Quincy Jones (whom Charles had taught to write music as a teen in Seattle). These distinguished musicians were not sure if this twenty-seven-year-old blind piano player deserved all this; New York jazz cats with their typical attitudes about rhythm and blues. In the middle of running the score, Ray called Nesuhi over. "Fourth bar, third trumpet, there's a bad note," he said. Quincy didn't hear it, so they had the trumpets play one by one. Third trumpet, fourth bar, wrong note. Transcriber wrote it down it wrong. The entire band broke into applause. Who had ears like that? The tone of the session suddenly changed, as Charles led the assembled multitude through a peerless romp of jazz standards, rhythm and blues, ballads and blues. They called the album *The Genius of Ray Charles*, and at Atlantic, that's what they thought of him.

Atlantic was like a river in spring. Ahmet told the trades the label was forced to hold back spring releases because they were having so much success, he knew there wasn't room for that much Atlantic product on radio station playlists. By summer, the company was billing $1 million a month in sales. And the best was yet to come.

Bobby Darin hated rock and roll. "I sing rock and roll because it sells records," he told *Billboard* in September 1958. "The young kids like it and want it and I can do it. But I try to be versatile. It's the only way to build a future in this business. In the nightclubs, I lean to other things, ballads done fairly straight, special bits, etc. I even do 'Mack the Knife' from *Threepenny Opera*."

He and Ahmet went into the studio in December 1958 and cut an album's worth of big band pop, including Darin's swaggering version of the Kurt Weill–Bertolt Brecht song that had recently been reprised by Louis Armstrong. Ahmet used an arranger he found through Darin's publicist and always claimed that he knew "Mack the Knife" was a hit on the first run-through in the studio. But the label proved to be in no hurry to release this decidedly adult fare from their resident teen idol. The album, *That's All*, came out in March 1959. The next month, the company released a new single from sessions Ahmet conducted in March, "Dream Lover," more teen beat pop romance, although a slightly larger session than on his previous outings. The label didn't even release a single of "Mack the Knife" until August, by which time demand had already built up.

The record was the best-selling record of the year in 1959 and, again, the best-selling record of 1960. Even more unimaginable, at the second annual Grammy Awards in November 1959, "Mack the Knife" won Record of the Year—over Sinatra and Presley—and Darin himself was named Best New Artist, the first year that award was given. "Mack the Knife" is often seen as an anti–rock and roll statement, a blow by reactionary forces that sided with the Sinatra/Mitch Miller viewpoint on rock and roll as garbage for kids, but what "Mack the Knife" really turned out to be was an anomalous, final hit from the swing era, the last time the big band sound would top the charts. It was a record they understood around the Broadway music offices. Between "Mack the Knife" and "What'd I Say," the dominion of Atlantic ranged far and wide.

Russell Byrd on *The Clay Cole Show*

VI.

A Little Bit of Soap **[1961]**

B OBBY MELLIN WAS a stout, short man in his fifties who dyed his gray hair. When Berns joined his firm in 1960, Mellin was running his publishing empire from his Knightsbridge district office in London, while his posh second wife lived in a five-hundred-year-old manor in the Surrey countryside, where he joined her for weekends. The great Gus Kahn had shown the kid the ropes. The ubiquitous Chicago lyricist of the twenties ("Yes Sir, That's My Baby," "Makin' Whoopee") took a shine to young Bobby Mellin, a Russian Jew immigrant kid working behind the counter at a music publisher, and took him on the road with him for several years.

Mellin was never much of a songwriter. He paid someone to ghostwrite lyrics to his big standard, "My One and Only Love," one of the first songs Frank Sinatra recorded with arranger Nelson Riddle on his comeback swing for Capitol Records in 1953. It was a rewrite anyway of an existing number called "Music from Beyond the Moon" that Mellin—or someone on his behalf—simply fitted with new lyrics. Mellin's biggest hit, "You You You" by the Ames Brothers, one of the most unbearably puerile songs of its day, was simply his English lyrics to a German pop song. Mellin turned suiting English lyrics to foreign language songs into his specialty as a songwriter.

As a music publisher, Mellin made his money off songwriters and kept offices in both London and New York. He was a tuberculosis carrier, so he had difficulty entering the United States and rarely showed up on these shores. Russ Miller managed the office on the sixth floor of 1650 Broadway, next door to where Berns, Ray Passman, and Herb Wasserman ran their music business hustle. When Miller offered him the $50-a-week song plugger job in early 1960, Berns sold his desk and file cabinet to Herbie, who closed the office shortly thereafter.

Like all the old-line publishers, Mellin was afraid of rock and roll, and Miller sensed in Berns someone who could bring the office up to date. Mellin approved, but he was a remote presence in the small office suite above Broadway. At the time, rock and roll's future seemed uncertain. Folk music was the latest threat on the horizon. The Kingston Trio was selling albums by the truckload. Anything seemed possible. Music publishers like Mellin, their catalogs mired in post–swing era glossy pop songs that suddenly sounded very old-fashioned, had no idea what was happening. At age thirty-one, Berns hardly qualified as a teenager, but he had fresh, hungry ears.

Starting out in the music business, Berns spent the first year looking for his voice. His initial efforts were gimmicky and pedestrian, but he managed to get songs recorded. Berns was a man with ideas. He sold Gene Schwartz at Laurie Records his "The Ballad of Walter Williams," a song commemorating the recent death of the last Civil War soldier, which Schwartz cut with a rockabilly singer named Jack Carroll. Berns and Russ Miller wrote "White Oak Swamp," more sentimental claptrap about a Civil War battle, for a single by one Johnny Yukon on the Versatile label. Berns now had a new songwriting name—his first two names, Bert Russell.

With the release of the epic John Wayne motion picture looming—and Berns still laboring under the impression that American history was a hot topic for the hit parade—Bert Berns made his debut as a recording artist with "The Legend of the Alamo" in October 1960 on a Laurie Records single destined for obscurity. With banjos strumming, martial choirs singing along on the choruses, lyrics half-recited, half-sung, Berns no doubt meant to strike a patriotic chord, but this was no "The Ballad of Davy Crockett." Berns shared the writing with Bobby Mellin and another recent Mellin songwriting signing, a young rockabilly singer from Texas named Bob Johnston. (Years later, as staff producer at Columbia Records, Johnston would oversee hit albums by Johnny Cash, Simon and Garfunkel, Leonard Cohen, and Bob Dylan.)

On the flip side, Berns sang the folky "Gotta Travel On," which country singer Billy Grammer made a Top Ten hit the previous year, covering a song that had been "written"—well copyrighted—by Greenwich Village folk song discoverer Paul Clayton, who based his song on a nearly identical piece of mountain music long in the public domain. Buddy Holly used the song to open his shows the year before on his fatal "Winter Dance Party" tour. *Cashbox* liked both sides. "A lively folkish stand which takes very good advantage of the upcoming 'Alamo' flick," noted the trade magazine. "Deft folk-beat sound."

Berns had found a sympathetic ear in Gene Schwartz at Laurie Records, but Schwartz was a solid square who was just learning the business himself. He and his brother Bob Schwartz were accountants who thought the record business would be fun. They looked the part; horn-rim glasses, crew cuts, and bow ties. Their partner, Allen Sissel, had put up the money and they cut in Gene's best friend, Eliot Greenberg, who happened to be an arranger and musician, making him useful in the actual making of the records.

The label struck gold on the first release in 1958, "I Wonder Why," a volcanic epiphany of white doo-wop and Bronx soul by Dion and the Belmonts that the Schwartzes had stumbled over. By 1960, when the group broke through to a widespread audience with a straight-faced cover of the Jerome Kern standard, "Where or When," Dion and the Belmonts were certified rock and roll stars. Of course, the lead vocalist and the group went their separate ways later that year, and Dion was considering different options to pursue as a solo act when he ran into Berns walking down Broadway. Berns pulled him over to the curb and, pounding on the fender of a parked car, gave Dion an impromptu song demonstration. Dion couldn't help but like the guy.

The first demos Berns cut for Mellin Music were not a distinguished lot. He tried out some pseudofolk ("Sally"), morbid country and western ("(I'm Gonna Carve Your Name on) Cold Prison Walls"), and another jailhouse ballad ("I'm Coming Back"), a trifling whistling novelty feature that actually was recorded as "Whistler's Twist" by someone named Elson Smith. "The World Is Mine" was intriguing—a sultry Cubano vamp banged out on piano. Also there was the rocking bare bones of a song titled "In a Room In a House," Berns shouting out the lyrics over his pounding piano and a buzzing electric guitar. The song is a stark, almost metaphorical lament for a life without love. He gave the song to Dion, who cut a big band version in a kind of Bobby Darin–style experimental session after splitting with the Belmonts. Dion sounded ballsy and bluesey in front of the blasting brass, but Gene Schwartz decided to stick with the teen scene for Dion and the track was shelved.

But Berns did land a record with Schwartz on a song titled "Push Push" with a singer named Austin Taylor. The record moved on an insistent bass and supple rhythmic groove straight out of the mambo. Cowritten with Phil Medley, an older black gentleman who worked down the hall at Roosevelt Music and also wrote the current Jimmy Charles hit, "A Million To One," the song itself was more frankly sexual than standard chart fare of the day with its repeated chorus, "Push, push . . . you've got to give a love a shove."

Schwartz customarily made indifferent, unexciting recordings that depended on the vocal performance and the song for everything. With Berns in the studio kibitzing, the Caribbean undercurrent of the arrangement is clearly Berns insinuating himself into the record. The entire production sounds considerably more animated and lively than Schwartz's usual job, whipped up by some of Berns's enthusiasm.

Little noticed at the time, "Push Push" spent two entire weeks on the *Billboard Hot 100* in November 1960 and reached as high as ninety. It may have been only a modest beginning, but Berns was on the charts.

Berns started making the scene, meeting people, getting known, developing contacts. When Dante and the Evergreens showed up from Los Angeles to sing their hit "Alley Oop" at the Brooklyn Paramount, Berns introduced himself in a hotel lobby to lead vocalist Don (Dante) Drowty, handing him a business card and identifying himself as a music publisher.

Drowty and his three associates were Santa Monica College students whose record exploded on a small label. The song had been recorded by a number of groups, but Dante and the Evergreens and the Hollywood Argyles, a group whose members had gone to the same high school as the Evergreens, were battling for supremacy pretty much market by market. In New York, Dante and the Evergreens went to number one in three weeks after the June 1960 release. The group came to town to play the Apollo Theater—after Buddy Holly and the Crickets and Duane Eddy, only the third white group to play there— and James Brown was on the bill. Harlem is a long way from Santa Monica. Berns went with them.

Berns took Drowty the next day to the Mellin office and, before Drowty and company went back to California, he and Berns were writing songs and singing together into Drowty's portable Wollensak wire recorder in Berns's room at the Hotel Woodward at Fifty-Sixth Street and Broadway, where Berns lived with a pair of Siamese cats and a litterbox. He was scuffling, trying to make things happen. He often ate cheap at the automat and sometimes he shared of a can of tuna with the cats for dinner.

Bobby Mellin also managed a vocalist named Hoagy Lands, who had worked as a solo in clubs around Jersey after his high school vocal group, the Dynaflows, flowed apart. Lands didn't know whom she was talking about when Mellin's secretary called to say "Bert Berns wants to see you." With Mellin in England, Lands was informed, Berns was a songwriter who was going to work with him. They rehearsed two songs Berns wrote with Phil Medley. The session was produced by Morty Palitz, an old-time record man who ran Columbia Records during the forties, and the arranger was Teacho Wiltshire, a tall, light-skinned black pianist who had been around the scene for years, arranging and even producing a few jazz sessions for Prestige and others with the likes of Thelonious Monk and Annie Ross ("Twisted").

Lands, whose father was Cuban and mother part Cherokee, sounded a lot like Sam Cooke without the smooth sheen. For the rest of his life, Berns would work with Hoagy Lands. "Lighted Windows," the B-side, was another take on the old mistaken-identity gag Bob Crewe and Frank Slay worked with such success on the Rays' "Silhouettes," but "(I'm Gonna) Cry Some Tears" gave Lands what he needed to rip it up. Berns would spend his life putting his singers in tears—tears of joy, tears of shame, tears of rage, tears of despair—this was just the first time. But when Lands hit that chorus—"I'm gonna cry-y-y-y-y, yeah"—it was pure pay dirt.

Mellin paid to have some singles pressed on a label named Judi, after his daughter. The record attracted enough attention, and they sold the master to ABC-Paramount, after which it was never heard of again. But, in Hoagy Lands, Bert Berns had found a voice that could bring his songs to the edge of heartbreak.

Things were starting to happen and Berns was beginning to get songs recorded. Frankie Brent, ex–Freddie Bell and the Bellboys gone solo, cut his manic "Bangin' on the Bongo." Some sappy white singer on Laurie named Tom Gullion did "Precious" (Berns lifted the melody from the Jewish hymn "Ein Keloheinu") and "Turn Around," both terrible songs, but Berns was getting around.

When Berns went to visit Jerry Wexler at Atlantic Records, he pulled out the Goya nylon-string. The first thing he played Wexler in that first meeting was a little dance song with an Afro-Cuban wrinkle that he had written with Phil Medley called "Twist and Shout."

Berns based the number on his favorite song, "La Bamba." In fact, he started writing the song one morning in his office at Mellin Music with Ray Passman, sitting behind his desk, strumming the chords to "La Bamba," and humming, while Passman beat a tattoo on Berns's desktop with his fingertips. They had only just gotten a good groove going when Berns's secretary interrupted, reminding Berns about a lunch appointment. Berns told Passman to come back after lunch and they would finish the song. When Berns returned from lunch and didn't find Passman, he went down the hall and found Phil Medley. They wrote the song, using large hunks of an unrecorded song they published the previous year as "Shake It Up Baby."

Berns had made an impression on Jerry Wexler. He used a song Berns and Ersel Hickey wrote, "A Little Bird Told Me So," on a LaVern Baker session. Wexler also decided to take "Twist and Shout" for a new r&b duo on Atlantic called the Top Notes. Derek Martin and Howard Guyton, who were going by Derek Ray and Guy Howard, had been singing together in groups since the Five Pearls recorded for Aladdin in 1954. As the Top Notes, they had released a couple of singles that went nowhere the previous year on Atlantic and were due to cut a couple more at this February 23, 1961, session at Atlantic Studios.

Sitting in the producer's chair next to Wexler that afternoon was a nineteen-year-old boy wonder from the West Coast named Phil Spector, who hit the Midtown music scene like an atom bomb since he showed up the previous May 1960. Spector, who had written and sung a 1958 number one hit when he was still in high school based on his father's epitaph, "To Know Him Is to Love Him" by the Teddy Bears, told his mother he was going to New York to work as an interpreter at the United Nations. Actually, he spent his first few nights in town sleeping on a couch in Leiber and Stoller's office, after their esteemed benefactor Lester Sill sent him their way. They didn't like the little squirrel but were impressed with Spector's musical skill and signed him to a publishing deal.

Spector had written a couple of songs with Doc Pomus and managed to promote himself into a writing session with Jerry Leiber that produced the song "Spanish Harlem" (although the uncredited Stoller added the descending triplets that stitch the whole song together the first time Spector and Leiber played it for Ertegun and Wexler). In October 1960, Spector attended the Leiber-Stoller session at Bell Sound on West Fifty-Fourth Street just off Broadway, where Ben E. King, making his first solo recording session since leaving the Drifters, cut two of the songs he wrote with Doc Pomus, "First Taste of Love" and "Young Boy Blues," along with "Spanish Harlem." With only about fifteen minutes remaining in the session, Leiber and Stoller pulled out a song based on an old hymn that Ben E. King had brought to their office several days earlier for them to polish, called "Stand By Me."* The session ran a half hour overtime and Wexler was furious.

Only a couple of weeks before the Ben E. King date, Spector had produced his first New York session. Leiber made it happen. Johnny Bienstock ran Hill & Range's record label, Big Top Records, for his cousins the Aberbachs. The Aberbachs had been convinced to start the label to compensate for the decline in revenues from sheet music sales, but there was a built-in conflict. The Aberbachs always viewed the record label as music publishers and Johnny Bienstock knew that successful record men looked at things differently. He wanted Leiber and Stoller to cut a record with singer Ray Peterson, coming off the Top Ten hit "Tell Laura I Love Her." Leiber, who couldn't be bothered, handed off the job to an eager Spector, whose production of Peterson doing "Corinne, Corinna" also made the Top Ten.

Cocky, contentious, obnoxious, Spector caught the attention of Ahmet Ertegun, who brought him around Atlantic, eventually offering him a job as staff producer. By the time Berns saw him sitting there

*Leiber and Stroller used their pen name on the songwriting credit, Elmo Glick, a Leiberesque contraction of the names Sammy Glick, from the novel *What Makes Sammy Run?*, and bluesman Elmore James.

between Wexler and Dowd, Spector had done only a couple of sessions for Atlantic with vocalist Billy Storm—a Wagnerian cover of the Turbans' "When You Dance"—and a singer named Jean DuShon, but nothing anybody noticed. He was really almost as much a nobody as Berns, but he was getting the shot.

In the studio with "Twist and Shout," Spector took charge. He changed the tempo of the song, rewrote the middle section, and lost all the Afro-Cuban rhythms. Wexler urged him on. They turned a surefire natural hit into a bland, banal shuffle. Berns watched from a gallery. He was horrified. "You fucked it up," he told Wexler.

"Shut the fuck up," Wexler said.

THE RECORD WAS dead before it left the studio and scarcely noticed when it was released, but Berns had learned an important lesson. He hadn't been in the record business long before he came to understand that the producer held all the power. He was the commander of the session, the architect of the record, the final arbiter on all matters creative. The fate of the song was in the producer's hands. If only out of self-defense, Berns needed to take control of his songs' full creative lives.

The whole idea of record producers was new. Some old-time artists and repertoire guys might have done little more than bring the beer, but there was no doubting the kind of influence a cunning, expert a&r man could have on a record. Milt Gabler at Decca Records, who made all those jump-and-jive Louis Jordan records in the forties, clearly steered the yodeling hick cowboy Bill Haley down that road on early rock and roll hits such as "Rock Around the Clock," "See You Later Alligator," or Haley's barn-burning 1956 Little Richard cover, "Rip It Up." The man who probably invented record production, Mitch Miller, the grand and elegant head of a&r at Columbia, earned a lifetime of bad publicity from his fevered denunciation of rock and roll, but the controversy obscured his genuine contributions.

At the 1958 disc jockey convention in Kansas City, Miller famously accused the assembled radio programming executives of having abdicated their responsibilities "to the eight-to-fourteen-year-olds, the preshave crowd that makes up twelve percent of the country's population and zero percent of its buying power once you eliminate the ponytail ribbons, Popsicles, and peanut brittle."

His real crime was to suit deed to word and keep Columbia almost entirely out of rock and roll and rhythm and blues. As a result, companies a fraction of the size of the industry leader were beating out Columbia's brains on the hit parade.

But Miller was an authentic visionary of the recording studio. By adding sound effects to his forties hits with Frankie Laine, Miller instinctively understood the science of recording to be something more than making mere replicas of live performances of music, and unwittingly paved the way for rock and roll (his fifties hits with Johnnie Ray have been described as the missing link between Sinatra and Presley). Miller's experiments were more than rambunctious inventions; they were purposeful recording industry strategy. Not only were his double-tracked vocals on Patti Page records a technical breakthrough, but also the records established Page as the country's leading female pop vocalist.

By the time he went to work at Columbia Records in 1950, with the label's top-drawer artist roster, Miller had developed a robust, charismatic approach to record production that boldly asserted the art of phonography—the art of making phonograph records—into the second half of the twentieth century. He knew that phonograph records were an entirely different entertainment experience than listening to live music and that the modern recording studio expanded the number of tools and resources available to the contemporary composer. Miller was a classically trained oboist and composer and a bit of a snob, but no useless square. He loved to smoke weed and hang out with jazzmen. He played oboe next to Bird's alto on the classic *Charlie Parker with*

Strings sessions—almost a duet at times—and was standing next to Bird on the album jacket photo.

The record producer was somewhat analogous to a motion picture director. The work is, by nature, collaborative, but the record producer, like a film director, was signatory of the piece, the one who signed off on all the creative decisions. More than the performer, the songwriter, the arranger, the musicians who provide the accompaniment, the record belongs to the producer. He is the responsible party.

Producers began to sign the records. George Goldner ran a somewhat imperial credit on singles he produced for his End and Gone labels: "Under the Personal Supervision of George Goldner." Leiber and Stoller may have been the first independent producers in the business, but Atlantic didn't start giving them label credit until "Save the Last Dance for Me" by the Drifters in 1960.

The growing recognition of the role of the producer was one of the signs that the record business was moving beyond the seat-of-the-pants approach of the independents only a few years earlier. Just as the promotion methods and distribution operations had rapidly expanded to meet the market, the ways these men made records in the studio were changing in fundamental and profound ways. Berns understood the record producer was the man in charge and he wanted to be that man. He started to produce sessions where he could. That was the lesson of "Twist and Shout."

He conducted a split session at Bell Sound for Johnny Bienstock and Big Top Records with gospel-voiced Dottie Clark and Sammy Turner, a greatly underrated vocalist three releases past his 1959 Top Ten moment, "Lavender Blue," a sappy song originally sung by Burl Ives in a Disney movie, retooled for Turner on Big Top by producers Leiber and Stoller. Turner gave Berns's "Pour It On" an earnest affability, but the record wasn't particularly distinctive. Dottie Clark got some good words on her single's A-side, a cover of the Vera Lynn World War II chestnut, "It's Been a Long Long Time" (" . . . strong, moving reading from the thrush with a slow rockaballad tempo . . ." said *Billboard*), but nothing happened with the record.

Berns cut Little Jimmy Dee doing his "I Should Have Listened" for the Infinity label ("an interchange of his vocal and chorus effects, on a touching weeper," said *Billboard*). He produced a girl-group version of the Mellin catalog's key nugget, "You You You," by a female quartet called the Flamettes on Laurie, but that was in no way a good idea. Berns didn't get any production credit for the Arthur Prysock record of his "One More Time" on Old Town, but Berns's stamp is all over the record—from the call-and-response gospel chorus to the Cuban rhythms and flute part that could have come from an Esy Morales record.

Jimmy Jones had one of the hottest records of the previous year with "Handy Man," and the follow-up, "Good Timin'," hadn't done too badly either. But he was already two stiff singles beyond that when Berns took him in the studio. Jones was a savvy old hand at the game. He recorded for Herman Lubinsky's Savoy Records with the Sparks of Rhythm in 1954 and spent a couple of years making records for George Goldner. He did some things with Bobby Robinson up in Harlem and produced a couple of groups on his own. He had made about twenty-five records when he cut "Handy Man," a record that took almost a year to break.

Jones had seen his songs come back from the pressing plant with new coauthors on the label. He knew the game and he liked Berns—he related to people. Berns gave him a song, "I Say Love," that came wrapped in an explosive Cuban big band sound straight off the dance floor of the Tropicana. The record burst open with a salvo of brass and drums, driven by a jungle beat straight out of Beny Moré and Havana in the fifties, a confident, commanding production unlike anything Berns had done. He was quickly finding his way in the studio.

He wasn't credited as producer again, but Berns is all over "A Little Bit of Soap" by the Jarmels, his first real hit, a song written solely by

Berns as Bert Russell, that peaked at number twelve on the *Billboard* charts in September 1961, after eight weeks on the way up. He played the song on guitar for the five fellows who were going to sing it at the Laurie Records offices and they practiced it in the subway on their way back to the hotel.

The five young men hailed from Richmond, Virginia, where their vocal group first attracted the attention of blues singer B.B. King, who recommended the college students to a New York agent and a record deal. The record company named the group after a street in Harlem. The first record went nowhere. At the May 1961 session for the second single, Berns stood beside the Schwartz brothers in the control room. The group did something like twelve takes. The record would have been just another Drifters knockoff if it wasn't for the way the lyrics seared the melody into the brain. Nathaniel Ruff's lead vocal gave the piece the requisite urgency, and the clinking clave put the Latin under-beat into overdrive.

> *A little bit of soap*
> *Will take away your perfume eventually*
> *But a little bit of soap*
> *Will never wash away the memory*
> *Of your name in the night*
> *That I call through the lonely years*
> *A little bit of soap*
> *Will never wash away my tears*
> —A LITTLE BIT OF SOAP (BERT RUSSELL, 1961)

Berns had barely been in the music business one year, but he had made the rounds and it was starting to pay off. He was a likable guy and he was getting his songs recorded. When Russ Miller left Mellin, Berns moved up to office manager. His salary doubled to a hundred bucks a week. He hired Ray Passman, who had been working selling handmade furniture by his pal Paul Colby, a former music publishing counter man running his own showroom on Second Avenue. Berns was selling songs and making records any way he could, but it was Luther Dixon of Scepter Records who thought Berns should be the recording artist.

Dixon was a classic r&b hustler who was riding high, running Scepter Records, home of the Shirelles, whose "Will You Love Me Tomorrow" hit number one in February 1961. He had met his boss, Florence Greenberg, during an elevator ride, but that was long enough. A middle-aged suburban New Jersey housewife, Greenberg not only managed the Shirelles, but also financed the group's first single after her daughter told her about the group. Mary Jane went to Passaic High School with the quartet and attended the high school assembly where the four girls tore up the place with a simple song they wrote, "I Met Him on a Sunday."

After the record started to catch on, Greenberg leased the master to Decca Records, who ran it up the charts and dropped the group. Greenberg was determined to start her own record company and she had crossed paths with Wally Roker, a former bird group bass vocalist who had been promoting records uptown for Bobby Robinson's labels. It was Roker who introduced her to Dixon in the elevator. They went and had a cup of coffee and exchanged phone numbers.

Florence Greenberg grew up in the Lower East Side and took the first proposal that came her way, to get out of her parents' home. She had been married for a lifetime to an accountant for a potato chip company. Her son Stanley was blinded in a delivery room accident and she became very involved in civic issues, summer camps for the handicapped, Republican county committee, that sort of thing. At an early age, Stanley showed some talent on piano and writing songs. It was his songwriting that led her to investigate the Brill Building and the music business. Her first taste was success—she made a tidy $4,000 profit on "I Met Him on a Sunday" from Decca—and she was intrigued. She called Dixon back and the next time they met, he introduced her to the joys of interracial sex and the full madness of rhythm and blues. She started Scepter Records and hired her new boyfriend to run the company.

Dixon had knocked around the music business for years. He was a tall, thin knife of a man, and he liked to drink. Although Dixon almost never wrote a song without a collaborator, he had some good covers. Pat Boone cut his "Why Baby Why." The big notch on his belt when he met Greenberg was "Sixteen Candles," the 1958 hit he wrote (cowrote) and produced for the Crests. Working with some lyrics by the group's lead vocalist, Shirley Owens, about a young girl deciding to give it up, Dixon fashioned a credible Top Forty hit for the Shirelles with "Tonight's the Night" in 1960, enough to keep Scepter in business.

Around the same time, Carole King, an eighteen-year-old mother of a six-month-old in Sheepshead Bay, recorded a piano part and left a note propped up against the Norelco tape recorder for her songwriting partner husband, who would be coming home from work at the chemical plant and his Marine Corps Reserves meeting after she went off to play mah-jongg: "Donny needs a new song for the Shirelles tomorrow. Please write."

Donny Kirshner was the music publisher who had signed King and her husband, lyricist Gerry Goffin. They had submitted fifty songs, so far without any appreciable success, to Kirshner, partner in Aldon Music of 1650 Broadway, a burgeoning teen pop enterprise. Aldon's top writer was hitmaker Neil Sedaka, who knew King as Carol Klein at James Madison High School in Brooklyn and had originally steered her and her husband to Aldon. That night, Goffin had most of the song sketched out by the time his wife returned around midnight. By two in the morning, they had it done.

Kirshner liked the song so much, he took it to all-powerful Mitch Miller at Columbia Records and pitched it for Johnny Mathis. Miller told Kirshner it was a woman's song. When Luther Dixon heard the demo, he immediately wanted the song for the next record by the Shirelles. The girls didn't like what they heard—they thought the demo sounded like a country and western record—but Dixon ruled at Scepter. Carole King, self-assured musically beyond her years, wrote a string arrangement after checking out a book about scoring from the public library. She played the kettle drums on the session. The Shirelles changed their minds about the song when they heard the track. "Will You Love Me Tomorrow" was the first number one hit by a black female vocal group, a huge breakthrough for the r&b independents, and Dixon was walking tall.

He had pieces of current hit songs by r&b crooner Gene McDaniels ("A Hundred Pounds of Clay") and blues singer Jimmy Reed ("Big Boss Man"), and he continued to openly conduct his affair with his label boss. Florence Greenberg was a not especially attractive older woman, happy to be out of her suburban exile, set free into the big-city world of r&b and the Midtown record scene. But she was no cream puff. Fiercely protective of her girls and her interests and quick to act on anything that she perceived as a threat, she had a foul temper, a whiny, reedy voice, and the mouth of a sailor. Dixon walked a fine line with her, but she depended on him in the studio.

Chuck Jackson was the first artist Dixon signed to Wand Records, a second label Dixon started with Greenberg that was supposed to handle more gritty r&b than Scepter (Greenberg liked to name her labels after things queens owned; she called her first label Tiara). Jackson was the handsome lead vocalist of the Del Vikings, who had been encouraged to go solo by Jackie Wilson. Dixon saw Jackson appearing with Wilson's revue at the Apollo and wanted to sign him. Despite interest from RCA Victor and Wilson's label, Brunswick, Jackson went with the smaller label after praying to God for a sign. That sign came when the pair went to Dixon's apartment and wrote Jackson's first solo hit, "I Don't Want to Cry," released the week before the Berns record, which Dixon also put on Wand.

Dixon heard a demo Berns had made and wanted to know who the singer was. As a recording artist, Berns decided to call himself Russell

Byrd, yet another professional identity. The Russell Byrd record, "You'd Better Come Home," rode on a swinging, sawing string part written by Carole King, who also played piano on the track. Berns does his Elvis imitation on the vocal, but the percussive repeated chorus—*you better, better, better, better come home right now*—gave the record a certain offbeat appeal.

Berns posed for Russell Byrd publicity photos in a jaunty suede cap, the Goya on his lap. His thumbnail was full of bull about his attending college and all the famous artists who had recorded his songs. He was photographed for the trades with Ray Passman and a publicist holding copies of the records on their fingers like donuts. Wally Roker, Scepter's promotion man, took him off to afternoon TV dance shows in places like Pittsburgh and Providence. He did the *Clay Cole Show* in New York with Adam Wade ("Take Good Care of Her"). He primped his waterfall hairdo endlessly before lip-synching his record on camera, although he was already sporting a hairpiece. He did *American Bandstand* on the same show that Bobby Lewis played his big hit, "Tossin' and Turnin'." "You'd Better Come Home" spent the month of May 1961 on the charts, climbing all the way to number fifty on the *Billboard Hot 100.* Halfway there.

In August, with the Jarmels winding their way up the charts, Berns had songs on releases by Dottie Clark, Arthur Prysock, Sammy Turner, all of which he also produced, and Conway Twitty, the Nashville-based rock and roll star who cut a crazy little number Berns wrote with Passman called "It's Driving Me Wild." Berns also went back in the studio and made Hoagy Lands cry some more. He did four numbers for MGM Records, including one of Mellin's old Ames Brothers songs, "I'm Yours," under Mellin's instructions to work the catalog.

Lands enters "My Tears Are Dry" sliding, gliding, sailing across a slow dirge, his voice fluttering over the descending chords and a bass vocalist. His confident, showy entrance frames the song in high drama. Comparisons with Sam Cooke would be inevitable. "It's Gonna

Be Morning" starts with wistful acoustic guitars setting the smoldering track in motion as Lands dances with the melody, dropping little sobs and gospel wails into the verse. The Bert Russell song is hopeful, but the sense of a troubled past hovers like a dark cloud over the song's protagonist. He sounds as if he is trying hard to convince himself. *I'm never gonna cry, never gonna cry another wasted tear*, Hoagy sings, but it doesn't ring true. It sounds more like a desperate prayer from someone who knows he is doomed to cry.

Luther Dixon liked Berns, even if Berns thought Florence Greenberg was an unpleasant old bag. Dixon and Berns were both street corner guys. They knew where they stood with one another. Phil Spector was supposed to produce the next Russell Byrd single and he did cut a Berns-Passman song, "Nights of Mexico," with Berns/Byrd as vocalist that sat in the can waiting for a second side. Berns pitched Dixon still more material and Dixon put him together with a male-female vocal group called the Renaults, who had been around a couple of years without getting anywhere. But they could sing. It was a little noticed record at the time—or since—but it was on "Just like Mine," where Berns started writing his own story in his songs.

If everybody's heart
Was made of glass
And broken in little pieces like mine
If everybody's heart
Was made of glass
They would feel the sands of time
Just like mine
—JUST LIKE MINE (BERT RUSSELL, 1961)

Berns had not yet been in the record business a second full year. Maybe he hadn't made it in any final, definitive way, but he could hold his head up at the weekly Sunday dinner with Charlie and Sadie in the Bronx. Berns had already lived longer than doctors told him he was going to live. He was in a hurry and didn't talk about it much. He told Don Drowty about his heart—Drowty also had rheumatic fever as a youth—but he laughed it off, as if it were a joke, no big thing. Drowty didn't buy it. He thought it was a very big thing.

But Berns wanted more. He knew he had places to go and he was running late.

1619 Broadway

VII.

Brill Building [1961]

THE BRILL BUILDING, an eleven-story office building at 1619 Broadway, was built by Abraham E. Lefcourt, a skyscraper builder who changed the face of New York. He originally intended the tower to be one floor taller than the Empire State Building, which would have made it the tallest building in the world, but the builder ran into financial problems and his real estate empire collapsed. The three Brill brothers, haberdashers who operated a store in the neighborhood for decades, took over the building in 1932, although Lefcourt left behind a bust of himself at the top of the building and, above the front door, a bust of his son Alan Lefcourt, who died a year before of leukemia. Like all the pluggers, Berns took the elevator to the top floor and worked his way down, going office to office selling songs.

The music business adopted the building in the early thirties. Old-line publishers like Irving Mills and Southern Music still kept offices there, and other relics of the swing era were listed in the building's directory—from Duke Ellington to "Swing and Sway with" Sammy Kaye. Irving Ceasar, the old-timer who wrote "Tea for Two" and "Is It True What They Say about Dixie," could be found in an office just down the hall from Leiber and Stoller, when he wasn't at the race-track. Amateur singers loitered outside on the sidewalk. Two restaurants flanked the lobby on Broadway, the Turf, where you had to push past music business insiders such as Jackie Wilson or Brook Benton to get a drink at the bar, and Jack Dempsey's, favored by the older crowd, watched over by the champ himself.

There were arrangers, copyists, bandleaders, song publishers, record labels, distributors. Recording studios were nearby in the bustling Midtown neighborhood. Colony Records was on the corner, where the latest records and hit sheet music were always available. This was the music business, baby.

While Berns was starting out down the street, the biggest and the best were at the top of their game at Forty-Ninth Street and Broadway. The Brill Building was only around the corner, but it was a long way from 1650 Broadway. This was the high-rent district of the music business, and the firms inside were the gold standards.

Songwriter Doc Pomus worked in a little cubbyhole in the penthouse office of the Brill Building. He wrote "Save the Last Dance for Me" late one night at his home on the back of his wedding invitation. Crippled by polio at age six, he never expected to get married and became a songwriter only reluctantly, after he gave up his career as New York's first white blues singer. He cut "Heartlessly" for RCA Victor in 1955, and of all the thirty or so records he had out, he never had a shot like that before. Alan Freed slammed the big ballad nightly on WINS and the record exploded on jukeboxes. But RCA dropped the record. It was over like someone switched out the light. Pomus never knew why, although he suspected it might have something to do with the fact that the singer was a thirty-year-old, overweight Jew living in a fleabag hotel who couldn't stand without crutches and leg braces.

Ray Charles recorded his "Lonely Avenue," and the Atlantic guys, who knew Pomus from before there was an Atlantic, started feeding his material to Big Joe Turner, Pomus's idol since he was a sickly kid listening to Turner sing "Piney Brown Blues" over the radio late at night. Big Joe did good with his "Boogie Woogie Country Girl." Pomus first met Mike Stoller in Atlantic's waiting room, where Stoller recognized

Pomus as the vocalist behind a hip radio commercial Pomus used to sing on Symphony Sid's *Make Believe Ballroom*. Pomus struck up a friendly relationship with the two younger songwriters and, some months later, slipped Stoller a tape of a song he thought might be something for the Coasters, "Young Blood," and shortly thereafter forgot he ever did.

Anyway, Pomus married actress Willi Burke in 1956 and they were returning from a honeymoon in the Catskills when Pomus stopped at a diner and absentmindedly checked the jukebox only to see a new single by the Coasters with a song called "Young Blood." He watched carefully as the record loaded to play and saw the label spinning around reading "Leiber-Stoller-Pomus." He pumped coins into a pay phone outside and reached Jerry Wexler at Atlantic, who told him the record was a smash and that he would wire Pomus a $1,500 advance. It was more money than Pomus had made all year.

Three years later, he sat at home alone in a postmidnight haze, smoking cigarettes and turning over the wedding invitation in his fingers. That afternoon, his songwriting partner, Morty Shuman, had played him a florid, flamenco-flavored melody and Pomus had already decided he wanted the lyrics to sound as if they had been translated from Spanish. He wrote long lines of percolating one-syllable words— "You can dance every dance with the guy who gives you the eye, let him hold you tight"—as he remembered sitting by himself on their wedding night and watching his bride dance with, first, his brother and, then, one friend after another. He couldn't quite put all the pieces together, but he scrawled "Save the Last Dance for Me" across the top and went to bed.

Pomus and Shuman had written ten chart songs in 1959, more than anybody except Leiber and Stoller, who had twelve. In 1961, they wrote thirteen, more than anybody, period. After "Young Blood," Pomus had determined that writing grown-up blues for adult singers such as Big Joe Turner and Ray Charles wasn't going to buy the groceries for a newly wedded family man and Shuman was going to guide him to the teen-age market. Mort Shuman was a high school student to whom, at first, Pomus gave 10 percent simply to sit in the room while Pomus wrote, serving as kind of an instant test market. Slowly Shuman became more of a collaborator and their stuff started to get better. Shuman lived at home with his mother in Brighton Beach—his father drank himself to death around the time Doc got married. He took occasional philosophy courses at City College, made indecent proposals to black co-eds, drank wine, and slept on the subway home to Brooklyn. Shuman and Pomus made the rounds of the Brill Building publishers, often in company with Pomus's wife, Willi—the hipster teen and his older, crippled songwriting partner with his blonde ingénue wife.

They landed at the Brill Building almost by accident. They started out at 1650 Broadway. Pomus met a former Arthur Murray dance instructor who had married a rich widow and needed a front so he could get away from the old dame. He loaned Pomus $10,000 of the lady's money to start a record label. Pomus rented an office at 1650 Broadway and opened R&B Records (the name was his idea). When a group walked in off the street from Harlem wanting to audition called the Five Crowns, Doc and Morty found themselves interested in making records for real with this group, which revolved around lead tenor Charlie Thomas and shy, bass-voiced Benny Nelson. "Kiss and Make Up" in 1958 was a decent-enough record, and even started to take off in Pittsburgh, but the dance instructor's widow figured out the charade and R&B Records was quickly no more. The Five Crowns found work. Manager George Treadwell hired the group to be the Drifters, and the Five Crowns started their career as the Drifters by recording "There Goes My Baby."

Otis Blackwell used to come by the R&B Records offices. Pomus knew Blackwell from their days singing at blues joints in Brooklyn during the forties, long before Blackwell hit it big with Elvis Presley songs such as "Don't Be Cruel" or "All Shook Up." Blackwell wrote the Little Willie John number "Fever," and Peggy Lee had a big record with it. His latest was Jerry Lee Lewis—Blackwell wrote "Great Balls of Fire" and "Breathless." He took Pomus and Shuman to meet Paul Case, the savvy professional manager of Hill & Range, the publishing firm that occupied the penthouse suite at the Brill Building.

Pomus and Shuman were signed to Hill & Range and the first assignment Paul Case gave them was a teen idol candidate from Philadelphia named Fabian. He had been discovered by his manager sitting on his front stoop minutes after his father had been taken away in an ambulance with a heart attack. He had no evident musical skills. His vocal range didn't go much past four or five notes and his pitch was iffy, but he was a beautiful boy who looked the part. Case watched his effect on teen girls at record hops and thought there was gold there, if Pomus and Shuman could tailor some material that would, at least, downplay his insufficiencies. They wrote a string of successful hits for Fabian that launched him. They concocted a gimmicky rock and roll hit for Bobby Darin, "Plain Jane." Case gave them more teen idols—James Darren, Bobby Rydell, Frankie Avalon. They wrote "Go Bobby Go" for Bobby Rydell, who didn't like it, so they handed it to Jimmy Clanton as "Go Jimmy Go," telling Clanton they wrote it for him.

Elvis Presley Music put Hill & Range in the penthouse of the Brill Building in 1956, when swing-era bandleader Tommy Dorsey choked to death in his sleep after stuffing himself full of Thanksgiving turkey, booze, and sleeping pills, leaving an unexpected vacancy that holiday season at the top of the Broadway office building. The music publishing firm occupied a lavish twelve-thousand-square-foot office, the walls decorated with dreary paintings by Bernard Buffet, the French artist whose career was sponsored by the Aberbachs, major collectors of modern art. Office wiseacres called the Picasso lithograph of mating doves "The Fucking Pigeons."

With all their hits, Pomus and Shuman were rewarded with an eight-by-ten cubicle with a couple of chairs and an upright piano, and a small window with a ledge. Pomus parked his family in an enormous Long Island home and took a room around the corner at the Hotel Forrest, where he stayed during the week. Damon Runyon Jr. lived in the penthouse. Surrounded by gamblers, con men, whores, and lowlifes of all kinds, Pomus held forth in the lobby nightly. Paul Case had introduced him to Phil Spector while the kid was still sleeping in Leiber and Stoller's office. They wrote songs together in the hotel lobby and retreated to Doc's room, where Doc played him his jazz records.

When a vocal group from Brooklyn called the Mystics turned up in the office looking for material, Morty recognized them from his old neighborhood. They tried out a song the pair had already written, "It's Great to Be Young and In Love," but Pomus wasn't satisfied. He rewrote the entire lyrics, saving one line (*each night I ask the stars up above*), and gave them a new song, "Teenager in Love." Gene Schwartz at Laurie Records, the group's label, thought the song was too good for the Mystics and gave it instead to the label's leading act, Dion and the Belmonts. Pomus and Shuman, chagrined, came up with another piece expressly for the Mystics, a nursery rhyme–like lullaby, "Hushabye."

Three different versions of "Teenager in Love" climbed the U.K. charts and British television producer Jack Good decided to devote an entire episode of his weekly musical variety show, *Boy Meets Girls*, to the songs of Pomus and Shuman. Doc and Morty made the trip to London, where they were greeted like pop music royalty. In London, they ran into Lamar Fike, one of Elvis's friends from Memphis on his way to Germany, where Presley was currently finishing his Army stint. Fike said he could get a song to Elvis. Neither Pomus nor Shuman gave that much of a chance, but Morty went into the studio and knocked out a piano and voice demo of a few songs. When Elvis got out of the army, he cut their "A Mess of Blues" at his first recording session. Paul Case gave them the next Presley single, which involved putting English lyrics to an old Italian ballad. Shuman wanted nothing to do with something so cornball, but Pomus didn't mind. He gave Presley "Surrender," another number one.

Pomus and Shuman dashed off a couple of songs for Bobby Vee while staying at the Roosevelt Hotel in Hollywood, but Vee didn't like them. Since they were in Hollywood, they took the songs to their old pal Bobby Darin, now a big movie star living in a Hollywood Hills mansion with his starlet wife, Sandra Dee. Darin took several passes at both songs, but never got them right. They handed the songs over to Paul Case when they returned to New York and he passed them along to another Hill & Range client. Elvis cut both "(Marie's the Name) His Latest Flame" and "Little Sister" in a marathon all-night session in June 1961 in Nashville, at one point phoning Pomus and waking him up from his sleep to ask a question. It was the only time the singer and songwriter ever spoke and Pomus thought it was a prank.

Hill & Range founders Jean and Julian Aberbach were behind-the-scenes masterminds to the whole Elvis enterprise. Jean Aberbach was a protégé of the great Max Dreyfus—publisher of the Gershwins, Rodgers and Hart, and Cole Porter; and founding member of publishing rights group the American Society of Composers, Authors, and Publishers (ASCAP)—and Aberbach learned music business intrigue and chicanery at the feet of the master, the man who invented the game. Long before Presley was scouted by a Hill & Range operative named Grelun Landon in Tupelo, Mississippi, in May 1955, the Aberbachs made piles with Presley's manager Colonel Tom Parker on partnership publishing deals with his clients Eddy Arnold and Hank Snow that were modeled after deals Dreyfus first constructed with Gershwin, Rodgers and Hart, and Porter.

They formed Elvis Presley Music and made certain that any material Presley recorded was published by them. Jean Aberbach was a severe taskmaster and harsh disciplinarian. His brother Julian was more informal, but both were old-world European gentlemen who still spoke in thick Austrian accents. Under their strict, merciless control from virtually the very start, they developed Elvis Presley into the big-gest money machine the Broadway music business ever saw. They kept teams of writers squirrelled away turning out enough dreck for two Elvis movies a year.

Leiber and Stoller were also a daily presence in the Hill & Range offices. They knew their brand of satiric social comedies that worked so well with the Coasters would never serve the Drifters, who spe-cialized in romantic fantasies, so the producers looked elsewhere for material. Pomus and Shuman loved the group since they were the Five Crowns. Their song "(If You Cry) True Love, True Love" was slated to be the A-side on the next Drifters single, following the group's million-selling breakthrough, "There Goes My Baby." The other side was another song written by Benny Nelson (Ben E. King) and owned by Drifters manager George Treadwell. King sang the lead on his song, but lead tenor Johnny Lee Williams was brought in to do "(If You Cry) True Love, True Love." Mike Stoller knew arranger Stan Applebaum because they were both students of avant-garde classical composer Stefan Wolpe, and between them, they built a sumptuous, soaring car-pet of sound, littered with tinkling, glistening percussion—bells, tri-angles, gourds, shakers. King Curtis played the sax break. These men were making records that sounded like no records ever did. They were lustful, ambitious musicians moving into wondrous realms entirely of their own creation.

For "This Magic Moment," the next Drifters epic, arranger Applebaum posed the Pomus-Shuman song on a whirlwind of strings, producers Leiber and Stoller accenting the arrangement with tympani and softly-strummed acoustic guitars. By the time they all reconvened in May 1960 at Bell Studios to cut "Save the Last Dance for Me" and three other songs, they had elevated the entire art of American popular music.

Leiber and Stoller moved up from their Fifty-Seventh Street offices to a ninth-floor Brill Building suite in January 1961. They started their own publishing company, Trio Music, and another company, Tiger Records, that was a partnership with Atlantic Records and Hill & Range, in addition to Quintet Music, where Hill & Range was already partners. Hill & Range had different pieces of so many Leiber and Stoller songs, only Mike Stoller could remember them all.

They were both permanently located now in New York City. Leiber was married in 1958 to actress Gaby Rodgers, whose father was an old-line Manhattan blue blood art dealer, and they had two sons. They lived in a sumptuous eleven-room apartment at the Langham on Central Park West. Acting coach Lee Strasberg lived on the top floor and Leiber used to see Marilyn Monroe in the elevator. Rodgers introduced Leiber to off-Broadway theater and the New York art world and they socialized with artists such as Mark Rothko, Robert Motherwell, and Larry Rivers.

Stoller and his accountant wife, Meryl, lived in a brownstone on Seventeenth Street with their daughter and two sons. He grew a goatee and carried a rolled-up umbrella with him wherever he went. Stoller, who studied classical composition with twelve-tone specialist Wolpe, even had one of his egghead pieces performed at the Ninety-Second Street Y. They were kings of Broadway in three-piece suits and cashmere socks.

They sometimes liked to write in the imposing surroundings of the Hill & Range office, amid all the garish modern art. But they were gravitating away from songwriting toward record production and music publishing. They continued to make Coasters' records, but the group had slipped from popularity. The records, if anything, were even more refined and sharply tuned social commentary.

"Run Red Run" told the tale of a fellow who taught his pet chimpanzee to speak and play cards, only to have the ape catch him cheating and pull a gun on him. "You made a man out of me," he tells the song's protagonist, "now I'm going to make a monkey out of you." The other side, "What about Us," was undisguised Marxist rhetoric about class warfare, posed as broad stroke *Amos 'n' Andy* blackface comedy, originally recorded at the same 1959 session as the hit "Poison Ivy," their sly take on VD. ("Sexy," less sly, from an earlier 1958 session that also produced million-seller "Charlie Brown," had gone entirely unreleased.)

The 1960 Coasters release "Shoppin' for Clothes" was a hilarious monologue, brilliantly delivered, a minor masterpiece and house favorite at Atlantic that spent only two weeks on the charts and turned out to have been lifted straight from a little-known record on a small-time label by some nobody. Leiber and Stoller undermined the poor sucker's lawsuit, when the flagrant copyright infringement was brought to their attention, by buying the publishing company that owned the rights. Their exquisite "Little Egypt" restored some of the group's chart luster in spring 1961. "Girls, Girls, Girls," recorded at the same session, didn't do much for the Coasters, but Elvis picked it up the next year as title track to one of his cinematic epics.

When Leiber and Stoller's accountants recommended an audit of Atlantic Records, Stoller, married to a former accountant, thought the audit was simply good business, but Leiber suspected it meant trouble. Wexler never liked the idea of the audit. Leiber and Stoller had been making a fortune from their association with Atlantic. Of course, Leiber and Stoller's remodel of the Drifters franchise saved the label in 1960 after Atlantic lost Ray Charles to the greener pastures, long greener, of ABC-Paramount Records. When the audit showed Atlantic owed Leiber and Stoller $18,000, Wexler went nuts. He screamed at them. He called them names. He told them they could have their money, but they would never work with Atlantic acts again. Leiber said no problem, keep the money. "I'm going to teach you a lesson," Wexler told them. "Not only are you not going to get the money, but you're not going to work with our artists again either."

While he couldn't afford to cut all his ties with the successful producers, Wexler never forgave them and would have as little as possible to do with them after that. Leiber and Stoller were going to have to expand their horizons beyond Atlantic if they wanted to continue to thrive as record producers, which had proved a key ingredient in their publishing success.

Art Talmadge came from Chicago, where he ran grubby Mercury Records, tasteless traders in such *pop ordinaire* as the Crew Cuts and Georgia Gibbs. A long way from the urbane, witty, and hip Atlantic chiefs who brought Leiber and Stoller into the business, Talmadge was a dull curmudgeon who took over the United Artists operation the previous year and was paying the rent with piano bar duo Ferrante and Teicher ("Theme from 'Exodus'") and a flukey folk hit, "Michael (Row the Boat Ashore)" by the Highwaymen.

Their attorney Lee Eastman negotiated a cute deal for Leiber and Stoller with the label that, *Billboard* speculated, could pay a producer's royalty of two to three cents a side. But the United Artists roster was also a long way from Atlantic. Leiber and Stoller, who hadn't worked with many white acts other than Elvis, found themselves making records with distinctly B-grade talents such as the has-been Johnnie Ray, a would-be teen idol named Kenny Chandler, and former *Arthur Godfrey's Talent Scouts* winners the Shepherd Sisters five years after their hit "Alone."

They found Jay and the Americans at an audition. Vocalist John Traynor, who left the Mystics after "Hushabye," hooked up with some other scuffling Brooklyn vocalists from a group called the Harbor Lights and, after a couple of nowhere singles, wound up trying out for Leiber and Stoller. Jerry Leiber gave the group a new name. With his eye on an American Airlines ticket on his desk, he suggested Binky Jones and the Americans. Traynor, not wanting to be known as Binky Jones, perhaps understandably, offered his own nickname as a compromise and Jay and the Americans were born.

With the movie version of *West Side Story* due to be released—a return engagement on Broadway had been running across the street at the Winter Garden for more than a year—they made a *baion* version of the show's hit ballad, "Tonight," as the first United Artists single by Jay and the Americans. The record never made the charts, although it got quite a lot of airplay around New York City.

When they went back into Bell Studios with the Drifters in February 1961 to follow up the number one success of "Save the Last Dance for Me" for Atlantic, producers Leiber and Stoller took two new songs from Pomus and Shuman, "Sweets for My Sweet" and "Roomful of Tears," along with songs from two teams they had never used before. "(Don't Go) Please Stay" came from Bob Hilliard and Burt Bacharach at Famous Music, a pair of professional songwriters who had both been around a while, still waiting for their big break. "Some Kind of Wonderful," on the other hand, was written by Carole King and Gerry Goffin, the husband-wife team whose first hit, "Will You Love Me Tomorrow" for the Shirelles, was riding the top of the charts that week.

LEADING THE CHARGE on the Brill Building aristocracy was an upstart publishing company out of 1650 Broadway that was on the verge of emerging as the top commercial force in American pop music. Teenage mom Carole King came to work every morning at Aldon Music, pushing a baby stroller with her one-year-old daughter, Lou Lou. After "Will You Love Me Tomorrow" hit, her husband quit his job at the chemical plant and drove away in a limousine. The whole enterprise was taking off. Aldon Music, a young pup teen pop factory, was hotter than any of the carriage trade publishers in the Brill Building.

Twenty-seven-year-old Don Kirshner had built a bustling hive and was making honey. His partner, Al Nevins, an older, more experienced music business professional, came from another era. He had belonged to a successful instrumental recording group since 1939 called the Three Suns, who made easy listening records for RCA Victor. He wrote the Platters hit "Twilight Time." In 1958, he and Kirshner had started Aldon—taking the title from their first names. Before that, Kirshner had been an amateur, pushing songs he wrote with a friend he first met at a drugstore in Washington Heights before he changed his name to Bobby Darin and finally launched his own singing career with "Splish Splash."

The first Aldon writers, Neil Sedaka and Howie Greenfield, had simply shown up at the office Kirshner and Nevins opened at 1650 Broadway in 1958. They signed Sedaka and Greenfield to long-term exclusive contracts the next day. Sedaka was a classical piano student on a scholarship at Juilliard. Greenfield ran errands for National Cash Register. Kirshner took them to Connie Francis, whom he had first met pitching her songs with Bobby Darin. She was looking for material to follow her first hit record, "Who's Sorry Now," and she found their song "Stupid Cupid" a cutesy rock and roll novelty that qualified as a left-field move for the girl singer. When Sedaka made the charts himself later the same year with their song "The Diary," which was supposed to have been the next single by Little Anthony and the Imperials, Aldon was off to the races.

By 1961, Kirshner had eighteen writers, all between the ages of nineteen and twenty-six. On Fridays, they demonstrated their best song of the week in front of one another on the red piano in his office. A competitive spirit prevailed. A songwriter coming back from lunch might hear the same set of chords he'd been working on all morning now coming out of another cubicle. Kirshner had boundless energy, enthusiasm, and a golden ear for a hit tune. Not satisfied with the measly two cents from every record sale the publisher was forced to share with the writer, Kirshner had expanded the services of Aldon into talent management and independent record production.

He signed Goffin and King's sixteen-year-old Aldon demo singer, Tony Orlando, to Epic Records, and he and Nevins supervised his recording of Goffin and King's "Halfway to Paradise," which sailed up the charts in May. They had their eyes on another Aldon song for the follow-up by writers Barry Mann and Larry Kolber, "I Love How You Love Me," but *enfant terrible* Phil Spector also wanted the song.

Spector had come to Aldon in June when he wanted material for Gene Pitney, even though Pitney was managed by the label owner, Aaron Schroeder, a songwriter and music publisher himself. Customarily, Schroeder would have been very protective of his own copyrights—he turned down Ozzie Nelson, who wanted a piece of the Gene Pitney song "Hello Mary Lou," before he would let Ozzie's son Ricky record the number (which Ricky went ahead and recorded anyway).

As a songwriter, he had more than twenty Presley titles. Schroeder was the king of Elvis Presley B-sides, not so much because of his songwriting skill as his willingness to kick back a hefty chunk of his royalties to Freddy Bienstock at Hill & Range, who really didn't care what was on the other side of Presley singles. It was a free ride; the B-sides earned the same amount as the hits. As a music publisher, Schroeder bought Dick Clark's Sea-Lark Music at a fire sale price when Clark was called before Congress to testify in the payola investigation.

Schroeder practically started Musicor Records to release Pitney recordings, and their first single did respectably. But the second didn't even chart. Pitney's record career was on the line. Schroeder had a feeling about this crazy kid Spector, dressed in capes, his long hair over his collar. He ceded to Spector on all fronts, including going to Aldon for material. Pitney met Spector only once before their epic session, over lunch at the House of Chan, a Chinese place on the corner of Seventh Avenue and Fifty-Third Street. "My sister's in an asylum," he told Pitney, "and she's the sane one in the family."

All of Broadway crowded into the control booth that night at Bell Sound to watch the boy wonder record Pitney singing the Goffin and King song "Every Breath I Take." The studio was stuffed with players, tympani, horn and string sections. Surrounding Spector behind the board as the session progressed were Leiber and Stoller, songwriters Goffin and King, fellow Aldon writers Barry Mann and Cynthia Weil, songwriter Burt Bacharach, Donny Kirshner, Aaron Schroeder, and his associate, Wally Gold.

The session ran way overtime. The single was the last track of the night. Spector made everybody do take after take. He went out in the studio and practically dictated how he wanted the drum fill to go with drummer Gary Chester. Pitney lost his voice and was forced to retreat to his falsetto to reach the final notes. The $500 budget ballooned to more than $14,000. But Schroeder knew, after all that, Spector had bottled some high-voltage electricity. At the end of the session, he tried to slip Spector a $50 bill, but Phil wouldn't take it.

Spector got what he wanted at Aldon. Even Nevins and Kirshner stepped aside for the hot kid and gave him the song he wanted, "I Love How You Love Me." Spector brought the Mann-Kolber song back to the West Coast, where he had recorded the Paris Sisters earlier in the year for Lester Sill's Gregmark label and done surprisingly well. Spector spent grueling hours in the studio working on the follow-up, painstakingly crafting a self-conscious masterpiece.

He slowed the ¾ time of the song down to a funeral dirge and rehearsed the vocal parts endlessly around a piano in the studio, carefully polishing the echo on lead vocalist Priscilla Paris (whom Spector was seeing on the side). He obsessively worried about the string sound and went back into the studio many times to remix. When he was done, Spector had created an eerie evocation of his old Teddy Bears hit. The record made the Top Five when it was released in September, by which time songwriter Barry Mann was already writing with a new partner.

Cynthia Weil, one of the few of the young songwriters not from an outer borough, actually raised in Manhattan, fell for Barry Mann pretty much as soon as she laid eyes on him at an audition in the offices of producer Teddy Randazzo. She had started out at Broadway composer Frank Loesser's office but had most recently been working out of Hill & Range. She spent time around Aldon, waiting for Mann to notice her.

They started to date and they started to write. Kirshner heard her sing on one of Mann's demos and hired her. Mann's "Who Put the

Bomp," a nutty, semiautobiographical send-up he wrote with Gerry Goffin, hit the charts in September. Orlando finally recorded the follow-up to "Halfway to Paradise," the first song to be recorded by the new songwriting team of Barry Mann and Cynthia Weil, "Bless You," which made number sixteen in October. They were married before it slipped down the charts.

Spector went back to Hill & Range. He quit his job at Atlantic Records in April, the day his nightclubbing pal Ahmet Ertegun married his new wife, the estimable Mica Banu Grecianu. (Ertegun had courted his bride, an ex-wife of Romanian aristocracy, by, among other things, hiding a small orchestra in her bathroom at the Ritz-Carlton Hotel to play "Puttin' On the Ritz.")

Spector also had severed his association with Leiber and Stoller. Copies of Spector's contract had mysteriously disappeared from the files at Leiber and Stoller's office ("Jerry," asked Stoller on one memorable phone call, "did you give Phil Spector keys to the office?"). Leiber and Stoller had successfully blocked Spector from landing songwriting assignments for an upcoming Elvis movie he had been finagling at Hill & Range, but Spector was still working out of the publishing company's offices.

Through Hill & Range, he found three acts—the Ducanes, the Creations, and the Crystals. He farmed out his offhand productions of the out-of-style white vocal groups—the Creations to Philadelphia's Jamie Records, and the Ducanes to a grateful George Goldner for his Goldisc label. Spector kept the Crystals, although Hill & Range was under the impression he was rehearsing the girl group in their offices for their Big Top label. But secretly, Spector had gone into partnership with Lester Sill to start their own label, Philles Records (a contraction of their first names). He brought arranger Jack Nitzsche out from Hollywood for the sessions. The single "There's No Other (Like My Baby)" was the breakout record on New York radio and retail of the first week in November.

While Berns was still waiting for his first big break, his neighbors at Aldon Music in 1650 Broadway suddenly ruled the pop music world. Bobby Vee put out Goffin and King's "Take Good Care of My Baby" in August. It was their second number one hit. Pitney's "Every Breath I Take" was released the following week—the same week as Bert Berns's first hit, "A Little Bit of Soap" by the Jarmels. Sedaka and Greenfield, together and with other cowriters, were still writing Connie Francis hits—"Where the Boys Are" and "Breakin' In a Brand New Broken Heart" were the latest—and Sedaka's own singles of his songs still scored. By the end of the year, Aldon Music counted more than ten smash hits on the books. More than a hundred of the firm's songs had been recorded that year, reported *Billboard*. Even old-timers at the Brill Building couldn't fail to notice the upstarts.

Wexler, Berns, Nesuhi and Ahmet Ertegun

VIII.

Cry to Me [1962]

WHEN ATLANTIC LOST Ray Charles and Bobby Darin in 1960, those two artists alone accounted for a third of the label's sales. Ahmet always depended on his personal relations in business. Charm was his con. He thought his friendship with Ray Charles would hold sway. He knew Sam Clark and Larry Newton of ABC-Paramount. They were squares, grimy merchants without a speck of cool. They were exactly the kind of crass, low-class record men Ahmet especially despised. They weren't even characters. But they offered Ray Charles an unprecedented deal that would result in his owning his own masters after five years, which Atlantic chose not to match. Clark and Newton needed Ray Charles.

The company had started only five years earlier, a phonograph record wing of the entertainment corporation that produced movies and television. Clark had been a Boston-based record distributor and he brought onboard Newton, a veteran of independent record labels, who guided the label toward the hit parade with fluff like "A Rose and a Baby Ruth" by George Hamilton IV and "Diana" by Paul Anka. But the label desperately needed a cornerstone act like Ray Charles.

Ertegun, still waiting for Ray Charles to call him back for a second offer, read about the ABC-Paramount signing in the trades. He and Wexler were furious and disconsolate. They felt betrayed, bested by slimeballs. They thought—perhaps not unreasonably—they gave Ray

Charles the kind of creative freedom and artistic support he could never have found at any other label and saw his signing with ABC-Paramount as a heinous defection, a personal insult. Charles thought it was business.

Ertegun also invested a lot of time in Darin. He personally delivered Darin's first real royalty check to him backstage at the Copa. Ertegun thought the $80,000 check represented a substantial sum. Darin's manager Steve Blauner, whom the Atlantic guys called "Steve Blunder," looked at the check. "Is that all?" he said.

Ertegun even managed to keep Darin on the charts with trifles such as "Multiplication" and "Things." Darin's naked, fearless ambition had always been a palpable part of his appeal and he was living the life of a Hollywood star in his mansion with his starlet wife. When Frank Sinatra called and asked Blauner to meet with the president of his new label, Reprise Records, Blauner used the invitation as leverage to cut a favorable deal with Capitol Records, the label Sinatra had only recently abandoned. Blauner knew his client would never get proper attention at a label owned by Sinatra, and signing with Capitol would allow Darin to record in those same studios and have his records released on the same label as Sinatra. Atlantic had never even been in the running. Darin and Blauner had big-time show business plans that didn't include some small independent r&b company. Again Ertegun was crushed and Wexler was furious.

Atlantic quickly fell on hard times. Ahmet and Nesuhi Ertegun, raised in luxury, knew nothing of deprivation. They lived like pashas at a clambake. Ahmet drove his Bentley to Harlem. But Wexler grew up poor. He wanted to make his fortune. He worried about money. He bought the big house in Great Neck, but he was not set. He pushed for the sale of the company's music publishing firm, Progressive Music, which contained copyrights such as "What'd I Say" and "Shake, Rattle, and Roll." Freddy Bienstock at Hill & Range snapped up Progressive for a cool half million.

Wexler exiling Leiber and Stoller over chump change was an act of hubris the company could ill afford. They were making hit records over at United Artists. Wexler knew better than to pull them off the Drifters, but even their records weren't doing what they did. After the number one hit of "Save the Last Dance for Me" in October 1960, the company hit a dry patch. The next Top Ten hit on Atlantic, "Gee Whiz," came as a surprise to Wexler, who didn't even know it was his record.

"Gee Whiz" by Carla Thomas was released on a small Memphis label, run by a brother and sister, Jim Stewart, bank teller by day, and Estelle Axton, who also kept a day job while she operated a small record store in a black neighborhood that gave the label its name, Satellite Records. Wexler picked up a previous release by the little label that had stirred some local action, "Cause I Love You" by Carla & Rufus—a father-daughter duo featuring Memphis disc jockey Rufus Thomas and his high school senior daughter, Carla.

It took Wexler one phone call and a thousand bucks, and he promptly forgot about the deal. But when Hy Weiss of Old Town Records, working his day job for Jerry Blaine's Cosnat Distributors, heard the Satellite pressing of "Gee Whiz" and contacted Jim Stewart about leasing the master himself, he looked over the papers and called Wexler. The deal Wexler made for the initial master turned out to include options on future releases.

After "Gee Whiz" in March 1961, Atlantic was frozen out of the Top Ten for eight months. Ahmet and Wexler no longer worked together in the studio. Neither of them spent much time recording. Ertegun, freshly married to the elegant socialite Mica, bought a bus, so he could take entire parties on his nightly rounds of Manhattan nightlife, starting every night at El Morocco. It was the time of the twist and Ertegun soon discovered the Peppermint Lounge on Forty-Fifth Street, between Broadway and Eighth Avenue, where the house band was Joey Dee and the Starliters and the owners were wiseguys. Mike Stoller ran into the handsome Mafia don Sonny Franzese there one night. Franzese, cold-blooded enough to shoot a man in the face at a Jackson Heights bar and calmly return to his drink, liked music business types. He took Stoller out to Third Avenue where Franzese and the boys operated a few more exotic clubs and they watched a lesbian love act. Ertegun tried to sign Joey Dee, but before he could, the act landed on Roulette. Morris Levy had the inside track. Ahmet was less interested in making records anyway these days.

Wexler wasn't doing much more in the studio. The little Memphis label, Satellite, now distributed by Atlantic, also came up with another lucky hit for the company, the instrumental "Last Night" by the Mar-Keys. He spent long hours working disc jockeys and distributors over the phone and using his contacts to find masters from other regional labels like Satellite. He was buying other people's records, but he wasn't making them himself anymore. Atlantic's fortunes were at an all-time low.

SOLOMON BURKE'S BIRTH was foretold. He came to his grandmother in a dream twelve years before. In anticipation, she founded Solomon's Temple: The House of God for All People in Philadelphia, and when Solomon finally was born, there was considerable excitement. He gave his first sermon at age seven. By nine, he was known as the Boy-Wonder Preacher. At twelve, he began weekly radio sermons and went out on the road on weekends, taking his ministry into the world.

When he was eighteen, Solomon spent a week writing a song as a Christmas present for his grandmother, who was sick in bed. The day after he finished, she told him she wanted him to see his Christmas present early and, under her bed, he found a guitar. He sang her the song he had written, "Christmas Presents from Heaven." She spent the rest of the day telling him how his life was going to be. She told him about the loves he would have, big houses, fancy cars. She told him his spiritual message would reach millions, but that he would descend to the pits of hell before he would emerge victorious. The next morning, a week before Christmas, his grandmother died in her sleep.

Shortly after her death, there was a talent contest at Liberty Baptist Church, but Solomon couldn't convince his group, the Gospel Cavaliers, to enter. One fellow had just bought a TV and another had tickets to the football game. So Solomon borrowed pants and a too-short coat from his uncle, went down and entered the contest by himself. The wife of a local deejay liked what she heard enough to introduce young Solomon to Bess Berman, the tough old dame who ran the New York–based independent label Apollo Records, where Mahalia Jackson made her name. Burke cut a number of inspirational-style records for the label that did quite well. But when Burke raised questions about getting properly paid, his manager warned him he would never record for anyone again and he dropped out of the music world entirely. It was his first descent into hell.

Encouraged by his aunt, who operated A.V. Berkley Funeral Home in Philadelphia, Burke went to mortuary school, earned his doctorate, and joined the family business. He married and started a family. After several years, he made a couple of small singles for a local Philadelphia label. The Atlantic brass all knew Burke through the Apollo singles, and *Billboard* editor Paul Ackerman, Wexler's old boss, kept bugging Wexler to sign him. He was an obvious candidate for the Atlantic treatment. When Burke dropped by the Atlantic office in New York unannounced, Wexler signed him to the label on the spot with a handshake. To Atlantic Records, Solomon Burke was deliverance.

When Wexler took Solomon Burke into the studio in December 1960 for his first Atlantic session, Wexler had been missing in action for a while. He rarely faced record production without a partner, but he and Ertegun were no longer as close as they had been. He cut three songs with Burke that day. Two were unremarkable and those were the two Wexler chose for Burke's first Atlantic single, which quickly came and went. The third song was a country and western number that Burke's champion and Wexler's mentor Paul Ackerman suggested, "Just Out of Reach," a song previously done by Patsy Cline on Four Star in 1958.

(At the session, Solomon Burke didn't even stay long enough to hear the playbacks. With a heavy blizzard slamming the East Coast, Burke, an always-enterprising father of eight, was in a hurry to return to Philadelphia, where he had a $4-an-hour job shoveling snow waiting for him.)

Rhythm and blues singers did not often attempt country and western material, but there was more common ground between the two audiences than most people realized. Southern blacks often grew up with a love for country music, but singing it in public was a different matter. Burke's plaintive tenor sailed over a pillowy cushion provided by a background chorale that gave the record a distinctly white touch, although nothing Solomon Burke sang was ever likely to be mistaken for pop.

The record took an agonizing eight months to break. Released in February, it finally climbed on the charts in September 1961 after it started to pick up a little airplay on the radio chain owned by former cowboy singer turned broadcast mogul Gene Autry, who happened to own the publishing on the tune. A lone wolf promotion man working the record for $50 a week blew on the ember. By the time the record fully caught fire and burned, Atlantic was selling thirty thousand copies a week.

But Atlantic had been having a tough time coming up with any hit records. The rhythm and blues style the label helped invent was ancient history. The company denied reports the label had been sold when *Billboard* called, but admitted they were talking to several possible suitors. It was stretching into a long drought. Atlantic's three best-selling singles in 1962 weren't even records they made. One of them Wexler didn't even know they owned.

From the newly renamed, already affiliated little Memphis label, Satellite, which was now called Stax Records, came the miracle instrumental "Green Onions" by Booker T. and the M.G.'s. "Alley Cat" was a perky, cloying piano piece from the man who owned the company that distributed Atlantic in Denmark. His name was Bent Fabricius-Bjerre, which Nesuhi shortened to Bent Fabric. The third was "Stranger on the Shore" by Mr. Acker Bilk, a British trad jazz clarinetist in a bowler hat who cut this string-laden easy listening instrumental that broke out as a hit single all over Europe. Wexler, pissed off that he licensed the damn album but had not been given the hit single, called the European record label and complained. He was told the song was already included on the album, under a different title. If he had listened, he could have heard it. But these were not Atlantic kind of records. These were fluke hits the label could not be expected to repeat. With the success of "Just Out of Reach," Solomon Burke looked like the most promising potential star on Atlantic in many moons. His coming release would be crucial.

Into this breach stepped Bert Berns. He had worked for Mellin Music for almost a year and a half and he had made a lot of records—his Jarmels song had even hit the charts that summer—but Berns was still waiting for his big chance. This was it, producing the next Solomon Burke single under the watchful eye of Jerry Wexler himself. He had no real credentials that would qualify him for the job. Berns and Wexler both knew this was a potentially propitious opportunity, a crossroads for Berns and for Atlantic Records. Burke was a formidable talent, no doubt, but there was much at stake on this session for everybody, especially Berns.

Wexler always said there was something in the way Bert Berns demonstrated the song that led him to take Berns into the studio to produce Solomon Burke. Berns did have an ebullient, enthusiastic manner. He could sing, play guitar and piano, and get inside a song. He could show other musicians how it could go, what you could do with the song. Although Berns was twelve years younger and didn't grow up poor, Wexler knew who Berns was. Wexler's father used to clean the windows at the Berns family's dress shop on the Grand Concourse. Wexler knew the territory. He understood the street corners. That Berns was talented was obvious. He was an eager puppy, brimming with music and ambition. He had all the musical knowledge Wexler lacked, and in his enthusiasm, he radiated a kind of innocent joy that was the polar opposite of Wex's cynical cunning.

At his first meeting with Berns, Solomon Burke had hardly been impressed. He took one look at Berns, wearing a strange hairpiece, scraggly hair that extended past his collar, no necktie, and blue jeans, and took Wexler aside. "What's with this paddy motherfucker?" he said.

Atlantic had installed studios that Tom Dowd designed at the company's new Sixtieth Street headquarters. The big room was almost fifty feet long, more than thirty feet wide, with fifteen-foot ceilings. The room had been instantly successful. Atlantic, almost alone among New York studios, recorded on modern eight-track machines with one-inch tape. On December 6, 1961, Wexler took Berns to the Atlantic studio to produce Solomon Burke singing his song, "Cry to Me."

Wexler produced the first two songs that day, indifferent, uneventful ballads that would have been out of date years before (including a listless cover of the 1950 Ivory Joe Hunter hit, "I Almost Lost My Mind," already twice reprised in 1956 by Ivory Joe for Atlantic and Pat Boone for the big hit). Burke sleepwalked through the vocals. But when Berns's song took center stage, things started to happen. Wexler had admonished Berns. "Keep him rhythm and blues—don't go pop with him," he said.

A descending figure opens the record with a cascading downbeat, sharp little offbeat accents lending the track a calypso feel. Burke opens up in rich voice, and as the lyrics turn and twist their way through the song, he drops down into some of his most golden, resonant tones. But the record doesn't really take off until Berns gets him crying.

Berns and Burke tangled in the studio over the tempo and Burke won out, taking the song at a faster pace than Berns envisioned. Gary Chester's drumming propels the song into each verse, building to Burke digging into the repeated line *Don't you feel like crying*. The question is rhetorical. The song is actually a proclamation of love, but the lyrics dwell on the pain and despair of loneliness. As a songwriter, Berns is less concerned about continuity than he is prodding his singer into desperation. Burke brings the song to a neat emotional epiphany, ad-libbing *cry-ca-cry-ca-cry-cry* over the final chorus.

When you're waiting for a voice to come
In the night, but there is no one
Don't you feel like crying
(Cry to me)
Don't you feel like crying
(Cry to me)
Here I am, honey, come on
Cry to me
—CRY TO ME (BERT RUSSELL, 1962)

For Berns, 1962 would be a watershed year, starting with the release of Solomon Burke's "Cry to Me" in January 1962. The record would soar to number five on the *Billboard* R&B charts (number forty-four Pop) and ignite Burke's inexorable ascension into the ranks of the music's great stars. The record would also be a turning point for Berns, as he sought to capitalize on the success and establish himself in the exclusive inner circle of rhythm and blues.

While his Solomon Burke record started its ten-week run on the charts that January, Berns and his new partner, Wally Roker, were ensconced in the studio, like everybody else in New York, making a twist record. The twist spread through the music business like a virulent flu that winter. Chubby Checker's 1960 number one hit version of the 1959 Hank Ballard song came back to life like Frankenstein's monster after Checker performed the song and his subsequent hit, "Let's Twist Again," on *The Ed Sullivan Show* in October 1961. More than back from the dead, the song spent three weeks at the top of the charts in January 1962, immediately followed by a three-week run at number one by "Peppermint Twist" from Joey Dee and the Starliters. The twist had exploded into a major cultural phenomenon. They were twisting in nightclubs all over the world.

The twist swept through the record business in those intoxicating months. Unlike rock and roll, the twist also had an adult constituency. Society bandleader Lester Lanin had a twist record. So did Sinatra ("Everybody's Twistin'"). No less an authority than Ahmet Ertegun told *Billboard* in February the twist was here to stay. "The Twist is going to be with us for a long time," he said, "certainly for another year at least."

Atlantic came up with two albums, *Do the Twist! with Ray Charles* and *Twist with Bobby Darin*, cobbled together from old recordings by the label's departed stars. Ahmet also announced the introduction of a new label, TwisTime Records, with new releases by the Edwards Twins, the Vocaleers, and the Hi-Lites.

A couple of months later, under a headline "Has the Twist Had It," *Billboard* noted that Atlantic had quietly folded the label.

Wally Roker first met Berns when he was hanging out with his old Bronx pal, Sid Bernstein, who now worked as a booking agent at Shaw Artists on Fifth Avenue. Roker, a large, genial black man, had kicked around the music business since even before his teenage vocal group, the Heartbeats, hit the charts with "A Thousand Miles Away" in 1956. He had introduced Berns to Luther Dixon (he had also introduced Florence Greenberg to Luther Dixon). He could tell Berns had talent. Roker and Berns formed Lookapoo Productions, a name Roker took from the trademark jive talk of Philly deejay Jocko Henderson, and Roker cut a deal with Capitol Records.

Capitol Records was based in Hollywood, where it was founded by songwriter Johnny Mercer in 1942 and flourished through the fifties with Frank Sinatra, Nat King Cole, and others, who made their records in that sumptuous studio in the basement of the label's landmark Hollywood skyscraper, built like a stack of records. The Kingston

Trio was currently selling long-players by the millions for the company, but Capitol needed help on the hit parade, especially after the
recent Sinatra defection. The East Coast office was assigned the job of
building up that end of the label's business and they had been talking
to Roker about working on radio promotion for Capitol, who certainly
could use the assistance. The label had success in the pop and country
fields, but didn't know r&b from their elbows. Roker understood his
first problem with the new affiliation would be his credibility among
the tight little world of rhythm and blues broadcasters, which is how
he hit on the idea of George Hudson and the Kings of Twist.

George Hudson's *Downbeat Club* was the long-standing morning
show on Newark's WNJR, the small station across the river where Alan
Freed first staged his assault on the New York market. Hudson was an
old-timer, charter member of the r&b station's first all-black staff in
1953, a figure of repute in the New York market and among other black
deejays, although he was certainly no musician, not that that mattered.
Berns and Roker took one day to knock out the first George Hudson and
the Kings of Twist album, *It's Twistin' Time*.

Long-playing albums weren't staple items in the r&b world of 1962.
The game was strictly singles, little records with big holes in the center. *It's Twistin' Time* was nothing more than a calling card for deejay
Hudson, an opening gambit in a revamped r&b program for Capitol. A
simple four-piece band (driven by drummer Gary Chester) and a two-
piece horn section featuring King Curtis on tenor sax ran down instrumental versions of a couple of Fats Domino songs, a couple of public
domain oldies ("I've Been Working on the Railroad," twist-style) and
a few specialty numbers, vocals provided by a new kid from Florida,
Gil Hamilton. Berns even recut "A Little Bit of Soap" and another new
original he wrote with Ray Passman, "Little Twister." Might as well
work the catalog.

The session with the Edsels for Capitol was more serious. The
Youngstown, Ohio–based group's 1958 record on a tiny Little Rock,

Arkansas, label had been unearthed three years later by resource-
ful deejays, and after licensing the original master to Hy Weiss's Old
Town label, by May 1961, "Rama Lama Ding Dong" was headed up the
charts. In the wake of the group's sudden rescue from oblivion, other
old recordings by the Edsels surfaced and the group won a new contract with Capitol Records.

Berns produced the group singing a couple of his songs for
Capitol—the single's B-side "If Your Pillow Could Talk" and the
unreleased "Don't You Feel," which he wrote with Don Drowty—
and a pair of songs from a new songwriter named Jeff Barry, whose
"Shake Shake Sherry" was the record's A-side when it was released in
December 1961. A screaming rocker with a scorching saxophone solo
from King Curtis—"a wildly rocking disc with a lot of excitement,"
said *Billboard*—the record started to break on New York radio in late
February, but never spread and then fizzled. But it had looked good for
a minute.

Berns took a powerful singer named Sylvia Hill into the studio for
Capitol and recorded four songs in January 1962 at a full session with
strings and horns, arranged by Teacho Wiltshire. Berns chose two songs
for the single by songwriters Bob Elgin and Kay Rogers—pseudonyms
for Stanley Kahan and Eddie Snyder, a couple of characters who also
shared songwriting credits with Scepter's Luther Dixon on the recent
Gene McDaniels hit, "A Hundred Pounds of Clay." Berns also recorded
one of his own songs with Hill, "Tell Him," that he kept in the can.

He also cut a new Hoagy Lands single that month for MGM Records,
where his old pal Julie Rifkind ran promotion and operated the r&b
label Cub Records. Berns recorded Lands on a roaring version of
"Goodnight Irene," the Leadbelly song the Weavers had introduced to
the pop charts many years before. Hoagy soared over the single-string,
solo guitar introduction and jumped on it when the band slammed in
behind him on the chorus. The flip side was another Bert Russell song,
"It Ain't as Easy as That," started by Lands gaily singing *la-la-la-la*,

skipping into a lighthearted verse about how difficult it is to meet girls, but building to a near-hysterical finish two verses and two choruses later—*I have lost and I've been tossed into the sea of lovers' lonely tears*—Lands pleading desperately, *It ain't easy for me, baby.*

Berns and Roker knocked out two more quickie George Hudson albums in rapid order. *George Hudson Presents Dance Time* featured three new "dance" songs from Berns—"Do the Bug," "C'mon an' Slop," and "Bronx Stomp," along with another piece cowritten with Passman, "Hully Gully Firehouse," that was a shameless appropriation of the song's namesake. Gil Hamilton supplied the vocals again. The third album, *Give 'Em Soul*, used the year's new buzzword in the black community—"soul"—and featured a slight instrumental of the same title credited to Berns and Roker, little more than an extended guitar solo by session player Jimmy Spruill with the title repeated over the track every so often by young Hamilton. The single was released under the name Apple Adam, only the first pseudonym Hamilton would be adopting in his recording career. Hoagy Lands also helped out on vocals and sang some of the songs. It was a kind of nothing album, but Berns wrote evocative liner notes.

Give 'em Soul! Okay . . . so you scratch your head, you look at the guy who represents the company and he's dead serious. Furthermore, he's telling you all the sweet things a weary producer loves to hear: "Money's no object . . . get all the down cats you need . . . just give 'em soul . . . " So you finish scratching your head and you reach for the nearest phone. You're cooking, you're really cooking! So you call Teacho Wiltshire to make the arrangements, and he says "okay." Then you get tensed up because it hits you like a rock about all the things you'll need—songs, the right artists, the right sounds . . . give 'em soul. The next couple of days your desk is piled up with all the great R and B records of the past, including a few original things which will knock everyone out. And then, right smack between all that sweet confusion, all the empty and grotesque coffee containers and crushed cigarette butts, it was there. I mean pow!

I don't think I can express the actual recording session with mere words. The studio was electrified. The musicians, engineers, and invited friends of the artists were gassed as each playback poured through the speakers. . . . Well, it was almost over. Someone called a five minute break. The piano looked inviting to me, so I walked over with a cup of coffee and began to groove, myself. Nothing much, but the big grand responded to a grinding beat. Someone picked up a guitar and fell in. Then the drums and bass gave it a rhythmic pattern that caused us all to lay on it with an uncanny drive. A voice came booming through the studio speaker to keep it going, so we did. The strings returned and, man, did they moan for us. It was too much! Nobody wanted to stop. My fingers were killing me, but I kept going. The knowing smiles in the rhythm section kept egging each other on as if to say: "Keep it moving man, we're saying something." Once again, the huge suspended speaker: "Okay . . . okay . . . great . . . just great. Thank you everybody, that's it." After the playback, everybody in the studio knew it . . . that was the title song of the album: Give 'Em Soul. It was four o'clock in the morning when I started walking home. I was beat but it was a real good kind of tiredness that was hanging on me; just light enough to let my imagination half dream of the people in Tennessee, Pittsburgh, Baltimore, Washington, Detroit, St. Louis, Chicago, California, Georgia, and down home U.S.A. who would be poppin' their fingers and leaning in and understanding—really digging why we call the album Give 'Em Soul.

Also during the *Give 'Em Soul* album sessions, Berns pulled out the instrumental track he recorded in January with Sylvia Hill of his song "Tell Him" and cut Gil Hamilton overdubbing his vocals to the song as "Tell Her." The record was a little jewel—Wiltshire's slashing string line darts back and forth across a thumping bass figure as the introduction leads to the brash opening couplet, *I know something about love / You've got to want it bad*—but it went almost entirely unnoticed when the single came out on Capitol. Hamilton, who was fresh from Florida and thrilled to be making $55 for a day in the studio, had recently finished a couple of months' work on the road as a member of the Drifters and barely noticed himself.

Both Roker and Berns also retained their association at Scepter Records. Florence Greenberg, the queen of Scepter, didn't care much for Berns, but she let Luther Dixon run the musical end of the company. It was practically the only part of the lives of the people around her she didn't try to control. She certainly stepped into Dixon's affairs anytime she felt so inclined. She refused to let him pick up the Four Seasons' "Sherry," which Dixon thought was a surefire hit, because she couldn't stand the record's producer, Bob Crewe, quietly homosexual but excruciatingly eccentric.

She could be openly cruel with her blind son, Stanley, whom she kept around the office in various menial jobs, some thought just so he would be handy to humiliate. She did have a temper. Jerry Leiber watched in amazement one night at Al and Dick's, the West Fifty-Fourth Street steakhouse where the music crowd met for drinks, as Florence beat Luther into submission with her purse. She often treated her good-looking beau, eighteen years her junior, like a child. But Dixon managed to keep the Shirelles in business and the Shirelles were Scepter. The girls had "Baby It's You" in the Top Ten in January 1962 and, glory be, a second number one hit that May with "Soldier Boy," a treacly, obvious piece of sentimental manipulation cowritten with Dixon by the distinctly unmusical Florence Greenberg.

They cut a second Russell Byrd single—a weird song Berns wrote called "Little Bug" that has Berns in deep discussion about his loneliness with an insect (*My heart is pumping a whole lot of tears*)—released in early 1962 on the Scepter subsidiary, Wand Records, with the B-side Phil Spector produced the year before, "Nights of Mexico." It passed with slight notice ("attractive tune and moving performance make this a record with a chance . . . " said *Billboard*). Berns cut a second session for Wand with the Renaults, who had recorded his autobiographical "Just like Mine" the year before, this time retooling the Platters hit "Only You" to little effect.

Berns also undertook for Scepter the case of Lori Rogers, Broadway teen ingénue, not yet fifteen years old, who had a small but cute part in the Broadway production of *Bye Bye Birdie* and now a similarly small but cute part in the new musical *All American*, starring the old Scarecrow himself, Ray Bolger, at the Winter Garden, around the corner from 1650 Broadway. Berns and Ray Passman fashioned a bit of tongue-in-cheek teen fluff, "Seymour," for her perky persona that veered clearly into parody. It was a typical Broadway deal, but at least Berns got a plug in Walter Winchell's column.

Berns was making fun of a type of record he himself never made. This kind of frankly adolescent pop usually came without irony, but could also contain a wholesome amount of self-deprecating humor (like Barry Mann and Gerry Goffin's "Who Put the Bomp"). It was often difficult to tell the sincere from the caricature and the difference frequently didn't matter. Teen pop in all forms flourished. The Aldon songwriters were all over the charts. Carole King and Gerry Goffin were crafting pop songs with great musical and lyrical gifts with near industrial precision. Neil Sedaka could be annoyingly frothy and lightweight, but his instinct for melody, his musical sense, and the precision of his performances could never be faulted. Donny Kirshner decided to move into the label business himself, launching Dimension Records that summer with a number one hit from Carole King and Gerry Goffin,

"The Loco-Motion," by Little Eva. *I know you'll get to like it if you give it a chance.* Berns may have been too funky to be that candy-ass, but he was about to meet his match.

Originally there were four Isley brothers—Ronald, O'Kelly, Rudolph, and Vernon—sons of Kelly and Sallye Isley of Cinncinati, Ohio. Three-year-old Ronald won a $25 war bond in a church spiritual contest and, by the time he was seven, he was singing onstage at the Regal Theater, alongside Dinah Washington and others. With their mother as chaperone, the four young Isleys toured Midwest churches until youngest brother Vernon was killed in a traffic accident. The parents convinced the brothers to regroup a year later and they left for New York in 1957 with bus fare and $20 from the family's savings. They made a couple of small-time vocal group records. George Goldner discovered them and cut a few sides with them.

But it was for RCA Victor that the Isley Brothers recorded the classic "Shout, Parts I and II" in 1959. The six-minute opus featured organist Herman Stevens from the boys' hometown church and represented a definitive distillation of the Pentecostal experience translated into secular terms, a work of sheer genius. It was never a big hit—forty-seven on the pop charts; never made the r&b charts at all—but almost immediately entered the literature as a standard. The Top Ten version by Joey Dee and the Starliters in March 1962 even brought the Isley Brothers original back on the charts for a couple of weeks.

After cutting three singles with Leiber and Stoller on Atlantic the previous year, the Isleys signed with Luther Dixon and Wand in 1962 and had already failed to click with a dance song called "The Snake" when they went into the studio a second time with Dixon, who, this time, had Bert Berns in tow.

Dixon spent most of the three-hour session at Bell Sound in March 1962 trying to get the Isleys to lay down an acceptable vocal take on top of a prerecorded track for a song written by Burt Bacharach, coauthor of the Shirelles hit "Baby It's You." The new song, "Make It Easy on Yourself," was somewhat tricky, hardly conventional pop fare and certainly unlike anything the gospel-fueled Isleys had ever previously encountered. Dixon and the Isleys were working with the song's original demo, recorded by Bacharach with a studio singer named Dionne Warwick. But the Isleys were not up to it. The song was abandoned.

Berns stepped forward with "Twist and Shout," the song he watched Wexler and Spector butcher a year before. This time, he would be the producer. The Isleys didn't know Berns. They hated the song. They didn't want to do any twist song. Wally Roker and Luther Dixon, representing the label management, expressed a contrary viewpoint. It had been a frustrating day already and angry words were exchanged. Furniture was broken. There were a lot of brothers arguing loudly in the control booth, and when the smoke cleared, Bert Berns, Solomon Burke's "paddy motherfucker," took over and produced the record in what remained of the session. At last, Berns was in command of his song's creative destiny.

"Twist and Shout" hit the charts as soon as the record was released that June, a smash on both the pop and r&b charts. The record was everything Berns wanted it to be. On the Isley Brothers record, Berns gave the song the sound he always intended—the Cuban *guajiro* rhythm he first strummed to the chords of "La Bamba" that morning in his office with Ray Passman. The Isleys breathed gospel intensity into the simple, spare arrangement. They climbed all over the song's architecture, building to two walloping crescendos in the record's two and half minutes. Teacho Wiltshire's horn parts were straight from any Latin dance band songbook, but this was not some distant American cousin of the Brazilian samba. This was Afro-Cuban rock and roll. The mystery of the mambo lurked at the heart of this record.

The record ran four months on both the pop and r&b charts. The Isley Brothers were selling a ton of records that summer. Florence Greenberg hadn't had a record this big by anybody on her label other than the Shirelles. So, Berns went back into the studio with the

brothers to record an album he filled from the catalog, including num-
bers such as "I Say Love," "You Better Come Home," and "Don't You
Feel" that he had already tried with other acts. He used his old pal
Herbie Wasserman on drums. Now he was in the record business.

Berns (top) with Phil Spector (bottom), Jerry Leiber (right), Mike Stoller (left, holding glass), Sam Cooke (next to Leiber), others, BMI Awards dinner, 1962.

IX

If I Didn't Have a Dime (To Play the Jukebox) [1962]

B ERNS WAS ALL over the place. He went straight from finishing the third George Hudson LP the next day into Atlantic Studios for his second Solomon Burke session with Wexler. Burke, who found Berns's suggestion he record "A Little Bit of Soap" almost laughable, had sketched out lyrics on the train from Philadelphia to an old folk song he only barely remembered, "Down in the Valley" (the copyright wound up credited to Burke-Berns). Berns also gave him a song he wrote during his earliest days in 1650 Broadway with Mickey Lee Lane, "Baby I Want to Be Loved," a Don Covay song called "I'm Hanging Up My Heart for You," and the old folk song Berns himself recorded two years earlier on the flip side of "The Legend of the Alamo," "Gotta Travel On."

He cut a second session with Jimmy Jones ("Handy Man") for Julie Rifkind's Cub label, including another version of his and Passman's "Nights of Mexico." His Lookapoo partner Wally Roker, working a few angles for Capitol, signed saxophone sideman King Curtis as an artist, fresh off his number one r&b instrumental for Bobby Robinson's Enjoy label earlier in the year, "Soul Twist" (one of the first records to use the term "soul" in the title). Looking ahead to summer and mindful of the surf music from California that had been recently making itself known on the charts, Berns had session guitarist Billy Butler turn up the reverb and cut a fairly typical King Curtis instrumental single that he called "Beach Party"—this surf music could turn out to be the next twist—before moving on to an album of instrumental versions of country and western songs by the saxophonist. "Beach Party" spent the entire summer on the pop charts.

He conducted a session for Capitol with the Cadillacs, or at least Bobby Ray and the Cadillacs, a late-edition version of the group behind the 1955 oldie "Speedo" that, over the years, had more members than a Mason Lodge. Berns wrote a florid little melodrama set in the bull-fight ring, "White Gardenia," with Brill Building background vocal specialist Carl Spencer. A richly evocative song that owes something musically to Jerry Butler's "He Don't Love You" (with a tip of the hat to "Spanish Harlem"), the bogus Spanish ambience hails back to the bullfight music albums from his days in the West Village with Rita Constance. He also finally recorded a version of his all-time favorite song with the Cadillacs, "La Bamba."

On his third Solomon Burke session in June, during the middle of the two-month chart run by "Down in the Valley," Berns forged the style that would forever be identified with Solomon Burke. He balanced four pieces of material, each judiciously decorated to frame Burke's remarkably expressive vocals in the foreground. With a young arranger Berns knew from Philadelphia, Jerry Ragovoy, who had done some records with Frankie Avalon and Fabian, producer Berns marshaled a large session orchestra that included stalwarts such as drummer Gary Chester and pianist Paul Griffin.

"I Really Don't Want to Know" followed the blueprint laid down by "Just Out of Reach"—a country standard given a stately, extravagant reading by Burke, gently prodded along by pianist Griffin. Another song, "Home in Your Heart," was gutbucket blues from old hands Winfield Scott and Otis Blackwell, working out of Hill & Range. But it was the other two pieces where Berns staked out his own territory. "Tonight My Heart She Is Crying" floats on a gentle Afro-Cuban *danzon* with xylophone, flute, and a bed of tinkling percussion, as Burke philosophically laments, *love is a bird that spreads his wings and flies away.* "You Can Make It If You Try" comes straight from the church— pure unvarnished soul music.

The productions are all recognizable Atlantic Records–style r&b, but these records also bring fresh vigor to the sound. Coproducer Wexler could tell. His records never sounded so good. Berns could get his ideas across to the musicians and communicate with Burke. His enthusiasm was contagious. Wexler felt his heart warm to the task of making records again. A beautiful friendship was beginning to bloom.

It also looked as if Berns might be landing the next Gene Pitney single. Berns only had to walk up a couple of flights at 1650 Broadway to show Pitney "If I Didn't Have a Dime (To Play the Jukebox)," another song he wrote with Phil Medley. He loved Pitney's records and thought the song would be right for him. He met the singer upstairs in the office of Pitney's manager, Aaron Schroeder, the kind of bare-knuckles music publisher who would hand out six different exclusives on the same song. Schroeder also ran the label Musicor Records, where Pitney made his records.

Berns sat on a chair, picked at the battered nylon-string acoustic, and played Pitney only the one song. Pitney liked the song, but he was fascinated with the sound Berns got out of the beat-up guitar. He knew the guitar part tied the song together and didn't think anybody else could get the same sound. He told Berns he would record the song only if Berns played the guitar. That would not be a problem, Berns assured Pitney.

Pitney was poised for stardom. Writing the next hit single for Gene Pitney would have been a big step up for Berns, but that was not going to happen. Berns's potential pop breakthrough was buried by the sudden emergence of one of the great American songwriting teams of their day from the other side of the record.

Pitney liked the Berns song and didn't particularly care for the other song, which Schroeder had picked for the session. To Pitney, it didn't feel like it had enough words. It had some strange chords and odd time signatures. The Berns song sounded like the hit to Pitney, not "Only Love Can Break a Heart" by Burt Bacharach and Hal David, a couple of Famous Music songwriters in their midthirties who had been around a while without really striking gold.

Burt Bacharach was born and raised in Kansas City. His father was a nationally syndicated newspaper columnist and best-selling expert on menswear and grooming. Young Bacharach studied music under avant-garde classical composer Darius Milhaud, and his first gig after he left the army in World War II was backing pop singer Vic Damone. He worked as an accompanist for a number of old-time show business musical acts—Polly Bergen, Imogene Coca, Georgia Gibbs, the Ames Brothers—before signing with Famous Music as a songwriter in 1956. He was teamed at Famous with lyricist Hal David, and the pair wrote a procession of forgotten B-sides through the late fifties, beginning with "Peggy's in the Pantry" by Sherry Parsons. Bacharach, handsome like a movie star, made his living as accompanist to aging screen siren Marlene Dietrich, who took the young gentleman to all the great cities of the world. He was the last great, albeit unconsummated, love of her life.

Hal David had been encouraged to pursue songwriting by his older brother Mack David, already a working songwriter himself. The younger David had some success almost immediately after he mustered out from the war and, two years after that, cowrote "The Four Winds and the Seven Seas," by Vic Damone, one of the biggest hits of 1949. The following year, Frank Sinatra made it big with his "American Beauty Rose," and Teresa Brewer scored with "Bell Bottom Blues" in 1953.

Bacharach and David managed some modest hits—"The Story of My Life" by Marty Robbins, "Magic Moments" by Perry Como— but both continued to write with other partners. David coauthored "Broken-Hearted Melody" with his collaborator Sherman Edwards that became the biggest hit of her career for Sarah Vaughan in 1959. Leiber and Stoller used a number of songs with the Drifters ("Please Stay,"

"Loneliness or Happiness," "Mexican Divorce") that Bacharach wrote with an older cowriter named Bob Hilliard, a nonconformist in beat-up tennis shoes and worn-out windbreaker, considered odd even by Alley standards.

Luther Dixon at Scepter started to work with Bacharach on the Shirelles. He liked a song Bacharach wrote with Hal's older brother, Mack David, called "I'll Cherish You" but wanted Mack to rewrite the lyrics into something darker. Dixon came up with the *cheat . . . cheat* line and the new title, "Baby It's You," and took a songwriting credit under his ASCAP pseudonym of Barney Williams. Dixon liked the song so well, in fact, once the new lyrics were finished, he simply overdubbed the Shirelles vocals on top of Bacharach's original demo.

Bacharach and David liked to fool around on the "Stardust" piano at Famous Music, where Hoagy Carmichael loomed large. Since Paramount Pictures owned the music publisher, songs by Famous writers were frequently funneled into motion pictures (which is how Bacharach ended up writing and recording the theme song to the 1958 science fiction quickie, *The Blob*). They wrote "(The Man Who Shot) Liberty Valance" for the John Wayne film directed by John Ford. After Pitney's searing vocal performance on "Town Without Pity" that not only took the record Top Twenty, but also earned the song an Oscar nod for Hollywood soundtrack composer Dimitri Tiomkin, he was the obvious candidate to sing "Liberty Valance." By the time Pitney was in Bell Studios recording the song, however, the movie had already been released without it. Still, Hal David's gem-cut lyrics were a detailed three-minute reduction of the movie's plot, and Bacharach's thunderous underpinnings gave Pitney some explosive lines (*The point of a gun was the only law that Liberty understood . . .*).

The record was well on its way into the Top Five and Pitney was going to have two straight hits when the next session was called that June at Bell. Berns was on hand to play his Goya on the track. Bacharach was there to conduct his arrangement of his song. It was going to be either "If I Didn't Have a Dime (To Play the Jukebox)" or "Only Love Can Break a Heart."

When it was released in September, trade advertisements trumpeted "If I Didn't Have a Dime" as the A-side of the new Gene Pitney single and the song entered the charts. "Twist and Shout" was still lodged in the upper reaches of the charts. The King Curtis single "Beach Party" hadn't finished its summer run, so that when the new Solomon Burke single "I Really Don't Want to Know" made its chart debut the next week, Berns had four records on the *Billboard Hot 100*.

The next week, however, the other side of the Gene Pitney record, Bacharach and David's "Only Love Can Break a Heart," started up the charts and didn't stop until it made number two. "If I Didn't Have a Dime" stalled at number fifty-eight and fell by the wayside. The Bacharach side was blocked from the top only by Phil Spector's first number one hit, "He's a Rebel" by the Crystals, recorded in Hollywood, where he was running his Philles Records label; ironically, a song written by Gene Pitney.

Money was starting to roll in. Berns took Wally Roker with him the day he rented his penthouse. The doorman building was at 301 East Forty-Eighth Street at Second Avenue, a block from United Nations Plaza and the East River. It was a sumptuous perch by any Manhattan measure—a three-bedroom aerie thirty-four floors high, surrounded by terraces on three sides—and it required a royal $700 monthly rent. Berns brought $10,000 in cash with him when he made the deal. There were fireplaces in both the living room and bedroom. He put a grand piano in front of the window. He kept a fishbowl on a side table in the living room where he stuffed royalty checks he was too busy to take to the bank.

Through Ray Passman, Berns met Paul Colby, recently divorced man-about-town who lived in the same East Side neighborhood. Colby worked in the music publishing business during the forties, where he became close friends with Frank Sinatra. Colby used to beard for

Sinatra with Ava Gardner when Sinatra was still married to his first wife. He took dames up to Sinatra's rooms at the Drake Hotel when Sinatra was out of town. He left the music business to get married and started making furniture. He built rough-hewn, handmade tables for Duke Ellington and Cy Coleman. Miles Davis bought furniture from Colby and became a friend. Morris Levy was a client, and as usual, he proved more trouble than he was worth. Levy loaned Colby $25,000, and when he unexpectedly called in the loan, Colby was forced to close his showroom.

His business—and marriage—over, Colby was making a living restoring antique elevator cabs when he ran across Berns. They were bachelors on the town together, going to clubs, bars, and parties, picking up women. One time, after a night of tomcatting, Berns and Colby returned to their respective apartments, having each taken prisoners. In the morning, Berns invited Colby over for breakfast, who arrived to find Berns and last night's date nonchalantly sitting around in the nude, acting like they were at a tea party. Colby went along with the gag. These guys were a panic.

Sometimes they brought along Jerry Ragovoy, who had moved from Philadelphia and landed a job as a song plugger for Swing and Sway with Sammy Kaye. Berns would no longer take women out on the dance floor, wary of his heart condition, but he would drink, smoke endless Pall Malls, and stay up all hours.

Berns was making the kind of records that would bring him to the attention of Leiber and Stoller. He was Wexler's new bright-eyed boy and nobody who knew any better could mistake the vibrancy of the Solomon Burke records for Wexler's usual studio fare. They liked Berns, but Stoller had to smile, standing behind Berns, while he sat at the upright in Leiber and Stoller's office and demonstrated some songs. The back flap of his toupee had peeled away from its adhesive and Stoller could see that Berns used gum to hold his rug down. But they dug his Cubano thing.

Leiber, in particular, was fascinated with the Gil Hamilton record Berns produced on Capitol, "Tell Her." He thought it was a hit song. He handed a copy of the single to the four young ladies, high school seniors from Queens, who called themselves the Masterettes, when they came to audition for him and Stoller at their Brill Building office. They came recommended by saxophonist "Big" Al Sears, who had a piece of the girls' management, and had been accompanied by his part-ner, Rene Roker, brother of Scepter promotion man Wally Roker, as well as a young man who played piano with them. Leiber thought the girls had something, but wasn't sure. He switched their lead vocalists and tried the youngest, sixteen-year-old Brenda Reid, who had never been to Manhattan before. He liked what he heard and told them to learn the song and come back.

When they did return, one of the girls was missing—her father didn't approve—so their pianist filled in on her vocal part. The young man also arranged the background vocals and turned the Gil Hamilton solo performance into a group vehicle. Leiber liked it and suggested the pianist, twenty-one-year-old Herb Rooney, join the group. Leiber also announced to the group they would now be known as the Exciters, a name that did not necessarily sit well with all its members, but who nonetheless chose not to say anything.

In short order, these young, starry-eyed teens and their older brother figure were standing in the center of a full-scale Leiber and Stoller ses-sion call at Bell Studios; strings, horns, additional vocalists, a half dozen percussion players. Arranger Teacho Wiltshire adjusted the key and accelerated the tempo slightly, but otherwise it was the same basic arrangement Berns had used on the Sylvia Hill session that previous January. Brenda Reid scorched the lead vocal. They didn't even notice the songwriter standing in a corner and nobody pointed him out.

Berns did not write teenage romance. His songs contained the very real presence of sex and obsession. The stakes are high and the prices are dear. Reid, this young innocent from Jamaica, Queens, a self-taught singer without a soupçon of artifice, carries the knowledge of deeper, fiercer emotions than she can possibly understand because they are bricked into the lyrics. *If you want him to be the very part of you that makes you want to breathe* . . . Leiber was right. As the record sailed into the Top Ten on United Artists, they decided to give Berns more work.

Leiber and Stoller didn't care for the teenage slant the whole market had taken. Music publishing was their game and the only way Leiber and Stoller knew to promote their publishing was to make records with the songs. They certainly didn't feel qualified to write songs for these acts. They were comfortable writing and producing "I Keep Forgettin'" sung by Chuck Jackson on Wand, a brilliantly devised instrumental track heavy with trademark percussion matched to some of Leiber's most pungent recent lyrics, but that kind of sophisticated r&b was increasingly scarce on today's hit parade.

They were losing their enthusiasm for making music, as they felt themselves sliding further out of touch with the market. They started to rely more on writers they signed to their publishing company, Trio Music, to provide songs for the records they produced. There was no way they put the kind of pride and joy they did in Drifters records into Jay and the Americans, a wholly inferior white version of the black original that Leiber and Stoller recorded for United Artists.

They got "She Cried" from Greg Richards and Ted Daryll, two young contract writers at Trio, and that hokum sold more than a million records. Brylcreemed and ready for his close-up, Hollywood pretty boy Mike Clifford was signed to a West Coast–based manager, Helen Noga, the old battle-axe who handled Johnny Mathis. His syrupy hit, "Close to Cathy," must have made Leiber and Stoller want to vomit, but they were rewarded with another big hit for United Artists. They wrote lyrics to "My Clair de Lune" for square Steve Lawrence, which is nowhere near as hip as writing lyrics to "Flyin' Home" for swinging Chris Connor, as they once did when they were still working with Atlantic.

They did continue to produce the Drifters and, once again, revital-
ized the group's failing fortunes in September 1962 with "Up on the
Roof," one of the most rich and bracing pieces yet from the pen and
piano of Gerry Goffin and Carole King. Leiber and Stoller rewrote the
bridge, after Goffin and King got stuck, but declined credit.

THAT WAS THE fall of the great bossa nova scare. "Is Bossa Nova the
New Twist?" asked *Billboard*. The smooth, cool combination of guitar-
ist Charlie Byrd and saxophonist Stan Getz on an album of contempo-
rary Brazilian compositions titled *Jazz Samba* started the flash flood.
More than fifteen recording artists rushed to the market with versions of
"One Note Samba" by Antonio Carlos Jobim and Newton Mendonça—
Count Basie, Lionel Hampton, Tito Puente, Dizzy Gillespie among
them—and Ella Fitzgerald was rush-releasing her version of Jobim and
Mendonça's "Desafinado," backed with "Stardust Bossa Nova."

Getz and Byrd played their version of "Desafinado," the record that
started all this fuss, on *The Perry Como Show* on TV in October, but no
Elvis-style rumblings occurred. Former teen idol Paul Anka bowed his
bossa nova original, "Eso Beso," on *The Ed Sullivan Show*. A sold-out
Carnegie Hall concert in November featured Byrd and Getz, Brazilians
Jobim and João Gilberto, plus Dizzy Gillespie, who also had a bossa
nova album. Bacharach watched from the audience in rapture. There
was no dance yet to accompany the craze, but Fred Astaire Studios had
their best people working on it. The record business, poised to catch an
incipient trend, held its breath.

In Brazil, bossa nova expressed a new national spirit rising from
the ashes of the long-run regime of dictator Getulio Vargas, who first
came to power in a bloodless coup in 1930 and ruled Brazil like his
role model, Benito Mussolini of Italy, until his suicide in office in 1954.
Under the spell of a wave of optimism, as Brazil, with a new, dem-
ocratically elected leader, rallied for sweeping industrial and social
changes, bossa nova emerged as a reflection of the country's buoyant

new mood. A 1958 record called "Chega de Saudade" was the starting point. The song was sung by guitarist João Gilberto. Bossa nova was modern Brazil—fresh and sleek, sensual yet nonexotic.

Leiber and Stoller couldn't resist the bossa nova. They took three members of the Clovers—the old Atlantic vocal group whose last hit, "Love Potion #9," Leiber and Stoller wrote and produced three years before in 1959—and their new lead vocalist Roosevelt "Tippie" Hubbard and cut "Bossa Nova, Baby" and "The Bossa Nova (My Heart Said)," neither of which were, strictly speaking, bossa nova records. They were comical/musical gems that recalled their finest work with the Coasters.

Leiber and Stoller liked the record so much, they decided to go back into the record business for the first time since they folded their Spark label and moved east seven long years before. They formed Tiger Records and released the Tippie and the Clovers single in November 1962. Ahmet and Wexler had shielded Leiber and Stoller from many of the tawdry inner workings of the record business and the songwriters knew next to nothing about graft and corruption. They received a "Pick of the Week" from *Billboard* and the brilliant little record withered away and died (although Elvis would make a million-seller of "Bossa Nova, Baby" the next year). The record label was quickly forgotten.

Leiber and Stoller not only turned to contract songwriters to provide the material for records, but also started to use other producers to make the records, farming off the results to United Artists under their deal there, down the hall with Johnny Bienstock at Big Top, or elsewhere. They used Burt Bacharach and Hal David to conduct sessions of their own material for Leiber and Stoller productions, including the brilliant "I Just Don't Know What to Do With Myself" by Tommy Hunt and "It's Love That Really Counts (In the Long Run)" by the Shirelles, for Scepter. They formed a music publishing partnership with Bacharach and David, fresh out of Famous Music, called U.S. Songs, another key acquisition in their growing publishing portfolio.

They tried out Berns on a couple of oddball assignments. Myrna March was a voluptuous 39D redhead with a va-va-voom act that Leiber and Stoller had previously tried to conjure on a piece called "I Can't Say No," set to a stripper's beat with arranger Artie Butler shouting his head off in the background. It was a sign of how low Leiber and Stoller had sunk that they were doing the job for Morris Levy's Roulette Records. At their behest, Berns also cut three songs with the sex kitten, including "Baby," a slinky remake of "Baby (I Wanna Be Loved)," the old song he wrote with Mickey Lee Lane and which he had recorded only six months before with Solomon Burke as a gospel-based number.

Trio Music songwriter Tony Powers found Beverly Warren singing with some friends under the elevated tracks in Sunnyside, Queens, just across the river. He was on his way for burgers at the White Castle, but he stopped and left his card. When she and her all male associates showed up at the Brill Building for their audition, fifteen-year-old Warren was wearing her trademark cat's eye makeup, white lipstick, and teased hair. Powers's songwriting partner, Ellie Greenwich, who sported a teased blonde beehive herself, liked what she heard.

When young Warren and the rest of her vocal group arrived at Bell Sound for the recording session, they were told the producers wanted only the girl. The guys went home. Suddenly all by herself, Beverly Warren nervously walked into the crowded control room, where busy engineers and other record business types surrounded Jerry Leiber, Mike Stoller, and the session's producer, Bert Berns, who looked up. "Here comes our new star," said Berns, and a feeling of well-being washed through the young girl.

They also sent Berns to cop Phil Spector's licks. After Spector launched a rumbling, echoey, reverbed cover of the old song from the Disney movie, "Zip-A-Dee Doo-Dah," by a group of Hollywood session singers Spector named Bob B. Soxx and the Blue Jeans on his Philles label, Berns found a set of New York session singers and took them into the studio to cut a near-identical model of the song "How Much Is That Doggie in the Window."

The four women who sang the record had worked around town since they were Bronx high school kids going as the DeVaurs. They had been singing sessions with background vocal contractor Arthur Crier, who pitched them at Berns. Carl Spencer, sometimes Berns's songwriting collaborator ("White Gardenia") and one of Crier's regular singers, handled the showpiece bass vocal on the bridge. When the record came out on United Artists that December, the singers were astonished to discover that, without anybody telling them, the group had been named Baby Jane and the Rockabyes—the Jerry Leiber touch—after the recent movie *What Ever Happened To Baby Jane?* The record did surprisingly well. "Sold 175,000 1st Ten Days," said the trade ads, and that ain't Purina. "Produced by Leiber and Stoller," said the label. "Directed by Bert Berns."

If working with Leiber and Stoller was almost inevitable, Berns pairing with Juggy Murray was somewhat less likely. Raised in Hell's Kitchen, Murray made his money in Harlem's numbers racket before deciding to try his hand at the record game. He was a street-smart hustler with a few connections to Harlem disc jockeys and no experience. His first hit on Sue Records—named after both his mother and his daughter—came the next year in 1958, "Itchy Twitchy Feeling" by sometime Drifters vocalist Bobby Hendricks, backed up on the session by some sidelining Coasters.

Juggy pretty much invented Ike and Tina Turner. He flew to St. Louis to meet with Ike Turner after hearing the demo of "A Fool in Love" and told Turner that he should feature the gal in the band. They racked up big numbers on Sue in 1960 with "A Fool in Love" and others such as "I Idolize You" or "It's Gonna Work Out Fine." Murray kept his own counsel and worked his side of the street. He used top Brill Building arrangers and contracted with the best sidemen. He produced his own sessions and he worked his own releases. He and Bobby

Robinson were the only two black label operators in New York. He was wary of prejudice. Murray didn't mess much with cats like Berns.

Juggy Murray, in fact, financed a bold black musicians' collective in New Orleans, a little worker-run cooperative to control the means of production in the local music business down there. Organizer Harold Battiste was a deep thinker with an inflamed sense of racial injustice. He pulled together fellow New Orleans musicians to form AFO Productions—All For One—a revolutionary effort to allow musicians to share in a record's revenue. He signed up some of the town's leading black musicians—saxophonist Alvin "Red" Tyler, pianist Allen Toussaint—and hired a black attorney. With Juggy Murray, they had a black national distributor.

They printed up black business cards with their names embossed in gold. Battiste envisioned nothing less than a black-owned major label, and the second AFO single Murray released, "I Know" by Barbara George, was indeed a nationwide smash Top Five million-seller in 1961. But Murray bought her contract and pulled the plug on AFO after a half dozen releases, pissed off that Battiste cut "Ya Ya" by Lee Dorsey for his crosstown rival Bobby Robinson. Brotherhood only went so far.

With Berns, Murray produced a third Russell Byrd record, "Hitch Hike," a two-part dance epic with considerable debt to the 1960 Ray Bryant Combo hit, "The Madison Time," Berns calling out moves—*Now make a three-step turn, baby, you're on your own*—in front of a cooking band on dance floor overdrive, King Curtis snaking his saxophone through much of the track ("Soul twisting," says Berns). There is nothing to even vaguely suggest white people might have been involved in the making of this record, including Berns's raspy vocalisms.

Murray didn't make records for the pop charts like Luther Dixon; his records were all for a black audience.

Murray produced almost all the records on his label—"A Juggy Production" was a trademark on every single—but he let Berns give the Isley Brothers treatment on Sue to Glen and Francis Hockaday, a pair of brothers with strong voices, on the only record they would ever make. Berns reworked the Russell-Medley "Hold On Baby" from the Isley Brothers for the Hockadays, keeping a little "Twist and Shout" in the introduction, but giving these voices a great, roaring ride on another one of his sparkling little Cuban rock and roll songs, a much improved version over the Isley Brothers recording. Nobody else was making records that sounded like this.

Berns and Murray even went in the studio together again in January 1963 with Murray's favorite artist, vocalist Baby Washington, when Murray produced her pop chart breakthrough, "That's How Heartaches Are Made." Murray was not known for creative collaborations and he didn't expect white people to give him a fair shake in the business. Justine Washington, also known as Jeanette, had been around since she sang with her vocal group, the Hearts. She had made more than twenty records since 1956, including a couple of decent r&b chart entries. Murray wanted to move her to larger, grander ballads, but first she had songs of her own she wanted to record and he waited her out. When the day came, he brought Berns in on the session and gave Berns the production credit on the single's B-side, "There He Is," recorded at the same session, his way of sharing production credit. Murray did not suffer fools—especially white fools—but he knew Berns was a real record man, whatever color he was.

Next, Berns took the Isleys back in the studio after "Twisting with Linda," the tepid follow-up to "Twist and Shout," came and went. For the A-side of the group's fourth single of the year, Berns harnessed the gospel fervor of the Isleys on their own rip-snorting "Nobody but Me," but Florence Greenberg pressed the case for the single's B-side, an unremarkable piece of typical Aldon pop, "I'm Laughing to Keep From Crying," produced by Luther Dixon. (Overlooked in the Isleys' original version, "Nobody but Me" would become a 1967 Top Ten hit and garage band classic by the Human Beinz.).

Whenever Greenberg did exercise her taste, the results were usually dreadful. Even Burt Bacharach, who had been delivering hit songs to the label, felt the chill of Greenberg's controlling hand. She relegated Bacharach and David's "It's Love That Really Counts (In the Long Run)" to the B-side of the next Shirelles single, a quietly elegant piece, one of their finest, something that could have lifted the Shirelles out of the realms of the purely teenage. She submarined for purely personal reasons the exquisite Bacharach-David production of their "I Just Don't Know What to Do With Myself" by Tommy Hunt, the former lead vocalist of the Flamingos, because the singer was dating both Beverly Lee of the Shirelles and the girlfriend of a Mafia don on the side and Greenberg didn't approve. She had never thought much of Hunt's voice; he was strictly Luther Dixon's signing, but now Luther was gone.

Tired of the daily strain of running interference between Florence and the rest of the record company, being responsible for writing, rehearsing, producing virtually the label's entire roster, all tangled up in his tormented personal relationship with his boss, Dixon accepted an offer to run his own label for Capitol Records. Under the same mandate that landed Berns and Roker their Lookapoo deal, not to mention the big money for Bobby Darin, Capitol Records, looking to expand their reach on the *Billboard* charts, set up Ludix Records. Dixon, according to *Billboard*, would continue to produce the Shirelles for Scepter. But with Dixon gone and the Isleys at the end of their string at Scepter, Berns would be a long time darkening those doors again.

"Pops" Maligmat owned a Filipino restaurant in Manhattan and wanted inexpensive entertainment, so he trained his four sons to play music. He kept their five sisters in Manila and put the boys out on the road at an age when most kids still needed babysitters. When former Roosevelt Music songwriter Neil Diamond saw the little cuties on *The Ed Sullivan Show*, he thought they'd be perfect for this Christmas song he wrote with a Latin beat. He took the idea to another former Roosevelt writer, Stanley Kahan, who had opened an office of his own at 1650 Broadway. He told Diamond to send in the group to audition, never dreaming for a minute that they would. When "Pops" showed up with his four boys, ages nine to fourteen, and Kahan heard them play and sing, he signed the group in an instant.

With some money from United Artists, he took the Maligmat brothers, now called the Rocky Fellers, into the studio and cut Diamond's Christmas song. When United Artists passed on the master, he took the tapes down the hall to Scepter Records. Kahan presumed Diamond's frequent absences from the project had to do with the young songwriter's college studies. But it turned out that Diamond suddenly had bigger fish to fry. He had signed a record deal with Columbia Records and was trying to wriggle free of any commitment he might have made to Kahan, who had given Diamond a piece of the Rocky Fellers. As a result, Diamond didn't meet Bert Berns when Kahan brought Berns onboard the next Rocky Fellers record.

Berns had previously used songs by Kahan and his partner, Eddie Snyder, writing as Bob Elgin and Kay Rogers, on some of his Lookapoo Productions records at Capitol. Kahan was a tall, older guy with a big personality and winning ways. He wrote lyrics, and Snyder supplied the music. Berns and Kahan dreamed up a song, "Killer Joe," that took its name from the dancer Joe Piro, known as Killer Joe, famous-at-the-moment around Manhattan discotheques. But Berns also built into the song a male jealousy angle that perhaps inserted a little more rage and angst than was appropriate for nine-year-old lead vocalist Albert Maligmat, cute as a Pres-to-Log. Even in dumb teenage dance songs, Berns liked to see his singers tortured.

Because the original production deal was still in place, Berns could only help produce the session uncredited, but that didn't matter. He liked Kahan. Like Berns, he had come into the music business relatively late in life. He had managed a hotel in Miami and dabbled in songwriting, but there had been problems with finances and the IRS, and he moved back to New York to pursue songwriting full-time. He had only recently opened his own office after being fired from Roosevelt Music three floors below. He was a wheeler-dealer, an entertaining, sociable fellow, life-of-the-party sort of guy. But there was something else about Stanley Kahan. It was something that people whispered about him, yet it hovered over him. Everybody knew it about him and it changed the way they saw him. It had to do with shadowy associations. There was a phrase for it. He was connected.

Ellie Greenwich at Mira Sound

X.

On Broadway [1963]

N EW YORK CITY in the early sixties was the center of the modern universe, the largest city in the country, second largest in the world.
Europe was still shaking off the dust of World War II and the domi-
nance of American industry, commerce, and culture went unquestioned, much of it run by men with offices high in Manhattan skyscrap-
ers. This was the big time, a sprawling, brawling mess of a city where
money talks and the most goes.

These men running the rhythm and blues racket in New York were
kings of what they liked to do. Provincial backwaters such as Chicago,
Memphis, New Orleans, or Los Angeles could produce records, but
nothing on the level of the New York scene. Behind the music publishers
and record labels lay a skilled cadre of arrangers, studio musicians, and
engineers, the best anywhere. Their world was invisible to the union
musicians in the Broadway pit orchestras or the society dance bands,
but to them, they were playing the only game in town. They loved these
records and they brought their scientific best to bear on every session.

Studio musicians were a new, well-paid underclass of professional
musicians. Many came out of the jazz world, gravitating toward lucrative work in recording studios as big bands disappeared and bandstand
jobs evaporated. The work required flawless technical ability, a collaborative ethos, and rewarded the flexible, adaptable musician more than

the rigid stylist with the forceful, individual vision. Tenor saxophonist King Curtis was such a versatile musician.

Born Curtis Ousley in Forth Worth, Texas, he won the amateur contest at the Apollo while visiting relatives in New York and returned to Texas to go to college on a music scholarship. By the time he landed on the Atco label in 1958, he had played with Lionel Hampton, formed a trio with pianist Horace Silver, and recorded under his own name for a number of independent labels. By the end of the fifties, he was the first-call saxophonist for any r&b dates in New York, a musician who could find a place for himself in many different kinds of music, still retaining a readily identified sound and never descending into cheap, gaudy showmanship or screeching, honking histrionics.

He could play ropes and snakes with the beboppers, and even did a couple of jazz dates for Prestige as a leader in 1960 with some Miles Davis sidemen, but he more comfortably followed a mainstream style patterned after Lester Young, Arnett Cobb, and Gene Ammons. He could be tough on a bandstand. Other players would step up, thinking they were going to burn him, and Curtis would call something like "Giant Steps" in F sharp. He would routinely play notes two or three harmonics above the horn range, and fly through the traditional horn range itself, leaving the other players looking at their fingers.

Curtis became an integral part of Leiber and Stoller's records with the Coasters, offering sly, insinuating commentary between verses written expressly for him by the songwriters. Leiber would sometimes stand beside him in the studio, whispering phrases in his ear as he played. He spent thousands on his wardrobe and always carried plenty of cash for his high-stakes gambling. A large, commanding presence in the studio, he grew to become a big man on the scene, often contracting the recording dates, lofting the occasional instrumental hit under his own name such as "Soul Twist" or the "Beach Party" single he did the previous year with Berns (his subsequent experiment in vocals that Berns also produced, "Beautiful Brown Eyes," did not fare so well).

The brilliant but troubled pianist Paul Griffin was playing with the King Curtis band at Small's Paradise in Harlem when he first met Bert Berns. The producer approached the young pianist, who grew up in Harlem and was in his second year of college, and asked him if he wanted to do some record dates. Griffin didn't know what he meant. Berns told him to take out his datebook. Griffin still didn't understand. Berns explained it to him and booked Griffin for a Solomon Burke session later that week. One day Griffin didn't have a phone; the next day he had to get one and it wouldn't stop ringing.

Gene Pitney watched as Phil Spector and Griffin lay on a studio floor, Griffin sketching out charts as Spector hummed in his ear. Burt Bacharach wouldn't do a session without Griffin. He was unhappily married to an aspiring songwriter with a deal at Scepter named Valerie Simpson and he drank, but Griffin's fluid, graceful, articulate playing was the backbone of every session he did.

Drummer Gary Chester replaced Panama Francis, a grumpy old man out of the Lucky Millinder band who handled most of the fifties r&b dates, as drummer of choice almost as soon as he played his first Leiber and Stoller session, backing LaVern Baker on "Saved" in 1960. Chester, an Italian raised in Harlem, ran away from home as a kid and never went to school. He won the Gene Krupa drum contest when he was fourteen years old and traveled with the jazz great for a while. He worked all over the Midwest and had settled into a routine of club dates and jingle sessions when he fell into the r&b work.

Chester was an unusual blond-haired, blue-eyed face behind the kit in the rhythm and blues world. He had his signature tricks, like resting a tambourine on his hi-hat or putting a sand-filled ashtray on his snare, but Chester was both a human metronome and a remarkably musical drummer who could smoothly navigate his way into the heart of a song. Whether he was reading or playing without charts, his drumming told a story. He memorized tempo changes. He could make the track heavy or make it skip along. He became an integral part of almost every record by Leiber and Stoller, Bacharach, Berns, and others, burrowing himself into whatever music he was playing. Bacharach, in particular, liked to tie Chester's drumming to Griffin's piano playing and even encouraged the association by making those two set up next to one another in the studio.

Vocalist Cissy Houston came from so far deep in the gospel world, she didn't feel comfortable even simply talking with white people when she first started doing sessions in New York. She sang with a family gospel group, the Drinkard Singers, under the direction of her minister father in Newark. The group was nationally known, played regularly on gospel bills at the Apollo, appeared at the 1958 Newport Jazz Festival, and cut an album for RCA Victor in 1959, but she supported herself with a factory job making television picture tubes, ironically, for RCA Victor.

She was suspicious of pop music—her father never allowed it to be played in their home—when her husband first suggested singing on recording sessions. Instead he took the Gospelaires, a group started by Cissy's teenage nieces Dionne and Dee Dee with some other kids from the New Hope young people's choir. He shepherded the girls on the bus to the Port Authority and off to Times Square recording studios for sessions that would often run past midnight.

Even as her husband and nieces were making good money and booking work with producers like Leiber and Stoller, who used the girls on Drifters sessions, and Henry Glover, who made jazz and blues records for Morris Levy at Roulette, Cissy remained reluctant to take her music out of the church into the world. The night, however, when her niece Dionne was called to a Shirelles session, leaving the other girls without a top voice, she went along and sang rather than disappoint Glover and Levy with their underworld connections.

Burt Bacharach heard the girls at rehearsals for a Drifters session he arranged and noted the young funny-looking one in pigtails and tennis shoes with the high, piping voice. Soon he and Hal David were using the twenty-one-year-old college student and substitute Shirelle to sing their demos. Dionne sang their demo for "Make It Easy on Yourself," which turned into a breakthrough for the songwriters when it was recorded by Jerry Butler in 1962.

Butler had been the lead vocalist of the r&b group the Impressions who had the 1958 hit "For Your Precious Love." With his colleague from the Chicago-based group, guitarist and songwriter Curtis Mayfield, he also cut the 1960 Top Ten hit, "He Will Break Your Heart." His silken baritone proved perfect for the aching Bacharach and David melodrama.

When Florence Greenberg heard Dionne singing on the Bacharach demos, she loved the voice so much, she signed the young singer. Greenberg, however, didn't care for the song "Make It Easy on Yourself," so they recorded the number instead with Butler for Vee-Jay. Their first record with her for Scepter, "Don't Make Me Over," came back from the pressing plant with her name misspelled as Dionne Warwick—instead of Warrick—but her career was launched with the December 1962 release under the new name.

After a pair of more modest successes, Bacharach and David cut Dionne Warwick singing both "Anyone Who Had a Heart" and "Walk on By" in the same morning session. They went to lunch and argued about which one to release first.

Cissy Houston took her place in the group. These women had been singing together since their days in the New Hope choir—Cissy Houston, Sylvia Shemwell, Estelle Brown, and Dionne's sister Dee Dee, who started calling herself Dee Dee Warwick to conform to her sister's new last name. Most background groups had three members, but Houston liked to add a fourth voice on the bottom doubling the top part for a richer, fuller sound. She made more money recording two days in New York than she did working an entire week at RCA. She quit the factory job and devoted herself to singing with the girls on other people's records. They brought the power and majesty of a gospel choir to every session they did.

The arrangers customarily wrote charts to the producer's specifica-
tions. Obviously with a Burt Bacharach record, the arrangement was as
much a part of the composition as the lyric and the melody. He broke
open the songs' tempos, using different time signatures to surround,
support, and expand on Hal David's lyrics. He wrote what the passage
required and, if that meant going from 5/4 to 7/8 or 7/4 and then back
again to 4/4, that's what he wrote. His charts used to intimidate the session players, although these guys all prided themselves on being able
to read fly dung, but the tempo changes threw them. Bacharach would
tell them to run through the number with him and let the interior logic
of the piece open up and, invariably, it did.

Old-time guys like Teacho Wiltshire or Bert Keyes would be pen-
ciling in changes at the start of the session, going over the charts with
the producer, before passing them out at the last minute to the musicians, already tuning up, getting ready to play. Garry Sherman was
new to the r&b scene. He was a podiatrist who shared a private practice with his brother in Jersey and took some time off to write music.
He recorded an album, *Percussion Goes Dixieland*, that came out on
Columbia and Mike Stoller discovered. Stoller hired the jazz doctor to
write some pop charts for them and tore apart the first thing Sherman
brought them. The second was "She Cried," the Jay and the Americans
million-seller.

Sherman was more orchestrator than arranger, but worked with
each producer differently. Leiber and Stoller always wanted to thin out
the palette, make every stroke, tinkle, and plunk count. Berns spent
long evenings in his penthouse with Sherman, playing him records
and pointing out this horn part, that guitar break, just generally introducing his new favorite arranger to the vocabulary of the funky blues.

Bell Sound on Broadway and Fifty-Fourth Street had been the
top independent studio in town since it opened in the early fifties.
Eddie Smith's crack engineering crew kept the equipment running, as
opposed to Mira Sound, a dump on the second floor of the Americana,

a hotbed hotel for hookers on West Forty-Seventh Street, where nothing worked, but everything sounded great. The horrid bathroom doubled as a first-rate echo chamber.

Tommy Dowd always ran a tight ship at Atlantic Studios. He installed the first Ampex eight-track recorder and never looked back. His clean, clear engineering was a hallmark of his recordings, whether the Drifters or John Coltrane was on the other side of the glass. The former nuclear physicist was always Atlantic's secret weapon.

In 1958, engineer Phil Ramone opened his A&R Studios on the site of a former film studio on West Forty-Eighth Street, a massive forty-eight-by-thirty-eight-foot room with a soft cement floor and a miracle sound. He was a child prodigy violinist who played for Queen Elizabeth at age ten and graduated from Juilliard when he was sixteen. He recorded in studio orchestras around town as a musician, but gravitated toward an interest in recording science.

Ramone knew the signature of a studio was its echo, and he and his partner installed adjustable tempered steel plates called EMTs that worked better than tiled bathrooms. When Dowd couldn't use Atlantic because he needed a larger studio for an orchestral date, he would take the session to A&R, beginning with the *The Genius of Ray Charles* album. Other producers started to come to A&R when Bell Sound was booked. By the time Ramone engineered at A&R the shimmering Stan Getz/João Gilberto record, "The Girl From Ipanema," in March 1963, the studio's reputation was secure.*

Studio insiders compared A&R's sound to the fabled cavernous Thirtieth Street studio of Columbia Records, one of the hallowed halls of New York recording, along with Decca Records' Pythian Temple, where Bill Haley and His Comets recorded the rim shot heard round the world

---

*Vocalist Astrud Gilberto, who spoke some English and accompanied her reclusive husband to the United States for his Carnegie Hall appearance, was talked into singing the English lyrics on the recording of "The Girl from Ipanema," convinced it was only a demo version, even though she was a housewife who had never before sung outside her home, which may help account for the stark, undecorated innocence of the vocal performance.

on "Rock around the Clock," and RCA Victor's Webster Hall, home of all those sumptuous Living Stereo classical recordings. A&R made that kind of rich, luxurious sound available to New York independents.

The public thought of the singers as the artists, the people with their names large on the labels, but the industry knew better. The singers were almost interchangeable, in some ways, the most disposable part of the equation. At the sessions, more attention would be paid to the highly paid instrumentalists, the arrangements, the studio setup, or even background vocalists than the titular star of the recording. These were the workers who actually made the record. The producer pulled all the parts together—the songs, the musicians, the studio, the arranger, the record deal, even the artist—but everything depended on the song, which made the songwriter king.

The remarkable songwriters of the era were at the center of what was happening in New York. A few songwriting teams in particular began to blossom above all others and started to produce extraordinary work, many under the encouragement of Leiber and Stoller, who directed the evolving art form from their offices in the Brill Building.

The songwriters began to stage their songs in New York. Barry Mann and Cynthia Weil's "Uptown" by the Crystals used the uptown/downtown geography of Manhattan to vividly represent class struggle, a song whose decided big-city ethnic flavor was brought out even more by Phil Spector's faux-Spanish production. Leiber dreamed up another romantic urban fantasy, "Spanish Harlem," with young Spector. In their most elegantly crafted song yet, Carole King and Gerry Goffin built an imaginary world that could have been nowhere else on this planet in "Up on the Roof."

Most pointed of all, Mann and Weil fashioned an epic out of their own life, setting the song on the pavements beneath their office windows in "On Broadway," the colossal Drifters record Leiber and Stoller produced in January 1963. Leiber and Stoller also worked on the Mann-Weil song, writing the bridge, straightening out the lyric.

Stoller messed around with the key and changed the finish of the crucial opening line, going up instead of down on the word "Broadway."
On their way to lunch before the session, they ran into Phil Spector
on the sidewalk and invited him. He showed up at the studio with his
guitar and ended up playing the solo on the instrumental break.

With "Up on the Roof" and "On Broadway," Leiber and Stoller once
again reprieved the Drifters from slipping off the charts entirely. It had
been two long years since "Save the Last Dance for Me." In April 1963,
they returned to the studio with the Drifters and another Mann-Weil
song they had remodeled. Originally "Only in America" was more of
an angry, straightforward protest song (*Only in America, land of opportunity, do they save a seat in the back of the bus just for me*). The
civil rights movement was reaching crisis proportions. New harrowing
headlines came daily from the South. Dr. Martin Luther King Jr. was
arrested and placed in solitary confinement on the day of the session
a thousand miles away in Birmingham, Alabama. Leiber and Stoller,
from their rarified, socially advanced perspective, as only two smart-
ass, New York Jews could, recast the song as a coolly ironic sendup
(having black people sing lines like *Only in America can a kid without
a cent get a break and maybe grow up to be president*).

Wexler was predictably blunt in his assessment. "Are you guys
nuts?" he said. "They'll lynch us."

The world was not ready to hear black people sing *Only in America,
land of opportunity*. Leiber was way too hip for the room. Leiber and
Stoller still liked the track immensely. They took off the Drifters vocals
and replaced them with Jay and the Americans. White people singing
the same song entirely eliminated all irony, turning the record into
the kind of cornball sentimentality that Leiber and Stoller previously
assiduously avoided. Wexler hated the record so much, he was happy
to sell the track to United Artists for something he was never going to
release and didn't even mind as the thing scooted up the charts. Not
much anyway.

Leiber and Stoller's next record with Ben E. King showed up almost out of the blue. They tumbled to an Italian pop song called "Uno Dei Tanti (One of Many)" written by Carlo Donida and lyrcist Giulio "Mogol" Reppti and sung in Italian by Joe Sentieri. Leiber rewrote the song in English and they had Ben E. King put his vocal on top of the original Italian orchestral track. "I (Who Have Nothing)," a Top Thirty record that summer, sounded like nothing else to ever come out of the New York r&b world—stormy, gothic, melodramatic—although it was more a feat of legerdemain by cunning record men than a musical creation all their own. Ultimately, they were becoming ever more remote from the source of their original inspiration. If they thought Wexler was a pain, they were also having problems over at United Artists with Art Talmadge. He kept pressing them for a bigger piece of their publishing and he was having political problems of his own at the label. He had them producing such hogwash as easy listening piano duo Ferrante and Teicher doing "The Theme from 'Lawrence of Arabia.'"

CAROLE KING AND Gerry Goffin were flying high. They moved to suburban splendor in a new development on a treeless hillside in New Jersey—the doorbell played "Will You Still Love Me Tomorrow," swimming pool and barbeque in the back—only a short distance from where Aldon publisher Donny Kirshner lived in a mansion. His limousine would stop by to pick up demo tapes (Kirshner never learned to drive). They had their fourth number one hit in two years with Steve Lawrence singing "Go Away Little Girl," pure piffle, but piffle that sold.

Kirshner was close friends with the staid show business couple Steve Lawrence and Eydie Gorme—Berns's first great discovery all those years before in the Bronx—and also supplied his wife with "Blame It on the Bossa Nova," featherweight fluff from Mann and Weill. Barry Mann played an energetic organ riff on the cutesy record, which also featured vaguely soulful background vocals by the Cookies,

Aldon's own girl group, whom Gerry Goffin had taken under his wing as a producer for the in-house label, Dimension.

Kirshner started the label the previous year because Carole King's demo for "It Might as Well Rain until September" sounded so much better than the Bobby Vee version. Gerry Goffin sweetened the track a little and the King single loped into the Top Thirty in fall 1962, but her husband ruled out any further singles by his wife. King had recently given birth to their second daughter, Sherry. Lyricist Goffin, who was smitten with Broadway musicals and had ambitions as a songwriter beyond the simple pop songs he and his wife composed, couldn't read music or play an instrument. He struggled to communicate with his songwriting partner, who was a deft musician with a solid commercial sense. With Goffin frustrated at trying to explain his musical vision, their writing sessions would break down into yelling matches. But the young mother was clearly in love with her husband, who may have seen her more as the girl he got pregnant.

Goffin had produced the irresistible "The Loco-Motion" for Little Eva, the label's number one hit the previous summer, but fumbled at follow-up efforts. He and another Aldon writer, Jack Keller, slapped together a dance song novelty, "Let's Turkey Trot," Keller substituting the melody from the Cleftones' "Little Girl of Mine" for a finished melody he would supply later. Kirshner loved the song as it was, and when it was released, it turned out that George Goldner's writer's share of the 1955 hit he produced now belonged to Morris Levy, who insisted that both he and Herbie Cox of the Cleftones be added as writers to the Little Eva song and collected an appropriate apology, even though the original song was lifted directly from a public domain gospel song. Levy liked his copyrights.

Goffin also was producing the Cookies, Aldon's girl group with a pedigree. The original Cookies cut r&b hits for Atlantic and sang backgrounds on a Ray Charles session where they so impressed the singer, he hired them for his band and renamed them the Raelettes. When her older sister went off with Ray Charles, Earl-Jean McCrea, a shy, pretty young lady with a sweet, attractive voice who grew up in largely white Coney Island, took her place in a reconstituted edition of the Cookies. Goffin recorded the new Cookies on the Goffin-King song "Chains," which made the Top Twenty at the beginning of the year, followed in March 1963 by the Top Ten smash "Don't Say Nothin' Bad (About My Baby)," a steely admonition of a song featuring the saucy riposte *So girl, you better shut your mouth.*

In February 1963, Aldon swept the BMI Awards for the second year in a row. But, at the end of March, with the new Cookies hit flying up the charts, the bombshell went off. Aldon songwriters first read about it in the trades—Donny Kirshner was negotiating the sale of Aldon with the motion picture–television studio Columbia–Screen Gems. When the deal finally went down, Kirshner and partner Al Nevins took somewhere around $2.5 million in cash and stock. Kirshner stayed on as Columbia–Screen Gems vice president in charge of music. The office at 1650 Broadway moved to new quarters at 711 Fifth Avenue, next door to Tiffany's.

Kirshner, who was not yet thirty years old and was now a millionaire, built a large, impressive corner office for himself, a far cry from the homey cubby he used to occupy with the red piano and the honor roll of hits on the wall. From someone who had made so much of Aldon being a family, who had used his personal relationship with the writers to get them to sign extensions on their contracts, the sudden, secret sale seemed like a betrayal. Most of the top writers never even set foot in the tony new office.

JERRY LEIBER TRIPPED across the last great songwriting team Leiber and Stoller would find by accident in his own Brill Building office. It was a case of mistaken identity. Leiber thought Carole King was the loudest piano player he had ever heard. When he wandered into one of the cubicles at Trio Music and glimpsed the back of a young lady banging away extra loud at one of the pianos, he didn't really look to see who it was. "Carole," he said.

Eleanor Louise Greenwich was a twenty-two-year-old who quit teaching high school to write songs. She was at the Leiber and Stoller office meeting a friend, who had stepped out for a few minutes and left her alone with the piano. Leiber introduced himself, listened to her song, and made a few suggestions. He told her that she could use the Trio office anytime she liked, as long as she gave them first look at anything she wrote. When she went home to her parents' house in Levittown and found out who he was, the young blonde was beside herself.

She had moved when she was seven years old with her family to builder Bill Levitt's experiment in affordable middle-class housing on Long Island when the trees were freshly planted, the very beginning of postwar suburbia, twenty miles outside New York City. Her Catholic father was a failed painter turned electrical engineer and her Jewish mother ran the women's department of a J.C. Penney's. They celebrated both Easter and Seder at different aunts' homes. Her father played balalaika and she picked up the accordion at an early age.

She listened to Alan Freed's radio show in her bedroom and bought 45s avidly at the nearby record store in Hicksville. Her mother arranged the meeting with Arthur Godfrey bandleader Archie Bleyer, who ran Cadence Records and made records with Godfrey's boy tenor, Julius LaRosa (Bleyer counseled the teenage girl to finish school before trying the music business). But it was through the Hicksville record store owner that Greenwich wound up with RCA Victor, who released a single of her singing two songs she wrote while she was a freshman music major at Queens College in 1958. Her music teacher was not impressed. She changed majors and graduated from Hofstra University, where she reigned as Spring Queen, then went to work teaching high school, a delicious prospect sabotaged by reality. She left the job after three weeks and started lurking around the Brill Building, selling occasional songs for thirty-five or fifty bucks, sometimes more.

Paul Case of Hill & Range introduced her to Doc Pomus and they wrote a couple of songs together. Case had been trying out a number of different collaborators with Pomus. His customary partner, Morty Shuman, flush with success, dressed like a country squire and rode around with an endless procession of new girlfriends in a hip little convertible British sports car. Shuman smoked Gitanes and changed apartments frequently. He left the country at every opportunity. Doc still spent weekdays at the Hotel Forrest and weekends in Long Island with his family. Pomus and Greenwich didn't get much going, although their "Who Are You Gonna Love This Winter (Mr. Lifeguard)" made a little noise in Scandinavia.

Leiber and Stoller's Trio Music was no song factory. The company existed primarily to publish their own work, but they kept a few writers around to help knock out material for the teenage market such as Tony Powers. Like Greenwich, Powers had been one of those kids on the sidewalk outside the Brill Building, until he managed to bluff his way into a publishing office. He caught a hit with "Remember Then" by the Earls, a catchy little number that played off the oldies but goodies wrinkle of 1962, nostalgia for a recent past that was some of the first evidence rock and roll was developing a literature of its own.

Powers and Greenwich started writing together and sold a song to Aaron Schroeder, after giving Leiber and Stoller first look. Schroeder thought the song might be right for Phil Spector, "(Today I Met) The Boy I'm Gonna Marry." Schroeder previously gave Spector "He's a Rebel," the number one Crystals hit written by Schroeder client Gene Pitney, so he arranged a meeting between the songwriters and the producer.

While Ellie Greenwich played "That Was Me Yesterday" for Spector in her cubicle at Trio Music, Spector barely paid attention. He kept checking a mirror on the wall. He left the room. He fixed his hair. He made little noises. Greenwich blew up and chewed him out ("you little prick"). Spector stormed out in a fury. A couple of weeks later, he finally heard the demo to "(Today I Met) The Boy

I'm Gonna Marry," and summoned the writers through their publisher. Powers and Greenwich cooled their heels for several hours
in the lobby of the apartment building at Sixty-Second Street and
York, where Spector lived in the penthouse and kept an office off the
lobby. When Spector finally did show up and Greenwich gave him
hell again, he remembered her from Leiber and Stoller's offices. This
time, they hit it off.

Spector recorded both "The Boy I'm Gonna Marry" and their "Why
Do Lovers Break Each Other's Hearts" at the same session in October
1962 in Los Angeles. Studio vocalist Darlene Wright, who sang lead on
the Crystals records beginning with "He's a Rebel," sang both. "Why
Do Lovers Break Each Other's Hearts" became the next single by Bob B.
Soxx and the Blue Jeans and "(Today I Met) The Boy I'm Gonna Marry"
was the first solo single by Wright, whom Spector renamed Darlene
Love for the occasion.

Leiber and Stoller cut a couple of their songs. They used "This Is
It" as the follow-up to "She Cried" for Jay and the Americans, though
it failed to chart. They took Greenwich and Powers's "He's Got the
Power" into a marathon session at Bell Sound for the Exciters, intended
to produce an album and a new single to follow the Top Ten success of
Berns's "Tell Him." Also among the handful of songs they were going
to cut that night was "Get Him," a song Berns and Passman had on
Dottie Clark the year before as "Get Him Alone." Leiber and Stoller
gave it a facelift along the lines of "Tell Him," giving it the inside track
as the most obvious follow-up (especially considering that Leiber and
Stoller were now also participants in the song's copyright).

Greenwich was still living at home in Long Island and her father
drove her to the session, which ran long past midnight. Sometime
just before dawn, Leiber and Stoller came out of the booth and told
Greenwich her song would be the next single. She woke up her sleeping father, who drove the elated young lady home before turning
around and driving back to work in Manhattan. She soon signed a deal

with Trio Music, negotiating Leiber and Stoller's original $50 a week offer to $100 a week.

She met Jeff Barry at a family Thanksgiving in 1959, but they didn't start working together for several years. That first night, she brought her accordion to the dinner. He brought his wife. They made music together. His wife was not pleased. Barry was working as a songwriter for E.B. Marks publishers, having temporarily shelved his own ambitions as a singer. She was fascinated. He was attracted. His latest single was titled "Lenore," after his wife, but the flip was "Why Does the Feeling Go Away."

Barry was born Joel Adelberg. His father was blind and his sister was mentally retarded. His father made a good living selling insurance over the phone. He took the spring out of the rotary dial and could make calls at lightning speed. When his parents divorced, his mother refused any money and took the two children, along with her father, to live in her mailman brother's attic. Back in Brooklyn four years later, the four of them crowded into a one-bedroom apartment.

He was a funny, dreamy kid who watched too many cowboy movies. He sang on the street corner and, after a stint in the Army Reserve following high school, he entered City College to study industrial design. Before long he dropped out of NYCC to try his luck as a singer and changed his name to Jeff Barry. A family connection won him an audition with Arnold Shaw of E.B. Marks. Barry, who could play only two chords on the piano, knew only his own songs to sing. Shaw asked him about the songs and Barry confessed he knew only G and C. Shaw asked him if ever considered a career in songwriting and offered him a $75-a-week job.

He wrote "Tell Laura I Love Her" with Ben Raleigh, an older songwriter around the Brill Building. Barry originally envisioned the teenage car crash song as a horse opera. He rewrote the song when it was pointed out to him that teenagers didn't care about horses; teens liked cars. Texan singer Ray Peterson, a ninety-eight-pound polio victim in leg braces, made a Top Ten hit in summer 1960 out of the sob song, not to mention ushering in a slew of other teen death records.

Barry left E.B. Marks on West Fifty-Second Street for Trinity Music at the Brill Building in March 1961. Over the next couple of years, Barry would have almost a hundred other songs recorded without ever coming close to having that kind of hit again, until he started writing with Ellie Greenwich.

Their personal relationship warmed. Barry would bring records over to Levittown. She would take the train into the city and sing on his demos. She quickly became a favored demo singer with her crisp, clear tones and brisk efficiency in the studio. She and Barry produced a novelty side, "Red Corvette," under the name Ellie Gee and the Jets. But Greenwich was leery of using her boyfriend to make it in the music business. She wanted to succeed on her own terms. Ensconced in the bosom of Trio Music, watched over by the lions of Broadway, Leiber and Stoller, she felt secure. She and Barry were married October 28, 1962, in a lavish party at Leonard's, the elegant prom date restaurant in Great Neck where every princess from Long Island wanted to stage her wedding. Berns led everybody on the dance floor in the hitch hike. He had hosted the bachelor party the night before at his penthouse: booze, cigars, and stag films.

Barry, meanwhile, turned down an offer from Bobby Darin, who had acquired Trinity Music and wanted Barry to move to Hollywood and manage the publishing firm, which Darin renamed TM Music. Barry flew to California and Darin wined him and dined him. But even after hanging out with Hugh Hefner in Tony Curtis's cottage on a Hollywood movie set, Barry came home and accepted a much lower offer to sign with Trio Music. He knew Leiber and Stoller were the top men in the field and the opportunity was not lost on him. It only remained for Barry and Greenwich to break the news to their respective songwriting collaborators. They had successfully kept their romance under wraps and the news came as a sullen surprise to Tony Powers, for one.

The newlyweds returned to their own cubicle in the Trio offices, their names on the door and leather chairs waiting for them inside.

Greenwich introduced her new collaborator to Spector and the three of them locked themselves in Spector's Sixty-Second Street office for two days, Greenwich pounding on a piano, Spector strumming a guitar, urgently coming up with a new song for the Crystals. Spector had quickly pulled the group's first follow-up to the number one "He's a Rebel" after radio instantly rejected the bizarre Goffin and King song, "He Hit Me (And It Felt Like a Kiss)," which was, strangely enough, inspired by their babysitter, Eva Boyd, before she became Little Eva and cut "The Loco-Motion." Apparently, she showed up for work one day sporting a black eye and a big smile. "He loves me," she told Goffin.

Working on writing the new song at Spector's office, when promotion man Bill Walsh stopped by, the songwriters wrote him into the opening couplet: *Somebody told me his name was Bill*. Barry and Greenwich had used some nonsense syllables as a placeholder until they could think of the chorus line, but Spector insisted the line stay and "Da Doo Ron Ron" was finished. Spector cut the song with Darlene Love on lead vocals, but reconsidered and brought in fifteen-year-old LaLa Brooks, one of the girls who actually belonged to the Crystals and who had never been kissed. Her unmistakable innocence was dramatically juxtaposed on the final production against the thunderous, explosive volley from Spector's Hollywood sidemen, led by the detonating tom-toms of drummer Hal Blaine.

The Top Five smash was the first of nine chart hits that Barry and Greenwich would write for various artists on Spector's Philles Records over the next sixteen months, records that would make Spector a towering figure in his little world and Barry and Greenwich the leading songwriters of the year.

They sketched out a song riding the train to town from their apartment in LeFrak City, the massive new housing development on the edge of Queens where they moved after they married. They went straight into Associated Recording that morning and, in a little more than an hour, cut a demo of the song "What a Guy." Greenwich sang the vocal and overdubbed the harmonies. Barry added a few *dip dips*. Jerry Leiber heard something he liked in the demo and insisted they let him sell the recording as-is to Jerry Blaine's Jubilee Records. He offered the pair a whopping 5 percent royalty, a good two points above the usual. What Barry and Greenwich didn't know was that Leiber and Stoller were collecting 16 percent from Blaine and splitting it with Barry's publisher. Both publishers were making more than the songwriter-artists. They called the group the Raindrops and the record made its way up to the middle of the charts. Still Greenwich was astonished to see the first royalty check for $28,000, having no idea how much her publishers were pocketing. They hired a couple of other girls (including teenager Beverly Warren, who cut Greenwich's "That Was Me Yesterday" with Berns) and another guy because Barry was stage shy and made the rounds on weekends lip-synching the song on TV shows and package concert bills.

Unlike Leiber and Stoller, who were older and came into the music from rhythm and blues, Barry and Greenwich actually belonged to the audience for their music; a shade on the older side, but they were both rock and roll children. They wrote songs that reflected the basic innocence and optimism of teenage life because they were fresh from its glow and unspoiled by cynicism and greed.

Greenwich was all music and theirs was a romance in song. There was music for them everywhere. They sat in a car parked at a lovers' lane, laughing at the other couples making out, as they scribbled a half-baked song they called "Hanky Panky" that they would record as the Raindrops. Adorable Greenwich wore white lipstick and bouffant beehives. Long, lanky Barry dressed like the Marlboro Man, cowboy hats, jeans, and boots. They were a welcome addition to the Leiber and Stoller world.

Leiber and Stoller parted company with Talmadge and United Artists, but they still needed an outlet for their songs. They decided to revive their Tiger Records label, defunct since last year's Tippie and the Clovers bossa nova novelty. They always modeled themselves after Tin Pan Alley titans such as Gershwin, Berlin, or Porter, and they were like the old-time moguls themselves now, managing their publishing portfolios, keeping young writers on staff, cutting deals to make records. They were earning more on their end of the Barry and Greenwich hits with Spector than they were with their own songs.

They were living out the destinies that began when they composed their first songs at a piano under a photograph of George Gershwin inscribed to Stoller's mother. They dressed like bankers and ate and drank like rajahs at Midtown watering holes like the Russian Tea Room. Since splitting with United Artists, they had developed a stockpile of recordings that they owned, now that UA wasn't paying for them, and putting them out seemed like the best way to get their money back.

Their first record on the new label, "Big Bad World" by Cathy Saint, produced by Jeff Barry, was released the same week President Kennedy was assassinated in Dallas. Not a good week for a record titled "Big Bad World." (The nation's dour mood also chilled the response that year to Phil Spector's masterpiece Christmas album featuring all the Philles Records artists, *A Christmas Gift for You*). It was a bad start to something that wasn't going to end well at all.

Jeff Barry, Ellie Greenwich, Phil Spector, Bert Berns, BMI Awards dinner, 1963.

XI.

Cry Baby [1963]

THIS WAS THE golden era of rhythm and blues. Berns's records with Solomon Burke not only bailed out Atlantic Records, but also made Burke one of the music's crown princes, alongside such regal peers as Sam Cooke and Jackie Wilson. James Brown was emerging as an inexhaustible, indomitable showman. Ray Charles had reached a mainstream audience previously thought impossible for any black entertainer, chiefly through his 1962 breakthrough album of country songs, *Modern Sounds in Country and Western Music*, that included the massive hit "I Can't Stop Loving You." The music had evolved into sophisticated, ingenious realms of expression, far beyond its humble beginnings only a few years earlier.

Bert Berns was also very much in the Leiber and Stoller orbit at the start of 1963. His "Tell Him" by the Exciters (number four Pop) was the biggest hit Leiber and Stoller had managed for United Artists. His production for them on Baby Jane and the Rockabyes did better than anyone expected. He brought them some music. Ahmet Ertegun said it reminded him of Gypsy music and gave the song its title, "Gypsy," (and himself a piece of the songwriting). Leiber and Stoller finished the song and cut it in January 1963 with Ben E. King, while Berns watched. It was the first time he and Ben E. King met.

The same four writers shared credits on another number. Ertegun again supplied the title, "You Can't Love 'Em All," and Berns gave the piece a Cubano lilt, while Leiber finished the song with his trademark comic touch. Stoller went over to Berns's penthouse one afternoon and the two of them batted out another pair of songs, "His Kiss" and "You'll Never Leave Him." Leiber and Stoller let very few associates into their charmed songwriting circle, but now Berns qualified as one of the elite. His records with Solomon Burke established his bona fides by themselves.

Burke was now the big Atlantic star, and when Wexler found a song he wanted to record, it went to Burke. Berns's next session with Burke in March 1963 revolved around a song Wexler found on a tape that came in the mail from Detroit. Of the eight songs on the tape, only one impressed Wexler, called "If You Need Me." He paid $1,000 for the publishing to the song but, for some reason, failed to acquire the rights to the demo. Other labels would have simply purchased the demo and released it, but Atlantic liked to build their artists and sought out suitable material from all kinds of outside sources. Arranger Garry Sherman hewed close to the arrangement on the demo and Burke sang it down to the ground.

"Can't Nobody Love You," also recorded at the same session, led off with a blues figure picked on an acoustic guitar, as the song slowly built to the gospel chorus entrance. Berns gave his soul–folk touch to "Hard Ain't It Hard," a Woody Guthrie song popularized by the Kingston Trio that Berns outfitted with big acoustic guitars and a female background chorus. He also cut the Berns-Leiber-Stoller-Ertegun piece "You Can't Love 'Em All," a supple, Cubanized take on the Leiber-Stoller formula for the Drifters with Afro-Cuban percussion instead of Brazilian and a booming bass straight off a mambo record. With mariachi horns punctuating the chorus, the track glides into Burke's wheelhouse. He moves easily into Leiber's sly braggadocio.

You can't love them all, the girls sing.

No, I can't 'cause I'm only one guy, Solomon sings.

No, you can't love 'em all, sing the girls.

No, you can't love 'em all. No, I can't, sings Solomon, *but I'm sure gonna try.*

These were robust productions, delicately flavored, superbly crafted with authority and grace, all in service of Burke's iridescent vocals and the song. Berns had matched Solomon Burke's formidable character with a musical style that made him one of the leading rhythm and blues performers of the day. Burke may have been the star, but they were Berns's records. Other record men like Ertegun and Wexler or Leiber and Stoller knew how good these records were, even if they didn't call attention to themselves like Phil Spector's bombastic productions from the coast. In the closely watched, highly competitive insular world of New York rhythm and blues, Berns had made his mark.

Before Wexler could release the new Solomon Burke single of "If You Need Me," he got wind that singer Lloyd Price and his partner Harold Logan, an unpleasant and unscrupulous man even in the relative morality of the rhythm and blues world, had purchased the demo of the song, which featured a former gospel vocalist named Wilson Pickett, fresh out of the vocal group the Falcons, who put "I Found a Love" on the charts the year before. Wexler met with Logan, who wanted Atlantic to kill the Burke record and lease his Wilson Pickett record instead. Wexler offered them a piece of the Burke record, in exchange for giving him the Pickett version, which he would release later (maybe). They could not come to terms and Lloyd and Logan put out the Wilson Pickett single of "If You Need Me" on their own Double L label, which they got Liberty Records to distribute, the same week that the Solomon Burke record hit the chutes on Atlantic (the same week also as Phil Spector's "Da Doo Ron Ron" by the Crystals).

Wexler went to work. He knew Liberty couldn't promote a record like he could. He burned up the phones. He wheedled, cajoled, did anything he could to pump that record. He was furious at the effrontery and a little pissed at himself for not coming up with another grand for the demo in the first place. Wexler went to war. When the smoke cleared, he had clobbered Liberty. Solomon Burke's record went all the way to number two on the r&b charts and blew the Pickett version off the charts after only one week. A year later, Wexler walked into a hotel bar during a disc jockey convention, and Al Bennett, chief of Liberty Records, spotted him. "Don't mess with this man," Bennett announced to anyone who could hear.

Under their deal with United Artists, Berns went back into the studio for Leiber and Stoller with Baby Jane and the Rockabyes. In addition to a follow-up to the surprise hit, "How Much Is That Doggie in the Window," Berns cut a pair of his songs with only the female vocalists in the group. He called this girl group configuration the Elektras and gave the record to United Artists. He had made "It Ain't as Easy as That" before with Hoagy Lands, but "All I Want to Do Is Run," cowritten with Baby Jane bass vocalist Carl Spencer, was pure Berns heartache and despair.

Leiber and Stoller may have split with United Artists, but Berns started bringing acts on his own to United Artists without missing a beat, beginning with the Isley Brothers, who were done with Scepter. Berns cut a surprisingly desultory session of two songs written by the Isleys, "Tango," a patently silly dance novelty that Ronnie Isley nonetheless sang the crap out of, and "She's Gone," the kind of plodding, lifeless ballad Berns knew would never be commercial. But the door at UA was open to Berns and he wanted to make a move.

Jerry Ragovoy found Garnet Mimms and the Enchanters in Philadelphia. A friend took him to see Mimms and his group singing gospel in a nightclub. Ragavoy, who grew up in Philly, dropped out of school and left home when he was sixteen. He had always fooled around on the piano and, outside of a few weeks of lessons when he was a teen, was entirely self-taught. Nevertheless he wound up making a living as a children's piano teacher. He studied classical music and learned to write orchestrations.

He landed a job, little more than a gofer, working for Peter DeAngelis and Bob Marcucci, the Philadelphia record producers behind teen idols Frankie Avalon and Fabian. Ragovoy wrote a couple of charts for Frankie Avalon sessions, found a song or two, soaked up some experience. He studiously composed a song he felt contained all the elements of a hit record and found a vocal group called the Majors to sing his song. Financing the session himself with his $1,200 savings, Ragovoy took the master around New York and was roundly rejected by every label in town, before finally selling the track (and half the publishing) to the East Coast office of Hollywood-based Imperial Records for $500. In the meantime, he quit his job in Philly, moved to New York, and started working for Sammy Kaye at the Brill Building. When "A Wonderful Dream" by the Majors came out in fall 1962 and hit the charts, three weeks later he left that job.

Ragovoy knew Berns from Philadelphia, when Berns would come down to represent Mellin material to DeAngelis and Marcucci. Berns gave him studio work in New York and showed him around town. He took an amazed Rags to a bar where a couple of dozen young Jewish women were drinking and talking loudly. He wrote a friend that New York Jews made Philadelphia Jews look like *goyim*. Although Ragovoy had dark-complexioned good looks, he marveled at Berns's bachelor ease. He also admired Berns's intuitive musical gifts, nose for talent, and street smarts.

Garnet Mimms was a twenty-six-year-old from Philadelphia who made his first gospel record as a member of the Norfolk Four in 1953. After a stint in the service, he started singing with vocal groups in Philly in 1958. The Gainors cut eight singles over the next three years for a number of labels. Their first, a cover of a pop song by *Oklahoma!* star Gordon McRae called "The Secret," even made some noise around town. But Mimms had disbanded the group and returned to singing gospel by the time he met Ragovoy. He and Sam Bell from the Gainors found another couple of singers, but they didn't call themselves Garnet Mimms and the Enchanters until Ragovoy signed them.

Ragovoy had been working on the song "Cry Baby" for a couple of years. He had the title. He had the melody. He wrote the lyrics. But he could never fit it together. He kept the song in the drawer, and every couple of months, he would pull it out and fuss with it. One afternoon at Ragovoy's Upper West Side apartment, he sat at the piano and played what he had for Berns. In no time, Berns wrote the recitation that serves as the song's bridge and figured out the ending. The gospel-flavored ballad was right down his alley.

After weeks of rehearsing Mimms in Philadelphia, Ragovoy brought him up for the session. Mimms arrived at Rags's apartment the day before to find Berns and Ragovoy still buffing the song, before running him through one last rehearsal. It was the first time he met Berns, who laid out and let Rags run the show. At the session, his sole direction to Ragavoy was to put Mimms's voice in "a flood of echo." There were no Enchanters on the session; Cissy Houston and her two nieces, Dionne and Dee Dee Warwick handled the heavenly harmonies. Paul Griffin's stately piano opens the track under a gleaming electric guitar introduction. Gary Chester's drums tumble into the gospel choir's wail *Cry, cry, bay-ay-by*, Mimms's arching tenor piercing the blend. It is Ragovoy's record, but it is Bernsian to the core. Berns took the master to Talmadge at UA and this time the label read A Bert Berns Production—Directed by Jerry Ragavoy. He was moving up.

A couple of weeks later, Berns was back in the studio for United Artists, taking over from Leiber and Stoller at propping up a quickly fading former stalwart of the label. Marv Johnson came to UA in 1959 and managed nine chart records for the label over that time, including two Top Ten hits, "You Got What It Takes" and "I Love the Way You Love," in 1960.

He was signed to a Detroit-based songwriter who had some success with Jackie Wilson named Berry Gordy Jr., who wrote and recorded Johnson's first record as the initial release on his own Tamla label, before selling the master and signing Johnson to UA. Gordy closely supervised Johnson's recordings, at the same time beginning to build a stable of writers and performers in Detroit that would form the nucleus of Gordy's Motown Records empire. Gordy understood Johnson's low-key appeal. Without the flamboyance of a singer like Jackie Wilson, Johnson was cast by Gordy as a kind of genial everyman. He gave him midtempo songs that didn't test his limited range and a conservative, almost white-sounding production that had been responsible for his surprising durability. Johnson moved to New York and started taking his star status seriously.

By the time Gordy was too busy with his rapidly blossoming enterprise in Detroit, he was pissed off at Johnson and glad to be rid of him. Leiber and Stoller had outfitted Johnson with dramatic material more suited to Chuck Jackson. They had tried him with Bacharach and David. His last three releases had failed to make the charts when Berns took him in the studio.

"Come On and Stop" was one of Berns's most exciting productions yet, but he buried Johnson in the arrangement. He has Cissy Houston and her girls blasting the chorus of the Bert Russell song in counterpoint until Garnet Mimms leaps out of the fray and sails away with the song. By the time the song gets back to Johnson's solo vocal, he is an anticlimactic bump in the road on the way to the next explosive chorus by his background singers. The record never amounted to anything when it was released, but Berns noted the electric guitar lick he used to anchor the verse. It would turn up again.

Berns also handled for UA a session with another group on the label that turned out to be the last record in the surprisingly long-lasting career of the Wanderers, an old-fashioned vocal quintet modeled on the Mills Brothers that had been recording since 1953 without ever having a hit record. It probably didn't hurt the group's longevity that the Wanderers were managed by Roy Rifkind, brother of Julie Rifkind, Berns's pal at MGM Records. Roy was widely thought to be connected, and whether he was or not, he knew those guys. Berns gave Wanderers vocalist Ray Pollard something to dig into on "You Can't Run Away from Me," a tuneful Bert Russell song tied to an acoustic guitar figure and seductive Latin drive.

Don Drowty came east to do Dante solo sessions with Berns for UA. Dante and the Evergreens had broken up after the fellows all ate something and got ill, one of them so severely the other guys had to leave him in the hospital in New York and returned to Los Angeles without him. Drowty went back to college. Every so often, he would find a $100 bill in the mail from Berns "for books." Berns talked Bobby Mellin into hiring Drowty to run a Los Angeles office and Drowty rented a small space on Sunset Boulevard, although he continued to go to school and showed up to open the office only around noon. Mellin got angry and closed the office when he found out Drowty had been letting musician friends sleep on the office sofa. Drowty never did the firm much good in Hollywood anyhow. Berns, ever the loyal friend, cut a set of demos with Drowty in New York, but nothing ever came of that.

Berns was the unquestioned big dog songwriter at Mellin publishing. He had at least one record on the *Billboard Hot 100* every week since "Tell Him" entered the charts in December 1962, sometimes more than one. He was working with all the tops in the field. He was making money for everybody. Over at Atlantic, Wexler had taken a special interest in Berns. The new junior songwriter Mellin hired, twenty-three-year-old Doug Morris, former boy singer, fresh out of the Army, used to take Berns's checks over to him at Atlantic Studios on Sixtieth Street, where he was spending more time than at the Mellin offices (in 1980, Doug Morris would be named president of Atlantic Records; he produced the 2002 collection *The Heart and Soul of Bert Berns* for Universal Records).

Berns and Wexler were becoming the best of friends. They even went into the studio and cut another Russell Byrd record, Berns singing a song he wrote with Wexler, "That's When I Hurt," and a bit of dialect comedy, "Chico and Maria," that went unreleased by Atlantic.

Berns would spend weekends out at Wex's Long Island place, tooling around the sound with him on Wexler's boat in his little yachting cap, listening to his endless line of patter.

Berns liked voices. His records were all carefully constructed to support and enhance the lead vocal performance. He wanted to push singers to the brink of hysteria. He needed to feel the urgency, the power, the passion in the singing. One of his signature stunts was to have the vocalist saunter through the opening line, almost casually, and then step on the gas with the second line, a sudden turn into despair that deepens the plot in the opening scene. He liked the sound of women in distress—from Baby Jane and the Rockabyes' Madelyn Moore to powerful, gospel-drenched singers like Sylvia Hill or Ruth McFadden whom he recorded the previous year for Capitol. Betty Harris was the same model, exactly Berns's type.

She didn't know Berns wrote "Cry to Me" when she auditioned for him by singing the song. She didn't know that he originally envisioned the song the way she sang it, slowed down to a crawl. She knew the Solomon Burke record and she liked to sing the song slowly, as she did in her a cappella audition in Berns's 1650 Broadway office.

Harris was a nineteen-year-old soul ingénue, reasonably fresh out of Florida (by way of Philadelphia), brought to Berns by Babe Chivian, a Philadelphia insurance salesman who doubled as Solomon Burke's manager. She was a stagestruck cutie with a big gospel voice who spent a month or so under the tutelage of blues singer Big Maybelle, whom she sought out backstage at the Apollo after watching her perform several times in one day. Berns signed Harris to Jubilee Records through Leiber and Stoller, who cut the deal with Jerry Blaine, took a taste for themselves, and left the work entirely in Berns's hands. It was the young girl's first time in a big-city recording studio.

From the first sob that bursts almost involuntarily from her throat, Betty Harris slowly, deliberately, picks her way through the pathos of Berns's breakthrough composition. She sings the song with a bitter authority that draws a lot of its strength from the funereal cadence at which the song in her retelling creeps. Garry Sherman eases in voices and strings, but Harris dangles in front of everything, alone in her pain, writhing in agony. The record did much better even than Burke's original hit on the Pop charts (number twenty-two) and made Top Ten R&B when it was released in September.

The song on the other side of the record is the remarkable "I'll Be a Liar." Songwriter Berns is dealing with compulsive behavior. The song's protagonist is under the spell of her lover so much that she will tell lies for him—*for the rest of my days*—although there is no specific lie mentioned, or any exact deed to be refuted. He drives the vocalist to almost disturbingly abstract extremes. Much of the song's emotional furor is rooted in an invisible subtext. Harris didn't understand the song and didn't like it, but she sang this odd piece of psycho-soul with a terrifying ferocity.

Nothing was more remote from Times Square than Southern California beaches, which was one reason the surf music boomlet was slow to register with the Brill Building crowd. The only major label located in the provincial outpost of Hollywood, Capitol Records, jumped in the water. Their group, the Beach Boys, struck the Top Ten that spring 1963 with "Surfin' USA," nothing more than watered-down Chuck Berry. Capitol also won the fevered bidding to sign surf guitarist Dick Dale, who had been presiding over capacity crowds of barefoot dancers across the street from the beach at the old big band haunt, the Rendezvous Ballroom in Newport Beach, outside L.A. His album *Surfers' Choice* had been the best-selling LP the past year and a half at Wallichs Music City, Hollywood's big retail record store at Sunset and Vine, down the street from the Capitol tower. He was a phenomenon, although he was entirely unknown outside the five Southern California counties. The question was, would surf music's California appeal work with East Coast youth? Capitol was betting it would. The label gave Dick Dale an unprecedented $50,000 advance, more than RCA Victor paid Elvis. The twist. Bossa nova. Surf music. All in the space of a year. Who knew anything?

Berns did know that he had floated a routine King Curtis instrumental the entire previous summer simply by calling it "Beach Party." Even so, there was no excuse for "Surf and Shout" by the Isley Brothers, a combination of "Twist and Shout" and Jan and Dean's "Surf City" that should have never been allowed to happen. Some surf record. But the flip side, recorded at the same session, was exquisite, prime Berns heartbreak, "You'll Never Leave Him," one of the two songs he wrote with Mike Stoller at his penthouse. Berns himself plays the acoustic guitar figure on the record that pulls the entire arrangement together.

Carl Spencer introduced Berns to Jimmy Radcliffe, who worked for Aaron Schroeder as a songwriter and Gene Pitney's recording manager. He also sang a lot of demo recordings, especially for Bacharach. A large teddy bear of a fellow, Radcliffe wrote a couple of songs with Berns, and Berns cut a couple of songs Radcliffe and Carl Spencer wrote. He sang background vocals on Berns sessions, his deep, rich voice often rounding out the bottom end of the vocal mix with the Cissy Houston singers.

Radcliffe, who also played guitar, was one of those all-around talents that always seemed to be on the sidelines of the scene. He cut Bacharach and David's "(There Goes) The Forgotten Man" for Schroeder's Musicor label, released about the same time Berns took him in the studio and did the elegiac "Through a Long and Sleepless Night," an old song out of a late forties Hollywood movie from Hal David's older brother, Mack David. Radcliffe gives the sonorous ballad a powerful performance, his vibrato carefully rimming every line, Berns keeping his vocal poised on a rising bed of strings in his commanding, panoramic production— another brilliant record nobody heard.

Another Berns-Radcliffe-Spencer song, "My Block," was recorded by the Chiffons under the name the Four Pennies and released in June 1963, although the pseudonymous record hardly fared as well as the

Goffin-King song "One Fine Day" by the Chiffons, a Top Five hit under the group's real name that came out only three weeks earlier.

Berns took one of Carl Spencer and Jimmy Radcliffe's songs when he went into the studio next with Tammy Montgomery, who was, along with Solomon Burke and Betty Harris, also handled by Babe Chivian. She was signed to the Chicago-based r&b label Chess Records out of the company's New York office.

She grew up in Philadelphia and won a talent contest on the Jersey shore when she was eleven years old. By the time she was fourteen, she was recording for Luther Dixon at Wand. She toured with James Brown and he produced a single with her on his Try Me label. The two fell in love, although theirs was a tumultuous affair. Chivian took Betty Harris to visit her in the hospital, where Brown had left the tiny teenager after one of their fights.*

The focus of the session was Berns's song, "If I Would Marry You," which Berns knocked into shape for the teenage soul singer. Berns anchored the record to a reverb-drenched electric guitar part that sounded as funky as something out of the Chess studios in Chicago, where they used a thirteen-foot piece of sewer pipe for an echo chamber.

Berns came back a changed man from his October trip to England, where a rock and roll group called the Beatles had made a huge hit out of his "Twist and Shout." Berns saw how backward the British record business was and he glimpsed the enormous talent pool in his quick introduction to the blooming English music scene. He had been greeted like a conquering hero and he began to see the vast reach of his music. Something was in the air. Berns felt the world turning. A new seriousness of purpose attended his work.

Outside the studio, Berns and Wexler were cooking up plans. Other than Berns, at this point, Atlantic Records had nobody making

---

*Montgomery would later record for Motown Records under the name Tammi Terrell, where she was best known for duets with Marvin Gaye. She died from a brain tumor after collapsing onstage in Gaye's arms.

hit records for the label. Leiber and Stoller still produced the Drifters and Ben E. King, but that relationship was growing even more strained. Wexler behind their backs referred to Leiber and Stoller as "Mr. Lust and Mr. Greed." The Stax/Volt deal with the small Memphis label looked good; their latest project was a promising young singer named Otis Redding, who was beginning to sell a few records.

Other than that, Atlantic had been dry as dirt when they picked up a master from a local producer in Detroit that went into the Top Five that summer of 1963, "Hello Stranger" by Barbara Lewis, a welcome drink of water in a parched landscape for Atlantic. "Just One Look" by Doris Troy, another happy gift, came in over the transom. The label couldn't stay in business counting on those.

Atlantic had opened the year by offering generous sales incentives to distributors—delayed billing, one in every seven records free—but the company had not rebounded. Wexler denied rumors to *Billboard* in November that the label was in talks for sale with Jerry Blaine and his Cosnat Distributing Corporation. While Cosnat was Atlantic's largest single outlet and undoubtedly held considerable receivables over the cash-poor company, the Blaines were unlikely to be able to put together that big a deal. "Our only relationship with Cosnat is that they distribute for us in some areas," Wexler told the trade magazine, "but I never mind taking Blaine's money on the golf course."

Wexler thought the entire market for singles had gone soft, by perhaps as much as 50 percent. His strategy was to double the number of Atlantic's releases. "But these are not just any records," Wexler told *Billboard*, "they have to be records the firm feels are potential hits. They must be worked on with great intensity throughout the country, so that each one gets a full shot at regional action that might bring it into national hit category." He needed Berns.

Meanwhile, Berns was chafing increasingly under Mellin's stingy adminstration. He had made tons of money for the poncy old bastard, and now Berns wanted a share of his publishing and he wanted his own record label. He negotiated a new music publishing contract with Mellin while conspiring with Wexler to go to work for Atlantic. Mellin and Berns discussed terms during his trip to England. Mellin agreed to start a new publishing company, fifty-fifty with Berns. He gave Berns more money. They signed a new deal in November, about the same time Atlantic's law firm was drawing up their contract with Berns.

Berns wanted his own label, and Atlantic and Berns agreed to start a record label that would be wholly owned by Berns and distributed by Atlantic, much like the deal with Stax. In addition, Atlantic also secured the services of Berns to produce artists already signed to Atlantic. They agreed to pay $300 a week advance on royalties.

The first single for Berns's new label was already in the can—a rocking little romp called "Baby Let Me Take You Home" that somehow managed to catch the fresh excitement of the new rock and roll records that were starting to appear. Berns wrote the song with Wes Farrell, professional manager at Roosevelt Music and another one of the cast of characters at 1650 Broadway, who had only recently started writing with Berns.

In his new post as staff producer at Atlantic, in the weeks before Christmas, Berns would take over the most successful brand name vocal group in the history of rhythm and blues and begin producing the Drifters.

Johnny Moore had rejoined the Drifters in April. He first sang with the old Drifters in 1955, before the Five Crowns took over the name. During the group's next recording session (where the group cut "Only in America," among others), gritty vocalist Rudy Lewis had also recorded a couple of solo sides, as if Atlantic was gearing him for a solo career along the lines of Ben E. King. But Moore and Lewis got along, so the group expanded to five members with two capable lead vocalists (not including guitarist Billy Davis, a fixture in the group's music for many years whose real name was Abdul Samad). During their final session with the group in August, Leiber and Stoller cut another Bacharach and David song, "In the Land of Make-Believe," which didn't even chart.

In December, Berns took over the Drifters recordings in a three-song session at Atlantic Studios. The Drifters had outlasted entire epochs of changing styles since the group first appeared ten years before on yellow label Atlantic 78s. They were the flagship of the Atlantic fleet. Berns immediately abandoned the glistening percussion and celestial strings of the Leiber and Stoller productions in favor of a more hard-edged, spare sound with prominent, swinging horns. "Beautiful Music" was a half-hearted rewrite by Leiber and Stoller (with Mann and Weil) of their "(My Heart Said) The Bossa Nova." "Vaya con Dios," the old Les Paul and Mary Ford hit, featured female voices in the foreground of a Drifters record.

It was "One Way Love," more than the others, however, that signaled the Berns era of the Drifters. Written by Berns and Ragovoy, the track glides along taut, clean lines, as lead vocalist Johnny Moore flies over the group vocal with the orchestra's stop breaks punctuating the title lyric. The song takes a darker look at relations between the sexes than the typical Drifters romantic fantasy. Handing over the production duties for the Drifters to Berns was more than a symbolic gesture. Berns needed to reinvest this valuable property with new life.

If taking over stewardship of the Drifters wasn't enough, within days of each other, he would also make his two most towering records yet with both Solomon Burke and Hoagy Lands.

Both sides of the Hoagy Lands record were epics; from the thumping twelve-string guitar introduction of "Baby Let Me Hold Your Hand" that could have been lifted from a Leadbelly record to the majestic finale of the other side, "Baby Come On Home," Lands pleading over the gospel choir's harmonies and Gary Chester's cymbal crashes. Unlike the pared-down version of the song Berns and coauthor Wes Farrell recorded as the Mustangs, Berns takes Lands through a fully orchestrated landscape of "Baby Let Me Hold Your Hand," booming guitars, chorale harmonies, and a fierce, driving charge led by drummer Chester, a powerhouse track that never lets up. "Baby Come On Home," a classic Bert Russell tune, moves grandly to a more elegant pace, Lands reciting the opening verse, leading to the wide-screen chorus, a curtain of voices draped behind him. The command, confidence, and personal vision Berns marshaled on this record was unequaled thus far in his career.

With Burke, he recorded one of the soul singer's own compositions, another cover of a country and western standard ("He'll Have to Go") and another new Berns-Farrell composition, "Goodbye Baby (Baby Goodbye)." Over the sweetly cooing Cissy Houston choir, Burke gives the song everything. He moves easily from a warm, calm intimacy to powerful, cantorial heights on the chorus. He drops his voice at the end of the verse into his deepest, richest tones, as the chorus explodes behind him and everybody goes to church. Burke's innate dignity lifts up a song that could easily be mired in its gloom.

> *You made me lonely*
> *You made me hurt*
> *Just like a fool, I gave you candy*
> *And you fed me dirt*
> *But I'm coming to your party*
> *And just before the break of day*
> *I'm going to kiss you one more time*
> *Then I'm going away*
> *Goodbye, baby*
> *Baby goodbye*
> —GOODBYE BABY (BABY GOODBYE), BERNS-FARRELL (1963)

With this new, upward juncture of his rocketing career, Berns was his own man. His rich, singular musical vision had been realized beyond anything he could have imagined as he was standing in the studio making "A Little Bit of Soap" a scant two years before. He arrived at the utter heights of the music game in New York just in time. Within weeks, forces nobody could have predicted would sweep through the pop music world from all the way on the other side of the Atlantic Ocean.

RECORDED BY THE BEATLES
TWIST AND SHOUT

by BERT RUSSELL
and PHIL MEDLEY

05509

ROBERT MELLIN, INC.

75¢

XII.

Twist and Shout [1963]

J OHN LENNON POPPED a couple of Zubes throat candies in his mouth
and lit a contraindicated Peter Stuyvesant cigarette. After more than
twelve hours in EMI's Abbey Road studios, the Beatles were one track
short of finishing the group's first album. Since it was past ten o'clock
at night, the official triple session was over. The last three hours, the
band had slammed down five songs from the group's well-practiced
stage act, finishing with a cover of Burt Bacharach's Shirelles song,
"Baby It's You."

The four musicians and producer George Martin repaired to the
cafeteria. While Lennon bathed his scorched throat in warm milk, the
others drank tea. They wanted to try one last song, "Twist and Shout."
The band had been using the song to close its shows starting the year
before. They had been playing the number, fresh off the U.S. charts
by the Isley Brothers, since the band's final nightclub engagement at
Hamburg's Star Club, whipping up hometown crowds with the song
during their last shows at the Cavern. They had picked up the tune from
another Liverpool group, Kingsize Taylor and the Dominoes, and had
even nicked the guitar part in the middle from the Dominoes' version.

Lennon took off his shirt and laid it across a bench. He gargled
quickly with a mouthful of milk and counted off the take. He tore into
the song—*Well, shake it up, bay-ay-bee*—pushing his ravaged voice

past the pain threshold. His throat would hurt for days. He staggered through the number, wrenching the vocal out of somewhere deep inside. His raw, inflamed flesh is there for all to hear, embedded in the performance. Paul McCartney's triumphant *Hey!* punctuates the close. A perfunctory run at a second take was made, but Lennon spent it all on the first. The group's manager, Brian Epstein, had to promise the tape operator a ride home to get him to stay for a playback. What they had committed to tape in that last half hour was nothing less than the most rugged, powerful piece of rock and roll that had ever been recorded in a British studio.

At the time the session was held in February 1963, "Please Please Me," the group's second single, was sitting on top of the British charts. The band had gone from down the bill on a tour starring Helen Shapiro, the British teenage pop vocalist best known for her 1961 hit, "Walking Back to Happiness," to third-billed on a show headed by two American rock and roll acts, Chris Montez and Tommy Roe. "Twist and Shout" closed the band's every show.

In July, on the heels of the Top Ten success of a cover of "Twist and Shout" by Brian Poole and the Tremeloes on Decca, a label still smarting from passing on signing the Beatles, EMI released a four-song EP by the Beatles titled *Twist and Shout*. The debut album, *Please Please Me*, had been released in March, hit number one on the charts in May, and stayed there for thirty consecutive weeks. No album since the *South Pacific* soundtrack topped the British charts from their inception in 1958 to 1960 had even remotely approached that kind of popularity. When the first $90,000 royalty check arrived for Berns's "Twist and Shout" cowriter Phil Medley, his wife insisted they buy a house with the entire proceeds, convinced they would never see another check like that again. Berns went to England to see for himself.

"Twist and Shout" may have been an unlikely rallying cry for a new generation of British youth from an American perspective, but rock and roll meant something entirely different to people growing up in postwar Britain. London still wore the scars of the Blitz. Bombed-out buildings stood on every block. A thin, charcoal blanket of coal dust, a hundred years old, covered the city. Few Londoners had central heat; most were warmed in the cold London winter by coin-operated gas heaters. London was still getting to its feet. War babies raised on rations were reaching their teens.

America looked like a shining New World, home of cowboys and Indians, gangsters and molls, enormous automobiles, Disneyland and all manner of exotic delights far beyond the gray realm of the British Isles. The country had watched one of the greatest empires in history crumble. Once the mightiest nation on earth, Britain had lost the lead to America in commerce, industry, communications, arts, world politics, culture, everything. English schoolkids marveled at Hollywood films such as *Rebel without a Cause* or *Blackboard Jungle* and wondered if life could really be like that in the United States.

Rock and roll arrived in Britain sounding like America. "Shake, Rattle, and Roll" by Bill Haley and His Comets slipped quietly into the British charts in December 1954, a fresh, raucous sound from over the sea with an impudent name, both vulgar and charming in a uniquely American way. Rock and roll in England, at first, was widely viewed as a harmless aberration, a transitory entertainment, certainly nothing to threaten the status quo or scare the horses in the street. But many young Brits immediately cracked the code and understood rock and roll was here to save them from a life of war widows, bus queues, ghastly English cigarettes, and fish and chips wrapped in newspaper.

Unlike in America, rock and roll in Great Britain was hard to find. The American records were only occasionally released by British labels, and the American 45s were highly prized treasures from another world, smuggled into the country by sailors and other world travelers. The English rock and roll hardly matched the American originals. The government controlled the airwaves and the BBC followed strict regulations about what kind of records they would play, concentrating on the most sanitized, safe programming. The BBC knew what was good for Britain and that generally excluded rock and roll. The one alternative was Radio Luxembourg, a commercial station from the Grand Duchy on the continent whose sputtering signal barely reached the UK. But, as it flickered on and off, static interrupting the broadcast, hypnotized listeners could glimpse a world beyond the Light Programme.

EMI and Decca dominated the British record business. The two giants both manufactured not only phonograph records, but also radios, record players, even needles. Decca was founded in 1929 by stockbroker Edward Lewis, later knighted for his company's work during the war developing radar. When Sir Joseph Lockwood, a successful flour miller, took over the chairmanship of EMI in 1954 and turned the company's ailing fortunes around, Lewis took the competition personally. He found some small comfort in the fact that, unlike himself, Lockwood owned no significant amount of EMI stock, so he was "just an employee."

Lewis brought onboard Dick Rowe, a third-generation stockbroker, to the Decca artists and repertoire department, at least partly because Rowe owned an impressive record collection. Rowe would have a long run on the British charts starting in the early fifties with such British pop stars as Dickie Valentine, Winifred Atwell, David Whitfield, Jimmy Young, the Beverley Sisters. He didn't know music, but he knew what he wanted on a record and he knew what was commercial. With Norrie Paramor at EMI's Columbia Records label doing fine with Cliff Richard and the Shadows, Rowe held his own at Decca with conservative, colorless records by clients of manager Larry Parnes: Tommy Steele, Marty Wilde, Billy Fury.

Rowe liked Americans, and when Shel Talmy showed up with a stack of acetates he claimed were demos he produced when he worked for Capitol Records in Hollywood that included recordings by Lou Rawls and the Beach Boys, Rowe hired him as a staff producer. Talmy turned out a smooth pop chart entry for Rowe's latest signing, the

Bachelors, two brothers and a pal from Dublin who all played harmonica and wore matching suits and bow ties. They were discovered
in Scotland by their manager Phil Solomon and his booking agent wife,
Dorothy. Talmy found the English music scene incredibly backward
and was thinking about trying to establish himself as a kind of independent producer along the lines of Leiber and Stoller back home, but
there was little precedent for that in Great Britain.

The only independent producer operating in London was eccentric Joe Meek, who used to conduct séances to try to contact the ghost
of Buddy Holly for help on sessions at his recording studio. Meek
was a RAF electrical engineer who built the EMI Lansdowne Studios,
before starting his own small operation above a Holloway Road shop
in Islington. Meek, who was obsessed with the occult, outer space,
and strange noises, presided over the transcendent "Telstar" by the
Tornados, a 1962 instrumental hit with a space-age sound that went
into orbit on even the American charts. Rowe leased the odd master or
two from Meek.

In the wake of the number one U.K. success of "Please Please Me"
by the Beatles in February 1963, after it became evident that the group
could well be the biggest thing in the British music business since
Cliff Richard and the Shadows, Rowe became unfortunately known
as the man who turned down the Beatles. He did give the group thor-
ough scrutiny. Mindful that the group's manager, Brian Epstein, also
ran his family's NEMS, Liverpool's leading retail phonograph record
shop, Rowe authorized an audition at the Decca studios. The group
cut fifteen songs New Year's Day 1962 under the supervision of Rowe's
assistant, Mike Smith, but the results were hardly promising, mostly
tame covers of American rock and roll hits from the band's stage show.
Rowe even traveled to Liverpool to catch the band's show at the Cavern
but turned back after encountering a mob in the pouring rain outside
the club blocking his entrance. It didn't occur to him until months later
that the crowd was waiting to see the Beatles.

Rowe mistook the Beatles for the Shadows ("Groups with guitars are on their way out," he famously told Epstein—seldom in history have men been more wrong) and signed, instead of the Beatles, Brian Poole and the Tremeloes, another nascent rock combo that auditioned the same day as the Beatles and had the distinct advantage of living in London. The British music business was always centered in London; Liverpool might as well have been on the other side of the world.

After Epstein and George Martin at EMI subsidiary Parlophone produced in the first few months of the year not only the Beatles but also Gerry and the Pacemakers and Billy J. Kramer and the Dakotas out of Liverpool, Rowe and the rest of the record industry looked differently at the northern seaport city. Rowe, in fact, ventured back to Liverpool to sit on a panel judging a talent contest and found himself seated next to Beatles guitarist George Harrison, who casually recommended to Rowe an up-and-coming rock group in London called the Rolling Stones. Rowe, more than eager to compensate for losing the most popular new act in years, acceded to demands from the Stones he wouldn't have considered a few months before. He needed to get with the beat group thing. The first Decca single by the Rolling Stones, a Chuck Berry song, "Come On," was released in June.

When he saw Parlophone leaving the track lying on the best-selling album without releasing a Beatles single of the song, Rowe had Brian Poole and the Tremeloes cover "Twist and Shout," a Top Ten hit single for Decca that summer. His Knightsbridge-based publisher, Bobby Mellin, was already working with Rowe and Phil Solomon pulling together material for an American-style folk album with the Bachelors. It was Mellin who suggested bringing over "Twist and Shout" songwriter Bert Berns to produce some sessions for Decca.

Rowe liked to ally himself with professional music business managers long before his string of hits with teen idols who were all handled by British rock and roll impresario Larry Parnes. The British music business did not deal with the amateur musician or songwriter. Philip

Solomon was an established figure in British show business. His father owned the Irish record distributorship Solomon and Peres and was a significant stockholder in Decca Records. His brother Mervyn Solomon, a jazz enthusiast who spent some time working in New York City, was involved in a record label and managed several record shops in Belfast.

Philip Solomon was instrumental in the career of Irish vocalist Ruby Murray, who had six Top Tens in the first half of 1955. He and his glamorous wife Dorothy moved to London in 1958 and opened Dorothy Solomon Artistes Agency. They met Dick Rowe through Solomon's family connections with Decca and found him the Harmonichords, whom Rowe renamed the Bachelors.

They hatched a plan to pull together a number of beat groups to audition for Berns. They went to Birmingham, the burly Midlands industrial center where Solomon had lined up a couple of groups, Gerry Levene and the Avengers and the Redcaps, and a female vocalist named Brenda Boswell. Solomon also had Miar Davies, a fifteen-year-old singing phenomenon off the TV show from the Midlands Programme, *For Teenagers Only*.

Rowe contacted Larry Page, a onetime teen idol candidate and recording artist known as "Larry Page—The Teenage Rage." Page, who once dyed his hair blue in a hapless bid for attention, had retired from show business to run a pub in Wales but was lured back. He was managing the Orchid Ballroom in Coventry and had developed a small stable of his own among the local punters. Page was bringing a singer who called himself Johnny B. Great, teenager Shel Naylor, a beat group called the Plazaents, and a trio of pubescent girls he dubbed the Orchids after his ballroom, whom he dressed in schoolgirl uniforms and photographed eating ice lollies.

The British music business was looking eagerly beyond London for the next Liverpool. When West Midlands groups the Redcaps and the Bruisers started making the tiniest noise, no less a figure than Norrie Paramor of EMI jumped on the scene, named it Brum Beat—pundits in the British press had already tabbed the new rock and roll sound from the north "Mersey Beat"—and he signed five acts from around the Birmingham area in the hope that Brum Beat was going to be the next Mersey Beat. Not to be outdone by EMI, Rowe signed all the acts Solomon and Page presented to Decca. He was also bringing in an American gunfighter.

No American record producer had ever worked in British studios before. When Berns arrived in London that October, the music newspapers took note. "US A&R MAN ON DECCA TALENT SEARCH," said *Melody Maker.* "American record manager, Bert Berns, who wrote 'Twist and Shout' and has had more than 100 songs in the U.S. hit parade [*sic*], will travel to Birmingham this week with Decca's Dick Rowe in search of new talent."

They'd never seen anything like Bert Berns in London before. He was an authentic character, a bit of *Guys and Dolls* in the flesh. He dressed like a racetrack tout, smoked like a chimney, and talked a mile a minute in the hip argot of the Broadway underworld. "Twist and Shout" was the new English national anthem. Even the Isleys version had made a brief appearance on the UK charts that summer. After checking in to the elegant Savoy Hotel and attending meetings at the nearby Decca headquarters on the Embankment, Berns went with Rowe and Solomon to Euston Station to board British Railways for Birmingham.

These new British beat groups had not yet proved successful at all across the Atlantic. New York attorney Paul Marshall, who had not only served since 1958 as chief counsel for Atlantic Records, but also started his entertainment law practice working for Sir Edward Lewis at Decca in London, also represented Brian Epstein and couldn't find a single American record label with the slightest interest in putting out the Beatles in the States. The first place he took the Beatles records was to Jerry Wexler at Atlantic, who dismissed the British group as "derivative" and wanted nothing to do with it. EMI's American wing, Capitol

Records, already turned the band down. Marshall licensed one record, "She Loves You," to a small Philadelphia label, Swan Records, who pipelined the side to *American Bandstand*'s Dick Clark, who didn't hear it either. Marshall made a nothing deal with Chicago r&b indie, Vee-Jay, just to get the records out in this country.

Nobody had any reason to believe these groups were anything more than a peculiar English aberration, unlikely to penetrate the vast American market in any meaningful way. But something was definitely going on in England. Berns had seen the royalty checks. He was a believer. So was Berns's music publisher, Bobby Mellin, running his publishing firm out of the London office, watching the British music scene practically explode under his feet all year.

"Twist and Shout" started paying like a jackpot, as the Beatles' success spread rapidly through Australia, New Zealand, Canada, and the rest of the British Commonwealth. He saw opportunities for his company's star writer. This scouting trip would give Berns a chance to see the British music business up close, where he and Mellin were already making plenty of money, even without the States.

Decca Records maintained three studios at their Broadhurst Gardens complex in West Hampstead, the smallest of which, Number Two, was reserved for pop sessions. The control room and the studio had relatively low ceilings around sixteen feet and the main room was about twenty-two feet across and forty-five feet long, large enough for a rhythm section and horns. The control room overlooked the studio from an oblong window and was reached from a flight of stairs at the end of the room. The studio staff wore white lab coats.

Dick Rowe introduced Berns to arranger Mike Leander, a twenty-two-year-old with untamed, woolly hair who had been working at Decca for two years. He landed the job by bluffing his way into the position with an independent production he had done. Born in East London, he went to boarding school on a scholarship, where he studied classical music and played in a skiffle band. He studied law briefly after school but was working in a music publishing office when he leased his master to Decca. The record flopped, but Rowe offered Leander a staff position and he made records with Billy Fury and other Decca acts, at the same time as he was learning orchestration at Trinity College of Music in Greenwich.

Berns rattled off five tracks with five different acts. Leander brought in a set of session musicians. Berns gave "It's Driving Me Wild," the song he wrote with Ray Passman that Conway Twitty recorded two years earlier, to Gerry Levene and the Avengers. He had Johnny B. Great do "You'll Never Leave Him," the Berns-Stoller number he had done earlier in the year with the Isleys. He cut Larry Page's homely Lolitas, the girl group called the Orchids, singing "Everybody's Love," the rewrite of "Just like Mine" he would also make with Betty Harris the next month when he returned to New York.

He handed the Redcaps "Come On Girl," a song he wrote with Stanley Kahan and had already tried a few times, including a version by the Jarmels, following up, without luck, "A Little Bit of Soap." He put Brenda Boswell together with Johnny B. Great as Brenda & Johnny and gave them a wacky doo-wop version of the Rodgers and Hart chestnut, "It Must Be Love." Leander caught the Mersey Beat sound on the tracks and Berns gave the records force and focus entirely absent from other British rock productions of the day.

These were experimental sessions for Berns. He had no idea what to expect and gave the acts retreads of songs that already failed to ignite much interest in the States, but at least he was working the catalog. The talent wasn't extraordinary, but there was a fresh energy in the air. Nothing much happened with any of the tracks he cut that day.

"Come On Girl" showed up on the B-side of the second Redcaps single. Rowe signed the group, whose claim to fame was having opened for the Beatles on four occasions. Rowe took Gerry Levene and the Avengers back into the studio and cut a handful of r&b songs, including "Twist and Shout." He had better luck with his Rolling Stones, who hit the UK charts that November with a number custom-tailored for the group by Beatles songwriters Lennon and McCartney, "I Wanna Be Your Man."

Berns went with Mellin to spend the weekend at his Surrey country manor. They hammered out a new publishing agreement and Berns couldn't help but be impressed by the baronial pastoral surroundings. Mellin's wife Patricia owned a Great Dane that entranced Berns, and before the weekend was over, she took him to visit the breeder and he ordered a dog to be shipped to him in the United States.

In the December 7, 1963, issue of *Billboard*, a few weeks after Berns returned to New York, tucked away in the back of the magazine with the international news, was a photograph of Sir Joseph Lockwood presenting the four Beatles with silver record awards, with the following caption:

> *Members of the Beatles, hottest British group, receive their two silver LP awards from EMI chairman Sir Joseph Lockwood for sales well over the 250,000 mark on each of their albums, "Please Please Me" and "With the Beatles." The latter award was given two weeks ahead of the release of the LP. Advance orders stood at an unprecedented 345,000. At the same ceremony, the group was given a miniature silver EP to mark sales of 400,000 for their first EP "Twist and Shout." The boys have racked up a total sale of four million on the sum total of all singles, EP's and LP's.*

IT WAS A photo of a tidal wave offshore and nobody saw it coming.

Bert Berns, Wes Farrell

XIII.

My Girl Sloopy [1964]

W ES FARRELL WAS the master of the short relationship. Well dressed and well groomed, he was the first man Dion saw with manicured nails. He wore custom-tailored mohair suits and monogrammed shirts and drove a Jaguar XKE. His girlfriend was a society doll, the beautiful blonde daughter of a prosperous Long Island car dealer. Luther Dixon brought handsome, dashing Farrell to the studio when he recorded the Shirelles singing the song he and Farrell wrote for the flip side of "Will You Love Me Tomorrow," "Boys," just so the girls could see what they were singing about. Farrell formed Picturetone Music in 1963 with Phil Kahl, a questionable character who ran Morris Levy's publishing empire for years. He and his brother Joe Kolsky had always been shadowy figures in the background at Levy's operation at Roulette Records (and before), but Kahl left the year before and started this new company with twenty-five-year-old Farrell in an office at 1650 Broadway.

Farrell had a certain kind of front that worked well in the music business. He could sing, but he wasn't much of a musician. He was slick, and he knew the score. He could get songs in front of the right people. When he was working as professional manager at Roosevelt Music, Farrell found himself hanging around the company offices with nine other songwriters, trying to come up with something on a dead-line for Pat Boone. He tossed out the title—"Ten Lonely Guys"—and supplied the bottle of Scotch.

Before the evening was through, they had not only knocked out a jokey country and western parody, but also gone downstairs and cut the demo at Allegro Studios in the basement, lead vocals provided by a junior Roosevelt writer named Neil Diamond. The crazy bastards liked the demo so much, they took it over to Joe Kolsky and Phil Kahl, who were running Diamond Records down the hall on another floor, and everybody was convinced for a minute that it was a hit.

Sanity did prevail, as Hal Fein, who ran Roosevelt, refused to grant the Diamond Records guys a license and instead gave the song after all to Pat Boone, who put the dumb thing on the charts. Farrell, like everyone else, had only a one-tenth writer's share, but he got his extra taste under the table from Fein.

Dion wrote a couple of songs with Farrell. He was off the charts, looking to find his way back, and Farrell impressed Dion with his affability and high style. He found Farrell good company, a collaborator who took him places he might not otherwise have gone, but otherwise someone who contributed little, not that Dion begrudged him the song-writing credits.

Berns and Farrell produced a flurry of songs that winter, while producer Berns busily slapped them on records within days of each other—"Baby Let Me Take You Home" by Hoagy Lands, "Goodbye Baby (Baby Goodbye)" by Solomon Burke. Farrell and Berns took to the studio themselves, singing together like a pair of deranged Everly Brothers. As the Mustangs, Berns and Farrell cut a rock and roll version of "Baby Let Me Hold Your Hand" and a couple of other pieces. Berns was absorbing the lessons of the British rock scene, incorporating the changes in his own music, even if he couldn't quite abandon all his trademark brushstrokes (the Mustangs, for instance, featured Cissy and the girls singing *giddyup* in the background).

They made a Wes Farrell single together for Capitol, a strange, calypso-flavored song about visiting a girlfriend's apartment when she's not home and leaving behind a note, Berns singing the payoff on the chorus in his exaggerated, Elvis-y vibrato.

I drank your coffee, I played your records
I touched your pillow and I talked to your cat.
I was happy for a little while
I just stopped by to thank you for that.
—THE LETTER (BERNS-FARRELL, 1964)

They wrote "My Girl Sloopy" at Berns's office at 1650 Broadway. As he did with "Twist and Shout," Berns drew the chords and the feel straight from "La Bamba," although "Guantanamera" was another obvious reference point. The Cuban love song was originally introduced in the late twenties by Joseito Fernandez, a shoemaker who started singing with *son* groups as a teenager. He first recorded the song in 1941, but it was his daily improvisations when he sang it as the theme song to a popular Cuban radio show through the forties and fifties that burned the airy melody into the country's brains. When orchestra leader Julian Orbon adapted verses to the song from the poetry of Jose Martí, the greatly beloved Cuban revolutionary who died fighting for his country's freedom in the nineteenth century, the song ascended into an unofficial national anthem. Folksinger Pete Seeger popularized the number throughout the English-speaking world, but nobody would find more utilitarian use for the piece's endlessly appealing chord changes and rumbling bass line than Berns.

As soon as Farrell left, Berns pulled songwriter Artie Wayne out of the hallway to play him the freshly minted song. Berns sat down at the piano and began pounding out the r&b *guajiro*, and by the time he reached the chorus the second time, Wayne was singing along at the top of his lungs and the girls from the office peered around the doorways to listen.

The presence of a collaborator notwithstanding, "My Girl Sloopy" was pure Berns, cut from the same blueprint as "Twist and Shout," a Romeo and Juliet story about a girl with a funny nickname cast in the authentic sound of the street. Solomon Burke turned the song down, but Berns didn't have far to look to find the perfect vehicle for his material. The Vibrations had signed a quick deal the year before with Atlantic and released a single on the label the previous fall written by one of the members, that had gone nowhere. The group actually boasted practically the perfect pedigree for the seriocomic "My Girl Sloopy."

The members first met at high school in Los Angeles in the fifties, when the group was called the Jayhawks. Their 1956 hit, "Stranded in the Jungle," written by a couple of the group members, brilliantly juxtaposed parallel narratives, each with its own signature rhythm, switching back and forth between the song's protagonist being boiled alive by cannibals in Africa and ("*meanwhile back in the States . . .* ") his girlfriend back home being romanced by some slick guy. Recorded for a tiny Los Angeles independent, the Jayhawks version got beat out on the charts by an uptown cover from the Cadets on the Modern label across town. Nevertheless the group managed to survive.

By 1961, now calling themselves the Vibrations, the five singers cut the Top Thirty pop hit "The Watusi" for the Checker label in Chicago. About the same time, they did a quick session off the books in Los Angeles for producer Fred Smith, whose regular vocal group, the Olympics ("Hully Gully"), was on tour in the East Coast. He released the track "Peanut Butter" by the Marathons, but Checker soon figured the ruse and handed the matter over to the attorneys. For a while, the group wore matching sweatshirts onstage with the letter *V* on their chests, changing to ones with the letter *M* when they did their other hit.

But the Vibrations did not depend on these comic, novelty hits for the group's longevity; they had a polished, acrobatic stage act—flips, splits, and leapfrogs, far more frenetic than the customary, almost military drill squad precision of most r&b acts of the day. By the time the Vibrations came to Atlantic, the group had made more than twenty records in nine years in the business. They met with Berns at his apartment, only to be greeted by a huge dog bounding up and slobbering on them as soon as they stepped off the elevator.

Dino had taken over the place since arriving from the British kennel a few months before. He joined the Berns menagerie already in progress, the two Siamese cats, Keetch and Caesar. The giant dog chewed to shreds what little furniture there was. Dog hair was everywhere, and since bachelor Berns was not the most diligent of dogwalkers, the terrace around the apartment where Berns allowed Dino to roam was filled with dog shit. He spoiled the beast shamelessly, routinely feeding him steak and burgers.

The Vibrations were not immediately impressed with the song, but Berns put them through rigorous paces. He knew what he wanted and he paid close attention to what some of the vocalists thought were minor details. After the end of the routining, the song sounded more promising. When the group faced a studio full of top sidemen and heard the badass backbeat they laid down, the Vibrations began to see the beauty of "My Girl Sloopy."

The record turned out to be a masterpiece of production by Berns. He brings the compact, expertly orchestrated piece to two brisk crescendos—shades of "Twist and Shout"—and manages to distill unfiltered Afro-Cuban voodoo for the pop charts. The obviously fake crowd noise turns up the heat on the track. He draws from vocalist Carl Fisher a peerless, loopy performance that straddles the borders of humor, lust, and hard soul, leavened with just the right touch of jive. As he did during rehearsals, Wes Farrell watched from a couch in the corner.

Berns dove into his work at Atlantic. A week after his session with the Vibrations, he went into the studio with Ben E. King for the first time. They cut a couple of songs, including "That's When It Hurts," a slight rewrite of the unreleased song Berns recorded as Russell Byrd for Atlantic a few months before. The songwriting credit was shared between Berns and Wexler, although Wexler did little more than pour the drinks and *kibitz* while Berns wrote the song one Sunday afternoon at the piano in Wexler's Great Neck mansion, where he spent many weekends.

His first single with the Drifters, "Vaya con Dios," the old Les Paul and Mary Ford hit he recorded in December, was heading up the charts. His Hoagy Lands single on Atlantic was making noise ("The singer really preaches on this one," said *Billboard*, "from the opening recitation to the wailing finish . . . ").

He was preparing Esther Phillips on four songs for a February session. The onetime Johnny Otis teenage protégé, whose "Double Crossing Blues" was a number one r&b hit in 1950 when she was known as Little Esther Phillips, had recently signed with Atlantic. She was handled by Alan Freed's old bagman, Jack Hooke, who was also her lover, and was coming off a 1962 Top Ten hit with the country and western song "Release Me" for a small Nashville label that subsequently went kaput. Her career on an upswing, she was off drugs for the time being.

In March 1964, Berns introduced Keetch Records, his own label to be distributed by Atlantic. The record label joined his new joint publishing venture with Bobby Mellin, called Keetch, Caesar & Dino Music, in bringing his animals into the act. A cartoon drawing of a Siamese cat decorated the label.

The first release was "Jose He Say" by Linda Laurie, the nutty kid whose off-the-top ad-libbing Phil Ramone turned into the hit record "Ambrose (Part Five)" in 1959. Part wacky beatnik, part naïve waif, she used her Brooklyn little girl voice talking to her boyfriend (*Ambrose, why are we walking through the subway tunnel?*) and dropped into a deep, trick voice to reply (*Just keep walking*). With the record set in a subway tunnel, "Ambrose" may have been a midchart record everywhere else, but in New York City it struck home. The modest hit spawned a series of "Ambrose" records that had played out its string when Berns found her. They collaborated on a couple of pieces of dialect humor, "Jose He Say," a Bert Russell number where Laurie got to again use her trick voice, and "Chico," which Berns and Laurie adapted from the other side of his unreleased Russell Byrd record, "Chico and Maria."

The record picked up some play here and there, but his own label wasn't Berns's top priority. As great as it was to have his own imprint, none of this mattered as much as the work at hand at Atlantic.

Only Solomon Burke was selling any records and Atlantic had gone ice cold after the previous summer. The company released around fifteen singles every month. Singles amounted to half the company's revenue, pushing $7 million annual sales, according to *Billboard*. Live by the hit single. Die by the hit single.

Wexler had been grooming Berns for this step, literally since he took him into the studio two years before to record "Cry to Me." Wexler was Berns's biggest booster, best friend, closest musical confidant. He was a hip father figure. To Berns, he offered the encouragement, the acknowledgement Berns always sought and never got from his own father. He had taken over at the label where Leiber and Stoller left off. At Atlantic, Wexler gave Berns the keys to the kingdom and told him to let them sing his songs and play his music. He was home.

On the *Billboard Hot 100* on May 9, 1964, the first week since February that the Beatles didn't have the number one (Louis Armstrong did with "Hello Dolly"), Berns had four records he wrote and produced for Atlantic on the pop charts. "My Girl Sloopy" reached the height of its chart life at number twenty-seven. "Goodbye Baby (Baby Goodbye)" by Solomon Burke was halfway up the charts after a month. "That's When It Hurts" by Ben E. King and "One Way Love" by the Drifters were just starting up. But that was only Atlantic. Way up above all these r&b records, scraping the bottom of the Top Ten at number eleven was "Twist and Shout" by the Beatles. Good week.

Berns continued to do a few independent productions with other labels. He and Paul Colby hung out all hours of the night before Berns had a session scheduled with Lou Christie ("Two Faces Have I") for Roulette. Colby wound up with half the songwriting credit on "You May Be Holding My Baby" largely by staying up with Berns while he pounded out the thing for the next day's session. Berns finished up at United Artists, where Art Talmadge was having problems hanging on to his job, with a one-off by a singer named Larry Hale ("In Front of Her House") and a marathon Isley Brothers session to finish an album that included Isley originals "Who's That Lady" and "Love Is a Wonderful Thing" (Ragovoy continued to produce Garnet Mimms at UA).

Berns cut more demos with Dante (Don Drowty), including a collaboration of theirs called "Jo-Jo" that baldly appropriated the melody from the current hit instrumental "Cast Your Fate to the Wind." Berns reunited with Gil Hamilton, who sang the original version of "Tell Him" two years before. Under the name Johnny Thunder, Hamilton had a Top Five smash in early 1963 with "Loop De Loop," a dim-witted dance song, and Berns outfitted Thunder with a couple of up-tempo numbers, "More More More Love Love Love"—a WABC "Pick of the Week" until some British group knocked it off the playlist—and "Send Her to Me," for Kolsky and Kahl's Diamond label. He invited Hamilton to join the chorus at the next Drifters session, where Hoagy Lands was also going to put his voice in the blend.

Drifters vocalists Johnny Moore and Rudy Lewis ate dinner together and talked about the session the night before it was scheduled. Later that night, Lewis was found dead in his hotel room from a drug overdose. Charlie Thomas of the Drifters was brought to Lewis's room the next morning and closed the dead man's eyes. Then he went to the studio for the session. Belonging to the Drifters was not for sissies.

Wexler blamed the union for not canceling the session, but of course he didn't want to spend the money. Weeks of preparation had gone into the planning. Berns had stormed out of Wexler's office after one meeting. He hated the song that Wexler found, "Under the Boardwalk," and he wanted baritone vocalist Charlie Thomas to sing lead on one of his songs, "I Don't Want to Go On without You," while Wexler was arguing for Johnny Moore. Berns's gifted British arranger Mike Leander had come over for the sessions and written a magnificent string orchestration for Berns's song. Leander couldn't be credited because of immigration and unions, but he was working shoulder to shoulder with Berns on this session. Berns felt so strongly about Thomas singing the song, he spent a number of afternoons rehearsing at his penthouse, just him on guitar and Thomas. Berns sent Thomas to a lady voice teacher on West Fifty-Seventh Street, who had the Drifter walking around singing through a trumpet mouthpiece.

Thomas and the other Drifters assembled, numbed and confused, at Atlantic Studios that morning in May 1964 after Lewis died. They genuinely liked Lewis, and since he had managed to keep his drug habit a secret from the group, his death came as a sudden shock. Berns considered "Under the Boardwalk" a lightweight throwaway by a couple of unknown Brill Building songwriters, Artie Resnick and Kenny Young, still looking for their first big song. He was banking on the dark, brooding dirge he wrote that he rehearsed in such detail with Thomas, "I Don't Want to Go On without You," a title that suddenly that morning took on deeper significance.

They ran quickly through "Boardwalk" and cut the session's second song, the Bert Russell number "He's Just a Playboy," in two different keys for vocalist Johnny Moore, not originally scheduled to sing the song's lead, some quick pencil work by Leander and Teacho Wiltshire, the official arranger of the session, as far as the union was concerned. Berns saved the big number for last. As Leander's lilting, sonorous chamber orchestra filled the room, Gary Chester tapping out quiet, stately waltz time, Thomas leaned into a carefully measured performance, tinged by a reservoir of incredible sadness.

Here in the gloom of my lonely room
I hold her handkerchief and smell her sweet perfume.
I can't stand to live on without you.
Oh my darling, hear my plea,
Come on back to me.
—I DON'T WANT TO GO ON WITHOUT YOU (BERNS-WEXLER, 1964)

THE DRIFTERS OFFERED Hoagy Lands the spot in the group. He asked Berns to look into it. They ate breakfast together the next day and Berns laid it out to Lands. Manager George Treadwell maintained his iron hand on the group. The performers did not participate in royalties or performance fees, and in fact, any songwriting compositions by group members were copyrighted by Treadwell. The pay was a flat $250 a week. Berns recommended Lands take it. Married with six children, Lands, who had started writing his own material, balked. Berns told him to ride out the contract and go solo in two years, like Ben E. King, but poor Lands didn't want to play ball.

As they spoke, Berns was remaking Ben E. King, as with the Drifters, taking over where Leiber and Stoller left off. After "That's When It Hurts," Berns had taken King back into the studio and cut four songs that steered the r&b balladeer of Leiber and Stoller's creation even more firmly into new territory. Berns gave King lower keys to sing and the songs settled into his power alley. He also gave King, last heard singing "I Could Have Danced All Night" from *My Fair Lady*, some gritty emotional depths to bite down on. Berns took him back to church. In May, King recorded the Bert Russell–Mike Leander song "It's All Over," and the chilling intensity of the song, the abject, naked heartbreak of the piece, was something entirely new for a Ben E. King record.

Two weeks after Ben E. King, one week after the Drifters session, Berns presided over another major epiphany in the studio at a Solomon Burke session. Berns had Burke cut a couple of clunkers—"You May Be

Holding My Baby," the song he finished the night before he cut it with Lou Christie only months before, and "Lili Marlene," the German beer hall song out of Marlene Dietrich's repertoire. It was Burke who took the session into another dimension.

Over a three-chord vamp drawn straight from his church service's "money march," Bishop Burke starts preaching wonderful nonsense about "there's a song I sing and I believe if everybody was to sing this song, it would save the whole world." Burke had never been modest in his ambitions, but as Cissy Houston and the girls stop shouting in the background and gather themselves into his gospel choir to kick the song into motion, Burke launches into sermonized soul that would be his grand moment, his greatest truth, nothing less than his magisterial summation of the whole human condition, "Everybody Needs Somebody to Love." The spirit pours out of Burke in a torrent. Arranger Phil Medley's horn punches barely contain him as he barrels his way through the message, the winds of love filling his sails.

If ever a pop song summoned the power of God, it was "Everybody Needs Somebody to Love." It is not a song so much as a performance, a blast of Burke's towering, commanding presence funneled into a three-minute sermon, but it still needed to be copyrighted.

Burke was appalled when Wexler told Burke he was taking half the writer's share for himself and Berns. Wexler told Burke he didn't think the song was a hit, so it wouldn't matter. The tempo was too fast for the teens. He didn't like Burke preaching—Wexler had told him that before—Atlantic wasn't a gospel label. The company leveraged Burke's publishing account against money he borrowed and he owed them. When the copyright went to paper, all three—Burke, Wexler, and Berns— shared the songwriting equally. Although Burke was signed as a writer to Atlantic's new publishing company, Cotillion Music, the song was published by Berns's new publishing venture, Keetch, Caesar & Dino.

Burke was furious. He was not just another soul singer who depended on Wexler and Atlantic for everything. He answered a greater calling. He believed in a higher power and he recognized Wexler's earthly greed for what it was. He had quit the music business once before over just such mortal matters. He also knew that since he had put his own name on that hundred-year-old folk song, he was not without guilt. He said it himself in the song—*Sometimes you get what you want, but you lose what you had.*

Berns had reached a new level; he was joining the ruling class of the record business. He had become one of the overlords who could take for the taking, who could play the great con game of the music industry for what it was worth, and who could reap all the rewards he could claim as his own. He learned from the masters. Nobody in this greedy, larcenous pit of vipers was more duplicitous, poisonous, and arrogant than Jerry Wexler, and Berns was studying up close. He was also falling in love.

She called herself Ilene Stuart, this gorgeous twenty-two-year-old blonde who danced at the Roundtable, the mobster hangout on East Fiftieth Street co-owned by Morris Levy. She still lived with her parents in Long Island, and her older sister, Marcy, recently divorced, had moved back home with her infant daughter. Since her sister didn't drive, she talked Ilene into taking her into Manhattan in their mother's brand-new Lincoln Continental on a Sunday afternoon. Their salesman father never made much money, but he always owned a new luxury auto.

The two sisters went for hamburgers at P.J. Clarke's on the Upper East Side and were seated at a table when Marcy sidled up at the bar next to Mickey Raygor, Berns's old friend from the Bronx who went to Cuba with him. He and Berns were having burgers and beer at the bar, but Raygor and Ilene's older sister struck up a conversation. They fed the little sister some line about a party at the penthouse and repaired to Berns's place not far away. Before long, the older sister and Raygor were back in Berns's bedroom and Berns was sitting around the living room with this innocent young thing who didn't even drink.

Ilene Holub, her real name, grew up in Los Angeles on the cusp of Beverly Hills. Her mother was raised Irish Catholic but converted to Judaism when she married Ilene's father. Ilene went to school with the sons and daughters of the rich and privileged and was so concerned about her appearance, she worked two jobs after school to save money to have her nose fixed. Her mother always favored her two older sisters and her younger brother, who almost landed a part in *Marjorie Morningstar*, except his blue eyes clashed with the brown eyes of star Natalie Wood. There were compensations. The music was great—Phil Spector's high school group, the Teddy Bears, played at her junior high—the cars were wonderful, and the beach was always there.

For a golden moment, her life was a teenage paradise in the Southern California wonderland—*American Bandstand* on TV every afternoon, burgers with the Fairfax High gang at Dolores' on Wilshire—but when her parents moved to Oakland, California, when Ilene was sixteen, she dropped out of the tenth grade rather than go with them. When her sisters both married *schlubs* from Brooklyn and the Bronx around the same time and moved back to New York, her parents took the other children and moved back East with them.

She went from teenage heaven to a roach-infested high-rise in Queens, where she shared the tiny bedroom with her brother, and their parents slept in a pull-out couch in the living room. After Ilene made a lame suicide attempt, her parents moved the family to Long Island, where the beach reminded her of California, and she started modeling. She started dancing. She worked as a Twister at the Roundtable in a cage across the room from an unknown Goldie Hawn. She danced at private clubs. She escorted an elderly Franchot Tone to a film premiere and got her picture in the paper and a limousine ride home. She was no longer a skinny, gawky kid—she looked like a Las Vegas showgirl—although she didn't know it.

This slob songwriter with hair over his collar was hardly her type. She went more for the blond-haired, blue-eyed model. He didn't make a move, but she offered him no encouragement. They talked about records. She knew "Tell Her" and "Twist and Shout" from dancing at the Roundtable. He played her some acetates and told her about working with Solomon Burke. The evening ended uneventfully and she took her sister back to Long Island.

Before the next weekend, her sister Marcy started bugging Ilene to take her into town again to see Mickey Raygor and Bert Berns. This time they went to dinner at an Italian restaurant before returning to Berns's place. Raygor and her sister disappeared in the back. Berns sat around playing guitar and talking with her.

She drove her sister in to see Raygor a couple more times and sat around having conversations with his funny, warm friend. She didn't feel attracted to him, but she was fascinated as he spoke to her about the Nazis and his passion for Israel. She knew he was a deep, sensitive man, and the night he reached over, turned out the light, and kissed her, she fell in love with him the instant he did.

At age thirty-five, Berns had outlived his doctors' most optimistic forecasts. His heart was helplessly swelling in his chest. Circulation problems caused him to perspire. He glowed with a sweaty sheen. He gulped pills and obsessively visited doctors. He saw Midtown specialists he met the week before and still went to his old doctor from the Bronx. He had money and success, but little else.

His sister had married an upright citizen, a likable guy who ran a knitting mill in Brooklyn, and was raising a family. Berns liked getting on the floor and playing with the kids, Neil and Robin.

Hip as he was, he was not sophisticated. He had vaulted virtually from living with his parents to living in a penthouse. He had loud, garish artwork on the walls. A large reclining nude hung above his sofa and in the corner another nude was beside his piano, the lid covered with knick-knacks, candles, and a framed photo of him and Wexler. There were only two raggedy chairs his cats tore up. He was called a genius by the people in his field and he didn't know about simple things like income tax.

Solomon Burke laughed as Berns messed up a pair of steaks he was grilling for the two of them on the penthouse terrace, feeding their dinner instead to Dino and ordering out for Chinese. Burke found Berns mooning over his new girlfriend and singing him uncharacteristic upbeat love songs. Burke told Berns he should marry the girl and get back in the heartbreak business.

After weeks of her coming into town to spend the night with him, Berns fired up the Corvette he owned but couldn't drive (too many speeding tickets) and cruised out to Long Island to meet his prospective in-laws, worried all the way that he would be pulled over. He walked in wearing his typical corduroy jacket with the arm patches, open-neck shirt, no necktie, his shaggy hair over the collar. Ilene was so smitten she didn't realize he was wearing a toupee. After that evening, Berns took her home and she never left.

Wexler not only was the best man at the wedding, but also paid for everything but the booze and the flowers, which the bride's dad covered. The band—featuring Berns session stalwarts such as Gary Chester and Paul Griffin—played for free. They decorated the penthouse terrace luau-style and set up tables everywhere. Dick Rowe and Phil Solomon and their wives came over from Great Britain.

It was a lavish, New York rooftop Jewish wedding on a sunny July day, visions dancing in Berns's head of the wife, family, and home of his own he never before really allowed himself to imagine in his life. His mother did not approve. She sternly warned him that marrying a woman so young and beautiful would kill him with his heart condition.

"Under the Boardwalk" by the Drifters spent all summer on the charts, rising to number four in August, Atlantic's first big hit after a long parched winter of discontent.* Arranger Mike Leander's crisp take on Berns's Afro-Cuban approach to the Drifters' trademark sound, first

---

*Billboard Hot 100 Top Five, week of August 15, 1964: 1. "Where Did Our Love Go" by the Supremes; 2. "Everybody Loves Somebody" by Dean Martin; 3. "A Hard Day's Night" by the Beatles; 4. "Under the Boardwalk" by the Drifters; 5. "The House of the Rising Sun" by the Animals.

tried out on the Solomon Burke album track "You Can't Love 'Em All" gave "Boardwalk" a familiar yet fresh sound for the tired vocal group, ten years down the road from Clyde McPhatter. Written in a cubicle at TM Music on the same Brill Building floor as Leiber and Stoller's office, Kenny Young strumming the guitar and Artie Resnick scrawling out the lyrics, "Under the Boardwalk" practically invented the summer song genre, in addition to revitalizing the Drifters' marquee value just when Atlantic needed it badly.

Solomon Burke's "Everybody Needs Somebody to Love" ran out of gas midchart, but having the two hits running at the same time rejuvenated the company. Berns put Atlantic back in the game. Kingpin Baltimore disc jockey Fat Daddy, a three-hundred-pound black gentleman named Paul Johnson who wore robes and a crown in public appearances and was a frequent weekend guest at Wexler's Great Neck place, wrote in his pick hits column in *Billboard*: "This is producer Bert Berns' year."

Berns tucked away two surefire follow-ups for the Drifters in August, cutting Resnick and Young's sequel to "Under the Boardwalk," a supple autumnal ballad explicitly redolent of the original hit, "I've Got Sand in My Shoes," and "Saturday Night at the Movies," another upbeat snapshot of teen life from Mann and Weil. He cut Solomon Burke preaching "The Price," no matter what Wexler said, and a song of his own, "Yes I Do." Berns did some incidental projects for the company; he supervised an LP of the Drifters singing supper club standards—both the Coasters and Ben E. King had made similar albums for the label.

He cut a protégé of Fat Daddy's named Kenny Hamber for a single on an Atlantic subsidiary of a song Berns wrote with Mike Leander called "Show Me Your Monkey." The premise of the song was that if the girl really loves the singer, she'll dance especially well for him, doing various dance steps of the day—the twist, the mashed potato, the hully gully, the monkey. On the other hand, it's pretty hard to get past the fairly obvious double entendre of the title line, especially when the band takes a stop break on the record just before Hamber shouts, *Show me your monkey*.

"Don't be misled by the title," said *Billboard*. The tidy, rocking little track picked up some play but, perhaps not surprisingly, never caught on.

Outside of Atlantic, now Berns did little. He produced a session with the great Roy Hamilton, long past the manly baritone vocalist's commercial peak, reprising his "She Makes Me Wanna Dance" for MGM Records, and dusted off an old Burt Bacharach instrumental track to have session vocalist Jimmy Radcliffe add new lead vocals to a Bacharach-David number, "Long after Tonight Is All Over," which Aaron Schroeder put out on Musicor. Atlantic was keeping Berns busy.

Behind the scenes at Atlantic Records times were changing and the partners were making important moves. They closed the deal in September 1964 to buy out Ertegun's old dentist, Dr. Sabit, who made a fortune on his original investment, and Miriam Bienstock, Atlantic founder Herb Abramson's ex-wife, long since remarried to Freddy Bienstock of Hill & Range, monocle-wearing cousin to the Aberbach brothers and former office boy to the great Max Dreyfus. Miriam vaguely tolerated Wexler, but she had no interest whatsoever in a street character like Berns, whom she regarded as Wexler's latest grubby fascination. She looked the other way. Berns was too uncultivated, too déclassé for her Park Avenue world. But Wexler loved the guy. He was practically exultant that he had discovered and groomed this brilliant record man leading Atlantic's salvation.

She remained steadfastly, vociferously opposed to any possible sale, so they made the tough broad walk the plank. Miriam Bienstock had been instrumental in the nuts and bolts of Atlantic's business since day one and was responsible for such key areas as music publishing and international sales. They asked her what she wanted and gave her the price she named—$600,000. As she walked out of the office with her check, she offered a parting shot. "I give you assholes six months," she said.

HERE COMES THE NIGHT

By BERT BERNS

RECORDED BY **THEM** ON DECCA F. 12094

ROBERT MELLIN LTD.
64 New Bond Street, London, W.1 • Trade enquiries: 46 Gerrard Street, London, W.1

2/6

XIV.

Here Comes the Night [1964]

THE BRITISH INCURSION on the American pop charts led by the Beatles that January, 1964 was so intense and unexpected that it swept away all before it. Even Wexler bowed down. Only a year before, he sent Paul Marshall away when his general counsel showed up wanting to give him the new Beatles records. Wexler now eagerly licensed an ancient recording of the Beatles, cut three years earlier in Germany when the band was hired to back British expatriate vocalist Tony Sheridan. He released the one track featuring John Lennon on vocals, the Jazz Age chestnut "Ain't She Sweet," and floated the single into the Top Twenty. British records suddenly suffused the American hit parade. The year before, there were none. The next year, somewhere between one-quarter and one-third of the big hits in this country were British.

Although British culture had been making inroads on the American scene over the previous few years on the Broadway stage and in movie theaters, nothing in those early signs suggested that British pop music would swell up out of London and become the single most significant trend in the American pop music marketplace since the original introduction of rock and roll ten years before. These guitar-playing British art school dropouts were practicing a distinctly American form of music, echoes of a raucous din first raised in the faraway former colonies, colored by the working-class, underdog, disaffected sensibilities of these British youth, oddly enough, not greatly unlike their counterparts in the American social substrata, the black musicians who made much of the original music in the first place. On levels they didn't even understand, these Brits connected with the American blacks.

Separated by geography, history, and culture, the postwar British public saw American life as exotic and adventuresome. American racial issues meant little in England, so that element of the music was absent from their understanding. It was all music from darkest America. The rank consumerism of America shocked and fascinated an England still recovering from the deprivations of war. In the austere, repressive British culture of the day, the carefree rebelliousness implicit in rock and roll stirred unimaginable emotions in young British musicians.

While some of the English enthusiasts were attracted to even more subterranean American musical currents represented by vernacular blues artists such as John Lee Hooker or Jimmy Reed—British audiences had been exposed to that fundamental music since midfifties performances by Chicago bluesmen Big Bill Broonzy, Memphis Slim, Muddy Waters, and a subsequent procession of others—most of these British pop upstarts drew their clearest inspirations from the New York rhythm and blues scene. Lennon and McCartney really just wanted to be Goffin and King.

Mickie Most was the twenty-six-year-old son of a regimental sergeant-major who sang as half of the Most Brothers at the 2i's Coffee Bar, the birthplace of British rock and roll in London, before moving to South Africa, where he essentially introduced rock and roll to the country and landed eleven consecutive records on the charts, largely covers of U.S. rock and roll hits that he basically produced by himself. He returned to England in 1962 and had some modest success as a recording artist ("Mister Porter," number forty-five U.K. 1963) but was working as a retail distributor, a position that would have been called rack jobber in the United States, when he signed as an independent producer the Newcastle r&b band the Animals and landed a deal with England's Columbia Records for the group.

Mickie Most admired and studied the New York maestros and visited New York in 1963 to look for material. He knew publisher Bobby Mellin from the London music business, and Most picked up fresh Berns demos from the New York office. After an initial session with the Animals concentrating on the band's r&b repertoire, Most brought the group back in the studio in February 1964 to record more commercial material, including the Bert Russell–Wes Farrell song "Baby Let Me Take You Home," which would be the band's debut U.K. single in March 1964.

Although Berns undoubtedly copped the basic blueprint for the song from the version of "Baby Let Me Follow You Down" on the first album by Bob Dylan, the song has a long history in the folk process, as Dylan himself alludes in his recording, crediting his version—although not sharing the copyright—to Boston folksinger Eric Von Schmidt. Arranger Garry Sherman heard Berns raving about a Dylan concert he attended. Berns and Farrell used the song's basic framework for a very slight rewrite, punching up the old blues lyrics for today's hit parade, moving the song into a driving closing section that owes more to the Isley Brothers' "Shout." But folksinger Josh White also has a version of the song well known in folk circles at the time (both White and Dylan also did the old blues, "The House of the Rising Sun," that Most likewise recorded with the Animals in the same February recording session).

Vocalist Eric Burdon recognized the song from blind New Orleans blues singer Snooks Eaglin's "Mama Don't You Tear My Clothes," another variant of the song, and knew that Berns and Farrell had given the old blues a pop slant that his group could work. The Animals' version of Berns and Farrell's "Baby Let Me Take You Home"—an arrangement almost identical to the demo Berns and Farrell recorded that served as the basis for their Mustangs record, not yet released—made a respectable showing at number twenty-one on the U.K. charts, but "The House of the Rising Sun" exploded into a worldwide number one smash after it was released in June 1964.

With his next signing, the Manchester group Herman's Hermits, Most went straight to Gerry Goffin and Carole King for a cover of "I'm into Something Good," a song Goffin and his wife King composed specifically for his pregnant mistress, Earl-Jean McCrea, lead vocalist of the Cookies. Goffin, who fathered a child out of wedlock with McCrea in July, produced the Earl-Jean version for the Columbia–Screen Gems label Colpix, which made a modest chart showing around the same time their daughter was born. Herman's Hermits took the song three months later to number one in the U.K. and number thirteen in the United States.

South African jazz pianist Manfred Mann arrived in the U.K. only in 1962, but quickly got with the program. His beat group cut the first theme song to British TV's *Ready Steady Go!*—"5-4-3-2-1"— which hit the British Top Five in early 1964, but when his band covered the Jeff Barry–Ellie Greenwich song originally recorded the year before by the Exciters, "Doo Wah Diddy Diddy," the Manfred Mann record went number one that fall on both sides of the Atlantic. British beat was coming from New York.

The English record business was light-years behind New York, but they could see the maw of opportunity yawning before them in London. Nobody in New York understood this better than Berns, whose visit the previous October at the British high tide for his "Twist and Shout" led him to nurture promising business relationships with associates such as Mike Leander, Dick Rowe, and Phil Solomon. Unlike every other hot shot in New York, Berns had gone to England.

It was Dick Rowe's idea to bring Berns back to produce Them, the new Irish r&b group Phil Solomon had signed for management and Rowe picked up for Decca. Rowe had personally supervised the group's first session at Decca's London studios in July 1964, cutting seven tracks including the first single, the Slim Harpo song "Don't Start Cryin' Now."

Mervyn Solomon found the band in Belfast, where Them had become an instant sensation when the group started the city's first r&b club only a few months before. A local rock and roll band called the Gamblers that modeled their sound on the American instrumental combo Johnny and the Hurricanes ("Red River Rock") was thinking about going r&b, when bandleader Billy Harrison auditioned the former saxophone player for the show band the Monarchs. He was a short, redheaded nineteen-year-old who also sang named Van Morrison.

Recently returned from a brief visit in London, Morrison had been dazzled by r&b night at Ken Colyer's Studio 51 club featuring an English r&b band called Downliners Sect. He had only recently accepted a job as vocalist with one of the city's top show bands, the Golden Eagles, but after his experience in London, Morrison was determined to play r&b. He joined the Gamblers on saxophone and harmonica, sharing vocal duties with guitarist Harrison. He was in the lineup when the band reemerged as Them in April 1964 at the Maritime Hotel in Belfast.

When Phil Solomon showed up with Dick Rowe in Belfast to see the band, his brother Mervyn Solomon paid to have fainting teenagers carried out of the hall, but Rowe had seen that before. He signed the group not out of any musical conviction, but because Phil Solomon was the band's manager. He watched at the airport the next day as Solomon collected the signed contracts from all but one of the lads (one minor member, whose parents had other plans for his career, declined).

After the group's Decca debut failed to leave much impression, Rowe suggested to Solomon they share the expense in bringing over Berns to produce the band's crucial next single. He thought Berns could also work with Elaine and Derek, sixteen-year-old twins, already show business veterans, whom Solomon recently placed with Decca, as well as possibly other Decca acts such as Dave Berry or the Bachelors. Rowe, who was beginning to show some progress Stateside with his other r&b signing, the Rolling Stones, thought an American producer might help the group make a hit record. The Stones finally broke through to the top of the U.K. charts in August with "It's All Over Now," and the Animals' "The House of the Rising Sun" was all over the place, so the climate for this music never looked better.

At Decca Studio Number Two in West Hampstead that October, Berns sat on a stool surrounded by the band, strumming his acoustic guitar and singing the group a song he wrote. He didn't have much more than the song and a guitar riff. He had played them other tunes—he tried out "My Girl Sloopy" on them—but "Here Comes the Night" was the song. The group spent the next four days in the studio slowly building the bare-bones song into a record, Berns showing them how. By the time Solomon's in-house musical director Phil Coulter, who was going to play organ, walked into the proceedings, it already sounded like a hit to him.

Berns was an American archetype, a species entirely unknown in Britain—the Broadway record man. He reeked of Pall Malls, cheap cologne, and hit records. Them's Morrison was impressed that Berns wrote "I Don't Want to Go On without You," the cool B-side of his new Drifters hit. Since he was the producer, Berns called the shots and Decca's rules were out. He allowed the evil overdubs and made the engineer reserve an empty track so he could bounce tracks and overdub as much as he wanted. He was not the British style—he won over surly Billy Harrison by walking through the room during a take, grabbing a drumstick, loudly bashing a cymbal several times, and telling the band, "Let's get something cooking, lads."

The band had already suffered through the indignity of having members replaced by session musicians during the first session with Dick Rowe. This time the group barely noticed when Berns brought in outside hands. Drummer Andy White, who substituted for Ringo Starr on the first Beatles session, took the kit, and on second guitar, Berns brought in a twenty-year-old British guitarist he met through Mike Leander and had used on the sessions the year before, named Jimmy Page.

Over the previous two years, the young guitarist had become a favorite session player whose guitar graced dozens of records, including a lot of work for Decca. On the previous Them session, Page played for Dick Rowe as the band members glared at him and the other side-men who took their places, but this time was different. And Page was used to that anyway. The Kinks had been irritated when producer Shel Talmy brought Page to play on the band's early sessions; the Who didn't care (Page played on sessions for both "You Really Got Me" and "I Can't Explain").

Berns showed Page the guitar part he salvaged from his Marv Johnson production the year before of "Come On and Stop." Page changed the guitar positions, turned up the reverb, and sprayed gold into the sound.

Berns cut two songs with Them that final evening in the studio, starting with the band's version of a John Lee Hooker blues. Page's snarling guitar gives "Baby Please Don't Go" a stinging introduction, rattling against an ominous rumbling bass, and Berns lets it run, but as with his American r&b records, it is the intensity of the lead vocal by Van Morrison that drives Berns's production. A couple of additional session vocalists provided harmonies on "Here Comes the Night," set off by Page's incandescent guitar parts, but the production is primarily powered by the vocalist's fierce commitment to the song's stark vision.

> Well, here it comes.
> Here comes the night,
> Here comes the night,
> Oh yeah.
> The long, the long, the long and lonely night
> The night, the night, the night, the night
> Here comes the night.
> —HERE COMES THE NIGHT (BERT BERNS, 1964)

Leander and Berns turned around and cut the song again in the same studio the next week with Lulu, this time as a huge, symphonic pop ballad, opening with Lulu chanting *The night . . . the night . . . the night . . . the long and lonely night . . .* as the tympani, strings, and, once again, Jimmy Page's guitar go to work behind her and open up the song to epic dimensions.

Born Marie Lawrie, this diminutive sixteen-year-old Glaswegian scored Scotland's first beat hit for Decca in May 1964 with her group Lulu and the Luvvers' cover of the Isley Brothers' "Shout" in her almost freakish raspy voice. Berns and Leander cut five songs with the budding star, including the monumental "Here Comes the Night"; the Berns-Stoller "You'll Never Leave Her"; a song credited to Bert Russell and Ilene Stuart, "I'll Come Running Over"; and covers of Jerry Butler's "He Will Break Your Heart" and the Rufus Thomas novelty, "That's Really Some Good," with Berns jumping in for a vocal duet on the choruses.

For the showbiz twins, Elaine and Derek Thompson, Berns churned out a piece of infantilized pop, "Teddy Bears and Hobby Horses" and a feckless cover of his Linda Laurie record from earlier in the year, "Jose He Say."

The Lulu version of "Here Comes the Night" spent one week on the U.K. charts in November, then disappeared forever, a lost pop classic. "Baby Please Don't Go" by Them was released in November with a song on the B-side from the initial Dick Rowe sessions written by vocalist Van Morrison, "Gloria." The single almost sank without a trace, except Phil Solomon wouldn't say die.

Long after Decca gave up, Solomon convinced producer Vicki Wickham of TV's *Ready Steady Go!* to use "Baby Please Don't Go" as the show's theme for two months. The record went back on the charts after two weeks and into the Top Ten in January 1965. When Them's "Here Comes the Night" was released in March 1965, the record sold a spectacular sixteen thousand copies the first day and went all the way to number two in England. (In the United States, "Gloria," long considered a rock classic, spent exactly one week on the charts at number ninety-three and "Here Comes the Night" crawled as far up the pop charts as number twenty-four.)

With the new breed of British producers such as Mickie Most or Andrew Loog Oldham of the Rolling Stones trying as hard as they could to make records that sounded American, Berns was the first American producer trying to make records that sounded British. He instantly understood the dynamics of the five-piece rock combo. The instruments on the Them session were voiced and recorded like no other British records of the time, but the way these young musicians handled their instruments was a different world from the New York classicists. There were also no shortage of parallels between these working-class youth of Great Britain and the black recording artists on Berns's records back in the States.

Berns cast a wary eye at what he saw happening in England. As a favor to Phil Solomon, he dropped by the London audition of a Welsh singer named Tommy Scott, whom Dick Rowe had recommended. Solomon lost interest in the singer after Berns told him his boy was "no Elvis." The singer went back to Wales and found another manager, who changed his name to Tom Jones.

Berns sat in a pub around the corner from the West Hampstead tube station one afternoon before one of the Them sessions talking with journalist Nik Cohn, who also came from Ireland. Surrounded by these scruffy hooligans and malcontents from the other side of Belfast, Berns was having problems understanding their thick brogues and tried to enlist Cohn into helping translate for him. Cohn was not tempted.

Cohn knew that Berns had a flair for the dramatic. He had interviewed Berns over lunch earlier at a fancy London restaurant for *The Observer*. Cohn had asked Berns, somewhat innocently, what pop was about. Berns turned from the table and loudly said, "Waiter." Three gentlemen in white appeared almost instantly and Berns produced a cigarette to face a wall of flame from the waiters. He turned back to Cohn. "Wouldn't you say," he asked, "that's what pop's about?"

But this afternoon in the pub, wrestling with the communication difficulties with his charges and other challenges of the evening's session and beyond that lay ahead, he was more rueful. Berns thumbed a British music magazine, opened to a photograph of the Beatles, which he regarded grimly. "Those boys have genius," he said. "They may be the ruin of us all."

Meanwhile back in the States, with Berns taking over at Atlantic and having walked on Art Talmadge at UA, Leiber and Stoller found themselves without any ready outlets for their music and running out of money. Without a label behind them, they had to pay the studio bills themselves. Mike Stoller had grimly informed his partner that their bank account was down below $20,000 only a couple of hours before Jerry Leiber walked into Al and Dick's steakhouse and found Hy Weiss cracking wise with George Goldner in March 1964.

In the twenties, boisterous singer Texas Guinan used to shout "Hello suckers" from atop a piano on the premises, but the West Fifty-Fourth Street institution had been the unofficial clubhouse of the record business for some time. Leiber pulled up a chair and joined the two pirates. Of all things, Jerry Leiber had never met George Goldner before.

"Can you believe this schmuck," said Weiss, puffing a cigar. Goldner had been going through tough times and he apparently had come to Weiss to see about working for Weiss's Old Town label, a marginal operation at best. Weiss, like a lot of his bunch, mistook being a pain in the ass for being funny. He took pleasure in rubbing Goldner's face in it for Leiber's benefit.

Goldner *was* one sorry son of a bitch. After losing his End and Gone labels two years earlier to, guess who, Morris Levy, Goldner spent the next year and change doing Levy's dirty work on record promotion, a field Goldner practically invented and at which his skills were unsurpassed. He left Levy nine months before and had not been able to get a single thing going in the meantime. He was broke, down on his luck.

He had submitted a remarkable letter in 1964 to the register of copyrights at the Library of Congress: "This is to acknowledge,"

Goldner wrote, "that the attached schedule of compositions which contain my name as writer should properly have the name Morris Levy in my place." The schedule listed forty-nine such compositions, including "Why Do Fools Fall in Love." He lost his publishing, his labels, and with this single document, his copyrights. By some inexplicable accident, all the songs previously credited to Goldner actually should have been credited to Morris Levy. Once again, Levy took everything.

His French cuffs, perfectly presented, Leiber noticed, were frayed. Weiss offered Goldner some chump change. Goldner tried to negotiate, but Weiss excused himself to go to the bathroom. Leiber turned to Goldner and asked if he would be interested in doing something with Leiber and Stoller. Goldner asked for the keys to Leiber's office and left Al and Dick's to listen to acetates.

The next morning, Leiber went to work and found George Goldner, not a hair on his head out of place, standing behind Leiber's desk, holding a disc. "On my life," he told Leiber, "this is a hit record."

Leiber hated the track, but his partner Mike Stoller always thought there was something there. Jeff Barry and Ellie Greenwich produced the number with a girl group called the MelTones brought to them by New Orleans bandleader and entrepreneur Joe Jones ("You Talk Too Much"). Barry and Greenwich wrote the song with Phil Spector, who first cut it with the Ronettes, and then with the Crystals, but refused to release either. After back and forth with Spector on the publishing, Barry and Greenwich and Mike Stoller took Jones's vocal trio—who thought they were going to be called Little Miss and the Muffets—into the studio and recorded the song "Chapel of Love."

It was one of a stack of unreleased masters left over from the UA deal that had built up since they closed down their Tiger and Daisy labels the previous November. Leiber and Stoller formed a partnership with Goldner, whom Stoller had never met before either, and started Red Bird Records. As Goldner predicted, "Chapel of Love"—by the time it was released, the group was renamed the Dixie Cups—shot to number one in a dizzying six weeks after it was released in April 1964.

They didn't know it at the time, but Red Bird Records was the beginning of the end for Leiber and Stoller. They were kids from Los Angeles who hit the big time in the record business before they knew what had happened to them. With their own musical career in decline, they had compensated with savvy, knowing work as music publishers, slowly expanding into the record business, a realm, as it turned out, they knew nothing about. With the label's first release number one and more hits in the pipeline, at first, they had to deal with success, which is infinitely more difficult to handle than failure.

RED BIRD LAUNCHED sixteen charts hits in twelve months during the absolute peak of what came to be called the British Invasion. Received wisdom holds that the onslaught of fresh, exciting young British beat groups wiped out the cobwebbed old music business in New York, which was hardly the case. Not only was much of the early days of the British beat movement based in the New York rhythm and blues scene, but many of the Broadway rhythm and blues moguls continued, regardless, to thrive and prosper. Berns was not the only one having the best year of his life on the charts.

Burt Bacharach and Hal David were also cutting through the flood of British pop clogging the charts the first quarter of the year. The team continued to have success with Gene Pitney after "Only Love Can Break a Heart" with songs such as "True Love Never Runs Smooth" and "Twenty Four Hours from Tulsa." They started a series of remarkable, underrated productions with vocalist Lou Johnson for Johnny Bienstock at Big Top with "Reach Out for Me."

Beginning with their Top Ten in 1963 for Bobby Vinton, "Blue on Blue," Bacharach and David became an exclusive songwriting-production partnership. They scored a massive, unlikely hit with a jazz waltz composed on assignment for the title song to the movie

Wives and Lovers, sung and swung by Jack Jones. But it was the back-to-back Top Ten hits—"Anyone Who Had a Heart" and, especially, "Walk On By"—that established not only Dionne Warwick as the new female pop vocal star of the year, but also Bacharach and David as the hot new young songwriting team after more than eight years of having their songs recorded.

That Dusty Springfield took an Anglicized version of their "Wishin' and Hopin'" into the Top Ten that summer only galvanized their growing standing. The Dionne Warwick hits reversed the thinning fortunes of Scepter Records, where Florence Greenberg was having difficulty adjusting to life after Luther Dixon.

Bob Crewe was also reaching new heights of success in the midst of the British onslaught with the Four Seasons, who were scoring the biggest hits of the vocal group's estimable career. Baroque pop productions like "Dawn," "Ronnie," and "Rag Doll" gave the group their best chart numbers since they blasted into business with three straight number ones two years before in 1962 ("Sherry," "Big Girls Don't Cry," and "Walk Like a Man").

Producer Crewe was an extravagantly extroverted personality, a onetime fashion model and pop singer himself, who lived in a sprawling penthouse in the nineteenth-century apartment building on the edge of Central Park called the Dakota. The offices of his company, Genius Music, were in the same office building as Atlantic Records, where a receptionist sat directly opposite the elevator doors in front of a sign that spelled out in six-foot letters GENIUS.

It was also a breakthrough year for Motown Records, the bootstrap independent from Detroit started by former car plant worker and the Jackie Wilson songwriter Berry Gordy Jr., who also wrote Marv Johnson's hits. His team of ambitious black professionals modeled their production methods on the automobile plant assembly line where Gordy worked and aimed their rhythm and blues records at white teenagers. Gordy liked to gear songs toward everyday experiences, looking for those low common denominators in his audience, and always, always had a tambourine on his tracks because he thought the radio was the call to church. He discouraged bravura performances and sought a sturdy tunefulness that acted as a reassuring agent against any melancholy or distress that might be part of the song's emotional landscape.

He often conducted the experiments in the studio himself, but also trained a platoon of songwriter-producers schooled in his philosophies. The unblinkingly candid "Money (That's What I Want)" by Barrett Strong in 1960 started it off for Gordy and company and they refined their attack until they began consistently hitting their target with uncanny accuracy. "My Guy," a Mary Wells performance written and produced by top Gordy acolyte Smokey Robinson, made number one in May 1964, followed before the end of the year by the first two of five consecutive number ones by Gordy's most superb creation, the Supremes, a group whose smooth assimilation of pop platitudes was as remote from the kind of raw desperation of Berns's records as you could get in rhythm and blues.

Phil Spector was also at the peak of his magnificence. Spector hated to fly, but he was convinced the Beatles were going to make it in America. So when he flew home from London in February 1964, he changed flights so he could fly on the same plane as the lads from Liverpool. He walked down the gangway in a floppy cap behind the boys, as thousands of cheering teens greeted their arrival in New York.

In London, Spector had spent a drunken evening in the studio with another new British rock band, the Rolling Stones, lending his hand to the production of what would become the group's breakthrough U.S. single, "Not Fade Away." He was involved in a torrid extramarital affair with lead vocalist Veronica Bennett of his new girl group stars, the Ronettes, whose smash debut single for his Philles label written by Jeff Barry and Ellie Greenwich with Spector, "Be My Baby," Spector's most Wagnerian production yet, went to number two in October 1963.

On his latest creation with the group, Spector marshaled nothing less than the heavens themselves, as he wove thunderclaps and rainstorms into the orchestrations on "Walking in the Rain," cowritten with Mann and Weil, an ethereal, billowy, self-conscious masterpiece that nevertheless only reached the midtwenties on the charts. Spector countered with his towering "You've Lost That Lovin' Feeling," a song he handcrafted for blue-eyed soul duo the Righteous Brothers once again with Barry Mann and Cynthia Weil.

On the grand, confident production, Spector plays a cat and mouse game with the two lead vocalists, only bringing them together finally over the bridge before the explosive final chorus, the conga drum leading the breakdown into a Latinized section that could best be described as a tribute to Bert Berns. The part could have been lifted straight from one of his records.

Outside Spector's domain, Barry and Greenwich were also flourishing at the new Red Bird Records, housed in the Trio Music suite in the Brill Building. They quickly followed "Chapel of Love" with "I Wanna Love Him So Bad," a Top Ten hit for the Jelly Beans, four gals and a guy, still in high school, from Jersey City. Right from the label's first release, Goldner was picking hits, promoting Red Bird records on the radio, and making his distributors work them. "George Goldner has the musical taste of a fourteen-year-old girl," said Jerry Leiber, with more than a trace of admiration.

With Leiber and Stoller acting as executive producers, Barry and Greenwich wrote the songs and produced the records. They conducted the sessions at Mira Sound with engineer Brooks Arthur, whom they knew from his days at Associated Sound where they made the Raindrops records and cut a lot of their demos. Arranger Artie Butler was a gifted young pianist and quick pencil artist whom Leiber and Stoller found working as the tape operator at Bell Sound. They hired him on the spot after watching Butler start the tape rolling in the control room and dash into the studio to play the piano and fix a part their hired hand botched during the session. George Morton was more of an accident.

Morton knew Ellie Greenwich from Long Island and, visiting their office one afternoon at Trio Music, shot his mouth off with Jeff Barry and walked out having promised to return in a week with a hit record. Of course, he knew nothing about anything to do with hit records, but within a week, he found a group, rented a studio, hired a band, and cut a demo of a song that he wrote in his car on the way to the session. The results, which he brought to Barry a week after his first visit to their office, intrigued Jerry Leiber, who signed the screwball kid and put him to work with Barry and Greenwich. They smoothed the oddball piece into shape, ready for the studio with his group, four girls from Cambria Heights in Queens called the Shangri-Las.

An offbeat pastiche of sound effects, spoken word, soap opera narrative, arrangements from outer space, and the oddly appealing, unaffected vocals by the girls, "Remember (Walking in the Sand)" streaked into the Top Five when it was released in August, although not before another production company surfaced with signed contracts on the group who had to be cut in on the deal.

Morton, whose erratic behavior—now you see him, now you don't—earned him the name Shadow Morton from Leiber, brought Barry and Greenwich the bones of the next Shangri-Las record, which the three of them (along with Artie Butler) hammered into "Leader of the Pack," a massive number one hit that vaulted the two sets of sisters out of Queens into the front ranks of the day's pop groups before they even knew how to pronounce "chateaubriand." Barry and Morton went out and bought motorcycles.

While Barry, Greenwich, and Morton were so successfully plumbing the lucrative Top Ten teen market, Leiber and Stoller even managed a slight return to making the kind of funky records they liked, such as the starkly mordant blues "The Last Clean Shirt (My Brother Bill)" by Honeyman and New Orleans badass Alvin Robinson's "Down Home

Girl," a Leiber-Butler composition that featured especially witty, pungent lyrics from Leiber, although neither record was a candidate for the pop charts. Red Bird was on fire. They could put out what they wanted.

Bert Berns, The McCoys (front), Jerry Goldstein (left), Bob Feldman (right)

XV.

Hang on Sloopy [1965]

I N MARCH 1965, his contract with Mellin expired and Berns formed a
publishing company with the Atlantic partners called Web IV, owned
50 percent by Berns and 50 percent by Wexler and the Ertegun brothers. The company's name stood for the four partners' names—Wexler,
Ertegun, and Berns—with the Roman numeral for all four. Although
the music publishing firm was announced first, it was always the plan
to also start a record company. They wanted his publishing and Berns
wanted them to bankroll him in a label. Wexler resisted, but Berns saw
how Leiber and Stoller were doing at Red Bird. Ilene Berns was the
one who suggested they scramble all their names together and they
came up with Bang Records for Bert, Ahmet, Nesuhi, and Gerald (only
his mother ever called Wexler "Gerald"). His partners put up $17,500.
Berns took an office in 1650 Broadway and placed a help wanted ad for
a secretary in *The New York Times*.

Berns wasn't exactly leaving Atlantic in a lurch, but Wexler and
the Erteguns were not only helping Berns start his record label, but
also helping themselves to his publishing. They couldn't lose, and they
could win on both bets. Ertegun's father would have been proud of
such Turkish diplomacy. "Exactly," his son Ahmet Ertegun would say
to anyone. About anything. It was one of his favorite expressions. It
almost sounded as if he agreed with you.

At the same time, in one of the record business's worst-kept
secrets, Atlantic was deep in negotiation to sell the company to ABC-
Paramount, the loathsome square record company that had wrested
Ray Charles from their bosom five years before. The label may not have
been hip, but with parent company ABC Television hovering in the
background, the label did have money. Still, Wexler complained that
when ABC-Paramount chiefs Sam Clark and Larry Newton came over
to his Great Neck place to talk about the deal, it took a week to get the
grease stains out of the sofa where they sat.

Atlantic had entered into serious discussions with ABC-Paramount
about selling the company. Atlantic chief counsel Paul Marshall spent
long hours over the coming months negotiating the terms. Although
Wexler and the Erteguns expected to be contractually tied to Atlantic
for a number of years after the sale, they set up Berns in a separate
partnership, outside the boundaries of the sale (although they did give
Berns a small piece of their music publishing firm, Cotillion Music,
when they cut the Web IV deal, something they would come to regret).

Wexler watched over every detail of Bang Records. When Berns
hired his secretary, an eighteen-year-old Queens College freshman still
living at home with her parents in Forest Hills named Sheila Silverstein,
Wexler sent her directly to Ahmet's steely assistant, Noreen Woods at
Atlantic, for training. When she returned to work at the Bang Records
office in 1650, it was only she and Berns in one small room.

Berns finally got his first number one through a screwy chain of
events nobody could have seen coming. When he did, it came first
class, hand delivered to him on his vacation. Berns hit the trifecta—he
owned the song, the group, and this time, the record label. It was the
kind of play only the big boys made.

Bob Feldman, Richard Gottehrer, and Jerry Goldstein didn't know
Berns, even though they'd been around 1650 a few years, and were
fairly well known themselves as the Feldman, Gottehrer, and Goldstein
who wrote the 1962 number one hit "My Boyfriend's Back" by the

Angels. They knew who he was, of course. They showed him some songs once. They remembered Phil Spector wanting to catch a train in Philadelphia to make a party at Berns's place.

Bobby Feldman was a kid from Brooklyn who danced on the Alan Freed TV show *The Big Beat*, a local New York City afternoon dance program that Freed ran from 1958 until he was fired during the payola scandal. Feldman showed Freed's manager Jack Hooke a poem he had written called "The Big Beat." When Hooke told him that if the poem had music behind it, it could be the show's theme song, Feldman went around the corner to see his stickball buddy, Jerry Goldstein, whose parents had providentially recently bought a new piano and who knew three chords. The song was recorded and used as the show's theme song.

The boys had their first published composition and everything was going great until Feldman showed up as always to dance on the TV show to find Hooke outside waiting for him. The mother of the lead singer from the group who sang their song had raised holy hell with her congressman or something after she watched her daughter take the check from the last week's TV show in front of the union official and then endorse it back to the producers after he left. Feldman's career with Freed had come to an end.

Feldman and Goldstein knocked around writing songs, recording the results. They were Evie and the Ivies. They cut a Buddy Holly memorial song, "A Letter to Donna," two days after the plane crash. They were Bob and Jerry who did the answer song "We Put the Bomp." They found themselves sitting around a Brill Building office for a couple of hours waiting to show some songs to Nat King Cole's publisher alongside another young songwriter, Richard Gottehrer, a tall, good-looking twenty-one-year-old, exactly their age, who grew up in the shadow of Yankee Stadium in the Bronx. They introduced themselves, started talking, and eventually left together to write songs rather than continue to sit around.

In 1962, the three of them sold "I'm Tossin' and Turnin' Again" to Beltone Records as a follow-up for Bobby Lewis a full year after his big hit, "Tossin' and Turnin'," and they wrote and produced "What Time Is It" by the Jive Five for the same label, although the label owner took the credit. Wes Farrell convinced them to sign with Roosevelt Music when he landed them the next Freddy Cannon single. They wrote the song in the car on the way to Philadelphia the next day to play it for his record label.

They moved from Roosevelt to a new publishing firm, April/Blackwood, and were pulling down $200 a week, serious money, supervising their own demos, hustling their own songs. They took an office next door to April/Blackwood in the 1650 building and started to become more involved in producing.

They were working with a female vocal trio from New Jersey called the Angels, who had a couple of singles a couple of years before. The girls were trying to make ends meet singing background vocals on sessions. It all fell together quickly after Feldman went to have a sentimental egg cream in Brooklyn across the street from his old high school and he heard the young lady in the back room screaming at the some guy in a black leather jacket, "My boyfriend's back and you're going to be in trouble."

Feldman scribbled some notes on a napkin and rushed back to Manhattan. The three songwriters finished the song before going out to a late-night dinner that evening. April/Blackwood wanted the song for the Shirelles, currently the top girl group in the country, but the fellows refused to play it for them. They wanted to produce the song themselves. They were locked out of their office. Their contracts were dropped. They scraped together enough money to produce a split session with the Angels and two other acts and sold all three masters, the first two for $1,500 apiece and "My Boyfriend's Back" for $10,000. Feldman, Gottehrer, and Goldstein were in business.

They produced more Angels records. They produced records that sounded like the Angels and the Angels stopped working with them. They started their own label, Stork Records ("delivering the hits"), with pink labels for girl artists and blue labels for boys. Morris Levy offered them $10,000 for "Lookin' for Boys" by the Pin-Ups—threw the cash on the desk—but they were so sure they had a hit, they held out.

Within weeks, they were sorting through old Angels tapes to see if they had anything that could make them a little money. By this time, of course, British bands had wiped girl groups off the charts when Feldman ran across the tape they made for the Angels of the old Jo Stafford song, "That's All I Want from You." He wrote some new lyrics and the three of them laid down vocals, but when Feldman got to the middle eight, he improvised some crazy stuff in this bad English accent. Can't beat 'em, join 'em. Marty Kupersmith, one of Jay's original Americans, was visiting their office, wearing those silly glasses and giving the arm salutes from the Peter Sellers character in the movie *Dr. Strangelove or: How I Learned to Stop Worrying and Love the Bomb.* Feldman snatched the glasses and started talking in his fake British accent, and the Strangeloves were born.

They sold the Strangeloves single, "Love, Love," to Swan Records in Philadelphia for $1,500 and it picked up a little airplay.* They started getting calls from WGH in Virginia Beach, where the record was doing particularly well, asking the Strangeloves to appear on the station's Halloween concert with Chuck Berry, the Shangri-Las, Gene Pitney, and Bobby "Boris" Pickett.

"We're not British, we're Yiddish," they told the deejay, who told them never mind—play his concert and he would make their record number one. They had never performed in public before, but they were not in a position to turn down work. Feldman didn't feel that confident of his British accent, so they decided to be Australians.

They took two cars and were arrested en route for speeding. The radio station had to bail them out, but they finally arrived at the Newport News airport. They boarded a private plane that taxied—never left the

---

*The B-side of the single, "I'm on Fire," was recorded by Jerry Lee Lewis as his last rock and roll record before going over to country and western music.

ground—down the runway to the Virginia Beach airport. Police lines were holding back thousands of teens. They held up signs and banners reading WELCOME TO AMERICA, WE LOVE YOU. They threw jellybeans, teddy bears, even stuffed kangaroos. The mayor gave them the key to the city.

The three counterfeit Australians in cashmere sweaters and jeans played their American debut—a forty-minute show, of which an elongated version of "Shout" accounted for almost half. The group also played a thunderous version of "Bo Diddley." Swan Records did not want another Strangeloves record, but a New York studio operator fronted them some time and they cut a monster version of "Bo Diddley."

Ahmet Ertegun met one of the songwriters at a party and took an interest in their work. They brought him the "Bo Diddley" demo. Ertegun liked it, but when they played it for Wexler, he hit the ceiling. He didn't want to hear white guys sing "Bo Diddley" and he said so in no uncertain terms, at the top of his voice, and threw them out of his office. Ertegun followed them down the hall. Atlantic had a new partnership starting out with Bert Berns, he told the Strangeloves. Take it over to him and see what he thinks.

They checked out Berns with a few people. Stanley Kahan, who wrote "Killer Joe" and other songs with Berns and worked with the Strangeloves when they were staff writers at Roosevelt Music, thought it was a great idea. "Bert Berns is the luckiest guy in the world," he told them.

The three songwriters began to develop an intricate cover story. The Strangeloves were three brothers—Niles, Miles, and Giles Strange—from Armstrong, Australia, on the edge of the outback. They were born to one mother, but have three different fathers, which accounts for the almost total lack of family resemblance. They were wealthy sheep farmers who made a fortune on a crossbreed called the Gottehrer sheep, registered with the Feldman-Goldstein Company. The band members adopted a severely exotic look with zebra-skin vests and matching African hair drums—not very Australian—carrying spears and brandishing boomerangs.

They met with Berns. He loved the track, but agreed with Wexler. He suggested writing a new set of lyrics—the sad truth of Bo Diddley's life was that a beat cannot be copyrighted—and he thought they should stick with the outrageous. Inspired by the X-rated novel and literary *scandal du jour, Candy* by Terry Southern and Mason Hoffenberg, that Berns had been reading, the four of them cooked up "I Want Candy." Berns also brought veteran session guitarist Everett Barksdale to drop some licks on the explosive existing track. Barksdale, who played for years in the Art Tatum Trio, used a jazzy arch-top electric and his playing has a crumbling, fleeting feel that skitters superbly across the bold, bashing beat of the drum-heavy track.

By the time the record came out in May 1965, Berns had brought Julie Rifkind to work at Bang. Rifkind, former promotion man at MGM Records and old-time record business guy, was well known enough in the industry to have his name featured alongside Berns in the trade advertisements announcing the label's first two releases—"I Want Candy" by the Strangeloves and "Shake and Jerk" by Billy Lamont, a fairly ordinary dance record Wexler picked up. The yellow label on the record showed a smoking gun.

"I Want Candy" took off, bumping the bottom of the Top Ten at number eleven on the pop charts (eclipsing the two other singles Berns had on the *Hot 100* at the time, "Here Comes the Night" by Them and "Baby I'm Yours" by Barbara Lewis on Atlantic). The Strangeloves hit the road on package tours with other top stars of the British Invasion— the Searchers, the Seekers, the Zombies, Freddie and the Dreamers, and the Dave Clark Five.

Berns sent them into Bell Sound for a week in July to cut an album. The three songwriters had recently caught the nightclub act of the Vibrations at an Upper East Side hot spot called Ondine's. Freshly reminded of the group's "My Girl Sloopy," written, as it was, by two key figures in their own career, the Strangeloves cut a version of their own that they called "Hang On Sloopy" for the album. When they went back out on the road, they included the song in their set.

At the end of a series of dates with the Dave Clark Five, the English rock group taped the Strangeloves playing the song and told the group they were going back to England to record the song as their next single. This was, like, the second biggest English rock group below the Beatles, thinking the Strangeloves' song was good enough to copy. The Strangeloves had been getting good response with it onstage. They decided they would release the song on a single as soon as they returned to New York, after one last show the next night in Dayton, Ohio.

The Strangeloves didn't play instruments other than their zebra-skin African hair drums and, without the tour's house band, backing them up in Dayton was a local group, Rick and the Raiders, who had been playing shows all summer for radio station WING. Guitarist Rick Zehringer graduated high school little more than a month before, and his fourteen-year-old brother Randy played drums in the quartet. Dressed in their new Beatles suits, ripping through Chuck Berry numbers, warming up the crowd for the Strangeloves, these raw, young rock and roll musicians set off bells for Feldman, Gottehrer, and Goldstein.

Backstage after the show, they asked the teenage musicians if they wanted to go to New York and make a record. They drove to the Zehringer home and woke up their parents. The next morning, they drove off together—the Strangeloves in one car and the mom and dad driving the other. The band members argued among themselves so much on the trip, the Strangeloves started calling them the Hatfields and the McCoys. They went straight into the studio. They used the instrumental track already recorded for the Strangeloves and had the boys sing over the existing recording. Sixteen-year-old Rick Zehringer—about to change that to Rick Derringer—laid down a guitar solo. When they heard the playback, people in the control room jumped up and yelled, "Number one."

Feldman, Gottehrer, and Goldstein went straight from the studio to look for Berns. They soon discovered that Berns and his wife were on his annual August vacation at Grossinger's, the same routine he had followed since he was a child. He and Ilene were there with Jeff Barry and Ellie Greenwich, Artie Butler and his wife. They had ridden their Harleys. The three Strangeloves piled in their car with an acetate and headed to the Catskills resort, hardly looking like typical patrons of the sedate, pastoral enclave. They walked up to the front desk, bearded, longhaired Feldman in cut-off jeans, Goldstein in shades and Hawaiian shirt, lanky Gottehrer looming behind them. The clerk took one look and said, "You must be looking for the Berns party."

They interrupted his dinner. The only place in the hotel they could find that had a phonograph player was the dance studio and it was locked. They broke in and played him the acetate on a portable phonograph. "That's my record," Berns said. "I want it."

Some cosmic movement in the rock and roll universe was bringing Berns's "My Girl Sloopy" back to life. Not only did the McCoys take the song number one on Bang Records in October, the label's first number one hit after less than six months in business, at the same time in England, the Yardbirds included a lengthy workout on the song on the band's first U.S. album.

From north of the border, Little Caesar and the Consuls, kings of Ontario rock and roll, recorded their slowed down, parenthetic "(My Girl) Sloopy" on Canada's Red Leaf Records, released in the United States the week before the McCoys single. Their version of "Sloopy" went number one in Canada, but made it only halfway up the Hot 100 in this country, where the band turned down offers to tour and appear on *American Bandstand* because all but one of the members had full-time jobs in Toronto.

Surf rock duo Jan and Dean included a version on their new *Folk 'n Roll* album. Hot on the heels of the McCoys hit, jazz pianist Ramsey Lewis, who made the hit parade that summer with an instrumental version of the r&b hit "The 'In' Crowd," was back on the charts with his "Hang On Sloopy." Berns and Farrell even made a reluctant Gil Hamilton—as Johnny Thunder—do "Everybody Do the Sloopy," which they put out on Diamond Records. By November, there were fifteen recorded versions of "Sloopy." The Dave Clark Five never got around to recording the song.

Arif Mardin, Ben E. King, George Treadwell, Ahmet Ertegun, Bert Berns

XVI.

Half as Much [1965]

B ERT BERNS'S SON, Brett Ben David Berns, was born on March 30, 1965. Jerry Wexler was the godfather. Bert's twenty-three-year-old bride was so unprepared for motherhood, his secretary had to be dispatched to buy the crib, the baby furniture, and all the rest before mother and child came home from the hospital. The birth of a grandchild brought no greater rapprochement with Berns's mother, who would infuriate her young daughter-in-law by showing up at the penthouse for Sunday dinner with her own food. Ilene took the baby to the park every day in his fancy English pram, the Rolls-Royce of baby carriages, and made her husband's dinner every night. Berns stopped on his way home at the butcher shop to pick up the bones and meat scraps that went into the Great Dane's nightly gluttony. His wife was not welcome at the office, but the dog was.

The world of rhythm and blues was changing and Motown Records was at the center of it. They were provong that rhythm and blues records oriented toward young whites could top the charts and that properly groomed and cultivated r&b acts such as the Supremes, the Temptations, Marvin Gaye, and others could be acceptable on the broadest levels of mainstream America. At the same time, Motown's acts and their records maintained enough authentic connection to the urban experience that they remained believable in the nation's black communities, where the mood was definitely darkening. The Motown acts represented the triumph of assimilation, the aspiration of integration, an ideal suddenly, surprisingly, coming under question. Rioters in the streets of Watts that summer appropriated the trademark cry of r&b disc jockey the Magnificent Montague when he especially liked a record, "Burn, baby, burn."

Soul was the word. Sam Cooke, shot to death in a seedy South Central Los Angeles motel in December 1964, moved strongly into the modern realm on his crowning posthumous single, the rousing, blaring big band blast of "Shake" that smelled richly of Memphis funk, and "A Change Is Gonna Come," the plaintive gospel cry that managed to articulate much of the deeper emotions behind the struggle for civil rights as almost pure metaphor. James Brown pledged his fealty to the new order, the announcement of his transformation carried by the very title of his latest hit, "Papa's Got a Brand New Bag."

At Atlantic, Berns was searching for his own sound on sessions with vocalists Tami Lynn and Wilson Pickett, trying to sail the shifting seas. His latest recordings with Ben E. King took the great vocalist even further into gospel-drenched emotions. These records were stamped with Berns's musical imprint. He was not jumping on bandwagons or copying already successful ideas so much as following his own natural progression, exploring new variations on the songwriting and production style he had been developing over the past four years, which, under Wexler's beneficent guardianship, was blooming with considerable magnificence.

Wilson Pickett made every kind of record a rhythm and blues artist could have over a career spanning more than four decades, but he never made another record like "Come Home Baby," the result of his three-song December 1964 session with Berns. Pickett had found a home on Atlantic by a circuitous route. He never earned a penny from "If You Need Me." Atlantic's Berns production of Solomon Burke buried Pickett's version, even though Burke and Pickett always admired one another and wound up performing the song together on concert stages occasionally.

Pickett, who spent more time picking cotton than going to school growing up in Alabama, began his career in gospel. He was singing both gospel with the Spiritual Five and secular music with the Falcons in Detroit, where he had moved at age sixteen to live with his auto worker father, when the Falcons' "I Found a Love" written and sung by Pickett, took off on the charts in 1962. He signed with Atlantic in early 1964 after Lloyd Price and Harold Logan were through with him. He produced his own first single for the label, a collaboration with songwriter Don Covay, "I'm Gonna Cry," that did nothing.

Instead of his customary gospel chorus on "Come Home Baby," Berns paired Pickett with the sole female voice of Tami Lynn, whose guttural growl rolls right into the foreground alongside Pickett's more mannered vocal, starting with a snaking *Ooh, yeah* inserted between the first two couplets over the introduction. The dialogue between the two vocalists takes hold on the chorus, while the horn section builds behind them, giving the production the grandeur of a Phil Spector record without the murkiness. Every detail of Teacho Wiltshire's arrangement—the spare verse accompaniment, the brassy crescendos, the muted trombone on the instrumental bridge—is in the front of the production. Pickett, unlike most lead vocalists on Berns productions, sounds slightly remote from the emotional content of the Barry Mann and Cynthia Weil song, reluctant to fully commit, but with the background vocalist singing rings around him on the chorus, literally, his reliance on a cool professionalism seems judicious. Wexler was astonished to find the session cost an astronomical $6,000, but he had to agree the record was beautiful. It never even charted.

Berns had already taken an interest in the Tami Lynn case, after Wexler signed the twenty-two-year-old jazz vocalist from New Orleans. Trumpeter Melvin Lastie, who was working with Latin bandleader Willie Bobo, had brought her to Wexler. Lastie knew Lynn from New

Orleans, where he and Harold Battiste started AFO, the sidemen's collective that produced the Barbara George hit, "I Know." Lynn started singing outside church as a teenager in New Orleans because the regular vocalist in the Alvin "Red" Tyler band didn't show up for a gig one night at a bar next door to where her aunt lived.

Lynn quickly became the favored younger sister to the group and they cut her singing a jazzy version of "Mojo Hannah" that Wexler heard her do at a disc jockey convention in St. Louis. When Wexler approached her about making records, she told him that she had other plans. "I'm going to be a speech therapist for retarded children," she said.

Two years later, she had moved to New York, where her father had always lived, and was singing jazz, opening for John Coltrane at Birdland, when Lastie brought her to Atlantic.

She stayed in the spare bedroom at the Bernses' apartment for several days. Lynn and Ilene were about the same age. They made dinner together and chattered. Berns played her dozens of records and acetates, trying to find material that she wanted to sing. He wanted her to pick the songs.

She selected a number written by Berns, "I'm Gonna Run Away from You"—a piece that recalled his 1963 record with the Wanderers, "You Can't Run Away from Me"—largely because she never heard anything like it. This exquisite record disappeared without a trace when it came out, also largely because nobody ever heard anything like it.* Songwriting was credited to Bert Berns, who started using that name instead of Bert Russell on his Web IV tunes, becoming just that much more his own man.

He also parked British session guitarist Jimmy Page in his spare bedroom on Page's first visit to New York. Page was stopping over at Berns's invitation on his way to Los Angeles, where he was romantically involved with songwriter/singer Jackie DeShannon (Berns cut

---

*Six years after its original release, British record producer John Abbey gave Berns's production a slight revision and the record went Top Five in the U.K. in 1971.

a song Page and DeShannon wrote together with Barbara Lewis). He introduced Page to Ahmet and Wexler and took him to an Atlantic session, where he strummed along uncredited because of the union and immigration.

Berns cut six tracks with Ben E. King on a double session in February, including Artie Resnick and Kenny Young's gimmicky "The Record (Baby I Love You)," which starts with the singer in a penny arcade recording the song. Berns plays it straight and King sings it to death, but it slipped off the charts after three unspectacular weeks. "Not Now (I'll Tell You When)" and the Berns-Ragovoy number "Cry No More" were strong records, but they didn't do any better. In all the fourteen songs Berns produced with King, nothing ever clicked. There were great records such as "Let the Water Run Down" or "That's When It Hurts," but Berns put King in such torment and despair, the singer could barely be recognized as the genial baritone of his previous singles from the Leiber and Stoller days.

At the same time, Berns was having no problems putting Barbara Lewis on the charts. Lewis, who two years before had come out of nowhere to rescue Atlantic after a long chart drought, was discovered by Ann Arbor deejay Ollie McLaughlin, a family friend who also discovered and managed the Battle Creek, Michigan, rock and roller who called himself Del Shannon ("Runaway"). Lewis had regional hits around Detroit before her big 1963 hit, "Hello Stranger," and even cut one session with the house band at the Motown studios while that operation was still small-time. Since her Atlantic hit, her subsequent releases had not performed up to expectations. Wexler decided to bring her to New York to record with Berns.

He found "Baby I'm Yours" by songwriter Van McCoy, who used to write for Florence Greenberg at Scepter and Leiber and Stoller at Trio but was now working out of April/Blackwood. It was the first time in her career that Lewis had been told what to sing—at age twenty, she wrote almost every song on the "Hello Stranger" album—and she didn't feel good about the number. It wasn't that she didn't like the song; it was that songwriter McCoy's assured vocal on the demo left little room for improvement, as far as she could see. Her first New York City session and she was not comfortable. Over the talk-back, her manager McLaughlin could not conceal his frustration, something she'd never seen before.

"Okay, Barb," he told her, "just go ahead and sing it, like what's good for you. Don't worry about your part. We can get that later. Let's just get the take. Get the orchestrations and the music right."

Lewis overdubbed her vocals weeks later in Chicago, kidded and chided into the performance by McLaughlin. She needn't have worried. Berns had her every step of the way. From the opening downbeat, he lays out a carpet of silken background vocals and soft, pillowy orchestrations that let the song do all the lifting. The effect is an effortless production that gently floats into streams of light and warmth, bathed in strings and horns. Lewis underplays the vocal magnificently and everything works. The song bubbled under the Top Ten at number eleven that summer.

Berns did two more sessions over the year with the subtle but immensely appealing songstress and came out of each with at least one powerful track: "Make Me Your Baby," which served as a fine follow-up for "Baby I'm Yours," likewise scraping the Top Ten at number eleven, and Goffin and King's "Don't Forget about Me," a tour de force production that may have been musically too demanding for the audience but featured Lewis brilliantly. She emerged from behind the mike at one session to find Berns in the control room wiping his eyes, moved to tears by her performance.

Berns worked hard keeping Atlantic in the Drifters business, pumping out a sparkling new single every three months by the vocal group, growing long in the tooth and far out of style. Including "Saturday Night at the Movies," which was released in December 1964, Berns managed to put six Drifters songs on the charts during the next year, although the group continued to experience diminished returns since the high point the previous summer of "Under the Boardwalk."

Berns ran into Tony Orlando in the elevator at 1650. "I always liked that record, 'Halfway to Paradise,'" he told the singer. "We ought to make some records together." Orlando, at loose ends since Aldon was sold, was between record deals. He had cut a lovely number with Bacharach and David for Epic that nobody heard and was beginning to work in publishing, thinking his singing career might be over at age twenty-one. A chance meeting in an elevator was all he needed for Berns to refresh his recollection.

Berns signed him to Atlantic. Orlando always wanted to be with the label and was even more thrilled when he was assigned to Atco, the label where his hero Bobby Darin had reigned. Berns did two of his songs with Orlando, a soulful vocalist who sang all those Drifters demos for Goffin and King, "Turn Around," and "Half as Much," but Wexler never released them.

Berns had very little time outside his Atlantic projects and the new company, although he did manage sessions with the Exciters, the group that made "Tell Him" a hit, now signed to Morris Levy and Roulette Records. Brenda Reid tore into two fiery new Berns compositions, "Run Mascara Run," and "There They Go," a bald rewrite of "Here Comes the Night," and Berns gave the productions the high drama of the other Exciters records ("Should hit fast and furious," said *Billboard*).

The Sal Mineo session was a favor for Miltie Ross, one of the regulars at Al and Dick's, a sleazy old big band pop singer who loved whores so much he married one. Ross was an oversized, shady character who always had something going in the background. If Miltie was around, the fix was in or somebody was looking for something they couldn't get regularly. He operated out of Award Music in the Brill Building, where he signed songwriters like Paul Kaufman ("Poetry in Motion") or Gregory Carroll ("Just One Look") when he wasn't at the racetrack. He had some deal with Atlantic to produce masters for the label with

Ruth Brown, Big Joe Turner, the Vibrations, and a few others. Berns cut the Hollywood movie star, just starting his slide down the backside of the bell curve, singing "Save the Last Dance for Me" for Big Miltie, who had a deal for Mineo at Fontana Records.

When Berns went back to England in May 1965, this time not only did Ilene and baby Brett join him, but also Wexler and his wife, Shirley. Phil Solomon installed the party in a service flat in Knightsbridge, around the corner from an old pub where Berns liked to dine. They arranged for an English nanny. Berns bought his wife her first British raincoat. Solomon called for them for dinner in a Daimler limousine.

Berns was scheduled to conduct sessions with Them for the group's coming debut album, but first he worked with another Belfast r&b act from the Maritime Hotel who called themselves the Mad Lads before Solomon renamed them Moses K and the Prophets, since there was already an American soul group called the Mad Lads. Berns met the group in a Soho nightclub and showed them a pair of songs on his acoustic guitar.

He took the band into Regent Sounds Studio on Denmark Street in central London, a seedy hole-in-the-wall where Andrew Oldham had been making all those Rolling Stones records. The control room was about the size of a small bathroom and the studio wasn't any bigger than a modest hotel room, but it got a great sound out of cramped conditions and egg carton ceiling. Berns knocked off a solid single with Moses K and the Prophets of a jaunty, Latinized Berns original, "I Went Out with My Baby Tonight," and a cover of the Drifters' "Answer the Phone," a record Berns had produced earlier in the year.

He spent most of the week at Regent Sounds recording Them, pretty much the hot new British rock group of the moment. "Here Comes the Night" was sitting atop the British charts. The band had been squeezed on the massive bill at the Empire Pool in Wembley in April for the year-end *New Musical Express* poll winners, even though the group's chart success was so recent Them hadn't figured in any of the voting. Nevertheless, there they were at a coronation of a new generation of British pop that assembled, under one roof, the Beatles, the Rolling Stones (the only occasion the two groups appeared on the same bill), the Kinks, the Animals, the Moody Blues, Freddie and the Dreamers, Dusty Springfield, among others. Them went on between Donovan and the Searchers and segued from their hit, "Here Comes the Night," into an unexpected seven-minute workup of "Turn On Your Lovelight," the staple barnstormer that closed the band's sets at the Maritime Hotel.

Berns did five songs at Regent Sounds with the band. "I Gave My Love a Diamond" was an old folk song well known from the version by Josh White (which Berns nevertheless copyrighted as songwriter), driven in this instance by a vibrato flourish from guitarist Jimmy Page. Berns's song about sending a lover away because she's too young, "Go On Home Baby," borrowed liberally from another old folk song, "Sloop John B," familiar from the Kingston Trio's first album, but sounded as tough as a Stones record. He pinched the background vocal part to the Berns-Farrell "My Little Baby" from Mickey & Sylvia's "Love Is Strange."

Van Morrison gives each vocal performance the kind of rusty razor blade intensity that Berns was accustomed to getting from his American rhythm and blues vocalists. His accent so thoroughly colored his singing, nobody noticed his ad lib at the end of his largely improvised "Little Girl," where he says "I want to fuck you." The gaffe was not discovered until it was released on a British charity album that was, as a consequence, subsequently recalled.

Berns also cut with Them the song he recorded the month before in New York with Tony Orlando, "Half as Much." It sounded like a goshdarn Garnet Mimms record.

If you find your baby's gone
And you don't know where or when.
You wonder, yes, you wonder

If you'll ever see him again.
Just remember, remember,
These simple words that I brought
Soon it won't hurt half as much
It won't half as much
No, it won't hurt half as much
As you thought.
—HALF AS MUCH (BERT BERNS, 1965)

The young men in Them sported bad attitudes, far beyond the cheeky wit of the Beatles or the surly hauteur of the Rolling Stones. After the band stood up the *New Musical Express* reporter three times for an interview, writer Keith Altham finally caught up with the musicians in a backroom of a pub near the studio. Morrison was sitting with Berns. "Fuck off," he told the reporter. "Can't you see I'm talking to Bert. You should be interviewing him—he's the genius."

Guitarist Billy Harrison picked his nails with a pocketknife while he gave short, angry answers to the hapless journalist, snapping off the interview by announcing he'd had enough "stupid questions." Morrison watched from the sidelines, while Berns strummed loudly on his guitar.

The Berns and Wexler party took a side trip to Paris, leaving infant Brett in the care of his English nanny. They checked into a deluxe suite at the Hôtel de Crillon, the seventeenth-century palace on the Place de la Concorde. While Shirley Wexler took Ilene Berns to the museums and showed her the Impressionists, their husbands did business with their French music contacts.

It was at dinner at the home of his French subpublisher, Gerard Tournier, where Berns made an alarming discovery. Tournier toasted Berns's great success over the meal and Berns pressed him for details. Tournier thought he had paid Bobby Mellin somewhere around $60,000 U.S. the previous year and estimated that 90 percent was for

Berns copyrights. Since Berns had been seeing checks from Mellin for something like $1,400, Berns smelled a rat.

Berns disliked the stuffy old bastard anyway, but to discover finally, irrefutably, that Bobby Mellin had been stealing from him, enraged Berns. But Mellin was prepared for subterfuge. He had learned of the pending sale negotiations between Atlantic and ABC. He threatened ABC privately that he was going to sue Atlantic over Berns and that buying the label would be "buying a lawsuit," thinking that Wexler would pressure Berns not to queer the deal. Berns nevertheless pressed litigation for an accurate accounting. Mellin countered by filing a dubious lawsuit against Atlantic (and other companies) over pieces of songs that didn't add up to much in the first place.

Regardless, documents for the sale to Atlantic Records were drawn up. ABC would pay $2,800,000 for Atlantic. The Erteguns and Wexler would receive three-year $35,000 contracts. It would have gone through, except for the pages and pages of warranties ABC's corporate attorneys demanded. Atlantic could never warranty the company paid all its royalties. Some company less scrupulous would have to be found if this company, which may have operated too long in the gray ethical/financial world of rhythm and blues, was going to be sold.

Mellin quickly lost a judgment to Berns and coughed up a $60,000 settlement. Berns also won the right to audit Mellin's international accounts. But now, Wexler was really growing panicky about selling the company.

Wexler went almost straight from Europe to Memphis with Wilson Pickett in May. He arranged with the Stax/Volt label that Atlantic distributed to bring Pickett into the Stax studio to work with the house band. Wexler was astonished at what he saw. After Tom Dowd came down to Memphis and tightened up the studio's equipment, engineering the classic *Otis Blue* album with Stax/Volt's Otis Redding in the process, the converted movie theater hummed with a sound all its own.

The house band was Booker T. and the M.G.'s, a tight-knit quartet, augmented by a few select regulars. There were no score sheets, no conductors, and no arrangers. They used what they called "head arrangements," which means they made it up as they went along, often communicated with nothing more than a discreet nod across the room. These musicians operated with a scary unity of purpose; eight arms and legs, one mind.

In this densely collaborative environment, Pickett shaped "In the Midnight Hour" with Stax guitarist Steve Cropper, and Wexler danced the jerk in the studio for the band so they could get the rhythm right. He came home with three fresh Pickett tracks, including this certain hit, and had been exposed to an entirely different approach to recording. The informality and ease that permeates Southern life extended to the Memphis recording sessions, far from the concert hall atmosphere of the New York studios.

At the same time, Ahmet Ertegun was eyeing the new rock scene. He recognized the male singer in Caesar and Cleo, a Los Angeles duo, as a former promotion man for his Los Angeles distributor and one of Phil Spector's toadies named Sonny Bono. His girlfriend was a background vocalist he knew from Spector sessions at Gold Star Studios in Hollywood, Cherilynn LaPier, known as Cher. Bono cooked up the act with arranger Harold Battiste, the brainy firebrand New Orleans sideman behind the AFO collective who moved to Los Angeles after it dissolved. They envisioned Bono as a kind of accessible version of Phil Spector and Cher as his girl groups. They cut a single for Warner Brothers, "Baby Don't Go," that flopped.

Ahmet flew to Los Angeles and signed the act, now called Sonny & Cher, unheard and unseen, for a $5,000 advance. The first record they made for Atlantic, "I Got You Babe," was not only a number one hit record three weeks in August in the United States, but also a huge smash across the world. Atlantic had never seen anything like it. The record was the company's saving grace, right as the ABC sale collapsed.

Ertegun next signed a rock band called the Rascals out of Long Island. The band, dressed in knee-high knickerbockers and Peter Pan collars, had been the summer's hot attraction in ritzy Southampton, where the Rascals pulled overflow crowds dotted with local celebrities such as Bette Davis to a funky wharfside discotheque called The Barge. Ahmet caught the band during the summer, but a number of labels showed interest. Sid Bernstein, busy producing the Beatles concert at Shea Stadium in August, managed the act (Bernstein, in fact, flashed a message, "The Rascals Are Coming," on the stadium scoreboard during the concert).

Phil Spector flew out to see the band play and made an offer, but the group signed with Atlantic largely because Ertegun would allow the Rascals to produce their own records (alongside Atlantic "supervisors" Tom Dowd and Arif Mardin, Nesuhi's new assistant, a brilliant Berklee College of Music graduate with the added advantage of being Turkish). The Rascals also liked the idea that they would be the only white rock group on the label. After a well-established outfit called the Harmonica Rascals screamed trademark infringement, the Atlantic legal department recommended a modifier and the group became the Young Rascals.

"I Ain't Gonna Eat My Heart Out Anymore," the group's first single, was recorded in September. Berns found the song by songwriters Pam Sawyer and Lori Burton, gave it to the band, and published it with Web IV. He was, above all, an Atlantic team player.

Bert Berns, Jerry Wexler

XVII.

I'll Take You Where the Music's Playing [1965]

B ANG RECORDS WAS exploding. With the label's first single, "I Want Candy," narrowly grazing the Top Ten, and five singles later, "Hang On Sloopy" grabbing the gold ring, the company was out of the gate like a shot. There was a power struggle from day one. Wexler wanted Julie Rifkind to report daily to Atlantic, even though he worked out of Bang at 1650 Broadway. Berns told him not to bother. Rifkind mapped out the distributors and handled the promotion and sales and Berns left him alone.

The quick success of Bang and Web IV caught the Atlantic partners by surprise. They never planned on the record label being successful—they had their own label, what did they want with another? What they did want was the half interest in Berns's publishing that they now held. Ertegun and Wexler forced out Rifkind and hired Bill Darnell, an old big band vocalist turned record plugger, to work out of the Bang offices. Wexler also put Atlantic's longtime independent payola consultant, Juggy Gayles, on the Bang account. Gayles had been around long enough to have plugged "God Bless America" for Irving Berlin.

Wexler called Berns on the phone three times or more daily. He carefully plotted with Berns the destiny of Bang Records, no detail too small for his attention. Berns may have thought he was running the label, but Wexler would go to any lengths to get what he wanted.

When "Hang On Sloopy" shot up the charts without benefit of a signed contract with Feldman, Gottehrer, and Goldstein, Wexler took over negotiations.

He staged a dinner for the fellows at his Great Neck place, a luxurious affair, servants waiting on everybody, bottles of fine wines uncorked, Cuban cigars smoked. Ahmet Ertegun was there, but not Berns. These outer borough kids had never seen anything like it. One bottle of the wine probably cost more than the clothes they were wearing, and Wexler, not much of a drinking man himself, made sure their glasses were always full. They signed the deal.

Berns met Andrew Loog Oldham and Tony Calder at the Bang office after George Goldner sent them over. These two British knuckleheads decided to start a record label while wheeling Oldham's Chevy Impala through London traffic down Park Lane on their way to a taping of the TV show *Ready Steady Go!* They pulled over at Marble Arch for Calder to make a call from a phone box to get price quotes on pressing records. The next weekend, they flew to New York to make business contacts.

Oldham, who discovered and managed the Rolling Stones, had long made a habit of flying to New York, if only to see the movies and buy the records. A former teenage assistant to fashion designer Mary Quant, Oldham idolized American record men like Phil Spector and George Goldner. These weren't people who simply had jobs in the record business and otherwise led dreary, vanilla lives. These were record men. Their work was their lives. They were a breed apart and operated by their own rules. They set the styles and pulled the strings. They had no British counterparts. Berns was one of these centurions of pop.

He played Oldham and Calder an acetate of the unreleased "Hang On Sloopy" by the McCoys. Oldham and Calder, who were about to start Britain's first independent record label, asked if they could acquire U.K. rights. Berns wanted a $500 advance. They had to pool their resources to give him the money, but they went home with the first single for their new company, Immediate Records. "Hang On

Sloopy" launched the label in high style; number five on the charts that fall in swinging England.

Berns went back into the studio for the first time in more than a year with Solomon Burke, using Felix Cavaliere of the Rascals on organ, and redid his magnificent "Baby Come On Home" with Burke. He cut a Motownesque girl group for Bang called the Witches singing the group's "She's Got You Now" and the Berns-Farrell song he did with Them in May, "My Little Baby," the first record he made for the new label, using the credit A Web IV Production.

He took the Losers, the house band from the Upper East Side niterie Ondine's, into the studio and did two songs written by the band's drummer for an Atco single. With the Lost Souls, another trendy Manhattan rock group from the East Fifty-Fourth Street discotheque Arthur, run by Richard Burton's ex-wife Sybil, Berns used three of his songs on a four-song session for Bang, including "I Gave My Love a Cherry" that he tried with Them.

Berns's "The Girl I Love" by the Lost Souls teetered on the edge of becoming a hit. (" . . . mighty impressive Bang bow," *Cash Box*; "Watch this one break out," *Billboard*). Over a jangly guitar drive, the vocalist moves from despair over losing "The Girl I Love" to entreaties for someone else to *come and get me before I fall in my tears and drown.* The second section of the song, the guitar now slashing, has the singer pleading with some new girl to *help me forget how she made me a man.* Over the course of a three-minute song, Berns juxtaposes these opposing emotions to keep the singer's turmoil in the foreground. The production catches the new rock sound of the moment, even though, as with his Them records, Berns used session musicians to substitute for some of the band's actual members.

At night, sometimes he and Ilene would climb aboard his Harley and ride down to the Village to grab a piece of pizza and catch a foreign film at the Waverly. Sometimes he would hit the art galleries on the weekends. He worked most of the time, office at day, sessions at night.

They had a modest sex life, tempered by his heart problems, but he couldn't fall asleep until his wife curled an arm and leg around him. He loved being a father. He thought his illness had left him sterile. He still flew through a couple of packs of cigarettes a day and there were always pill bottles lying around.

For his young bride, the routine was stultifying. He took her to Miami by train—Berns hated to fly—for the r&b disc jockey convention and she sunned herself by the pool while Berns schmoozed the dee-jays. He doted on the dog and she focused some of her resentments on Dino, who slept on their bed every night and could be powerfully flatu-lent. The giant Great Dane was untrained, clumsy, and liked to jump up and put his paws on people's shoulders. They quarreled about the dog. At one point, Ilene, who may have been somewhat unsophisticated, but was by no means any shrinking violet, laid down an ultimatum—the dog or me. Berns angrily moved out of the penthouse.

He complained aloud in the studio to Patti LaBelle and the Bluebelles, a girl group out of Philadelphia recently signed to Atlantic by Wexler. "I can always get another wife," he growled. The girls were a little shocked, but also secretly amused.

These four young ladies first hit the charts three years earlier with "I Sold My Heart to the Junkman" with a small Philly indepen-dent. Actually the record hit the charts before they did. They almost failed the audition without singing—the label head took one look and declared lead vocalist Patti Holte too plain looking and too black, but then he heard her sing.

The label chief named her Patti LaBelle and called the group the Bluebelles. The record by the Bluebelles was already on the charts—the recording had been done by another group signed to another label—but it was Patti Labelle and her three associates, Wynona Hendrix, Sarah Dash, and Cindy Birdsong, who lip-synched the record on *American Bandstand* before returning to the studio to rerecord the song themselves.

They had taken some decent shots on other labels and toured on r&b bills all over the country before Wexler signed the group. One of the first things they did for Atlantic was put some background vocals on a new Wilson Pickett recording from Memphis, "634-5789," and then Wexler turned them over to Berns to record.

Berns took them pop, pitching Patti LaBelle's high-flying vocals against a crashing wall of horns and strings on the powerful first single, "All or Nothing," from songwriters Pam Sawyer and Lori Burton, who wrote "I Ain't Gonna Eat My Heart Out Anymore," the song Berns gave to the Rascals. Berns tossed a song on the B-side cowritten with his wife, under the name Ilene Stuart, "You Forgot How to Love," a lot of the lyrics written by his wife after a marital spat.

Wexler had high hopes for the record. He circulated a typewritten letter over his signature to program directors and disc jockeys: "'Fantastic' is a word I rarely use, but I think our first Atlantic record with Patty and the Bluebells [sic] ALL OR NOTHING is just that— fantastic. I'm sure that after you listen to it, you'll agree that ALL OR NOTHING will be a Top 10 record."

The record sputtered around the bottom of the charts for a few weeks and then disappeared altogether. On the next single, Berns backed the A-side, LaBelle's star turn on "Over the Rainbow," with "Groovy Kind of Love," the first recording of a song by Screen Gems writers Toni Wine and Carole Bayer Sager that would become a number two hit the next year by British pop group the Mindbenders.

He did an updated version of "A Little Bit of Soap" with the Exciters on Bang that stirred some action but never charted. He also had them cover the old Russell Byrd song "You Better Come Home" and another Berns-Farrell piece, "You Know It Ain't Right," an echo from the "Here Comes the Night" rewrite, "There They Go." Berns didn't waste a lot of songs. He didn't like to waste even *parts* of songs. He was recording almost everything he was writing and working the catalog as hard as he could.

Ilene made her peace with Dino. There had probably never been any real question. She was clearly smitten with Berns, caught up in the world in which he walked, pulled into the whirlwind that was his life. Berns was a happy man, living a life full speed at the top, a prince of the industry, a master of Broadway.

He and Jeff Barry started spending a lot of time together, taking off during the day to shoot pool around the corner on Seventh Avenue for a nickel a ball. They bought each other pool cues. Berns, always flush with cash, was an easy touch for quick loans—twenty, fifty, a hundred, what do you need? He wasn't always so good at remembering to whom he loaned what. But when Barry owed him a quarter at the end of a pool session and had only bills in his wallet, Berns made him get change.

Barry, who liked to wear cowboy boots and hats, looked at Berns, a few years older, as a man's man. They tooled off on a road trip upstate on their Harleys. They left one of the motorcycles by the roadside after a flat tire and rode off on one bike into a rainstorm. By the time they found their way to the back door of an Italian restaurant, they were drenched and bedraggled.

They produced a Drifters record together, a serious effort at getting the group back up high on the charts, the first time the Drifters recorded any Barry-Greenwich songs. "I'll Take You Where the Music's Playing" made it halfway up the *Hot 100*. Although they hadn't spent that much time together before, Barry always liked Berns. When Barry had first started making hits, he found himself invited to Morris Levy's annual United Jewish Appeal fundraising dinner and seated between Levy and Berns. When the time came to write checks and Levy started to hound Barry to write a $10,000 check, Berns told Morris to leave the kid alone. Barry always recalled the kindness.

The fissures in the world of Jeff Barry and Ellie Greenwich were cracking open. The girl group sound that kept them at the top of the charts all the years before had evaporated. Barry was so busy running from studio to office to rehearsal, the New York police couldn't find him for ten days when they were looking for him on a murder charge (a case of mistaken identity). Greenwich, despite the blonde bouffant, eye makeup, and lipstick, was still basically the same innocent girl from Levittown. Barry, never a talker, grew ever more remote in their marriage. She felt the shadows play into her music. *Maybe I know that you've been cheating*, she wrote by herself in the back of a taxi, *but what can I do?*

Of course, she had to make it cheerful and use a major key.

With Shadow Morton, she and Barry cut an extraordinary Ellie Greenwich solo record for Red Bird, "You Don't Know," something slightly more mature than the teen romances they had been turning out for Lesley Gore and Connie Francis. It was going to be WMCA "Pick of the Week" until Jackie DeShannon's "What the World Needs Now Is Love" showed up. Leiber and Stoller made noises about sending her to England to promote the record, but Barry didn't see the point of her spending time working as a performer. There were always demos, sessions, new songs. Leiber and Stoller lost interest in the record and it slipped away.

Barry quietly started seeing a voluptuous young brunette who worked as studio receptionist at Mira Sound named Nancy Calcagno. In October, just before their third anniversary, Barry and Greenwich separated. Greenwich spent a lot of evenings at the Berns apartment with Bert and Ilene. They kept everything quiet for business reasons, but she was privately destroyed, trying to hang on to what she could.

The hits just kept coming at Red Bird. Leiber and Stoller came up with a lucky number one with the Ad Libs' "The Boy From New York City." They were looking for acts to launch an r&b subsidiary of Red Bird called Blue Cat and found a demo tape of this quintet from Bayonne, New Jersey, with the song written by an amateur, some friend of the group. Leiber loved the jive talk lyrics—*he's really down, but he's no clown*—and Artie Butler's cooking chart finished the package.

Goldner was a force of nature. He promoted those records up the
charts by himself. He had Johnny Brantley, one of Alan Freed's old bag-
men, running around the country distributing largesse. Goldner loved
hit records and he avidly attended playbacks at the studio. Dressed
impeccably, he would ceremoniously place a chair in the middle of
the control booth, and when the playback finished, he would stand up
and smash the chair against the wall and demand to hear it again. This
happened so often that the studio, understanding that he was a regular
client, built a breakaway stool for Goldner, but it wasn't as satisfying to
throw and didn't leave marks on the wall. Goldner was also losing at
the racetrack again. There were a lot of meetings behind closed doors
in his office with large, unattractive men. Everybody else in the office
looked the other way.

Goldner's wife's name was Grace, but he called her Mona, and they
could fight. She had that hot-blooded Latin temperament and a foul
mouth. They got into it during an awards dinner sitting next to Hy Weiss.
"Oh yeah," said Goldner's wife loud enough for all the table to hear,
"you didn't talk like that last night when I was licking your asshole."

At one point, Goldner left town on a business trip with his girlfriend, but sneaked back into town early without telling his wife so
he could spend still more time with the dame. His wife got wind and
went crazy looking for him. She phoned Jerry Leiber at home and interrupted his son's birthday party with all the little Rothschilds running
around their Central Park West place. She started screaming a blue
streak and all the children listening in on the extension picked up her
chant: "motherfucker, motherfucker, motherfucker." Goldner was not
Leiber and Stoller's kind of people.

Leiber hadn't heard from Jerry Wexler in some time and was mod-
erately surprised to find him on the phone. Wexler wanted to talk
about merging the Atlantic and Red Bird operations. He proposed a
meeting. Leiber and Stoller hated the record business. They hated
the record business when they were unsuccessful at it. If anything,

being successful only made them hate it more. They liked music. They retained both their youthful enthusiasm and gruff, hip cynicism about the music. It was the record business they hated. Goldner and his unsavory associates were difficult to ignore. The Erteguns and Wexler offered a possible solution.

A meeting was arranged for the Oak Room at the Plaza Hotel, a dark-paneled, subdued brasserie more accustomed to Park Avenue dowager luncheons than high-powered business meetings. Leiber and Stoller had come to increasingly distrust Goldner, but they weren't savvy enough in the sales and distribution end of the business to know if he was stealing from them. One of the advantages of joining forces with Atlantic was that Goldner would be fully contained, flanked by the Erteguns and Wexler, who would know. Stoller pointed out to Leiber, if they signed one more hit act, they could be stuck in this damn record business forever.

Leiber and Stoller brought Goldner and their attorney, Lee Eastman, to the luncheon. Wexler arrived with both the Erteguns. Goldner started gulping martinis. He quickly grew insulting toward Ahmet, which caught Leiber and Stoller by surprise. An uncharacteristically imperious Goldner acted as if he was going to run the company after the merger. Eastman, too, raised objections and argued with Wexler. Somewhere along the line, Ahmet got the idea that Wexler had sold him out to Leiber and Stoller.

He knew Wexler wanted desperately to unload the company—his company, not Jerry Wexler's company—for some time, but it never mattered to Ahmet, one way or the other. He was certainly less inclined to sell than Wexler. Since the ABC deal fell through, only the latest in a long line of Wexler scenarios, it had been Ahmet who rescued the company with the Sonny & Cher record. He felt utterly betrayed by Wexler, whom he knew to be capable of the worst sort of treachery, but that he would conspire with these two knaves whom they practically invented only added to the insult.

The meeting went haywire quickly. As Leiber and Wexler exchanged bewildered looks, the Erteguns were gone before anybody could say anything. Not only were Leiber and Stoller still stuck in the record business, but also, since Goldner clearly set out to sabotage the meeting from the start, it would appear that their suspicions about their partner were well founded.

A dark cloud hovered over the Red Bird offices. Their marriage may have been disintegrating, but Barry and Greenwich were still one of the top songwriting teams in the country. They had picked up another slew of awards at that year's BMI dinner and all Ellie wanted to know about was their marriage. "I don't know," he told her.

In December 1965, shortly before Christmas, Jeff Barry and Ellie Greenwich obtained a Mexican divorce. Now it was over, but their careers were still entwined. They agreed to continue working together and, for business reasons, would keep up a front. The divorce would be kept secret. She pondered her circumstances with some bitterness as she wrote out cheery replies to that year's Christmas cards to the couple.

Jeff Barry, Neil Diamond, Ellie Greenwich, Bert Berns

XVIII.

Up in the Streets of Harlem [1966]

EVER SINCE HE was a kid, Carmine DeNoia Jr. was always called Wassel. At six-foot-six, two hundred–plus, Wassel was not little anymore but a bookmaker who frequented Broadway and kept his finger in the music business. Wassel was no made man—his brother John (J. J.) DeNoia was—but he knew all those guys. His father was a famous Broadway character; Damon Runyon based Nicely-Nicely from *Guys and Dolls*, on Wassel's dad, a celebrated trencherman who once ate thirty-six servings of lasagna in an eating contest. Wassel grew up on the streets of East Harlem alongside Joey and Patsy Pagano.

Joey Pagano was a crazy, violent killer, short and swarthy, known by all the bosses of the New York families as uncontrollable and unaffiliated, a rare freelance thug. He went down in a bankruptcy fraud beef in December 1964 after milking dry the Murray Packing Company in New York City. Pagano helped arrange an $8,500 loan for the company, where he worked as a salesman. Before long, Pagano had been named president of the company, cosigner of every check. He sold meat at below-cost prices to a Mob-owned wholesaler and drained the company of $745,000 worth of merchandise in three months, leaving Murray Packing bankrupt and suppliers across the country holding the bag.

His younger brother Patsy Pagano, secretary-treasurer of Bricklayers Local 59, was fresh out of the joint. He had a varied background. He and his brother were nothing more than neighborhood punks when they were recruited by Joe Valachi. Long before he became the Feds' most celebrated stool pigeon, Valachi used the Paganos for a couple of hits in the early fifties. Patsy was a Genovese family soldier who ran the New Jersey docks for boss Tony Strollo. He put together an enormously successful heroin smuggling operation from France and, in 1956, took a three-year fall for bribing an IRS official and five more years consecutive on narcotics charges. Patsy and Wassel maintained such a close working relationship that singer Freddie Scott thought Patsy was his manager, not Wassel.

When Wassel signed the former Aldon demo singer to Columbia Records, the elite label's patrician president, Goddard Lieberson, gave Wassel an under-the-table signing bonus of twenty thousand "clean" albums to trade at Colony Records. In the Broadway music business, records were wampum and Colony was the trading fort.

A "clean" album—one that didn't carry any marks identifying it as a promotional copy—could be returned for full credit, and if a record company happened to press more copies of an album than the accounting department counted, they could easily end up entering this underground economy out the back door of the label. Even the white glove fat cats at Columbia Records understood how this worked. If you knew the right people, large amounts of records could be sold at discounts for cash, useful in certain off-the-book expenditures, and where there is cash, there are the racket boys. Hoods were plentiful in the record business, and not just small-time gunsels either.

Nobody had to look further than the card game at Roulette Records at 1631 Broadway, where the FBI kept a telescope trained from a room across the street in the City Squire Hotel. One of Levy's silent partners in Roulette, Dominick Ciaffone, was an older, respected member of the Genovese family also known by the name Swats Mulligan and a frequent visitor to the office. His nephew was Levy's long-standing associate, Tommy Vastola, Alan Freed's old manager who continued to keep his hand in show business, alongside fur warehouse heists, illegal gambling operations, loan sharking, and a wide variety of business enterprises that kept him in close contact with the DeCavalcante family of New Jersey, while maintaining ties with the Colombo gang and operating an outfit of his own around Manhattan.

Vastola took over handling the career of Jackie Wilson in 1961 with his associate Johnny Roberts. He previously had managed not only the Cleftones, but also r&b voodoo priest Screamin' Jay Hawkins, another fixture on the Alan Freed concert bills. He also picked up a piece of Queen Booking. Started by the queen herself, Dinah Washington, and run by her former maid, Ruth Bowen, the agency was one of the few black-owned operations in the business and booked dates for a wide variety of high-priced rhythm and blues talent. After Washington's death in 1963 at age thirty-nine from an accidental overdose of sleeping pills, Bowen took on a number of questionable partners.

Vastola, a fixture at the Queens office, met Sammy Davis Jr. through the agency, and the two struck up a relationship that spanned the business and personal. Jackie Wilson's previous manager, Nat Tarnopol, who ran Brunswick Records in partnership with Decca Records, turned over Wilson's affairs to the gangsters after he decided to devote himself full-time to running the label, where Wilson also recorded. Before long, Vastola's influence over the label extended to him cutting deals with other artist managers to sign acts to Brunswick and helping himself to kickbacks from the advance. Wilson, "Mr. Excitement," who made his living in the often treacherous, cash-only world of a rhythm and blues attraction on the road, found having ice-cold Johnny Roberts on the job meant fewer problems collecting fees.

Everybody knew Morris Levy was connected. It was what allowed him to be as difficult as he was. Levy prided himself on being a character. He could be disingenuously charming, but he could also be bluntly intimidating. He loved money and hated to pay royalties, rarely bothered to, in fact. He grew up in the Bronx running the streets as children with Genovese lieutenant Vincent "The Chin" Gigante. The doorman at the Majestic, where the target lived, made Gigante as the gunman in the unsuccessful 1957 hit of Mob captain Frank Costello, who earned the right to live out his life in quiet retirement by refusing to rat out Gigante.

The shooter made off that night in a car the cops always figured was driven by another rising Genovese star, Tommy Eboli, who knew Levy since he was a teenager running his little nightclub darkroom racket. Eboli, who was also known as Tommy Ryan, went back to the original Lucky Luciano gang. He managed Gigante's brief prizefighting career. His own career in the sport ended after he climbed over the ropes and beat the hell out of a referee whose judgment he disputed during a middleweight match by one of his fighters at Madison Square Garden in 1952 (he went back to the dressing room and, with his brother, also beat up the matchmaker). He was convicted of assault and banned for life from the sport.

Among Eboli's many and varied business interests were cigarette machines and jukeboxes, which made his company a valued customer of New York area record distributors—all long before he became the best friend of Bert Berns.

Nate McCalla often played in those card games at Roulette. He was an extra-large black man who could affix a highly severe look on his face but could also be warm and affable. Reputedly a former master sergeant in the military police, McCalla was Levy's close friend and enforcer. Physically imposing, tall, wide McCalla was the man for tough jobs.

In addition to his work with Levy, McCalla also ran a number of record business operations with Sonny Franzese, the dapper don of the Colombo family who looked like prizefighter Rocky Graziano and was tossed out of the army during World War II as a homicidal psycho. Among other enterprises, McCalla and Franzese managed girl group chart-toppers the Angels, whose "My Boyfriend's Back" put songwriters Bob Feldman, Richard Gottehrer, and Jerry Goldstein at number one for the first time.

Franzese loved the glamour of the record business and knew people all over 1650 Broadway. He was a silent partner in Kama Sutra Productions, independent production and music publishing guys who held the paper on the Shangri-Las before Red Bird signed the girls. When Goldner tried to muscle Kama Sutra out of the deal through Morris Levy, Franzese quickly straightened that out behind the scenes.

McCalla and Franzese were also welcome visitors to the Scepter Records office. Actually, Sonny Franzese was welcome pretty much anywhere he wanted to go. Songwriter Richard Gottehrer watched in amazement one night, joining Franzese for a sold-out show at the Copa, while waiters scurried around, pushing aside already seated tables, to bring a fresh table out of the back so that the don could have front-row seating for his party. He was the show business Godfather. Sinatra made a point of kissing his ring while Franzese was having dinner one night at Al and Dick's with his capo, Joe Columbo.

Nate McCalla owed some dough to a loan shark around Broadway named Sammy Bush. McCalla, who knew Sammy would be looking for him, dropped by Feldman, Gottehrer, and Goldstein's office and asked them to tell Sammy he was expecting a little money in a couple of weeks, he was leaving town in the meantime, but he was good for it.

A week later, Gottehrer and Goldstein, walking back to the office, were shocked to see their partner Bobby Feldman backed up against the office building by a pair of large, intimidating hoodlums who wanted to know where was Sammy's $7,500. These business associates of Sammy's were unwilling or unable to make any important distinction between the absent Nate McCalla owing the money and birds in hand. But, as they were not entirely unreasonable men, they agreed to meet the three at the same time, five days later, at the same place, on the sidewalk outside 1650 Broadway.

Five days later, still no McCalla, the hapless songsmiths decided to meet the thugs and frankly admit they didn't have the money. As they approached the pair in front of the building at the appointed time, Gottehrer noticed over their shoulders a taxicab pulling up to the sidewalk and emerging from the backseat his nightclubbing buddy John "Sonny" Franzese.

"Uncle John," Gottehrer shouted, steering a path around the waiting thugs to the outstretched embrace of the Colombo underboss. When he turned around, they were gone.

A week after that, Gottehrer was riding the elevator down at 1650 Broadway when it stopped at another floor and the same two hoods walked in the cab. Gottehrer braced himself. "Hey, sorry 'bout all that," said one. "You don't owe us any money. We didn't know you was connected."

Gottehrer went up to the racetrack at Monticello with Nate and Sonny and a Jewish fixer named Morris Spokane, who had his hooks into Florence Greenberg. She gave him a piece of the company to stop the bootleggers, who were Spokane's buddies in the first place. These guys had a horse wired in one race, but the trainer overjacked the nag with the drugs and the damn horse dropped dead on the track, only after everybody got their bets down.

There were guys running around under the clubhouse with their guns out, looking for the trainer. Spokane told everybody he couldn't get their money back, but he could get them some clothes. He drove them all into downtown Monticello to a men's clothing store and made the owner come down with his wife and open the store. They lost at the track, but they loaded up with sweaters and jackets on the way home. These guys were a million laughs.

Jerry Leiber was on his way to the office when he stopped and bought a pair of suspenders for his boys, Oliver and Jed, from a sidewalk stand. He was spending several days a week with the family at their East Hampton place those days, less time in the city. He was walking down Broadway when a large, genial black man sidled up beside him, stretched his arm over Leiber's shoulder, and smiled. "You're Jerry Leiber, aren't you?" he said.

Leiber did not know Nate McCalla, but he was frightened as the man explained that he and some friends wanted to talk to him and steered Leiber into a little Broadway deli on the same block as the Brill Building that he had never noticed before. In the back, sitting at the flimsy Formica tables while a couple of other large goons hovered behind him, was Sonny Franzese.

"I wanted to meet our new partner," he said.

Leiber sat in terror as the mobster bantered with him, ordering Leiber something to eat, talking in riddles about Catholics going to see their priest when they're in trouble. "Where does a Jewboy go when he's in trouble?" he asked.

"To his lawyer," said Leiber. Everybody laughed.

"No," said Franzese. "A Jewboy goes to his rabbi, and right now, I'm your rabbi."

Leiber quickly realized that George Goldner had fallen in arrears with shylocks, and all those recent closed-door meetings everybody tried so hard to ignore at the office, all those strange visitors using the conference room and leaving with stacks of albums, had led to this sordid, scary scene under fluorescent lights in the back room of this two-bit deli. Franzese noticed the paper bag with the suspenders. "You got kids," he said. "I got kids, too." A chill rippled through Leiber.

Back at the office, Leiber and Stoller angrily confronted Goldner, who picked up the phone and called Morris Levy. While his two partners listened, Goldner railed at Moishe about the mobsters snatching Leiber—he used the Yiddish term for gangsters, *richtiga*—but it was a charade strictly for the benefit of Leiber and Stoller. The songwriters were worried. Leiber sought the advice of his father-in-law Saemy Rosenberg, who invited Leiber to join him for lunch with his close friend Guy de Rothschild at Luchow's, a century-old restaurant near Union Square. "What do they want from you, Jerry, money?" his father-in-law said. "Anything you can buy for money is cheap."

On a chilly Monday morning in March, Leiber and Stoller walked into their partner's office at Red Bird Records, a Brill Building suite adjacent to the Trio Music offices. Goldner, dressed as always like a prosperous banker, his diamond pinkie ring matching his cuff links, was reading the *Daily Racing Form*, his feet on his desk.

"We want to sell you the company," they told Goldner, who thought they were kidding, at first, and then complained he didn't have enough money. They told him the price for their two-thirds of the label was $1.

That morning, afraid he would go to the track and lose anything he had, his wife had taken all Goldner's cash out of his wallet before he left for work. Goldner didn't even have $1. Stoller extracted a bill from his pocket and handed it to Goldner, who, somewhat bewildered, nevertheless passed along the dollar bill to Leiber. Leiber and Stoller left his office out of the record business. The next day workmen put up a wall between the offices.

STILL WORKING AT the Leiber and Stoller offices, Jeff Barry and Ellie Greenwich, freshly divorced, brought Neil Diamond up to the Bang Records office for him to play his songs for Bert Berns. He sat on the couch and strummed his blacktop Everly Brothers model Gibson. Berns liked what he heard.

Greenwich met the young songwriter when she was hired to sing background vocals on one of his demos ten months earlier, before her marriage collapsed. She and Barry first took Diamond to Leiber and Stoller, who signed him for three months as a songwriter at Trio Music. But Barry and Greenwich wanted more. They decided to sign Diamond to a partnership, Tallyrand Music, split fifty-fifty between Diamond and the then-married couple. They went into their own pockets to pay Diamond his $150 weekly salary, twice what he was making at Trio Music. Leiber and Stoller finally used one of his Trio Music songs,

"Sunday and Me," with Jay and the Americans. Diamond moved into a small Long Island house with his pregnant wife.

Diamond grew up in Brooklyn, where his father ran a dry goods store. As a teenager, he heard another camper at a liberal summer camp they attended play a song the other kid had written for folksinger Pete Seeger. Young Diamond went home and started writing songs. He made a couple of records, including a big-time single on Columbia that came and went. He showed songwriter Artie Resnick a crumpled cocktail napkin from his pocket with his name embossed, a souvenir from the label's little reception for his record release.

Despite many years knocking around the Midtown music scene, he had failed to make any lasting impression until Ellie Greenwich heard him.

The twenty-five-year-old songwriter had bounced among various Broadway music publishers for years without getting many of his songs even recorded. When he met Greenwich, he had been working for months by himself in a room he rented above Birdland on Fifty-Second Street where he installed a pay phone so he wouldn't be tempted to waste time and money making calls.

Berns shared the enthusiasm of Barry and Greenwich. He signed Diamond to Bang and took personal interest in every part of Diamond's work for the label. He participated in all the preproduction meetings and brought engineer Brooks Arthur onboard. Berns told Arthur he thought Neil Diamond was like an Elvis. When Barry and Greenwich heard a guitar lick they liked, Diamond expanded on the figure and came back with a piece of Latinized rock and roll right down Bert Berns's alley that he called "Money Money."

When they played it for Berns, he complained. "What's with this 'Money, Money' stuff?" Berns said. "It should be 'Baby, Baby' or 'Cherie, Cherie.' That's it—'Cherry, Cherry.'"

Barry put the finishing touches on the chorus in minutes. They took Artie Butler into Dick Charles Studios on Seventh Avenue to cut a demo. Diamond played guitar. Session musician Dick Romoff played upright bass and Butler handled piano and organ. There were no drums.

When Barry and Greenwich emerged from the first official Bang sessions for Diamond in February 1966, they had three songs—"Solitary Man," "I Got the Feeling (Oh No No)," and a fully produced "Cherry, Cherry" with drums and a horn section. Berns liked the demo better. He also liked "Solitary Man" as the first single for mid-February. BANG RECORDS PROUDLY ANNOUNCES THE BIRTH OF A GREAT NEW ARTIST said the full-page trade magazine ads.

In little more than six months, eight of the first fifteen releases by Bang Records had hit the charts. Berns was featured on the cover of *Record World* magazine in February, talking about his upcoming sessions with the Drifters for Atlantic and the pending release on Bang by a new artist who would use all three names, Neil Leslie Diamond.*

Berns told *Record World*,

I'll only record a song if I think it's a hit. Record the best artist with a mediocre song and results are going to be mediocre. And a good song has to have a strong point of view. That's what I've tried to write for the new Drifters session—a song with a point of view. Their best songs had it—"Under the Boardwalk," "Up on the Roof." When I record Solomon Burke, I have to give him a tune that is very meaningful in performance. He couldn't sing something like "Everybody do the something or other." I was with him once when a fan—a grown man—came up to him with tears in his eyes and said, "Solomon, when you sing, you're singing about me."

The rhythm and blues world struggled to keep pace with the changes in the black community. Berns knew the music was in transition. "I want to do more r&b," he told *Record World*, "because, for one

---

*Eice Cherry and Noah Kaminsky were two pseudonyms Diamond contemplated for his Bang Records debut before settling on his given first and last names, without the middle name, Leslie.

reason, r&b artists sustain longer than most pop artists. Right now I have the Exciters on the label, although they haven't recorded a soul song yet." Soul, he said, was elusive. "I can't think of any white artists who have it," he said, "because soul is more than saying 'ah' for 'I.' It's something that comes from within—an artist's singing, and frequently, writing, about something he uniquely feels."

The civil rights movement had long before entered the soul idiom. The songs gave voice to a nation's unspoken thoughts—a fresh soundtrack for changing times, a bulletin board on the country's wall—and, in turn, spread the word in profound, immeasurable ways. The Impressions brought "Keep On Pushing" to the charts, and even the steadfastly populist Motown label invoked the call for unity in "Dancin' in the Streets." At the same time Stokely Carmichael demanded "black power," the healing gospel impulse was trained on the black community from their radios.

Soul was the leading edge of black Americans' newfound sense of self-awareness; they heard their language in the songs and saw themselves in the music, where they could not as easily find their lives reflected or represented in all-white mass media such as *Leave It to Beaver* television or John Wayne movies. Stevie Wonder's "Uptight (Everything's Alright)" on the radio was not just pop music; it was the sound of liberation, a celebration of all-black America coming out from the shadows.

Also like the civil rights movement, soul music seemed to emanate most radiantly from the Deep South. "Hold On I'm Coming" by Sam & Dave, the duo Wexler assigned to the Memphis label Atlantic distributed, was only the latest killer soul side to come out of the Stax studios. Wexler sent Wilson Pickett back two more times to Memphis after "In the Midnight Hour" before Stax owner Jim Stewart banned any further outside production by the label.

Whether Stewart's slamming shut the door was a result of Pickett being such a pain in the ass or Stewart's desire to retain the signature sound of the studio and house band Booker T. and the M.G.'s for his own artists, he deprived Stax staff writers such as Steve Cropper of opportunities. Cropper's "634-5789" from Pickett's final Memphis sessions hit the charts in February. But almost as soon as Wexler was shut down in Memphis, a record came out of nowhere from a small Alabama backwater that brought a studio in Muscle Shoals to the attention of Jerry Wexler.

Rick Hall had been at the center of a small, disparate enclave of struggling music business professionals around Florence, Alabama, since he recorded the 1962 hit "You Better Move On" with local singer Arthur Alexander (who wrote the song) at his Muscle Shoals studio in an old candy and tobacco warehouse on the road to Wilson Dam. Joe Tex cut his 1964 breakthrough, "Hold What You've Got," at Muscle Shoals. Hall did okay himself putting out Jimmy Hughes records on his FAME label.

A small cadre of songwriters and musicians developed around the area. But Hall didn't hear the song as a hit when Percy Sledge, a twenty-five-year-old hospital orderly who was Jimmy Hughes's cousin, first brought his group, the Esquires, to Hall's studio. Songwriter Dan Penn did hear something and suggested they go see Quin Ivy, who Penn knew was starting a studio in nearby Sheffield.

They caught a magic instrumental track with a set of descending chords on the Hammond B-3 organ, but Ivy wanted them to change the lyric, so "Why Did You Leave Me" became "When a Man Loves a Woman." When they were done, they had no idea what to do other than take the tape over to play for Rick Hall, who immediately sent the track off to Jerry Wexler at Atlantic. Wexler quickly cut a deal for the master with the neophyte producer, who rejected Wexler's suggestion that he add his own name to the songwriting credits. Ivy thought that would be dishonest.

Wexler also sent the tape back to record over because the horns went flat on the fade. Back at the studio, they puzzled over the prospect, took a couple of passes at rerecording the track, but, in the end, sent the serendipitous original back to Wexler, who apparently didn't realize until sometime after the record was released that they put out the first version with the out-of-tune horns. "When a Man Loves a Woman" by Percy Sledge was not only a number one hit when it was released that April, 1966, but it was also one of the defining moments in the emerging sound of soul.

When Wexler sent Pickett down the next month to Muscle Shoals, the singer looked out the plane window as it landed and saw black people picking cotton. He was met at the airport by Hall, who Pickett had no idea was white. In fact, to Pickett's immense surprise, the entire Muscle Shoals scene—the songwriters, the studio musicians—were young white Southerners.

Hall came from country music, but he was trying to establish himself in the business, not pursue a particular musical vision, when this regional soul scene began to coalesce around his operation. The young musicians who came around were a different matter. Dan Penn pinballed between singing like Ray Charles, James Brown, and Bobby "Blue" Bland. He was a teenager as thoroughly drenched in this music as anyone. He wasn't pretending or imitating and he was like a natural wonder to the other Muscle Shoals musicians, who admired his level of expression.

These white Southern musicians belonged to a new generation schooled in black music at the source, from radio stations such as Memphis's WDIA, all-black broadcasters since 1948, that swept through the entire South in 1954 after adding a mighty fifty-thousand-watt transmitter. At nights on Nashville's WLAC, the white deejay John R.—John Richbourg—cut another clear channel swath through the South, reaching as far north as Brooklyn, playing the race records and making with his *Amos 'n' Andy* jive. A twist of the dial, and black culture, hidden away from their parents in a more segregated era, was readily accessible. For this generation of Southerners, the real divide was not so much black and white as rich and poor. These were the musicians behind the new Southern soul.

The Drifters practically epitomized the calcified, old-fashioned rhythm and blues, with the group's lineage extending back to the bad old days of conks and Jim Crow. As he told *Record World*, Berns carefully constructed "Up in the Streets of Harlem" as a bid for renewed relevance by the group.

Borrowing from the kind of social realism Mann and Weil used in the Animals' "We Gotta Get Out of This Place" (which would have been a Barry Mann solo single on Red Bird if his publisher hadn't pulled the plug at the last minute) or their "Kicks" by Paul Revere and the Raiders, an alarmist but tuneful antidrug screed apparently inspired by the ongoing dissolution of their colleague Gerry Goffin, Berns plants the Drifters almost defiantly at 125th Street, far north of their fabled neon lights on Broadway.

Berns gives the record an introduction with a distant echo of "Tell Him" and rides into the chorus on a lightly sinister Cubano groove, as he shoehorns a boy–girl subtext into his harsh landscape of *tenements and dirt*. It is a pseudoepic that tries too hard. *Billboard* figured the other side as the potential hit—baritone vocalist Charlie Thomas singing the old Solomon Burke album track Berns wrote three years before with Ertegun, Leiber, and Stoller, "You Can't Love 'Em All"—although the optimistic review ("should quickly re-establish the talented group on the charts") did not prove true.

The third song he cut at the January session at Atlantic Studios, a simple, sentimental remake of the old Dean Martin hit "Memories Are Made of This," made a little noise on the pop charts when it was released in March, but "Up in the Streets of Harlem" was really the last swing for the grandstands by the storied group. Neither side of the single even bubbled under.

Still, there was much to celebrate. Wexler sent a limousine to pick up Mr. and Mrs. Berns and bring them to the dinner at his Great Neck

mansion. In under a year, Bang Records had turned out to be successful beyond anybody's imagination. Wexler summoned all four partners
and their wives for a celebration dinner. Mica Ertegun attending such
affairs made it a rare event indeed.

Prosperity smiled on all their enterprises. Atlantic was once again
flush with hits. "Good Lovin'," the second single by the white rock
group the Young Rascals, earned a number one hit earlier in the year.
During the first quarter, the label kept nine or ten singles on the *Hot
100* every week. Stax was hot for Atlantic, with hits by Sam & Dave,
Otis Redding, and Carla Thomas on the charts.

Sonny Bono pulled something of a fast one and signed Cher as a
solo artist to United Artists. Her solo singles were currently doing better than their Sonny & Cher duo records for Atlantic, where the previous year they clicked with three crucial Top Tens on Atco (including
the worldwide monster "I Got You Babe"). But Wilson Pickett was selling records for Atlantic and there was that massive number one hit
by Percy Sledge out of Muscle Shoals. Furthermore, album sales on
Atlantic doubled from the previous year, the company benefitting from
an exploding market in long-playing albums of pop music. Ahmet even
brought Bobby Darin back to Atlantic, who earned his first Top Ten in
three years with "If I Were a Carpenter."

Life was good at Atlantic Records, although Wexler still hoped to
sell the company. He was putting together a package behind the scenes
that he hoped would play better than the abortive ABC sale. Wexler
could never be satisfied with success. He always wanted more. Berns
would be surprised to find out how much more.

After a lavish dinner, served by tuxedo-clad black servants,
washed down by vintage French wines, as the men lit cigars and
sniffed their brandy glasses, Wexler delivered his pitch. The entire
Web IV deal had been so successful—the publishing company, as
well as the record label—everyone was proud of Berns and felt it was
time to make a real partnership with all equal partners—25 percent

apiece. It was an outrageous proposal that was against Berns's own best interests.

As Wexler spoke, Ilene Berns felt anger rising. She knew her husband would be furious, but she also knew he would give the bastards what they wanted just because they asked. It wasn't fair. Even if he changed his mind, she knew he would never go back on his word. She spoke up.

"Why would he want to do that?" she said. "You already have your company. You already have half of Bert's company. This is Bert's baby."

Wexler slammed his hand down on the table, stood up, grumbled something about talking business around women, and stormed off.

She was right. Berns was angry with her. When they climbed in the back of the limousine, he told her she embarrassed him. "Bert, I love you," she said, and told him that Wexler and the Erteguns had no right to take what was his when they didn't have anything more than $17,000 at risk. They rode in silence for some time. Around the Midtown Tunnel, he put his arm around her and smiled. "I love you," he said.

Wexler was furious. He phoned Berns the next day and told him the deal was over. Berns didn't even know what he was talking about. "Either you buy me out or I buy you out," said Wexler, naming a price he thought Berns couldn't afford, but that he wouldn't mind paying—$300,000.

Berns was stunned. He had no idea what set Wexler off. He didn't have the money. Wexler had been his closest friend, his coconspirator, his biggest fan, his patient teacher, his father confessor, all that and more rolled into one all-encompassing relationship. Berns, who lived on the edge of death, saw Wexler's greed and anger as mortal betrayal. He would not allow him to prevail. Encouraged by his wife, who told him to sell everything, do whatever he needed, Berns begged, borrowed, cajoled the money. He inveigled his distributors into giving him advances. Whatever it took, he made it happen.

His last Atlantic session came in July 1966. He cut a couple of numbers with the Drifters, including a Bert Berns–Jeff Barry song, "Aretha." Tom Dowd was surprised to hear from Wexler that he needed to clear directly with Wexler's office any requests from the studio for tapes or whatever from Bert Berns. Berns was now persona non grata at Atlantic and Dowd always wondered what happened.

Berns was also now the sole owner of both Bang Records and Web IV publishing. Berns outlined big plans for the label when he talked to the trades. He unveiled a new r&b subsidiary, Shout Records, with releases by the Exciters and Jimmy Radcliffe. He announced the signing of Freddie Scott, Bobby Harris, and Roy C. to the new label. He spoke about plans to reach the Spanish market by signing the blind Cuban music great Arsenio Rodriguez, who had been living for many years in the Bronx, and Berns wanted to expand into folk music with another signing, vocalist Ronnie Gilbert of the Weavers.

Berns also noted the great new r&b sounds coming out of the South."The sound is happening down there, not up North," he told *Billboard* in July. "Joe Tex and Otis Redding are among a host of top talent, all from the South."

As for his former partners at Atlantic Records, Berns said the split was entirely amicable. "I will always be grateful to them for the help they've given me in getting Bang started," he said.

Carmine ("Wassel") DeNoia, Patsy Pagano, Bert Berns on his boat, *A Little Bit of Soap*.

XIX.

Are You Lonely for Me Baby [1966]

CARMINE DENOIA—WASSEL—knew Berns from when Berns was still scuffling and Wassel was making book on Broadway, but Wassel checked Berns out anyway before signing Freddie Scott with Bang. Wassel had admired Berns's spleen when he first met him eating at a diner at Broadway and Fifty-Third Street with some of the boys, Hy Weiss and Miltie Ross, when Berns told Wassel, "You don't know me well enough yet—I'll let you know when you can say 'You're my man.'"

Freddie Scott was an older guy, graduated college, some med school, sang gospel, did a tour of military duty, cut a couple of records, and wrote a few songs before Don Kirshner hired him to write with Helen Miller, coauthor of the Shirelles hit "Foolish Little Girl." Scott and Miller had songs they wrote recorded by Paul Anka and Gene Chandler, but when Goffin and King asked Scott's help putting a lead vocal on a song intended for Chuck Jackson, his demo of their "Hey Girl" turned out so well, Goffin took Scott back in the studio and polished the track into a master for Colpix, the Screen Gems label, and scored a Top Ten hit in 1963. His follow-up was a daring, slow cover of the Ray Charles hit "I Got a Woman."

Without anybody informing him, Scott suddenly found himself with a new manager, Wassel, taking over from his previous manager, and a new record label, Columbia Records, which directed the

magnificent vocalist to bland middle-of-the-road fare under the supervision of Brook Benton producer Clyde Otis. Still, inside the small
world of New York rhythm and blues, Freddie Scott was rated as one
of the finest vocalists on the scene.

When Wassel negotiated Scott's release from Columbia, one of the
label's lawyers told Wassel he would think about it. "Don't sit on it too
long," Wassel said, "or you'll have three holes in your ass."

Nat Tarnopol at the Mob-infected Brunswick Records offered
Wassel serious money for Scott, but Wassel had a good feeling about
this guy Berns. He already placed one of his other clients, the Exciters,
with Berns after pulling the group off Roulette. Wassel hated Morris
Levy, a touchy situation because Levy was a close friend of Wassel's
brother. That Levy hadn't paid the kids in the group a penny only
inflamed Wassel's sense of injustice. He once used iron bars rolled up
in newspapers to bust up the office of a recalcitrant music publisher to
encourage proper accounting on behalf of a client. The Exciters went
with Wassel for one reason, because they noticed that Freddie Scott
got paid. Wassel may have cashed in cartons of illicit free goods, but
after he signed with Columbia, Freddie Scott was driving a new gold
Cadillac Fleetwood.

Wassel became a part of the furniture at the Bang Records office.
Berns adored the goofy oaf with his colorfully mangled English.
He was a jolly, gentle giant. Under the right circumstances, Wassel
could be threatening and even dangerous, but he was more character
than torpedo. He didn't have a police record (although the FBI knew
who he was). If people mistook him for a mobster, they weren't far
wrong. Those guys all knew Wassel and he was especially close to
the Paganos, Joey even more than Patsy maybe, but Joey was away in
prison for some time to come. Wassel might not have been part of their
operation. Certainly he would have never hesitated to do any favor
they asked. Wassel knew how to mind his own business. Through
Wassel, Berns came to know Patsy Pagano. He and Ilene socialized

with Patsy and his wife, Laura. The couples had even taken cruises on Berns's new boat.

The forty-foot, steel-hulled Chris Craft was christened *A Little Bit of Soap*, and Berns berthed the unwieldy beast at the Seventy-Ninth Street boat basin. He knew nothing about seamanship, but he had tooled around enough with Wexler on his boat to think it couldn't be that difficult. He took a quick maritime course at City College and it was full speed ahead. Jeff Barry watched as Berns ripped a huge gash in some poor sucker's hull trying to dock his boat. An embarrassed Berns stayed below while the irate boat owner screamed bloody murder. Berns kept guns onboard and every so often would blast away at seagulls with a shotgun like a big kid.

Nobody knows when Berns met Tommy Eboli, but they quickly became such fast friends that Eboli bought a steel-hulled Chris Craft exactly like Berns's and kept his boat in the adjacent slip. Eboli invited Berns and his wife to dinner at his modest family apartment in Fort Lee. Ilene didn't fully appreciate their new friend's standing until she and Berns accompanied the boss on a stroll through Little Italy's San Gennaro Street during an Italian Day parade and she watched people, one after another, come up and kiss his ring. Eboli and Berns spent a lot of time hanging out on each other's boats. Jeff Barry didn't know what to think when Eboli looked over his shoulder at the helicopter that had been hovering in the distance the whole time they sat around the boat, tied to the dock. "FBI," Eboli said, and shrugged.

Eboli certainly knew he was under constant surveillance. He was one of the kingpin Mob bosses of New York City. When the Feds finally framed Vito Genovese and he went off to Atlanta in 1959 for fifteen years, Genovese left Eboli and another boss in charge of family affairs, with his consiglieri also minding matters. The leadership of New York's families had been in constant turmoil since Lucky Luciano tried to impose his will on them all from exile in Havana. Luciano was repudiated and sent back to Italy to live out his life like Napoleon in Elba by Vito Genovese, at least in part, who was also presumed behind—far behind—both the shooting of Frank Costello and the bloody massacre of Albert Anastasia, riddled with slugs while he dozed off getting a haircut and a manicure in the barbershop at the Park Sheraton.

Joe Bonanno, the last of the old bosses, showed back up in May 1966 after having been missing since October 1964, when he may have staged his own kidnapping outside his attorney's Park Avenue apartment building. He may have wanted to avoid testifying before a federal grand jury the next morning or he may have been beating the heat from the other bosses after he lost a power grab when boss Joe Profaci died in 1962. Ambitious Carlo Gambino and his ally Thomas "Three-Fingered Brown" Lucchese were strong with Cosa Nostra's ruling body, the inviolate Commission. But Lucchese was sick now, cancer eating him away, and the power was sure to shift again when he died. Lousy FBI wiretaps and stakeouts were the least of Tommy Eboli's concerns. But boats did offer a certain freedom from electronic surveillance that he no doubt enjoyed, cruising the Hudson with Berns and his music business pals.

The battle with Atlantic drained Berns. He was visibly nervous and sweaty. He sought treatment from a Park Avenue psychiatrist specializing in holocaust victims named Dr. Max Needleman. He was afraid of dying. When songwriter Artie Wayne underwent open-heart surgery at New York Medical Center, Berns quizzed him intensely about the procedure once Wayne was back on his feet, crawling the halls again at 1650. Wayne could tell that his fears about it ran so deep, they permeated every part of his thought process. He urged Berns to have the surgery, but Berns feared the operation would kill him.

He saw more heart specialists. He saw Dr. Needleman. He gulped medicine. He carried nitroglycerin pills in case of an incident. His nails were chewed to the quick. He sometimes clutched his chest and winced in pain. He scared Ilene, collapsing on their couch in the middle of a fight—she could see his heart pounding through his chest.

He frightened Brooks Arthur and Brooks's wife, Marilyn, driving back from upstate with Ilene in Berns's Jaguar XKE, when he had an attack. He turned white and burst into a sweat. He had to put a bag over his mouth and breathe, but he refused to give up the wheel and drove all the way back with his face in a paper bag. Berns was afraid of the risky experimental open-heart surgery that was being done at only a few hospitals, but he ordered the artificial valve and kept it on hand to help build up his nerve.

With Ilene pregnant again, their second child due in February, Berns rented his family a new home across the river in Englewood Cliffs, New Jersey, a suburban two-story house on a tree-lined street— Tommy Dowd lived in the neighborhood—while Berns started to make plans to build his own home in the area. Dino the Great Dane, who spent his life in a Manhattan penthouse, knew nothing about traffic. Somehow, he got loose from the house and was hit by a car in the street. When the veterinarian put a cast on the dog's leg, the open sores would not heal. Berns sat by the dog, sponged his wounds, and cried. It took him days to realize he had to put the dog to sleep. His heart was broken.

With all this *mishegas*, Berns had been out of the studio for months. His label needed records and he threw himself back into recording. With Sam Cooke imitator Bobby Harris, Berns cut a pair of new high-grade Bert Berns originals. "Sticky, Sticky" was a polished, commercial dance number with a Stax/Volt finish, a smooth piece of pop that even referenced "Hang On Sloopy" in the lyrics. But "Mr. Success" was dark soul that would have been fine for Solomon Burke. Harris, a veteran of more than a dozen previous records on various New York independents including a mawkish Sam Cooke tribute on Atlantic the year before, gave the songs a throaty roar. Berns did another one of his heartbreak soul ballads, "Gone Gone," with Roy C., who hit the r&b charts the year before with his own cracked soul side, "Shotgun Wedding." "Gone Gone" echoed Berns's growing fascination with Southern soul.

Seymour Stein, a promotion man for Red Bird, ran across a single on Chess breaking out in a few markets in the Midwest and played it for his pal, Richard Gottehrer. "Searching for My Love" by Bobby Moore and the Rhythm Aces, a snaking, smoky midtempo soul grinder, was recorded at Muscle Shoals, the first record by a veteran combo out of Montgomery, Alabama. Gottehrer and Stein gave the record to Berns, and the next time they saw him, he dragged them into his office to show them what he did with that record. He sat at the piano and pounded out the same song as he started to sing "Are You Lonely for Me Baby."

Berns grafted his song on top of authentic Southern soul—he even located the song's lyrics in the South (*the last train to Jacksonville . . .*). It was exactly what Berns needed for Freddie Scott. Arranger Garry Sherman pushed the stately pace with a groaning horn section, the production a little richer, a little more glossy perhaps than the Southern version, but Berns had unlocked the door to the world of soul.

His album with Arsenio Rodriguez was a joyous, festive labor of love. Rodriguez, who revolutionized Cuban music before the Second World War and lays claim to inventing the mambo, first left Cuba for Miami in the early fifties, but discouraged by the racism he encountered, relocated in the South Bronx, where the father of Afro-Cuban music stayed out of the limelight. He maintained his *conjunto* for a number of years, but he struggled to keep up with the rapidly changing waters of Latin music. He did an intriguing, almost folkloric session for Blue Note in 1957 with conga drummer Sabu as the leader. With five Cuban drummers on the session, Rodriguez, whose grandfather was a Yoruban slave who taught Arsenio all the ancient ways, led the ensemble on a succession of pure African chants.

George Goldner recorded him for Tico in the early sixties, but he was collecting dust when Berns found him. With Artie Butler arranging and Brooks Arthur behind the board, Berns brought Arsenio and his entire band into A&R Studios and cut a textbook Cuban album.

The great Cuban bassist Cachao, one of the fathers of the mambo, and Machito's *bongosero* Jose Mangual played on the session. Amid the shimmering brass and bright, sensuous rhythms, the clattering of Arsenio's *tres*—he was a master of the three-stringed instrument—percolated like horses' hooves on a dirt road.

Berns brought his "My Girl Sloopy" full circle with Arsenio's band giving the song a complete Afro-Cuban retooling, Arsenio wobbling his way through the lyric in thickly accented English (*Sloopy muchacha*), a minor masterpiece that would land Arsenio Rodriguez on radio station playlists for the last time in his historic career.

Berns then unleashed the second single by Neil Diamond on Bang, "Cherry, Cherry." He sent Jeff Barry back in the studio to put a spit shine on the original demo. The drumless track swung like mad and Diamond's vocal—supported by a raft of trademark overdubbed Ellie Greenwich background vocals—carried the record. The fully produced version turned out stilted, crowded with musical ideas. With the ghost of "La Bamba" hovering over the Latin-flavored pop song, "Cherry Cherry" was a record that had Bert Berns all over it. "Dance-beat disk of the week," said *Billboard*. Berns went to work on radio across the country.

"Solitary Man" had moved up the charts with blue smoke and mirrors. Before he was fired, Julie Rifkind performed nothing less than sleight of hand getting that record almost halfway up the charts on no sales, little airplay, and only isolated regional breakouts like Los Angeles, where the single went Top Ten. Berns greased sales by giving away records to distributors. Perhaps as many as three out of ten copies of "Solitary Man" had been giveaways. But the record did its job introducing Neil Diamond. "Cherry, Cherry" would clinch the deal.

Diamond was green. He made friends with Fred Weintraub, who ran the Greenwich Village folk club the Bitter End. Weintraub was a burly guy who did a lot of different things before opening the club in 1961, including play cocktail piano in Havana before Castro, where he was imprisoned on gun-running charges and pardoned only because he was an American citizen. In addition to operating the club, he also managed a few folk acts.

Weintraub started working with Diamond and used Diamond as the club's unofficial automatic opening act. He didn't even bother giving Diamond billing until "Solitary Man" came out. Diamond was so awkward, Weintraub told him not to talk between songs. The first out-of-town dates were three-song appearances one weekend around Florida and two appearances in California on "The Beach Boys Summer Spectacular" at the Hollywood Bowl in Los Angeles and Cow Palace in San Francisco, a panoply of pop acts with records on the radio that summer: the Leaves, the Sunrays, Sir Douglas Quintet, Percy Sledge, the Byrds, Lovin' Spoonful, Chad & Jeremy, and others. Diamond did his one semi-hit, "Solitary Man," and two songs he remembered from summer camp, "If I Had a Hammer" and "La Bamba."

Bert Berns

XX.

I Got to Go Back [1966]

H ER PIECE OF Neil Diamond was all Ellie Greenwich had left. She lost her husband to another woman, and her father figures Leiber and Stoller had abandoned her when they sold her songwriting contract to United Artists. Barry and Greenwich were done writing songs together, except for one last curtain call.

After several years of not working with them after "Chapel of Love," Phil Spector phoned Barry about writing together again. He either didn't know that they had split or didn't care, but Spector flew to New York to work with them. They met at Barry's West Seventy-Second Street apartment. Greenwich felt weird just being there. There was no real collaboration; everyone came with little pieces of melodies and lyrics that they just assembled like parts. The first, "River Deep—Mountain High," Greenwich had the verse melody and Spector brought the chorus, while Barry supplied most of the lyrics. They ended up writing three songs in a week, including "I Can Hear Music," all little suites as much as songs, different chunks of music pushed up against each other.

After the enormous success of "You've Lost That Lovin' Feeling," the Righteous Brothers and Spector went their separate ways. Spector was looking for a bigger, even more grand sound. He leased for $20,000 the recording contract from Loma Records of Ike and Tina Turner, r&b

stalwarts since their string of hits in the early sixties with Juggy Murray, and spent an astronomical $22,000 on the Hollywood recording sessions that produced the extravagant, titanic "River Deep—Mountain High."

During sessions concentrating on her lead vocal, Tina ended up stripped to her bra, belting out the song over and over for Spector, a perfectionist known to spend hours working over the same eight bars of music in the studio. When the record was released in May 1966 on his Philles label, Spector watched in agony as his greatest achievement, his most fabulous production ever, creeped and crawled in four weeks up to a pathetic number eighty-eight on the charts before dropping off entirely into oblivion. Spector was devastated. He sat in solitude behind the electronic fences of his Beverly Hills mansion and cried bitter tears.

Ellie Greenwich spent many evenings crying her own tears with Bert and Ilene Berns, whom she found warmly sympathetic. Ilene, young colt that she was, made several awkward attempts to get Jeff and Ellie back together, but stopped trying once Barry went public with his new girlfriend. Greenwich desperately needed the Neil Diamond project. She felt as though, without it, she would disappear.

Berns was definitely a full member of the creative team. He not only attended all the meetings, but also went to the sessions, although he left Barry and Greenwich more than capably in charge. He sang loudly in the background choruses and added handclaps. Berns would also return the next day to work with engineer Brooks Arthur fine-tuning the mixes.

Diamond, still wet clay, absorbed a lot from Jeff Barry, particularly in vocal mannerisms and phrasing. They were both a couple of Brooklyn cowboys who wanted to be Elvis. There was a natural understanding between the two, and Greenwich, after the divorce, felt increasingly cut out.

Don Kirshner loved "Cherry, Cherry" and called Diamond to see if he had anything suitable for the Monkees, the new hit TV series rock group controlled by Columbia–Screen Gems. The group's first single streaked to the top of the charts in September 1966. Kirshner loved one new Diamond song, "I'm a Believer," and offered to buy the copyright, along with a couple of others. Barry could produce the record and Diamond would retain his writer's share. The two partners in Tallyrand decided to take the songs out of the company and sell them to Kirshner without consulting Greenwich. They never asked her and they neglected to pay her. To Greenwich, it was the sign of her utter hopelessness, her total lack of power. She was hurt and despondent; all this meant more than dollars to her. This was her life.

She poured her heart out to Berns over dinner at La Brasserie, one of Berns's favored upper Broadway restaurants. She felt comfortable with Berns. She saw him as a boyish man, vulnerable and open, encouraging to be around. Berns's pet phrase—"I hear what you're saying"—applied equally to conversation or musical performances in the studio. He wanted people to know he was listening. Greenwich loved that about Berns. She didn't really expect his reaction.

Berns called Wassel and made him come to the restaurant. Greenwich repeated her story. Wassel asked how much money she was owed and assured her he intended no one any harm. Within days, Wassel collected the money.

But Greenwich could only be so close to Berns and ultimately started to drift away because his friendship with her ex-husband continued to flourish. Shooting pool, riding motorcycles, just bullshitting around, Berns and Barry got along like songs in the same key, but they could not collaborate musically. Ilene Berns watched in amusement as the two emerged from a writing session at the Englewood Cliffs place, each complaining about the other—"He's too pop," "He's too blues." They managed to eke out a couple of pieces together, and in Berns's world, no songs went unrecorded. Berns recorded their song "Ride Ride Baby" with a genuine rock and roll phenomenon he signed to Bang Records, Jack Ely.

As a teenager in Portland, Oregon, Ely had been a founding member of a high school rock and roll combo they named the Kingsmen. In one of the great harmonic convergences of rock and roll history, the Kingsmen entered a Portland recording studio the day after another Portland rock and roll band, Paul Revere and the Raiders, went into the same studio, and both recorded the same song—a cover of the Richard Berry original from the Los Angeles r&b scene in the fifties, "Louie Louie." Ely, who sang the song for the Kingsmen on the record, was fired shortly after the record's release by a bandmate who secretly trademarked the band's name and decided he wanted to be the lead singer.

That would have been that if disc jockey Arnie "Woo Woo" Ginsburg hadn't discovered the record for the "Worst Record of the Week" feature on his popular WMEX Boston radio show. Ginsburg ignited a firestorm of airplay that led Marvin Schlachter of Scepter Records to buy the master and release the record nationwide on Wand.

The Kingsmen—without Ely—sprang back to action and took off on a nationwide tour of television appearances and concert performances. Ely quickly formed his own outfit, Jack Ely and the Kingsmen, advertising himself as "The Original Singer of 'Louie Louie'." This was a blood feud, touched off when security guards barred Ely from entering the nightclub where the Kingsmen were recording the band's album, *The Kingsmen in Person, Featuring "Louie Louie."* Lawsuits flew.

The Kingsmen's "Louie Louie" (with Ely on vocals) went all the way to number two in December 1963, one of the last great blasts of American rock and roll before the Beatles swamped the charts.

"Louie Louie" would not go away. Word spread that Ely's incomprehensible vocals disguised dirty lyrics, a rumor so persistent, the FBI spent more than two years analyzing the record and investigating the song's background. The furor even brought the Kingsmen single back on the charts for a couple of weeks in May 1966.

Berns, never shy of the obvious, first cut Ely on Bang singing "Louie Louie '66" and, for the B-side of the next single, a cover no less of the Paul Revere and the Raiders' "Louie Louie" follow-up, "Louie Go Home." Ely didn't mind. He was a man on a mission. He wanted redemption and retribution. As part of the lawsuit settlement, he was forced to change the name of his band; the Bang singles were done by Jack Ely and the Courtmen.

"Ride Ride Baby," the A-side of the second single, did capture the joint sensibilities of Barry and Berns, a raucous rock and roll record riding on a riff redolent of "Louie Louie" with an erotic blues underbelly and Neil Diamond somewhere buried in the background chorus. Ely wasn't around Bang much, but he was there long enough to walk in on a screaming match over royalties between Berns and the parents of the McCoys, a group whose fortunes dimmed rather rapidly after the instant number one success of "Hang On Sloopy."

After the diminishing returns were not reversed by the group's snappy sixth single, Feldman, Gottehrer, and Goldstein's hip, funny, psychedelic bromide, "Don't Worry Mother, Your Son's Heart Is Pure," that ends with a clearly audible toke, Berns took the McCoys into the studio himself with Barry for another savory collaboration, "I Got to Go Back," the credit reading PRODUCED BY BERNS AND BARRY. Again, the song is Barry-brand pop plus sex with a Southern soul rinse, a vibrant, thumping distillation of their two distinct styles, a record far more strapping and appealing than its relatively anemic January 1967 chart performance might imply.

At Roulette Records, Morris Levy was back from the brink of insolvency after a stroke of lightning. Levy never made the records at Roulette. Records were only part of his racket. He made more off publishing. He still owned Birdland, still New York's premiere jazz club. He had other, less evident ways of making money.

Levy had fingers in many pies. At Roulette, he had to depend on other people's taste and abilities, which he would then subject to his own endless second-guessing. Teddy Reig hustled Latin records for him, the only thing keeping the label going for a while. Levy brought back Hugo Peretti and Luigi Creatore to handle artists and repertoire in 1964.

They had started Roulette off with hit after hit out of the blocks in 1957 and left a year later to run recording at giant RCA Victor for six years. Before they came back, Henry Glover, Lucky Millinder's old arranger and recording director for years at Cincinnati's King Records, had made r&b–flavored hits at Roulette with Joey Dee and the Starliters and others. His 1963 record with the Essex, "Easier Said Than Done," went number one.

Back at the label the next year, Hugo and Luigi found Roulette in sad shape. The big names on the jazz line were all gone. Levy was difficult. He would refuse to pay debts just for the hell of it. He was impossible to pin down about business matters. Hugo and Luigi couldn't deal with Roulette the second time around and split after less than a year, the label teetering on collapse. When Levy bought the Paramount Theater in 1964, the whole thing started to go down the drain.

Accountants were preparing the company for bankruptcy and the label was down to its last $10,000, when promotion man Red Schwartz ran across a record he thought could do something, "Leader of the Laundromat" by the Detergents, a group of New York studio brats making fun of the big Shangri-Las hit. Since the label would lose the money in bankruptcy anyway, Schwartz picked up the master and humped the dumb record into the Top Twenty.

Although it was hardly thriving, Roulette was back in business. The label had not managed another chart single since and showed a lot of debt with their distributors, who were always reluctant to pay the independent labels, especially if the line wasn't selling. Often how much you got paid depended on how good your next record was. Roulette was headed back in the toilet when Red Schwartz struck gold in Pittsburgh.

His distributor in Pittsburgh called Schwartz to tell him about a record that was a smash locally on a small label. He thought Schwartz could have it. Schwartz went to Pittsburgh and couldn't believe his ears—biggest piece of shit he'd heard in years, but a piece of shit that had already sold forty thousand pieces in the market and was number one and number three respectively on the yokel radio stations. He gave the group's manager $10,000 and agreed to buy two full-page trade magazine advertisements with his name at the top—BOB MACK PRESENTS TOMMY JAMES AND THE SHONDELLS.

Tommy James came from Niles, Michigan, where his band, the Shondells, had been one of a number of teen groups to record for a local disc jockey in 1964. The band covered the Barry-Greenwich song from the B-side of one of the Raindrops singles, "Hanky Panky." The disc jockey played the record on the Niles radio station WNIL for a couple of weeks and nothing more happened, until a year later, when a Pittsburgh deejay stumbled across the local record and started slamming it on his show as an exclusive.

James, at first, didn't believe the Pittsburgh disc jockey when he finally reached the teenager by phone, but James eventually made his way to Pittsburgh, where his old, forgotten record was already a hit. He signed with manager Bob Mack and put together a new set of Shondells.

Schwartz had no faith in the group, but he already collected more than $8,000 for the records sold in Pittsburgh. When Levy listened to the record and expressed roughly the same opinion that Schwartz held when he first heard it, Schwartz was able to calm down Levy by telling him it cost only $1,500. "Hanky Panky" went all the way to number one, one of the biggest records of the year. Levy was now truly back in the game.

Levy long provided certain services to the record business. He was the person to call if there might be problems that couldn't be solved any other way. If an artist's manager was being difficult and needed to be handled confidentially, Levy could help. He also had a pipeline for selling cut-rate albums, fast bucks for unsold inventory, cash transactions kept off the books. He had been the music industry's dirty little secret since he was pulling Alan Freed's strings. Wexler had made his deals with the devil before. He hated to have to do it—Wexler personally couldn't stand Levy—but there had been times when there was no suitable alternative.

Losing Web IV and Bang Records to Berns left Wexler embittered. It wasn't the money—it was the money. One final matter remained. Berns signed over the small piece they gave him of their Cotillion Music. Atlantic needed to consolidate ownership of their music publishing to package all the company's assets for sale. Berns signed off for a reasonable consideration, $70,000, but Wexler couldn't bring himself to pay, much as he had refused to give Leiber and Stoller the money their audit showed due.

In the giddy excitement of acquiring half of his publishing, the Atlantic partners had given Berns the small interest in their publishing, an act of generosity Wexler now felt that paying off would be unjustified punishment. Berns, who tapped himself out paying off Atlantic, needed the money. Wexler dodged Berns's persistent demands for payment, but he had no long-term strategy for dealing with Berns beyond not returning his calls. Wexler reached out to Morris Levy to see if Levy could bring some pressure to bear on Berns. He decided to muscle Berns, so Morris made a couple of calls.

Berns, meanwhile, had unloaded his problems on Tommy Eboli, who also made a couple of calls. Ilene made a secret, desperate call of her own to Jerry Wexler at his Great Neck place to urge him to stop. "You don't know what the hell you're dealing with," she told him. When Wexler rebuffed her, she asked Berns to call off Eboli, and Berns agreed everything had gone too far. He talked to Tommy. Too late, Eboli told Berns. Levy started something that needed to be finished. "It's out of my hands," he said. "You don't realize who I am."

A meeting was arranged at the Roulette offices. Wassel was so worked up about the meeting, Patsy Pagano made him wait at a nearby coffee shop. Miltie Ross came along. Big Miltie ran hookers up and down Broadway, made a bundle counterfeiting subway tokens, and kept his hand in the music business since the big bands. He did a lot of business with Ertegun and Wexler out of his Award Music office in the Brill Building. He ran their budget-line LP label, Clarion Records, which repackaged old Atlantic stock for bargain basement retail, a gray area of the business where wiseguys like Big Miltie liked to operate.

Levy invited his partner Dominick Ciaffone and a couple of their other gangland associates, highly ranked soldiers, but when Patsy Pagano showed up with Genovese boss Tommy Eboli, Levy's hand was trumped. Gangsters picked up Ahmet Ertegun walking down the sidewalk and brought him to the meeting. Whatever series of events Wexler set in motion when he first called Levy played out on an entirely different level than he originally intended. These guys carved up the deal and cut themselves a slice.

When it was done, Patsy Pagano and Big Miltie went to see Wexler at his office. Wexler was terrified just to be sitting across his desk from Pagano. They made jokes about breaking his daughter's legs. Wexler didn't laugh. They told Wexler that not only would he have to pay Berns the cash, but also as part of the settlement, he would have to turn over the recording studio the company just bought. Both parts of the settlement needed to be kept off the books, out of sight of the due diligence of any potential buyer of Atlantic Records.

The studio, Talentmasters, was a dump on the fourth floor above Tad's Steaks on Forty-Second Street off Times Square, an old fur storage locker where you could hear the rats in the elevator shaft and the shag carpet smelled of cat piss. Atlantic had only recently completed purchasing the operation. Atlantic's own studio had become so busy, the label had been booking overflow into Talentmasters, sending over a steady stream of Atlantic acts such as the Rascals, Ben E. King, Mary Wells, and others. Basically, Tommy Eboli wanted to get into the studio business with Berns, who took him to see Atlantic counsel Paul Marshall when arranging some of the details on the transfer of ownership. Wexler, scared for his life, hired bodyguards. He never forgave Berns.

Bert Berns, Van Morrison at "Brown Eyed Girl" session.

XXI.

Heart Be Still [1967]

FREDDIE SCOTT WAS doing a show in Philadelphia when his twin sister died unexpectedly of a heart attack. He came home the next day for the funeral, where Wassel found him and dragged him away from his grieving family through the snowy streets to the recording studio. His debut single for the Shout label, "Are You Lonely for Me Baby," was streaking up the charts, headed for number one r&b. Berns needed Scott to finish an album and he had just the song for Scott's next single, his Solomon Burke breakthrough, "Cry to Me." This time, he slowed down the track even more than he did with Betty Harris, painfully, excruciatingly slow. Tears rolled down Scott's face as he spit out every mouthful. Scott wasn't the only one crying. Everybody in the studio was crying.

Wassel came by the Bang Records office daily, sometimes just sat on Berns's couch for hours. Patsy Pagano stopped by occasionally. Pagano and Wassel dragged some poor son of a bitch they found downstairs bootlegging records up to the Bang office and threw him in a chair in front of Berns's desk. Ed Chalpin made soundalike records. He rushed out cheap covers of the day's hits and spread them around the world as fast as he could. Ironically, Berns used to play on some of his sessions when he was starting out.

They brought him into the office to admonish him. Berns turned away and looked out the window. While Berns wasn't looking, Patsy Pagano hit the dumb bastard so hard, he broke his own hand. Berns swiveled around. "See, I warned you," he said.

Wassel saw nothing wrong with taking vigilante action on bootleggers. He broke up a couple of operations—literally, with sledgehammers and pipes—in Brooklyn. He and his confederate threw steak to the guard dogs and climbed the fence. He liked to wear a large ring with his initials spelled out in diamonds that would leave cuts. He knew to swing down on people when you hit them in the face because they get frightened with blood in their eyes. Berns went along on one of their raids on some stupid sucker who had bootleg 45s stacked on broomsticks in his garage out on Ditmars Boulevard in Astoria, but he called off Wassel and his goons when he saw a baby sleeping in a crib in the garage. Wassel let the guy off with a stern admonition.

Pagano and his wife, Laura, showed up at the hospital in February when Berns's daughter, Cassandra Yvette, was born. Al and Sylvia Levine, Berns's sister and brother-in-law, were visiting. They didn't get along all that comfortably with Bert and Ilene, but they were family. Patsy handed Berns an attaché case. He clicked it open and showed his brother-in-law. It was full of cash—the Atlantic Records settlement. Al knew the Atlantic guys had cheated Berns and that he had the money coming, but he'd never seen so much cash.

There's something happening here, what it is ain't exactly clear, went the line in "For What It's Worth," the hit single by the new Atlantic Records recording artists from Los Angeles, Buffalo Springfield. Ahmet Ertegun was anxious to get Atlantic more deeply involved in this new rock movement that already proved rewarding with the Young Rascals and Sonny & Cher. He dispatched his brother Nesuhi to Los Angeles to see the band perform. Through the same Hollywood sleazebags that managed Sonny & Cher, Ertegun was able to sign the group away from Jac Holzman of Elektra and Lou Adler of Dunhill for a king's ransom of $12,500, without the benefit of having heard one song demo. There was a lot of excitement and interest in the industry over what *Billboard* called "pop/hippie acts," but there was also a vast amount of confusion and misunderstanding.

Canadian sociologist Marshall McLuhan called it "the hi-fi/stereo changeover." As inexpensive home stereo players became more available, the market for pop music began to shift from little 45 RPM singles to the 33 ⅓ long-playing albums, big records with small holes. This transition changed the pop music world in deep and fundamental ways. The audience and the music were both growing up. A key passage took place in November 1965, when the Beatles, the industry's leading act, released a new album, *Rubber Soul*, with no singles. A couple of weeks later, the band put out a new single not contained on the album, a double-sided instant smash, "Day Tripper" and "We Can Work It Out." The stereo production on the album was, at times, clumsy and awkward, while the monaural hit single sounded like a bullet coming out of cardboard car radio speakers, but the Beatles as recording artists were drawing a clear distinction between the kind of work they would do on albums and singles.

On the West Coast, new long-haired rock groups with funny names were launching records on the charts every week. In San Francisco, a hundred thousand hippies gathered in Golden Gate Park to listen to rock groups that didn't exist a year before. Peace and love, brother and sister. Jefferson Airplane loves you and the Peanut Butter Conspiracy is spreading. While old-time independents around New York were a vanishing breed, A&M Records in Los Angeles was installing new recording studios in the company's million-dollar headquarters, Charlie Chaplin's old studios on La Brea Avenue, after selling more than four and a half million copies of the long-playing album *Whipped Cream and Other Delights* by Herb Alpert and the Tijuana Brass, the *A* of A&M. Jac Holzman's Elektra Records was building a modern new Hollywood office complex and rapidly expanding beyond the Greenwich Village folk scene roots of the label into the pop charts with Los Angeles–based rock groups such as Love or the Doors.

Berns went to Los Angeles in March 1967, as soon as Ilene was well enough to travel after the new baby. For her, this was a triumphant return home and the first thing she did was have Bert take her to Dolores' on Wilshire in the limousine for a hamburger on the way to the hotel. She made Berns tour Beverly Hills real estate—they checked out actor Laurence Harvey's place—but he looked ill at ease and out of place, all pasty and paunchy, playing with baby Brett in the hotel swimming pool. They talked about moving to California, Berns getting into movie soundtracks, but he was such a New Yorker. She felt good being in California, back in shape after the baby, and enjoyed wearing a negligee to bed. Her husband took one look, offered his trademark "Ooh-la-la," and, one uncomfortable, slightly painful *schtup* later, Ilene was pregnant again.

Berns was in California to make a series of albums with the noted astrologer Sydney Omarr, author of countless books about the stars and signs and syndicated *Los Angeles Times* columnist. Berns cut Omarr doing one album for each astrological sign; one side about the particular sign and the other side about how that sign related to each of the other signs. This was a long way from *Rubber Soul*, but Berns was thinking about the growing album market.

He sought out Van Morrison through Phil Solomon, unaware that Them had crashed and burned the previous summer of 1966 in Los Angeles. The band took a three-week residency at Hollywood's Whisky a Go Go, where opening acts had included Captain Beefheart and his Magic Band, Buffalo Springfield, the Association, and the Doors, who finished their joint appearances with the two Morrisons—Van and Jim—sharing the stage singing "Gloria" and "In the Midnight Hour." During the Whisky run, Them fired Phil Solomon long-distance over money. Solomon washed his hands of the whole lot. After three months in California, the band splintered and most made their way home.

When Berns reached Van Morrison in Belfast, Morrison had nothing going on. There were several versions of Them touring. He was living with his parents and spending long hours spinning songs by himself into a reel-to-reel tape recorder he bought in the States. He was bitter, angry, and frequently drunk. Berns thought he could be a rock and roll version of the Irish poet Brendan Behan. He signed Morrison to a record deal with Bang, sent him $2,500, and flew him over to make an album in March 1967.

At A&R Studios on West Forty-Eighth Street, twenty-two-year-old Van Morrison was surrounded by the cream of New York session musicians—keyboard players Artie Butler and Paul Griffin, guitarists Eric Gale, Hugh McCracken, and Al Gorgoni, and drummer Gary Chester. Cissy Houston and her ladies were there. Garry Sherman wrote out the charts almost as quickly as Morrison could play him the songs. Brooks Arthur was engineering and Jeff Barry was hanging around. Guitarist Gale grabbed the electric bass on "Brown-Eyed Girl," an instrument Gale played with a flat pick, giving his downstrokes a rigid, hard-edged attack. Arranger Sherman had never seen anyone play the electric bass with a flat pick before.

Guitarist Gorgoni listened to Morrison run down the song on acoustic guitar and slowly put together the calypso-flavored introduction on his Gibson L-5 over the course of the first few run-throughs. By the time they cut the master on take twenty-two, Gorgoni had polished his sprightly, dancing guitar introduction into a solid, crafted piece. Berns, Barry, and Brooks Arthur joined the background chorus and Berns sang louder than anyone. Morrison originally called the song "Brown-Skinned Girl," but Berns knew better.

In two days, they cut eight songs. The nine-minute "T. B. Sheets" was an unprecedented improvisation with its claustrophobic images of a slow, languishing death. They were all Morrison's songs, except for one cover of something Berns did previously with Solomon Burke, "Goodbye Baby (Baby Goodbye)." Morrison was not comfortable with the professionalism of the accompanists. "I think it should be freer," he said between takes of "He Ain't Give You None." "At the minute, we have a choke thing going, know what I mean?"

Morrison flew home to an uncertain future the next day, after signing a publishing deal with Web IV for a $500 advance. He wrote his California girlfriend to listen to her radio and when she heard "Brown-Eyed Girl," he would be coming back to her.

Neil Diamond wrote "Girl You'll Be a Woman Soon," his second Top Ten record that April 1966, on his first real tour with a band the previous December of 1965, a thirty-two-city, twenty-eight-day ordeal with Tommy Roe, Billy Joe Royal, and P.J. Proby through the South and the Midwest where Diamond first encountered screaming teenyboppers. He was on a hot streak. His Monkees song, "I'm a Believer," earned him his first number one hit, five weeks at the top of the charts. He was turning out a procession of top-quality songs for his Bang singles. He wrote "Kentucky Woman" in the back of a limousine outside Paducah, Kentucky, on the same tour. He was starting to assert himself in the studio more. He asked Barry not to mix "You Got to Me" until he got back in town off tour because he didn't like the background vocals.

Berns went with Tommy Eboli, Patsy Pagano, and Wassel to watch Emile Griffith lose the middleweight championship to the Italian welterweight Nino Benvenuti at Madison Square Garden in April. Also sitting ringside was Frank Costello, the retired Mob boss. Costello knew Wassel from when he used to frequent Duke's Bar and Grill, a well-known Mob hangout in Cliffside, New Jersey, that Wassel's uncle owned in the thirties. Wassel was a punk kid who used to run around with a pickpocket pal and consider it a good day when they grabbed eight or ten wallets and made as much as $18. Costello joined the party for the ride home in the limousine. Berns concealed his excitement. Costello asked Berns, in the soft murmur in which he spoke, where was he from. Bronx, Berns said. Costello took that in. What kind of business are you in, Costello asked. The record business, said Berns, and the old man lit up.

"The record business," he said, "is a very good business."

Berns liked hanging around the wiseguys. These men wielded the ultimate unfair business advantage because implicit in all their dealings was the understanding that they would kill anyone who didn't do what they wanted. This was raw, vicious power, almost intoxicating in its purity and simplicity. Gangsters moved easily through the world of show business and have always found willing associates among the ranks—Frank Sinatra, for instance.

Berns came to be friends with these people, and his music business associates were both intrigued and frightened by his new pals. Berns took Patsy Pagano and his wife on cruises with music business buddies such as Jeff Barry and Jerry Ragovoy, with their wives and girlfriends. Freddie Scott huddled over a rail on Berns's boat with Pagano. "Don't worry," the gangster told the singer. "We're going to take care of you."

The more successful Berns became, the more impatient he grew. His fuse was shorter and his temper could be fierce. He was still the same warm, encouraging guy, but he could show a steely reserve when pressed. He could flash with righteous indignation in support of Israel, although not much of a practicing Jew, and he talked openly about volunteering for the Israeli army when war broke out in June. At his new studio, which he dubbed Incredible Sounds, the drawer in his desk was crammed with pill bottles and a .38-caliber revolver.

Jerry Wexler celebrated his fiftieth birthday with an industry dinner at the Hotel St. Regis in January 1967. Jerry Ragovoy didn't know anything was wrong when he walked in the ballroom with Berns and they brushed past Wexler and Ertegun in the hallway. Ragovoy was shocked at the tense, unspoken anger between them and Berns. He thought they were best friends. The chill in the air was almost palpable. Wexler and Berns ignored each other, Ragovoy couldn't help but notice.

Ahmet Ertegun delivered the keynote and toasted his partner. Privately, if they had been estranged before Wexler tried to pull that number with Leiber and Stoller and the Red Bird merger, Ertegun and

Wexler were now barely on speaking terms. Their relationship would never be restored; Ahmet could never fully trust Wexler again. That was also something the son of the Turkish diplomat would never let anyone know. He lavished praise on him at the birthday dinner.

AT THIS POINT, Wexler's Southern strategy was keeping the label afloat. Stax/Volt was turning out a steady stream of hits with the glorious Otis Redding, Sam & Dave, Booker T. and the M.G.'s, and others. Wexler had taken Pickett back to Muscle Shoals in October 1966 and came out with "Mustang Sally" and a half dozen or more other tracks. While in the studio at Muscle Shoals, Wexler received a phone call from a gospel deejay he knew in Philadelphia. She told him Aretha Franklin was ready to talk to him.

Aretha Franklin was certainly no secret. Even before she cut a chilling live album for the Chess Records label at age fourteen, she was widely known as something like a child prodigy singing in the New Bethel Baptist Church choir, where her father was pastor. Reverend C.L. Franklin ran one of the largest, most prestigious black congregations in Detroit. He was an important ally of Reverend Martin Luther King Jr. and a recording artist who made best-selling gospel albums of his sermons, such as "The Eagle Stirreth Her Nest." Franklin and her sisters grew up in a home that was one of the great black literary, political, and cultural salons in the country. Dinner guests ranged from Adam Clayton Powell to Dinah Washington. Young Aretha Franklin knew Sam Cooke, whose father led an important church in Chicago, since he was a young buck gospel singer.

She dropped out of school after she had her second child out of wedlock at age sixteen and devoted herself to music. For five years, she recorded for Columbia Records—signed by the venerable John Hammond, who brought Count Basie, Billie Holiday, and Bob Dylan to the label—but Mitch Miller turned out to be less than the ideal a&r man for her.

Her husband/manager Ted White cut a very simple three-song demo in Detroit that floored Wexler. From the opening blast of "I Never Loved a Man (The Way I Love You)," Aretha Franklin was bringing ecstatic gospel to the sound of soul. Wexler knew instantly. He invited her out to Great Neck. They talked music, played records, felt each other out. She agreed to sign with Atlantic. Wexler's first thought was to put her with the Stax/Volt operation, as he did with Sam & Dave, but Jim Stewart of Stax balked at the $25,000 price tag, so Wexler decided to take her to Muscle Shoals.

Aretha Franklin coming to FAME Studios was a big deal, the most important session yet at the tiny outpost. The all-white crew threw together on the spot an arrangement for "I Never Loved a Man" around a keyboard part by Spooner Oldham, one of the Muscle Shoals regulars. In rapid order, the track came together and the horn charts were scribbled down and overdubbed.

With one great cut done, celebration was in order. Colbert County was dry and it was against Rick Hall's rules to drink in the studio, but musicians will find a way. Ted White and one of the horn players, both nipping from the same bottle, got into it over something that White perceived as a racial slur. He and his wife were the only blacks in the room and they were in the Deep South. The session ended for the day with the instrumental track to the B-side, "Do Right Woman—Do Right Man," only partly completed.

During the evening, everything went to hell. Rick Hall and Ted White got into a fistfight. White and Aretha stormed out of the hotel in the middle of the night. Wexler told Hall he would never work with him again (he was back within weeks with Pickett again, cutting, among other things, a new song by Berns, "Mojo Mama," even if they were also on the outs).

Back in New York, Wexler sent acetates of the track to key disc jockeys, but he couldn't release the single until he had a B-side. Before Wexler would release the single, he took Franklin back for more sessions (importing the Muscle Shoals sidemen to New York City for the occasion). The second session she brought in the Otis Redding song "Respect" that she'd been doing in her live act for more than a year. She brought in her sisters Carolyn and Erma and drilled them on the vocals. By the end of February, before the first single hit in March, the entire album was done and on the last day of the sessions Wexler had one more track in the can recorded that sounded like another sure thing.

Wexler had been driving by Grand Central Station when he saw Gerry Goffin walking down the sidewalk. His limousine pulled over and Wexler rolled down the window. "I have a great title for an Aretha Franklin song," he told Goffin. "'You Make Me Feel Like a Natural Woman.'" A couple of weeks later, Goffin and King brought Wexler's custom-ordered song into the Atlantic offices. Wexler earned a third of the copyright for the title. He cut the song with Aretha the day after she finished her first Atlantic album and tucked away the string-laden, pop track for a later date. "I Never Loved a Man" vaulted into the Top Ten when it was released in March, but when "Respect" blasted its way to number one the following month, Aretha Franklin was crowned Queen of Soul by popular acclaim and Wexler had made it happen.

To Harold Logan, Aretha's coronation meant there might finally be a little money in her older sister, Erma Franklin, whom Logan had managed for the previous five years without much success. Aretha's sister had always been a singer. In fact, when Berry Gordy Jr. was first starting his record label in Detroit, he and songwriting partner Billy Davis were more interested in Erma than her sister, who they thought was too gospelish. They rehearsed young Erma Franklin on songs they eventually recorded with others ("All I Could Do Was Cry" by Etta James and "You Got What It Takes" by Marv Johnson) but never recorded her.

Reverend Franklin insisted his oldest daughter finish college before she commenced a musical career anyway. After graduating from Clark College in Atlanta, Erma moved to New York in 1961 and signed with

Epic Records, subsidiary of Columbia Records, where her younger sister was already making records. Harold Logan, a well-known tough bastard, signed her for management and put her out as opening act for his business partner, Lloyd Price. She made jazzy records nobody noticed for Epic and sang on the road with the sixteen-piece Lloyd Price Orchestra.

After five years, she was still making the same money as she did the first day. When she quit Logan and went to work in a day job for a downtown advertising agency, she started out making more money than she ever did on the road. After her sister hit the charts, Logan contacted Erma about making some demos and shopping a record deal. She agreed only if she could do the music in her spare time. They took the demos to Berns, and she told Berns she would only record at night. Berns liked the idea of signing Aretha's sister—there was definitely something to work with there, plus it would piss off Wexler. They went into the studio and cut an old Jimmy Reed song, "Big Boss Man"—she was a big blues fan from her college days—and a song from her other sister, Carolyn, "Don't Catch the Dog's Bone," which picked up some r&b airplay when it was released on Shout Records in June.

Hoagy Lands also came back into Berns's life. The singer and Berns parted ways after Lands declined to join the Drifters but went instead with Doug Morris, the onetime junior song plugger at Mellin who left music publishing to do a&r at Laurie Records with the Schwartz brothers. Morris made a few singles with Lands, all very much in the style of Berns, including a gorgeous remake of Berns's "White Gardenia," but nothing came of any of them. Berns took Lands into the studio and cut another piece of thumping faux Southern soul that went unreleased, "32 Miles Out of Waycross (Mojo Mama)," a song on which he shared songwriting credits with Wexler, who already cut the number with Pickett at Muscle Shoals.*

---

*The song was close enough to the 1969 Top Ten hit by Motown singer Edwin Starr, "25 Miles," that Berns and Wexler were awarded coauthorship.

Berns was still writing regularly with Jerry Ragovoy, who viewed Berns's new associates with growing alarm. Berns showed him his gun. "This is power," he told Ragovoy, who started to deliberately retreat from Berns's orbit after that. They continued to write together. Berns, who never knew Ragovoy was keeping his distance, would call with a song already underway. They continued to turn out luminous soul ballads for Garnett Mimms—"I'll Take Good Care of You" was only the latest—which Ragovoy produced on record. Berns would give Ragovoy a trademark look every time he tried out any kind of exotic chord and say, "Stop that bebop shit."

One afternoon with the wives at Berns's house, Berns took Ragovoy aside to run down another tune. All he had was the chorus—*Take it, take another little piece of my heart.* He had previously showed the song to Van Morrison, hoping to write a hit with him, but Van Morrison doesn't collaborate. He played the song for Ragovoy on guitar, while their wives chatted in the other room. They didn't work on it that afternoon, but Ragovoy took the song home and worked up the verse, both the melody and the lyrics. Berns added the *come on, come on*—pure Bert—into the chorus when they got back together and hammered the song in place. When they brought the song to the studio, Erma Franklin made Berns slow the tempo. In everybody's mind, they were just making another hit record and this was just another great song by Berns, but it was not that simple. In "Piece of My Heart," Berns was writing his own pathology.

Berns, about the same time, also brought Ragovoy another song, "Heart Be Still," that Rags recognized immediately as a note-for-note rewrite of James Cleveland's landmark gospel song, "Peace Be Still." Cleveland's 1963 recording of the eighteenth-century madrigal with the First Baptist Church choir of Nutley, New Jersey, sold an astounding 1 million copies, one of the biggest-selling gospel records ever, and vaulted Cleveland into the front ranks of gospel performers and suddenly made massed choirs fashionable with young people. Every black disc jockey in the country would recognize the tune. Ragovoy knew it was not a song to be messing with, but Berns didn't care. He gave his song one of the bleakest opening verses he ever wrote.

Baby, my heart is breaking
And there's no hope, no hope inside.
The sky is an ocean of darkness,
No one, no one, no one to hold me,
In the lonely night.
—HEART BE STILL (RAGOVOY-BERNS, 1967)

Ragovoy thought it audacious to tamper with a song held as sacred as "Peace Be Still," but he nevertheless cut the record with Lorraine Ellison, the former gospel singer from Philadelphia brought to Ragovoy by Sam Bell of Garnett Mimms and the Enchanters. Ragovoy had produced Ellison the year before singing his explosive "Stay with Me," an amazing record that fizzled out after a few weeks in the bottom reaches of the charts. "Heart Be Still" didn't even fare that well when it came out that fall. It never occurred to Ragovoy that his songwriting partner was writing a lot about his heart.

Jeff Barry, Bert Berns, Van Morrison, Janet Gauder, Carmine ("Wassel") DeNoia

XXII.

Piece of My Heart [1967]

TRUE TO HIS word, Van Morrison returned to New York as soon as "Brown Eyed Girl" started up the charts in August. He sent for his eighteen-year-old girlfriend from California, Janet Gauder, a beautiful divorcee who brought her young son, Peter, and they all squeezed into a small room at the City Squire Hotel, across the street from Bang Records. All eight songs Morrison recorded in March had been assembled on an album, slapped into a cheesy package with phony psychedelic artwork, and titled *Blowin' Your Mind!* Berns was a long way from *Sgt. Pepper's Lonely Hearts Club Band*, the new Beatles album.

Berns wrote the liner notes:

> *Van Morrison . . . turbulent . . . today . . . inside . . . a multi-colored window through which one views at times himself and his counterself. Van Morrison . . . erratic and painful . . . whose music expresses the now! The right now of his own road, the ancient highway.*
>
> *And Van blows and Van sings and Van screams and Van listens and Van says "up them all" and becomes Van and what the hell that's his friend and now he can live with himself. He's on the golden heels of success and his recordings are ubiquitous "baby please don't go" from the down home weed country of*

the United States of Negro America. This LP is Van Morrison.
We won't explain it to you. With this one, go for yourself.

He threw a cocktail reception for the album's release on the Circle
Line boat cruise around Manhattan. Some of his new friends mingled
in the crowd with the regulation suits and ties from the Midtown
music business. Wassel's brother J.J. went around passing the hat for
the United Jewish Appeal. Wassel took offense at the freakish ukulele
player Tiny Tim with his long hair and effeminate manner as he tried
to come aboard and Wassel dropped him overboard in the harbor. An
impossibly young Van Morrison, backed by his new trio of New York
musicians, just put together, delivered an earnest, vigorous set. He
smiled happily after for photographs, drink in hand.

Berns hired guitarist Charlie Brown, who was a great player,
not because he was a great player, but because he would make sure
Morrison got to the dates on time. At his shows the following week
at the Greenwich Village nightclub the Bottom Line, with members
of the press and radio in the audience, Morrison went berserk during
"T. B. Sheets," thrashing around the tiny stage with his microphone
stand. The female backup singers he hired for the dates had to duck.
He ended up crashing into the drums, sprawling onstage, as the girl
singers fled.

Moody, petulant Morrison spoke with such a thick accent he
couldn't make himself easily understood to anyone in New York,
which only added to his general level of frustration and resentment.
Trying to place a call through the hotel switchboard could take several
tries because he would get so angry, he would have to hang up and
calm down before he could start over. Morrison was not a social person. Berns dragged him out on his boat one sunny afternoon with his
family, but Morrison was sullen, uncommunicative.

He didn't have a lot of gigs, mostly local promotional events and
radio interviews. He holed up in the City Squire with his girlfriend,

drinking heavily, taking in occasional shows by the blues greats who were his idols: Muddy Waters, Howlin' Wolf, John Lee Hooker. He didn't understand someone like Berns, whose taste was tailored to the charts. Morrison had been surprised, talking to Berns about bluesman Sonny Boy Williamson. "He's nothing," said Berns. "In the States, people don't even know who he is."

Berns wanted Wassel to manage Morrison. Wassel found him foul-mouthed and unpleasant. He moved the Morrison party to less expensive quarters at the King Edward Hotel, where Wassel ran a poker game in the penthouse and professional wrestler Haystacks Calhoun lived across the hall. Wassel visited Morrison in his hotel room and found a drunken Morrison wearing a lamp shade, trailing window blinds from the hotel room, and singing "I'm Henry the VIII, I Am." Wassel discovered a radio he had given Morrison was broken. When Wassel asked what happened, Morrison let loose a stream of profanity. Wassel reached for the nearest thing handy—Morrison's acoustic guitar—and hit him over the head. The guitar was shattered. Wassel felt bad because it was a nice guitar, a Martin.

Even as the Aretha Franklin records Jerry Wexler was making pushed both Atlantic Records in specific and soul music in general further into the sunlight, he was still looking to sell the company and found some guys who might actually pull the trigger. Meanwhile, Wexler played Ellie Greenwich a rough mix of a new Aretha record and she immediately dreamed up a background vocal part on the spot that would tie the whole arrangement together to "Chain of Fools." Wexler took her into the studio and Greenwich sang these *whoop-whoop*s that locked down the track on Franklin's fifth consecutive Top Ten hit of the year. The hits just kept coming.

Eliot Hyman and Ray Stark started Seven Arts Productions in 1957, and while Stark produced movies for other studios all over Hollywood, Hyman stayed in New York consolidating other assets, such as buying the Warner Bros. film catalog and renting old movies to TV. They took the company public in 1964 and, in January 1967, acquired old Jack Warner's one-third interest in his film studio and record company for $32,000,000 and shortly thereafter purchased all the remaining outstanding stock. Hyman, who planned to sell Warner as soon as he could for a large profit, met with the Atlantic partners about a prospective purchase. Picking up undervalued companies and folding them into larger companies to make the combined companies more attractive to potential buyers—conglomerating—was very popular in the sixties. Hyman made Atlantic an offer.

Wexler hustled the Erteguns to and from the bargaining table. "This is the American dream," he said. "Capital gains." Ahmet Ertegun, living happily in his East Eighty-First Street townhouse, voted in favor of autonomy. His brother, Nesuhi, cast the deciding vote on the grounds of long-term survival. Few of the r&b independents Atlantic had started alongside were still standing. He did have mixed feelings, but he landed on the side of the sale.

There was only one problem. After years of cutting corners on costs, making records on the cheap, not paying royalties, and every other trick they could learn to put a few extra pennies in their pockets, the Atlantic partners apparently had no idea what their company was really worth on the market and drastically undervalued it. The price was surprisingly low. Hyman paid $4,500,000 in cash, $3,000,000 more in unsecured notes (IOUs), and the remainder of the $17,500,000 total in stock. Atlantic had $7,000,000 in cash, which became Hyman's the minute the sale went through, so his total net cost was not more than $10,000,000, less than half in cash, roughly equal to the cash on hand.

On the first of October, late at night under fluorescent lights in an office in a tall building in Manhattan, they signed about a thousand documents and turned over all outstanding stock in Atlantic Records to Warner Bros.–Seven Arts. Under Hyman's new W7 record division, they would merge with the existing Warner/Reprise labels. The creaky old Burbank film studio record label had undergone a complete transformation in recent years under the skillful leadership of chairman Mo Ostin, former accountant to Reprise founder Frank Sinatra (who retained a substantial interest in the label even after the Warner–Seven Arts deal), and president Joe Smith, ex-Boston rock and roll disc jockey. In August, for the first time in the label's history, Warner/Reprise had as many albums on the charts as industry leader Columbia—eighteen, including seven the label released that month. Although the labels were guaranteed autonomy under the terms of the acquisition, the combination was the beginning of conglomerating the entire independent record business.

In October 1967, Berns issued a new Neil Diamond single, "Kentucky Woman," over Diamond's objections. The singer wanted to release another song instead as his next single, a peculiar, offbeat number about a childhood imaginary friend named "Shilo." Berns gave that all the consideration it deserved. Diamond's last five singles went Top Twenty. He sold more than a million singles.

He was even moving a few albums, although his Bang albums were slapdash affairs. *The Feel of Neil Diamond* came out in the wake of "Cherry, Cherry" in August 1966 and featured his two big hits, "Solitary Man" and "Cherry, Cherry." His second album, *Just for You*, came out in August the next year and also featured his two big hits, "Solitary Man" and "Cherry, Cherry."

Berns ran his record company on his own strictly commercial instincts. They had something happening with Diamond—a kind of sulking, brooding sexuality that was going over big with teenage girls. "Kentucky Woman" would be the next single.

"Shilo" became a sore point with Diamond. Berns wanted hits and "Shilo" didn't sound like a hit to him. Diamond had two meetings with Berns. They argued. Berns told him he would put out the song if Diamond signed a one-year extension on his contract. Diamond told him he didn't want to give any more records to Bang. Berns also threatened Diamond. He said that it would be simple for the label to advance Van

Morrison's career at the expense of Diamond's in regards to promotion, advertising, the timing of releases, etc. Play ball, he warned Diamond.

Diamond didn't. As president and 50 percent partner in Tallyrand Music, without consulting his partners, Diamond the partner decided not to pick up the production company's option with Diamond the recording artist. He may have picked the fight with Berns, but he clearly didn't mind rolling over Barry and Greenwich to get what he wanted.

His attorneys advised him that Berns was in breach of contract on several counts. There were minor breaches involving "coupling" or releasing Diamond tracks on albums featuring other people's recordings, compilation albums such as *The Gang at Bang*, a collection of tracks by Bang acts. Also there was the matter of Diamond's legal representation. The contracts were drawn up by Paul Marshall, who happened to represent all parties, Diamond, Barry and Greenwich, and Berns and Bang, not to mention Bang distributor, Atlantic Records, even though Diamond himself allowed that nobody had any doubts as to Marshall's integrity.

But the key breach came from the omission—accidental according to Marshall, intentional said Diamond's new attorneys—of the term "exclusive" in describing Diamond's recording services in the contracts. Diamond's attorneys assured him that would free him to sign a new record deal with another label as soon as a judge looked at the briefs.

Berns was settling into a comfortable working relationship at his new Forty-Second Street studio, Incredible Sounds, with engineer Chris Huston, a British expatriate stranded in this country when his rock group broke up, who had been working with such other clients at Incredible in only the past few months as James Brown and the Who. The Young Rascals recorded "Groovin'" at the Times Square studio. Huston had a good idea who Berns's silent partners were and figured Wassel spent all that time hanging around the studio because he was keeping his eye on the business for those guys. He was leery, at first, but warmed up after Wassel took Huston to lunch at Jack Dempsey's and gave him a guitar.

Berns needed hits and his two main acts were not giving him what
he wanted. Van Morrison didn't have another "Brown Eyed Girl" in his
hip pocket, anymore than Neil Diamond had another "Cherry, Cherry."
Morrison spent endless hours at his mother's house in Belfast sitting in front
of his tape recorder, noodling, jamming, just inventing, trying to find pieces
of songs, images that stuck. He was pursuing a vision, dimly lit, elusive,
and faint. These brittle, half-finished tapes featured Dylanesque ramblings,
underscored by Morrison's rumbling, jangling guitar and punctuated by
the occasional thump and rattle of a tambourine. Morrison played the tapes
for Berns at his office as if he were unveiling precious cargo. Morrison mut-
tered something about preserving the spontaneity of the performances.
Berns joked about just releasing the raw, sketchy demo—"That's what we
should do," he said. For a minute, Morrison thought he meant it.

In November, when Berns reassembled the sessions at Incredible
Sounds, Morrison found a full ensemble of New York studio professionals waiting for him at the studio to start his new album. Morrison
was daunted and couldn't express himself. He was certain Berns
wasn't going to listen to him or that, even if he seemed to be listening,
Berns would go ahead and do what he wanted anyway. He threw his
guitar against the studio wall and yelled at the musicians. "You can't
understand me," he said.

Morrison had been living in tiny hotel rooms for months, spending
far too much time isolated. The warm camaraderie of the Circle Line
boat cruise had been replaced by a wary, tense relationship. Morrison
felt ignored by Berns, as if he was just another artist on the label. He
didn't have other options, but he was growing increasingly resentful,
drinking himself into dark, depressive moods.

The sessions with Van Morrison frustrated Berns, trying to make
sense out of his new material. Obviously brilliant but not brilliantly
obvious, the new Morrison songs vexed Berns. He dumped all sorts of
loud party noise on "Madame George," trying to give the obtuse, poetic
song some context, forcing the material into shape through production.

Morrison was right—Berns didn't understand these songs, but this time, he wasn't kindly and encouraging. Berns, exasperated, lost his temper with Morrison. He told him that, of the two of them, Berns was the one who knew what he was doing and that Morrison would be well advised to pay attention. Morrison was proving to be quite the headache and the new songs didn't sound like hits.

Berns conducted brief sessions with Freddie Scott and took Erma Franklin back in the studio at Incredible and cut a fine Berns-Ragovoy number, "Open Up Your Soul," while Ragovoy looked on, and a Goffin and King teardrops song, "The Right to Cry." After "Piece of My Heart" made the Top Ten R&B in November, Franklin decided to quit her job and signed with Queen Booking, the agency run by Ruth Bowen that also handled her sister. Berns restored her confidence. They were making an album. She was going back into the music business.

Berns decided to move his family back in the city while Ilene was pregnant. He wanted her to have ready access to her obstetrician. They rented a suite at the Oliver Cromwell Hotel on Seventy-Second Street, next door to the Dakota, across the street from Central Park. Construction of their dream house with the guitar-shaped swimming pool across the river in Tenafly, New Jersey, near where they had been living, was nearly finished. Mark Ben-Ari Berns was born December 12. His godfather Jeff Barry officiated at the bris. He held up the baby and remarked that it looked exactly like his father if somebody put a pin in Bert and let all the air out.

About the same time, session musician Al Gorgoni and songwriter Chip Taylor, who had been working as a production team, booked a date at Brooks Arthur's new studio, Century Sound, and showed up with Neil Diamond. Arthur was shocked there was no Bert Berns or Jeff and Ellie, but he didn't say anything. Arthur, Brooklyn boy that he was, cried as he recorded the song "Brooklyn Roads." Berns was on the phone a couple of days later, trying to sound cheerful. "I hear you cut Neil," he said. "Well, now it's out—we're not on terms."

The first week of December, Berns released another new Neil Diamond single, as if to let the entire industry know that he was still in the Neil Diamond business, the old Gary "U.S." Bonds song "New Orleans," one of the covers that filled out his first Bang album. A week later, Berns sent telegrams to every record company he thought might be talking to Neil Diamond:

> PLEASE BE ADVISED WEB IV MUSIC INC HAS EXCLUSIVE RIGHTS RECORDINGS OF NEIL DIAMOND FOR PHONOGRAPHIC RECORD PUR-POSES AND OTHER RIGHTS ANY INTERFERENCE AND ADVANTA-GEOUS RELATIONS IMMEDIATELY AND SUBSTANTIALLY DAMAGING

Berns went on the warpath. Not only was Diamond his label's top-selling artist, but also Berns felt protective of Barry and Greenwich, who were the real innocent victims of Diamond's fight with Bang and a stepping stone for his ambitions. They found Diamond when he was nothing, went into their own pockets to pay his salary, and gave him an unheard-of fair shake. Diamond used the equitable percentage they gave him to abandon their partnership and vacate the deal. He would have never been offered a deal like that from Leiber and Stoller or, for that matter, anyone else on Broadway. Berns did not want to see him get away with it.

When somebody tossed a stink bomb into the Bitter End during one of his engagements, Diamond knew Berns had it done. Ironically, Berns's old pal Paul Colby, who recently took over running the club for Diamond manager Fred Weintraub, cleaned up the mess. Then Weintraub was "mugged," beaten up pretty bad. Things were getting scary. Diamond borrowed a .38-caliber pistol from a friend and moved his wife and kid out of their new Manhattan apartment to stay in Long Island.

The week after Christmas, Berns ate dinner with Incredible engineer Chris Huston at Mamma Leone's. Berns had lots of plans for the future of the studio and was talking to Huston about working together.

Out of nowhere, his mood shifted, his voice dropped. "Have you ever had the premonition you were going to die?" he asked the twenty-three-year-old engineer, who sat there speechless, not knowing what to say.

On Friday, December 29, Stephen Prince, working as an assistant to Fred Weintraub, wheeled his boss's Cadillac Fleetwood uptown and waited while his passengers, Weintraub and Neil Diamond, went to have a meeting with Berns at his office. They returned shaken and upset. Berns scared them badly. They planned to call the district attorney and hire protection on Monday. "We'll get bodyguards," Weintraub said.

After the nasty confrontation with Diamond, Berns met Billy Fields that afternoon for a cup of coffee at the B&G Diner on Seventh Avenue. Fields, who knew Berns all the way back to the Trocadero Ballroom in the Bronx during the forties, worked at Weintraub's management office. He found a dispirited Berns, resigned to losing Diamond. But the working year wasn't over until Berns and Morrison held a shouting match on the telephone later that escalated to the point where Morrison hung up on him.

The long holiday weekend stretched out ahead. Soon it would be a new year, 1968. Bert and Ilene were going to a New Year's Eve party Sunday night at Artie Resnick's place.

On Saturday morning, Berns took out the new Cadillac convertible he bought Ilene and packed his wife and Brett off to inspect the new house. They drove across the bridge on the cold, gray day into the cul-de-sac in Tenafly. "Honey," he said, "I bet you never thought you'd fill up all these bedrooms."

They walked around back and looked at the guitar-shaped pool. Berns needed to check the shape of the hole before they poured the cement. He called Tommy Dowd, who lived in nearby Westwood, and dropped by to visit with him and his wife, Jackie. Bert and Ilene got in the car to drive home. "I don't feel so good," he said. "I feel a little tired. I think I'll go home and take a nap."

When they got back to the Oliver Cromwell, Ilene went out to Bloomingdale's. She had been in maternity clothes for eighteen months. She wanted to buy a new outfit for the party the next night. She left Berns with the baby's nurse and the Jamaican maid. The football game was on. When she called to check in, he asked her to come back. "I'm not feeling too good," he said.

She came home and went in the bedroom. "I'm not going to watch the game," he told her. "I'm going to take a nap." She turned off the television and shut the door behind her. The phone rang. It was Jerry Wexler. She shouted at her husband. Berns always wanted to talk with Wexler, even now, after all they'd gone through. "Tell him I'll call him back," Berns said from the bedroom.

The maid returned from downstairs with a pile of folded laundry and Ilene took a stack of socks and underwear in the bedroom. She opened the door and screamed. Berns was lying half off the bed, his eyes wildly dilated, wheezing, gurgling in his throat. Ilene grabbed him and threw him back on the bed. She scrambled looking for the nitroglycerin pills. She tried breathing in his mouth, but it was useless. The maid came in and started screaming and crying. "He's gone, he's dead."

Ilene knew. She slowly backed out of the room, horrified, shutting the door behind her. Two-year-old Brett pounded on the door. "I want my daddy," he cried. "I want my daddy."

She called her parents—her father had to be paged at an airport—and they came to take the two older children. The baby was three weeks old. Outside it was snowing. She called Jeff Barry and he came right over. He found Ilene a wreck and Berns's body lying on the bed. Tommy Eboli showed up in a cashmere overcoat. When Wassel got there, after running all the way from Sixty-Ninth Street and West End Avenue, tough guy Eboli was sunk into the couch, crying in his hands.

Barry knew about the cash in the safe at the office. Berns had showed it to him only recently. Barry thought Berns kept the safe combination in his right-hand desk drawer. Eboli left for Berns's office shortly thereafter. When he called back to say he couldn't find the combination, Barry knew what he needed to do.

He went into the bedroom, extracted Berns's wallet from the dead man's pants, and found a folded slip of paper from Massler's Safe Company. Eboli sent a car for Barry. By the time Barry arrived downtown, Patsy Pagano had joined the party at the office, and they stacked the $100 bills in a paper bag, almost all the $70,000 from the Atlantic settlement Pagano had brought to the hospital only nine months before. There were also three handguns in the safe and they brought those along. Back at the Oliver Cromwell, they gave Ilene the greens. The party at Artie Resnick's the next night was subdued.

On January 1, 1968, they buried Bert Berns at the Riverside Memorial Chapel on Amsterdam Avenue at Seventy-Sixth Street. Tommy Eboli came to the mortuary the night before to pay his respects. He asked Ilene to view the body. For everyone else, it was a closed coffin, but Eboli took one last fond look at his friend. He didn't feel comfortable going to the next day's services at the chapel, but Patsy Pagano and his wife did. Ilene was pudding. She needed help to walk. She left the children home. Freddie Scott stood in the back, sobbing. Ellie Greenwich came with Paul Marshall but didn't stay long because she was uncomfortable around Jeff Barry, who was there with his new girlfriend. Grown men were crying.

These people did not know death. Berns was their first take on the death of someone not old and infirm. He was their colleague and he was gone. Sudden, unexpected deaths always have a way of putting mortality in focus. Life for these princes and princesses of the music world had long been nothing but a frolic.

The curtain had rung down on more than Berns, truth be told, although they were all too stunned to take account. One of the great golden ages of American music had come to a close, although nobody may have noticed at the time. Atlantic Records was sold. Soul music would never grow greater than Aretha Franklin. Leiber and Stoller were as good as retired. They wanted to write a Broadway musical and shake free forever of the dirt and grime of the rhythm and blues that put them at the top of the Brill Building. Phil Spector was living like some kind of crazed recluse. He closed his Philles Records, fatally discouraged by the failure of his Ike and Tina single, "River Deep— Mountain High," and descended into a life lived on vampire hours behind around-the-clock security in a Beverly Hills mansion, where his jealousies and paranoias could run free. Doc Pomus, already long out of the music business, estranged from his family, divorced from his showgirl wife, was making a living running poker games in his room in the sleazebag Broadway hotel. Morty Shuman escaped to Paris, where he was writing songs for French rock and roll king Johnny Hallyday. Goffin and King split up and Carole King moved to California. Burt Bacharach had moved to Hollywood, where he was writing cheese for the movies, preparing a Broadway musical of his own with Hal David, and starting to develop his interest in racehorses. Donny Kirshner wasn't even in music publishing anymore; all he had left of his Screen Gems deal was a lawsuit. Barry and Greenwich were no more. Ellie Greenwich would never marry or write another hit song again. George Goldner would never put out another record. Wexler didn't come to the funeral, but Neil Diamond did. He went to ask the widow for his release. Van Morrison stayed away, too.

Brooks Arthur, Artie Butler, Gary Chester, and their wives stood around the cold sidewalk afterward and, without saying much, walked off together under the gray skies. They just wandered downtown, blocks after blocks, quiet for the most part, until they found themselves, without meaning to, in front of 1650 Broadway. An icy wind whipped down the empty streets. Some Broadway wiseacre, someone with nothing better to do than be downtown on this cold New Year's Day, recognized them and braced them. He asked what they were doing there, and they told him.

"Bert Berns," he said. "He coulda given Gershwin a run for the money."

Bert Berns, Garry Sherman

BERT BERNS DISCOGRAPHY

Compiled by Rob Hughes

with thanks to Kurt Mohr, Michel Ruppli, and Bob Hyde.

BOB MANNING & EYDIE GORME (Manny Levin & Edith Gormezano) (vo) with Les Elgart (tp,leader), Harry DiVito (tb), Tony Scott (cl), Harry Biss (p), Dante Martucci (b), Bob Barron (dm). Add Herb Wasserman, Alan Jeffreys (vo) omit Bob Manning (vo)-1. Arr. by Morty Craft. Prod. by Bert Berns and Sid Bernstein.

New York, 1949/50

M.N.X. (Herb Wasserman,Alan Jeffreys)	Magic
THE FLYING SAUCER (Herb Wasserman,Alan Jeffreys)-1	Magic

ESY MORALES AND ORCHESTRA: Ismael "Esy" Morales (fl) and his band. (same session as above). Prod. by Bert Berns and Sid Bernstein.

New York, 1949/50

AFRICAN VOODOO	Magic
NEGRO	Magic

THE LIMELIGHTERS (male vo-gp) with p, g, b, dm.

New York, June 1954

DB-2094 I LOVE A MELODY (PLEASE PLAY A SONG FOR ME) (Al Rubin,Bert Berns)	Pic 0006
DB-2095 MY BABY AND A LEMON-N-LIME (Al Rubin,Bernie Baum)	Pic 0006

MICKI MARLO (vo) with orch. cond. by Earl Sheldon: tps, tbs, as, ts, bs, p, g, b, dm. Add vb-1; bgo, male-cho-2.

New York, September 21, 1955

20869 HOW COME YOU DO ME LIKE YOU DO (Gene Austin,Roy Bergere)-1	Capitol 3346
20870 WAIT DOWN BY THE CHERRY TREE (Bert Berns)-2	Capitol 3346
20871 PET ME, POPPA (Frank Loesser)	Capitol 3266
20872 LIKE I LOVED NOBODY BEFORE (Bernie Wayne,E. H. Jay)	Capitol 3266

THE BEATNIKS: Bill Giant (Ethan Goldstein) and Bert Berns (vo) with King Curtis (ts), p, 2g, b, Herb Wasserman (dm). Add bs-1, as-2.

Allegro Sound Studio, New York, January 1959

K70W-2071 GET YOURSELF A READY (Sylvia Berns,Rene St. Charles)-1	Performance 500
K70W-2072 BEAT GENERATION (Ethan Giant,Bernie "Anna Shaw" Baum)-2	Performance 500

RITA CONSTANCE (vo) with Prod. by Bert Berns.
New York, January 1959
TROUBLES (Harry Belafonte)   Performance
NIGHT WINDS   Performance

BERT & BILL GIANT (Bert Berns and Bill Giant) (vo) with orch. dir. by Milton Delugg: ts, p, g, b, dm, male-cho. Add bjo; omit ts, p-1. Prod. by Joe Guercio.
New York, September 1959
MAH 10,770-1 WAYWARD MAN (Brown,Zimmerman)   Signature 12019
MAH 10,771-5 GETTYSBURG ADDRESS (Bert Russell,Ethan Giant,Jeff Lewis)-1   Signature 12019

JACK CARROLL (vo) with Eliot Glen (Eliot Greenberg) Orch.: 2tp, 2tb, tu, 2fl, bjo, g, b, dm, hca, mixed-cho.
New York, October 1959
ZTSP 62783 THE BALLAD OF WALTER WILLIAMS (Bert Russell   Laurie 3046

JOHNNY YUKON (vo) with bjo, g, b, dm, xyl, male-cho.
New York, March 1960
ZTSP 64532 WHITE OAK SWAMP (Ross Miller,Bert Russell)   Versatile 104
ZTSP 64533 THIRTEEN STEPS (Hal Gordon,Athena Hosey,Ora May Diamond)   Versatile 104

AUSTIN TAYLOR (vo) with Buddy Lucas (ts), p, g, b, dm, mixed-cho. Add vb-1; timpani, handclaps-2.
New York, June 1960
L70W-8545 A HEART THAT'S TRUE (Arlene Schwartz,Virginia Cleary)   Laurie 3067
L70W-8546 I LOVE BEING LOVED BY YOU (A.Smith)-1   Laurie 3095
L70W-8547 TOGETHER FOREVER (Ira Kosloff,Irving Reid)   Laurie 3095
L70W-8548 PUSH PUSH (Bert Russell,Phil Medley)-2   Laurie 3067

LAVERN BAKER (vo) with Al Sears (ts); Haywood Henry (bs,fl); Ernie Hayes (org); Bert Keyes (p); Mickey Baker, Carl Lynch (g); Abie Baker (b); Berisford "Shep" Shepherd (dm); Eddie Costa (vb,chimes); Malcolm Dodds, Nat Smith, Ed Barnes, Winfield Scott (bkd-vo). Arr-cond. by Jesse Stone. Prod. by Ahmet Ertegun and Jerry Wexler.
Atlantic Recording Studio, New York, August 17, 1960
A-4851 YOU SAID (Sara Wright)   Atlantic LP8071
A-4852 BUMBLE BEE (Leroy Fullylove,Lavern Baker)   Atlantic 2077, LP8050
A-4853 MY TIME WILL COME (Brook Benton,Bobby Stevenson)   Atlantic 2077, LP8050
A-4854 A LITTLE BIRD TOLD ME SO (Ersel Hickey,Bert Russell)   Atlantic LP8071

FRANKIE BRENT (vo) with tp, ts, bs, p, g, b, dm, bgo, mixed-cho.
Bell Sound Studios, New York, August 1960
C181 A-3 MORE OF EVERYTHING (Kal Mann,Dave Appell)   Cameo 181
C181 B-2 BANGIN' ON THE BONGO (Bert Russell,Bill Darnel, Kal "Jon Sheldon" Mann) Cameo 181

BERT BERNS (vo) with bjo, g, el-b, dm, mixed-cho. Add hca-1.
New York, August 1960
L07W-2295 GOTTA' TRAVEL ON (Paul Clayton)   Laurie 3074
L07W-2296 THE LEGEND OF THE ALAMO (Bert Russell,Don Johnston,
     Robert Mellin,Diane Johnston)-1   Laurie 3074

HOAGY LANDS (Victor Hoagland) (vo) with King Curtis (ts), p, 2g, el-b, dm, mixed-cho. Arr-cond. by Teacho Wiltshire. Prod. by Morty Palitz.
New York, September 1960
MP-13 LIGHTED WINDOWS (Bert Russell,Phil Medley)   Judi 054, ABC-Paramount 10171
MP-14 (I'M GONNA) CRY SOME TEARS (Bert Russell,Phil Medley) Judi 054, ABC-Paramount 10171

BERT BERNS (vo) with 2g, Bill Giant (vo)-1; g, el-b, dm, fem-cho -2; p, g, dm -3; p, dm, whistling -4.

New York, 1960

COLD PRISON WALL (Bert Russell,Bill Giant)-1	unissued demo
SALLY (Bert Russell)-1	unissued demo
I'M COMIN' BACK (Bert Russell,Phil Medley)-2	unissued demo
IN A ROOM IN A HOUSE (Bert Russell,Dion Dimucci)-3	unissued demo
WHISTLER'S TWIST (Bert Russell)-4	unissued demo

DION (vo) with tp, tb, as, ts, bs, p, g, b, dm, mixed-cho. Prod. by Gene Schwartz.

New York, November 1960

IN A ROOM IN A HOUSE (Bert Russell,Dion DiMucci)	Laurie unissued

ELSON SMITH (vo) with ts, Charles Macey (g), g, b, dm. Add Bert Berns (whistling)-1. Dir. by Chas. Macey. Ricar Production.

New York, January 1961

M80W-4088-2 WHISTLER'S TWIST (Bert Russell)-1	Fraternity 876
M80W-4089-2 COMIN' ROUND THE MOUNTAIN (Ralph Montello,Billy Dawn Smith)	Fraternity 876

THE TOP NOTES: Derek Martin (lead vo-1/vo), Howard Guyton (lead vo-2/vo) with orch. arr.-cond. by Teddy Randazzo: King Curtis (ts); Ernie Hayes (p/el-p); John "Bucky" Pizzarelli, Allen Hanlon (g); Abie Baker (b); Panama Francis, Gary Chester (dm,perc); Phil Kraus (xyl); 10 strings; The Cookies: Earl-Jean McCrae, Dorothy Jones, Margaret Ross (bkd-vo). Supervised by Phil Spector.

Atlantic Studios, New York, February 23, 1961

A-5356 HEARTS OF STONE (Eddie Ray,Rudy Jackson)-1	Atlantic 2097
A-5357 ALWAYS LATE (Howard Guyton,Esther Navarro,Derek Martin)-2	Atlantic 2115
A-5358 THE BASIC THINGS (Martin,Navarro)-1	Atlantic 2097
A-5359 TWIST AND SHOUT (Bert Russell,Phil Medley) 2	Atlantic 2115, LP8058

RUSSELL BYRD (Bert Berns) (vo) with orch. arr. by Carole King: p, 2ac-g, b, dm, strings. Add fem-cho -1. A Ludix Production (=Luther Dixon).

Bell Sound Studios, New York, February 1961

W107 A YOU'D BETTER COME HOME (Bert Russell)	Wand 107
W107 B LET'S TELL HIM ALL ABOUT IT (Bert Russell,Luther Dixon)-1	Wand 107

ARTHUR PRYSOCK (vo) with ts, bs, fl, p, g, b, dm, strings. Omit saxes; strings add cowbell; The Fiestas: Tommy Bullock (tenor bkd-vo), Eddie Morris (tenor bkd-vo), Sam Ingalls (baritone bkd-vo), Preston Lane (bass bkd-vo)-1. Prod. by Hy Weiss.

Bell Sound Studios, New York, March 1961

1043 SPEAK TO ME (Herbert L.Miller,Jack Finestone)	Old Town 1106
1044 THIS TIME (Herbert L.Miller,Johnny Lehmann)	Old Town 1101
1045 ONE MORE TIME (Bert Russell,Ray Passman,Phil Medley)-1	Old Town 1106
1046 I WONDER WHERE OUR LOVE IS GONE (Buddy Johnson)	Old Town 1101

JIMMY JONES (vo) with orch. cond. by Bert Keyes: p, 2g, el-b, dm, strings.bAdd 2tp, tb, ts, bs-1; mixed-cho -2. Prod. by Otis Blackwell.

New York, April 27, 1961

61-XY-617 I SAY LOVE (Bert Russell,Phil Medley)-1	Cub 9093
61-XY-618 WAVE THAT HAND	unissued
61-XY-619 DEAR ONE (Waldense Hall,David Parker)-2	Cub 9093
61-XY-620 TWO TON TESSIE (Gene Pitney,Aaron Schroeder)	unissued

THE JARMELS: Paul Burnett (lead tenor vo); Nathaniel Ruff, Earl Christian (tenor vo); Ray Smith (baritone vo); Tom Eldridge (bass vo) with orch. arr-cond. by Glen Stuart (Eliot Greenberg): p, 2g, b, dm, claves, timpani, strings. Prod. by Gene Schwartz.

New York, May 4, 1961

M70W-7042 THE WAY YOU LOOK TONIGHT (Dorothy Fields,Jerome Kern)	Laurie 3098
M70W-7043 A LITTLE BIT OF SOAP (Bert Russell)	Laurie 3098

TOM GULLION (vo) with p, bjo, g, el-b, dm, fem-cho. Lutz-Kipness Prod. (=Herb Lutz and Joe Kipness).

New York, June 1961

M80W-8813 TURN AROUND (Bert Russell,Audrey Saxon)	Laurie 3102
M80W-8814 PRECIOUS (Bert Russell,Ethel Haft)	Laurie 3102

SAMMY TURNER (vo) with p, 2g, el-b, dm, strings. Add ts, fem-cho -1; mixed-cho -2. A Lutz-Kipness Prod.

New York, June 1961

BG-1219 THE FOOL OF THE YEAR (Carl Spencer,Harold Johnson,Arthur Crier)-1	Big Top 3082
BG-1220 POUR IT ON (Mike Kelly,Bert Russell)-2	Big Top 3082

DOTTY CLARK (vo) with orch. cond. by Teacho Wiltshire: p, 2g, el-b, dm, tamb, marimba, strings, fem-cho. Prod. by Bert Berns.

Bell Sound Studios, New York, June 1961

BG-1221 IT'S BEEN A LONG LONG TIME (Sammy Cahn,Jules Styne)	Big Top 3081
BG-1222 THAT'S A STEP IN THE RIGHT DIRECTION (Bert Russell,Ethel Haft)	Big Top 3081

BOBBY ADAMS (vo) with p, 2g, el-b, dm, tamb, strings, mixed-cho. Arr.-1 or dir.-2 and prod. by Stu Phillips.

New York, July 18, 1961

M70W-9834 WHO KNOWS WHAT MIGHT HAVE BEEN (Bobby Adams,Bobby Stevenson)	unissued
M70W-9835 SAVE THOSE TEARDROPS (Fred Anisfield,Bert Russell)-1	Colpix 604
M70W-9836 I THINK YOU WANT MY GIRL (Jeff Barry)-2	Colpix 604

CONWAY TWITTY (vo) with Floyd Cramer (el-p -2/p); Al Bruno, Thomas Grady Martin, Ray Edenton (g); Floyd T."Lightnin'"Chance (el-b); Murray M."Buddy"Harman (dm); strings; mixed-cho. Add fl-1, scraper omit strings-2. Prod. by Jim Vienneau.

Bradley Film & Recording Studio, Nashville, July 24, 1961

61-XY-737 SWEET SORROW (Barry Mann,Cynthia Weil)	MGM 13034, LP4019
61-XY-738 A LITTLE BIRD TOLD ME (Harvey Brooks)-1	MGM unissued
61-XY-739 (tk6) IT'S DRIVING ME WILD (Bert Russell,Ethel Haft)-2	MGM 13034, LP4019

THE FLAMETTES: 4 females (vo) with tp, tb, ts, bs, p, 2g, el-b, dm. Prod. by Bert Berns.

New York, July 1961

ZTSP 69372 YOU YOU YOU (Robert Mellin,Lotar Olias)	Laurie 3109
ZTSP 69373 HEE HEE HA HA (Gregory Carroll,Sampson Horton)	Laurie 3109

LITTLE JIMMY DEE (vo) with orch. cond. by Teacho Wiltshire: p, g, b, dm, timpani, triangle, strings, mixed-cho. Prod. by Bert Berns.

Bell Sound Studios, New York, July 1961

INX-010-A I SHOULD HAVE LISTENED (Bert Russell)	Infinity 010
INX-010-B I WENT ON (Gene Redd,Ronnie Moseley)	Infinity 010

HOAGY LANDS (Victor Hoagland) (vo) with p, g, ac-g, el-b, dm, strings, mixed-cho. Add timbales-1, timpani-2. Prod. by Bert Berns.

New York, August 28, 1961

61-XY-833 IT'S GONNA BE MORNING (Bert Russell)-1	MGM 13041
61-XY-834 MY TEARS ARE DRY (Bert Russell,Selma Shifrin)-2	MGM 13041
61-XY-835 I'M YOURS (Robert Mellin)	unissued
61-XY-836 I'M GONNA BE A LONG TIME FORGETTING YOU	unissued

THE RENAULTS: 2 males (lead vo), 2 females (vo) with tb, p, 2g, el-b, dm, perc, strings. Prod. by Bert Berns.

Mirasound Studios, New York, August 1961

W114 A JUST LIKE MINE (Bert Russell)	Wand 114
W114 B ANOTHER TRAIN PULLED OUT (Bert Russell,Buddy Lucas)	Wand 114

RUSSELL BYRD (Bert Berns) (vo) with tp, g, ac-g, b, cga, scraper, triangle, marimba, strings, fem-cho. Prod. by Phil Spector.

Mirasound Studios, New York, September 1961

116B NIGHTS OF MEXICO (Bert Russell,Ray Passman)	Wand 121

THE EDSELS: George Jones Jr. (lead vo), Larry Greene, James Reynolds, Harry Greene, Marshall Sewell (vo) with orch. cond. by Teacho Wiltshire: 2tp, King Curtis (ts), p, 2g, el-b, Gary Chester (dm), scraper. Prod. by Manny Kellem.

New York, October 20, 1961

23922 DON'T YOU FEEL (Bert Russell, Donald Dean Drowty)	Capitol 4836
23923 SHAKE SHAKE SHERRY (Jeff Barry)	Capitol 4675
23924 IF YOUR PILLOW COULD TALK (Bert Russell)	Capitol 4675
23925 SHADDY DADDY DIP DIP (Jeff Barry)	Capitol 4836

GEORGE HUDSON AND THE KINGS OF TWIST: George Hudson (pesenter), Gil Hamilton (vo), King Curtis (ts), bs, g, el-b, Gary Chester (dm). Prod. by Andy Wiswell and Manny Kellem.

New York, October 31, 1961

23926 THE TWIST (Hank Ballard)	Capitol LP1578
23927 KANSAS CITY (Mike Stoller,Jerry Leiber)	Capitol LP1578
23928 IT'S TWISTIN' TIME (Mann,Lowe)	Capitol LP1578
23929 A LITTLE BIT OF SOAP (Bert Russell)	Capitol LP1578

GEORGE HUDSON AND THE KINGS OF TWIST: George Hudson (presenter), Gil Hamilton (vo-1), King Curtis (ts), bs, org, g, el-b, Gary Chester (dm). Add Bert Berns (bass bkd-vo)-2. Prod. by Andy Wiswell and Manny Kellem.

New York, October 31, 1961

23930 BLUEBERRY HILL (Stock,Rose,Lewis)	Capitol LP1578
23931 MY BLUE HEAVEN (Walter Donaldson,George Whiting)	Capitol LP1578
23932 (IF I KNEW YOU WERE COMIN') I'D 'VE BAKED A CAKE	
(Al Hoffman,Bob Merrill,Watts)	Capitol LP1578
23933 BABY FACE (Benny Davis,Harry Akst)-1	Capitol LP1578
23934 LITTLE TWISTER (Bert Russell,Ethel Haft)-1-2	Capitol LP1578
23935 THE RAILROAD TWIST (trad.)	Capitol LP1578
23936 LAZY RIVER (Hoagy Carmichael,Sidney Arobin)	Capitol LP1578
23937 THE DOODLIN' TWIST (trad.)	Capitol LP1578

SOLOMON BURKE (vo) with Leon Cohen (as), Jesse Powell (ts); Robert Mosely (org); Hank Jones (p); Don Arnone, Al Caiola, John "Bucky" Pizzarelli, Everett Barksdale (g); Art Davis (b); Gary Chester (dm); Phil Kraus (vb); Howard Roberts, David Vogel, Earl Rogers, Noah Hopkins, William Eaton, Sherman Sneed, Richard Kraus (bkd-vo). Omit saxes-1. Arr-cond. by Klaus Ogermann. Prod. by Bert Berns and Jerry Wexler.

New York, December 6, 1961

A-5843 A TEAR FELL (Dorian Burton,Eugene Randolph)	Atlantic LP8067
A-5844 CRY TO ME (Bert Russell)-1	Atlantic 2131, LP8067
A-5845 I ALMOST LOST MY MIND (Ivory Joe Hunter)	Atlantic 2131, LP8067

THE DESTINEERS (vo-gp -1) or **THE MARK FOUR** (vo-gp -2) with King Curtis and his Orch.: King Curtis, Seldon Powell (s); Bert Keyes (p); Everett Barksdale, George Barnes, Al Caiola (g); Milt Hinton (b); Gary C. Curcillo (=Gary Chester) (dm); Anita Darian, Christine Spencer, Elinor Ohms (bkd-vo -3). Arr-prod. by Ray Ellis.

RCA Studio B, New York, 7-11.30 PM, December 7, 1961

M2PB-5872-5 TAKE A LOOK (IN THE MIRROR) (Tommy Boyce)-1-3	RCA 8049
M2PB-5873-9 SO YOUNG (Tommy Boyce)-1	RCA 8049
M2PB-5874-11 ANYTHING IS BETTER (Bert Russell,Phil Medley)-2	unissued
M2PB-5875-3/6 GET UP (Eddie Carlton)-2	unissued

BERT BERNS (vo) with g-1; p, dm-2.

New York, 1961

MARY a.k.a. I'M GONNA HANG AND DIE (Bert Russell)-1	unissued demo
THE WORLD IS MINE (Bert Russell,Jacquie Silverman)-2	unissued demo

SYLVIA HILL (vo) with orch. cond. by Teacho Wiltshire: org, p, 2g, el-b, dm, vb, strings, fem-cho. Omit org-1, vb-2, strings-3. Add triangle-1. Prod. by Manny Kellem and Lookapoo Productions, Inc. (Bert Berns).

New York, January 11, 1962

24030 MAKE ME KNOW IT (Bob Elgin,Kay Rogers,Al Gardner)-2-3	Capitol 4706
24035 BE MY BABY (BE MY LOVE, BE MINE) (Bob Elgin,Kay Rogers)	Capitol 4706
24036 TELL HIM (Bert Russell)-1-2	unissued
24037 COME WALK WITH ME (WHERE THE RIVER MEETS THE SEA) (Kay Rogers,Robert Napoleon Taylor)	unissued

HOAGY LANDS (Victor Hoagland) (vo) with orch. arr-cond. By Teacho Wiltshire: tp, p, 2g, el-b, dm, mixed-cho. Add ts-1, fl-2. Prod. by Bert Berns.

Bell Sound Studios, New York, January 17, 1962

62-XY-352 GOODNIGHT, IRENE (Huddie Ledbetter,John Lomax)-1	MGM 13062
62-XY-353 WHITE GARDENIA (Bert Russell,Carl Spencer)	unissued
62-XY-354 IT AIN'T AS EASY AS THAT (Bert Russell)-2	MGM 13062
62-XY-355 MARY SUE (Bert Russell,Hoagy Lands)	unissued

GEORGE HUDSON (presenter), Gil Hamilton (vo) with King Curtis (ts), bs, org, p, Jimmy Spruill (g), el-b, dm, fem-cho. Add el-p -1. Omit fem-cho -2, org-3. Cond. by Teacho Wiltshire. Prod. by Manny Kellem and Lookapoo Prod., Inc. (Bert Berns).

New York, January 29, 1962

24041 HULLY GULLY FIREHOUSE (Bert Russell,Ray Passman)	Capitol LP1697
24042 THE PEPPERMINT TWIST (Joey Dee,Henry Glover)	Capitol LP1697
24043 (DO THE) MASHED POTATOES (Dessie Rozier)-1-2	Capitol LP1697
24044 DO THE BUG (Bert Russell)-3	Capitol LP1697

GEORGE HUDSON (presenter), Gil Hamilton (vo) with King Curtis (ts), bs, org, p, Jimmy Spruill (g), el-b, dm, fem-cho. Omit fem-cho -1, org-2. Cond. by Teacho Wiltshire. Prod. by Manny Kellem and Lookapoo Prod., Inc. (Bert Berns).

New York, January 29, 1962

24045	THE ROACH (Benton Willis,Sevastos "Steve Venet" Venetoulis)-2	Capitol LP1697
24046	DO THE NEW CONTINENTAL (Kal Mann,Dave Appell)-1	Capitol LP1697
24047	I'M POPEYE THE SAILOR MAN (Sammy Lerner)-1	Capitol 4717, LP1697
24048	COME ON AN' SLOP (Bert Russell)	Capitol LP1697
24049	IN TIME (Bob Elgin,Ed Snyder)-2	Capitol 4766

Note: Capitol 4766 issued as by **GIL HAMILTON**.

GEORGE HUDSON (presenter), Gil Hamilton (vo) with tp, King Curtis (ts), bs, org, p, Jimmy Spruill (g), el-b, dm. Add hca omit vo, tp, bs-1, add timpani-2; add fl, cga, bgo omit bs, org, dm-3. Cond. by Teacho Wiltshire. Prod. by Manny Kellem and Lookapoo Prod., Inc. (Bert Berns).

New York, January 30, 1962

24050	GONNA TWIST ALONG WITHOUT YA NOW (Milton Kellem)	Capitol LP1697
24051	SHIMMY SHIMMY WALK (Billy Lee Riley)-1	Capitol LP1697
24052	BRONX STOMP (Bert Russell,Harry Andrews,Jan Leslie)-2	Capitol 4717, LP1697
24053	DO THE LIMBO (Bert Russell,Yolanda Paterno)-3	Capitol LP1697

THE RENAULTS: 2 males (lead vo), 2 females (vo) with orch. arr. by Teacho Wiltshire: tb, p, 2g, el-b, dm, vb, strings. Omit vb, strings; add tamb-1. Prod. by Bert Berns.

Bell Sound Studios, New York, January 1962

WA120 A	ONLY YOU (Buck Ram,Ande Rand)	Wand 120
WA120 B	HULLY GULLY LAMB(Bert Russell,Don Drowty)-1	Wand 120

RUSSELL BYRD (Bert Berns) (vo) with ac-g, b, dm. Prod. by Bert Berns.

Bell Sound Studios, New York, January 1962

W121 A	LITTLE BUG (Bert Russell)	Wand 121

THE ISLEY BROTHERS: Ronnie Isley (lead vo), Rudolph and O'Kelly Isley (vo) with orch. arr. by Teacho Wiltshire: 2tp; King Curtis (ts); p; Trade Martin, another (g); el-b; Gary Chester (dm); tamb or on -1 backing track arr-cond. by Burt Bacharach: 2g, b, dm, vb, fem-cho or on -2 vo erased from 50172 and Jimmy Spruill (g) overdubbed. Prod. by Bert Berns. A Ludix Production.

Bell Sound Studios, New York, March 1962

	MAKE IT EASY ON YOURSELF (Burt Bacharach,Hal David)-1	Wand unissued
50172	TWIST AND SHOUT (Bert Russell,Phil Medley)	Wand 124, LP653
50350	SPANISH TWIST (Phil Medley,Bert Russell)-2	Wand 124, LP653

LORI ROGERS (vo) with orch. arr. by Teacho Wiltshire: 2tp, bs, p, 2g, el-b, dm, fem-cho. Omit 2tp -1. Prod. by Bert Berns.

Bell Sound Studios, New York, March 1962

S-1232-A	SEYMOUR (Ray Passman,Bert Russell)	Scepter 1232
S-1232-B	I LOVE YOU LORI (Bert Russell,Audrey Saxon)-1	Scepter 1232

GEORGE HUDSON (AND OTHERS) (presenter), Hoagy Lands (vo-1), Gil Hamilton (vo-2), King Curtis (ts except ss-3), bs, p, Jimmy Spruill (g), g, el-b, dm, strings, fem-cho. Omit strings-4, fem-cho -5. Add triangle-6. Or -7 Gil Hamilton (vo) overdubbed on track from 24036 (see SYLVIA HILL 1/11/1962 session). Arr-cond. by Teacho Wiltshire. Prod. by Manny Kellem and Lookapoo Productions, Inc. (Bert Berns).

New York, March 29, 1962

24130 tk14 TELL HER (Bert Russell)-7		Capitol 4766
24131 HE WILL BREAK YOUR HEART (Butler,Mayfield,Carter)-1-2-4-5		Capitol LP1730 to 1737
24132 WHEN MY LITTLE GIRL IS SMILING (King,Goffin)-2-3-4-6		Capitol LP1730 to 1737
24133 CRY TO ME (Bert Russell)-1		Capitol LP1730 to 1737
24134 LOVER PLEASE (Bill Swan)-2		Capitol LP1730 to 1737

Note: Capitol 4766 issued as by **GIL HAMILTON**.
Capitol LP1730 to 1737 titled GIVE 'EM SOUL.
The LP was issued eight times with different sleeves, each with a different DJ presenting the album.
LP1730 is GEORGE HUDSON PRESENTS.
LP1731 is SIR WALTER RALEIGH PRESENTS.
LP1732 is JOHN R. RICHBOURG PRESENTS.
LP1733 is RICHARD STAMZ PRESENTS.
LP1734 is DAVE DIXON PRESENTS.
LP1735 is PAUL JOHNSON PRESENTS.
LP1736 is LARRY D.I. DIXON PRESENTS.
LP1737 is HERMAN GRIFFITH PRESENTS.

GEORGE HUDSON (AND OTHERS) (presenter), Hoagy Lands (vo-1), Gil Hamilton (vo-2), 2tp, King Curtis (ts), bs, Jimmy Spruill (g), g, el-b, dm, fem-cho. Omit fem-cho -3. Arr-cond. by Teacho Wiltshire. Prod. by Manny Kellem and Lookapoo Productions, Inc. (Bert Berns).

New York, April 3, 1962

24135 ON TOP OF OLD SMOKY (trad.adapted Bert Russell)-1		Capitol LP1730 to 1737
24136 BATHTUB BLUES (Bert Russell)-2-1		Capitol LP1730 to 1737
24137 IT'S DRIVING ME WILD (Bert Russell,Ethel Haft)-1-2-3		Capitol LP1730 to 1737
24138 SPLISH SPLASH (Bobby Darin,Jean Murray)-2-1-3		Capitol LP1730 to 1737

GEORGE HUDSON (AND OTHERS) (presenter), Hoagy Lands (vo-1), Gil Hamilton (vo-2), King Curtis (ts), bs, p, Jimmy Spruill (g), g, el-b, dm, strings, fem-cho. Add scraper, triangle-3. Omit saxes add hca-4, omit unknown p add Bert Berns (p)-5. Arr-cond. by Teacho Wiltshire. Prod. by Manny Kellem and Lookapoo Productions, Inc. (Bert Berns).

New York, April 3, 1962

24139 STAND BY ME (Ben E. King,Elmo Glick)-1-3		Capitol LP1730 to 1737
24140 STRANGER ON THE SHORE (Robert Mellin,Acker Bilk)-1-4		Capitol LP1730 to 1737
24141 GEORGIA ON MY MIND (Hoagy Carmichael,Stuart Gorrell)-1		Capitol LP1730 to 1737
24142 GIVE 'EM SOUL (James Spruill)-2-5		Capitol LP1730 to 1737, 4768
24182 GIVE 'EM SOUL, PART II (Bert Russell,Wally Roker)-2-5		Capitol 4768

Note: 24142 retitled GIVE 'EM SOUL, PART I on single issue with writers as (Bert Russell,Wally Roker). 24182 was mastered from the continuation of the track at the SYLVIA HILL 4/24/1962 session below. The single was issued as by **APPLE ADAM**.

SOLOMON BURKE (vo) with orch. arr-cond. by Teacho Wiltshire: Lamar Wright, Wilbur "Dud" Bascomb (tp); King Curtis, Alonzo "Buddy" Lucas (ts); Haywood Henry (bs); Teacho Wiltshire (org); Alfred Williams (p); Jimmy Spruill, John "Bucky" Pizzarelli, Bob Bushnell (g); Charles Macey (el-b); Al Lucas (b); Panama Francis, Gary Chester (dm, perc); fem-cho. Omit fem-cho -1. Prod. by Bert Berns and Jerry Wexler.

New York, April 4, 1962

A-6089 DOWN IN THE VALLEY (Solomon Burke,Bert Berns)		Atlantic 2147, LP8067
A-6090 LOOKING FOR MY BABY (Solomon Burke)		Atlantic 2241, LP8067
A-6091 BABY (I WANNA BE LOVED) (Bert Russell,Mickey Lane)		Atlantic LP8067
A-6092 I'M HANGING UP MY HEART FOR YOU (John Berry,Don Covay)-1		Atlantic 2147, LP8067
A-6092 I'M HANGING UP MY HEART FOR YOU (stereo alt.take)-1		Atlantic LP8067
A-6093 GOTTA TRAVEL ON (Trad.arr.Paul Clayton,David Lazar, Pete "Tom Six I" Seeger,Ronnie "Tom Six II" Gilbert,Larry Ehrlich)		Atlantic LP 8067

THE HEARTBREAKERS (fem-vo-gp) with orch. arr-cond. by Teacho Wiltshire: Buddy Lucas, Bellino "Bill Ramal" Ramaglia (ts); Haywood Henry (bs); Bert Berns (p); Bill Suyker, Jimmy Spruill, Wally Richardson (g); Bob Bushnell (el-b); Al Lucas (b); Gary Chester (dm); Jack Jennings (triangle-1,vb-2). Add Leo McCorkle (vo)-2. Prod. by Bert Berns.

Atlantic Studios, New York, April 17, 1962

6158 POUR IT ON (Mike Kelly,Bert Russell)	unissued
62C-6159 THE WILLOW WEPT (William Leo McCorkle)-1	Atco 6258
6160 LEO	unissued
62C-6161 YOU HAD TIME (William Leo McCorkle)-2 (BB3/30/63)	Atco 6258

SYLVIA HILL (vo) with orch. cond. by Teacho Wiltshire: p, 2g, b, dm, strings, fem-cho. Add timpani-1, shaker-2. Prod. by Manny Kellem and Lookapoo Prod., Inc. (Bert Berns).

New York, April 24, 1962

24180 HERE SHE COMES (Bob Spencer)	unissued
24181 THE DRAMA OF LOVE (Phil Medley,Rose Bluestone)-1	Capitol 4767
24183 NO MORE HEART (Bob Spencer,Bob Elgin)-2	Capitol 4767
24184 LONELIEST TIME (Ron Miller,Leo Porter)	unissued

JIMMY JONES (vo) with p, g, ac-g, el-b, dm, strings, mixed-cho. Add chimes-1; marimba, maracas-2. Prod. by Bert Berns.

New York, April 30, 1962

62-XY-517 SMILE AGAIN	unissued
62-XY-518 YOU'RE MUCH TOO YOUNG (Teddy Vann)-1	Cub 9110
62-XY-519 NIGHTS OF MEXICO (Bert Russell,Ray Passman)-2	Cub 9110
62-XY-520 BLOW OUT THE SUN (Jeff Barry,Artie Resnick)	unissued

DORIS SWAIM (vo) with orch. cond. by Teacho Wiltshire: tb, ts, p, 2g, el-b, dm. Add triangle, timpani-1; mixed-cho-2. Prod. by Joe Rene.

New York, April 1962

BT-1106 DON'T FORGET TO FEED THE FLOWER (Carl Spencer,Bert Russell)-1	Beltone 2022
BT-1107 YOU'RE ALL THE DREAMS I'VE EVER HAD (Marlene Rothbort)-2	Beltone 2022

RUTH MCFADDEN (vo) with orch. cond. by Teacho Wiltshire: p, 2g, el-b, dm, strings, mixed-cho. Omit strings add bs, cow-bell -1. Prod. by Manny Kellem and Lookapoo Productions (Bert Berns).

New York, May 18, 1962

24234 FLY ME TO THE MOON (Bart Howard)	unissued
24235 STOP PLAYING THAT SONG (THAT'S WHAT YOU SAID) (Robert Spencer)	Capitol 4802
24236 PENCIL & PAPER (Bert Russell)-1	Capitol 4802
24237 I SAY LOVE (Bert Russell,Phil Medley)	unissued

KING CURTIS AND THE NOBLE KNIGHTS: King Curtis (ts); Ernie Hayes (org); George Stubbs (p); Billy Butler, Joe Richardson (g); Jimmy Lewis (b); Ray Lucas (dm). Prod. by Manny Kellem and Lookapoo Productions (Bert Berns).

Capitol Studio, New York, May 22, 1962

24291 TURN 'EM ON (Curtis Ousley)	Capitol 4788
24292-14 BEACH PARTY (Curtis Ousley,Wally Roker)	Capitol 4788

THE CADILLACS (4825)/ **BOBBY RAY AND THE CADILLACS** (4935): Bobby Spencer, Ray Brewster, James Ralph "J.R." Bailey, Roland Martinez (vo) with orch. cond. by Teacho Wiltshire: 2tp, King Curtis (ts), p, 2g, el-b, dm, cow-bell. Prod. by Manny Kellem and Lookapoo Productions (Bert Berns).

New York, May 31, 1962

24318 WHITE GARDENIA (Bert Russell,Carl Spencer)	Capitol 4825
24319 LA BOMBA (Ritchie Valens)	Capitol 4935
24320 I SAW YOU (Bob Spencer)	Capitol 4935
24321 GROOVY GROOVY LOVE (Bob Spencer,Ralph Bailey)	Capitol 4825

ROBERT BANKS (vo,p) with orch. arr-cond. by Teacho Wiltshire: Wilbur "Dud" Bascomb, Lamar Wright (tp); Frank Rehak (tb); Buddy Lucas (ts); Marlowe Morris (org); Bill Suyker (g); Bob Bushnell (el-b); Al Lucas (b); Gary Chester (dm). Prod. by Bert Berns.

New York, June 1, 1962

6216 I'M WAITING	Atlantic/Atco unissued
6217 WHOLE WORLD	Atlantic/Atco unissued
6218 MY BABY'S ARMS	Atlantic/Atco unissued

KING CURTIS (ts-1,vo) with Harold Johnson, Ernie Royal (tp); Bert Berns (org); Paul Griffin (p,el-p); Billy Butler, Carl Lynch, Charles Massey (g); Everett Barksdale (el-b); Jimmy Lewis (b); Ray Lucas, Gary Chester (dm,triangle,tamb,claves,shaker); fem-cho. Arr. by Paul Griffin. Dir. by Leroy Glover. Prod. by Manny Kellem and Lookapoo Productions (Bert Berns).

Capitol Studio, New York, June 5, 1962

24278 ANY TIME (Herbert Happy Lawson)-1	Capitol LP1756
24279 BROWN EYES (Curtis Ousley,Bert Russell,Jan Leslie)	Capitol 4841, LP1756
24280 YOUR CHEATIN' HEART (Hank Williams)	Capitol 4841, LP1756

KING CURTIS (ts-1,vo-2) with same except Bert Keyes (org) added; Bert Berns (org), Everett Barksdale (el-b) omitted. Arr. by Paul Griffin. Dir. by Leroy Glover. Prod. by Manny Kellem and Lookapoo Productions (Bert Berns).

Capitol Studio, New York, June 5, 1962

24281 TENNESSEE WALTZ (Redd Stewart,Pee Wee King)-1	Capitol LP1756
24282 WAGON WHEELS (Billy Hill,Peter DeRose)-2	Capitol LP1756

KING CURTIS (ts) with same. Omit tps-1, fem-cho -2. Arr. by Paul Griffin. Dir. by Leroy Glover. Prod. by Manny Kellem and Lookapoo Productions (Bert Berns).

Capitol Studio, New York, June 5, 1962

24283 HOME ON THE RANGE (Trad.arr.Ousley,Russell,Leslie)	Capitol LP1756
24284 NIGHT TRAIN TO MEMPHIS (Marvin Hughes,Owen Bradley,Beasley Smith)-1	Capitol LP1756
24285 I'M MOVIN' ON (Hank Snow)-2	Capitol LP1756
24286 RAUNCHY (Bill Justis,Sidney Manker)-1-2	Capitol LP1756

KING CURTIS (as,ts) with Sam "The Man" Taylor (ts); Ernie Hayes (org); Paul Griffin (el-p -1,p); Billy Butler, Carl Lynch, Charles Massey (g); Everett Barksdale (el-b); Jimmy Lewis (b); Ray Lucas (dm). Prod. by Manny Kellem and Lookapoo Productions (Bert Berns).

Capitol Studio, New York, June 6, 1962

24287 TUMBLING TUMBLEWEEDS (Bob Nolan)	Capitol LP1756
24288 HIGH NOON (Ned Washington,Dimitri Tiomkin)-1	Capitol LP1756
24289 WALKIN' THE FLOOR OVER YOU (Ernest Tubb)	Capitol LP1756

SOLOMON BURKE (vo) with Leon Cohen (as); Herb Wasserman (ts,fl); Dick Hyman (org); Paul Griffin (p); Bill Suyker, Chauncey Westbrook (g); Jimmy Lewis (b); Gary Chester (dm); Phil Kraus (xyl,scraper,triangle); Elise Bretton, Lois Winter, Trudy Packer, Lillian Clark, Howard Roberts, Jerome Graff, Robert Spiro, David Vogel (bkd-vo -1); Helen Way, Albertine Robinson, Doryce Brown (bkd-vo -2). No ts audible, Leon Cohen may also play fl and Herb Wasserman play part of perc. Arr.-cond. by Jerry Ragovoy. Prod. by Bert Berns and Jerry Wexler.

Atlantic Studios, New York, June 25, 1962

A-6288 I REALLY DON'T WANT TO KNOW (Don Robertson,Howard Barnes)-1 Atlantic 2157, LP8085
A-6289 TONIGHT MY HEART SHE IS CRYING (LOVE IS A BIRD)
    (Vic Abrams,Irving Reid,Morris "Moishe" Levy)-1   Atlantic 2157, LP8085
A-6290 HOME IN YOUR HEART (Winfield Scott,Otis Blackwell)-1   Atlantic 2180, LP8085
A-6291 YOU CAN MAKE IT IF YOU TRY (Ted Jarret)-2   Atlantic 2185, LP8085

THE ISLEY BROTHERS: Ronnie Isley (lead vo), Rudolph and O'Kelly Isley (vo) with orch. arr. by Teacho Wiltshire: 2tp, King Curtis (ts), p, 2g, el-b, Herb Wasserman (dm). Add bgo-1, cowbell-2. Omit horns, g add ac-g -3. Prod. by Bert Berns. A Ludix Production.

Bell Sound Studios, New York, June 1962

ZTSP 85596 TWISTIN' WITH LINDA (Isley,Isley,Isley)-1   Wand 127
ZTSP 85597 YOU BETTER COME HOME (Bert Russell)-2   Wand 127, LP653
ZTSP 89153 I SAY LOVE (Phil Medley,Bert Russell)   Wand 137, LP653
ZTSP 89154 HOLD ON BABY (Phil Medley,Bert Russell)-2   Wand 137, LP653
          NEVER LEAVE ME BABY (Bert Russell,Phil Medley)   Wand LP653
          DON'T YOU FEEL (Bert Russell,Donald Drowty)-3   Wand LP653

GENE PITNEY (vo) with orch. arr.-cond. by Chuck Sagle: Bert Berns (ac-g), ac-g, b, dm, xyl, claves, strings, fem-cho. A (Aaron) Schroeder-(Wally) Gold Prod.

New York, June 1962

7043 IF I DIDN'T HAVE A DIME (TO PLAY THE JUKEBOX)
    (Bert Russell,Phil Medley)   Musicor 1022, LP3003

THE JARMELS: Paul Burnett (lead tenor vo); Nathaniel Ruff, Earl Christian (tenor vo); Ray Smith (baritone vo); Tom Eldridge (bass vo) with orch. arr.-cond. by Glen Stuart (Eliot Greenberg): p, 2g, b, dm, triangle, xyl, strings. Prod. by Gene Schwartz (and Bert Berns).

New York, July 14 & 24, 1962

N70W-8957 LITTLE BUG (Bert Russell)   Laurie 3141
N70W-8958 ONE BY ONE (Lover Patterson,Benjamin Earl Nelson)   Laurie 3141
N70W-8959 COME ON GIRL (IT'S TIME TO SMILE AGAIN)
    (Bob Elgin,Bert Russell,Kay Rogers)   Laurie 3174

DOTTIE CLARK (vo) with p, 2g, el-b, dm, strings, fem-cho. A Bert Berns Production.

Mirasound Studios, New York, July 1962

BG-1305 CANDLE IN THE WIND (Stanley Kahan,George H.Brent)   Big Top 3120
BG-1306 GET HIM ALONE (Bert Russell,Ray Passman)   Big Top 3120

FRANK GARI (vo) with orch. arr.-cond. by Klaus Ogermann: Wilbur "Dud" Bascomb, Lamar Wright (tp); Tom Mitchell (tb); Peanuts Hucko (cl,ts); Ernie Hayes (p); Joe Richardson, Bill Suyker, Everett Barksdale (g); Jimmy Lewis (b); Gary Chester, Sticks Evans (dm,perc); fem-cho including Ellie Greenwich. Prod. by Bert Berns.

Atlantic Studios, New York, August 19, 1962

A-6465 AIN'T THAT FUN (Howard "Tony Powers" Puris,Jeff Barry)   Atlantic 2171
6466 ONE MORE TEAR (Jeff Barry,Ellie Greenwich)   unissued
6467 QUANDO QUANDO (Wes Farrell,Paul "Dee Marak" Anka)   unissued
A-6468 SHE MAKE ME WANNA DANCE (Bert Russell)   Atlantic 2171

RUSSELL BYRD (Bert Berns) (vo) with King Curtis (ts), org, g, el-b, dm, band members (bkd-vo). Prod. by Bert Berns.

Mirasound Studios, New York, September 1962

SY-917 HITCH HIKE PART I (Bert Russell)	Symbol 915
SY-918 HITCH HIKE PART II (Bert Russell)	Symbol 915

CLYDE AND THE BIRD WATCHERS: tu, ss, org, g, dm, fem-cho. Add p-1. Arr. by Andy Badale-1 and John Abbott. A Bert Berns & F. & M. Manfredi Prod..

New York, September 1962

ZTSP 85326 B VIENI QUA (COME HERE) (Frank Manfredi,Mike Manfredi)	Realm 1401
ZTSP 85327 A OLD SPICE (Angelo "Andy Badale" Badalamenti, John "John Abbott" Abatematteo)-1	Realm 1401

MYRNA MARCH (vo) with tb, ts, bs, p, 2g, el-b, dm, strings, fem-cho. Omit strings; add tamb; Bert Berns, Mickey Lee Lane (bkd-vo)-1. Add timpani-2, triangle-3. Prod. by Bert Berns. A Leiber & Stoller Production.

New York, October 10, 1962

17146 BABY (Bert Russell,Mickey Lane)-1	Roulette 4486
17147 WARM ARE YOUR LIPS (Myrna March,Steven Garrick)-2	Roulette 4463
17148 OUR LOVE, IT GROWS (Ellie Greenwich)-3	Roulette 4463

BEVERLY WARREN (vo) with orch. cond. by Jerry Ragovoy: tb, King Curtis (ts), bs, p, 2g, el-b, dm, strings, fem-cho. Omit horns-1. Dir. by Bert Berns. Prod. by Leiber-Stoller.

New York, October 1962

4299 IT WAS ME YESTERDAY (Ellie Greenwich,Jerry Leiber)	U.A. 543
4300 LIKE A MILLION YEARS (Ellie Greenwich,Tony Powers)-1	U.A. 543

THE EXCITERS: Brenda Reid (lead vo), Carol Johnson, Lillian Walker, Herb Rooney (vo) with orch. arr-cond. by Teacho Wiltshire: p; 2g; el-b; Gary Chester (dm); strings; Dionne Warwick, Dee Dee Warwick, Cissy Houston (bkd-vo). Add triangle-1; Al Sears (as), timpani-2. A Leiber-Stoller Production.

Bell Sound Studios, New York, October 15, 1962

4301 (tk.7) TELL HIM (Bert Russell)-1	U.A. 544, LP3264
4302 (tk.5) HARD WAY TO GO (Van McCoy)-2	U.A. 544, LP3264

SOLOMON BURKE (vo) with orch. arr-cond. by Klaus Ogermann: Ernie Royal, Jimmy Maxwell (tp); Tom Mace (ts); Jerome Richardson (bs); Dick Hyman (org); Paul Griffin (p); Bill Suyker, Everett Barksdale (g); Jimmy Lewis (b); Panama Francis (dm); Ted Sommer (xyl,triangle); Robert Henson, Robert Spiro, William Eaton, Sherman Sneed, Noah Hopkins, David Vogel (bkd-vo -1); fem-cho -2. Prod. by Bert Berns and Jerry Wexler.

Atlantic Studios, New York, October 17, 1962

A-6491 GO ON BACK TO HIM (Joy Byers)-1	Atlantic 2170, LP8085
A-6492 WITHOUT LOVE (Danny Small)-1	unissued
A-6493 WORDS (Solomon Burke)-2	Atlantic 2180, LP8085
A-6494 I SAID I WAS SORRY (Joy Byers)-2	Atlantic 2170, LP8085

BABY JANE & THE ROCKABYES: Madelyn Moore (lead vo), Yvonne DeMunn, Estelle McEwan, Yolanda Robinson (vo) with orch. arr. by Teacho Wiltshire: tp, ts, bs, p, 2g, el-b, dm, tamb. Add Arthur Crier (bass vo)-1. Dir. by Bert Berns. Prod. by Leiber-Stoller.

New York, November 1962

ZTSP 81926 MY BOY JOHN (Jerry Leiber Mike Stoller)	U.A. 560,
ZTSP 81927 HOW MUCH IS THAT DOGGIE IN THE WINDOW (Bob Merrill)-1	U.A. 560

THE ISLEY BROTHERS: Ronnie Isley (lead vo), Rudolph and O'Kelly Isley (vo) with 2tp, King Curtis (ts), bs, p, 2g, el-b, dm. A Bert Berns Production.

New York, November 1962

ZTSP 86889 NOBODY BUT ME (Isley,Isley,Isley)   Wand 131

THE HOCKADAYS: 4 males (vo) with 2tp, ts, bs, p, 2g, el-b, dm, cow-bell. Prod. by Henry "Juggy" Murray-1 or Bert Berns-2.

Mirasound Sudios, New York, November 1962

SY-923 FAIRY TALES (Hockaday,Howard)-1   Symbol 918
SY-924 HOLD ON BABY (Bert Russell,Phil Medley)-2   Symbol 918

GARNELL COOPER & THE KINFOLKS: Garnell Cooper (ts), Vonzell Cooper (org), David Walker (g), Marion Wright (el-b), Freeman Brown or Richard Waters (dm). Dir. By Bert Berns. A Leiber & Stoller Production.

Bell Sound Studios, New York, December 28, 1962

JB-11994 GREEN MONKEY (Garnell Cooper)   Jubilee 5445
JB-11995 LONG DISTANCE (Garnell Cooper)   Jubilee 5445

HOAGY LANDS (Victor Hoagland) (vo) with orch. arr.-cond. by Teacho Wiltshire: p, g, ac-g, el-b, dm, timpani, strings, mixed-cho. Omit timpani add marimba-1. Prod. by Bert Berns.

New York, December 1962

4449 I'M YOURS (Robert Mellin)   ABCParamount 10392
4450 THE TENDER YEARS (Bert Russell,Jacquie Silverman)   ABCParamount 10392
     TRUE LOVE AT LAST(Henry Vars,Sam H.Stept)   unissued

THE ROCKY FELLERS: Eddie Maligmat, Albert Maligmat, Tony Maligmat, Dorotao "Junior" Maligmat (vo) with orch. arr. by Alan Lorber: tp, p, 2g, el-b, dm, handclaps. Add tp, tb-1. S.M.N. Production (=Stanley Kahan, Mal Williams & Neil Diamond).

Mirasound Studios, New York, December 1962

50174 KILLER JOE (Bert Russell,Bob Elgin,Phil Medley)   Scepter 1246, LP512
      WHEN DO KIDS GROW UP (Bob Elgin,Bert Russell)-1   Scepter LP512

BERT BERNS (vo) with p, g el-b, dm, male bkd-vo.

New York, 1962

YOUR BEST FRIEND   unissued demo
ANYTHING YOU WANT ME TO DO aka I'M STILL WAITING FOR YOU
     TO MAKE ME DO ANYTHING (Bert Russell,Ray Passman)   unissued demo

THE EXCITERS: Brenda Reid (lead vo), Carol Johnson, Lillian Walker, Herb Rooney (vo) with orch. arr.-cond. by Teacho Wiltshire: p; 2g; el-b; dm; strings; Dionne Warwick, Dee Dee Warwick, Cissy Houston (bkd-vo). Add Al Sears (ts)-1, xyl-2, claves-3, timbales-4, timpani-5, triangle-6. A Leiber-Stoller Production.

Bell Sound Studios, New York, January 11, 1963

4611 (tk.4) HE'S GOT THE POWER (Greenwich,Powers)-1   U.A. 572, LP3264
4612 (tk.9) GET HIM (Bert Russell,Ray Passman,Elmo Glick)-2   U.A. 604
4613 (tk.17) I DREAMED (Charles Grean,Marvin Moore)-2   U.A. LP3264
4614 (tk.6) IT'S LOVE THAT REALLY COUNTS (Burt Bacharach,Hal David)-2-3   U.A. LP3264
4615 (tk.4) ARE YOU KEEPING SCORE (Ron Miller,Lee Porter)-2   U.A. LP3264
4616 (tk.2) SAY IT WITH LOVE (Van McCoy)-4   U.A. LP3264
4617 (tk.9) DRAMA OF LOVE (Rose Blueston,Phil Medley)-2-5   U.A. 572, LP3264
4618 (tk.3) REMEMBER ME (Brenda Reid,Herb Rooney)-6   U.A. LP3264
4619 (tk.3) SO LONG, GOODNIGHT (Brenda Reid,Herb Rooney)   U.A. LP3264
4620 (tk.4) HANDFUL OF MEMORIES (Ron Miller,Lee Porter)-6   U.A. LP3264

BABY WASHINGTON (vo) with orch. arr. by Bert Keyes: g, el-b, dm, strings, fem-cho. Add p-1; org, cga, castanets-2. A Bert Berns Production-1 or A Henry "Juggy" Murray Production-2.

Bell Sound Studios, New York, January 1963

SR-1083 THERE HE IS (Larry Weiss,Lockie Edwards Jr.)-1   Sue 783, LP1014
SR-1084 THAT'S HOW HEARTACHES ARE MADE (Bob Halley,Ben Raleigh)-2   Sue 783, LP1014

BEN E. KING (vo) with orch. arr-cond. by Klaus Ogermann-1 or Garry Sherman: Ernie Royal, Jimmy Maxwell (tp); Mike Stoller (p); Charles Macey, Al Shackman, Bill Suyker (g); Russ Saunders (el-b); Gary Chester (dm); George Devens, Brad Spinney, Bob Rosengarden (timpani,shaker,castanets); strings; Elise Bretton, Lillian Clark, Robert Davis, Eugene Lowell, Bob Mitchell, Peggy Powell (bkd-vo). A Leiber-Stoller Production.

Bell Sound Studios, New York, February 6, 1963

63C-6766 HOW CAN I FORGET (Ed Townsend,Bernard "J.Baird" Solomon,
        Murray "L.White" Cohen)-1   Atco 6256, LP165
63C-6767 I COULD HAVE DANCED ALL NIGHT
        (Allan Jay Lerner,Frederick Loewe)   Atco 6275, LP165
63C-6768 GYPSY (Bert Berns,Jerry Leiber,Mike Stoller,Nugetre)   Atco 6275

PATTI KOGIN (double-tracked vo) with oboe, p, 2g, el-b, dm, triangle, timpani/timbales, strings, mixed-cho. Prod. by Bert Berns.

Bell Sound Studios, New York, February 21, 1963

63-XY-407 BLESS 'EM ALL (James "Jimmy Hughes" Lally,
        Francis "Frank Lake" Kerslake,Al Stillman)   MGM 13164
63-XY-408 ARE YOUR LIPS LONELY DARLING (Bert Russell,Phil Medley)   unissued
63-XY-409 MR. MOON, MR. CUPID AND I (Gene Pitney)   MGM 13164

SOLOMON BURKE (vo) with orch. arr-cond. by Garry Sherman: Ernie Royal, Irvin Markowitz (tp); Sam Taylor, Ben Smith (ts); Haywood Henry (bs); Artie Butler (org/p); George Barnes, Bob Bushnell (g,12-string g); Russ Saunders (el-b); Bobby Donaldson (dm); Phil Kraus (tamb,scraper); prob. Cissy Houston, Dee Dee Warwick, Sylvia Shemwell, Estelle Brown (bkd-vo). Bert Berns Production.

New York, March 15, 1963

A-6880 CAN'T NOBODY LOVE YOU (James Mitchell)   Atlantic 2196, LP8096
A-6881 IF YOU NEED ME (Wilson Pickett,Robert Bateman,Sonny Sanders)   Atlantic 2185, LP8085
A-6882 HARD AIN'T IT HARD (Woody Guthrie)   Atlantic LP8096
A-6883 YOU CAN'T LOVE 'EM ALL (Bert Russell,Jerry Leiber,Mike Stoller,Nugetre) Atlantic LP8096

Note: A-6883 band-track and female background vocals were also used for the version by **MEL TORME** on Atlantic 2202, CD1 (A-7049, lead vocal and additional male background vocals overdubbed in New York 6/5/1963 produced by Ahmet Ertegun) (CB8/31/63).

BABY JANE AND THE ROCK-A-BYES: Madelyn Moore (lead vo), Yvonne DeMunn, Estelle McEwan, Yolanda Robinson (vo) with orch. arr. by Teacho Wiltshire: 2tp, ts, bs, p, 2g, el-b, dm. Add org-1. Omit horns, p add cga, bgo-2. Prod. By Bert Berns-2. Leiber and Stoller Production.

New York, March, 1963

GET ME TO THE CHURCH ON TIME (Allan Jay Lerner,Frederick Loewe)-1   Spokane 4004
HICKORY DICKERY DOCK (Ellie Greenwich,Jeff Barry)   Spokane 4001
SILLY LITTLE TEARDROP (Beverly Ross,Lor Crane) Spokane   unissued
HALF DESERTED STREET (Carl Spencer)-1-2   Spokane 4001

THE ELEKTRAS (Baby Jane And The Rock-A-Byes): Madelyn Moore (lead vo), Yvonne DeMunn, Estelle McEwan, Yolanda Robinson (vo) with orch. arr. by Teacho Wiltshire: 2tp, ts, bs, p, 2g, el-b, dm, maracas, male-cho. Add vb omit tp, ts, bs, maracas-1 Dir. by Bert Berns. Prod. by Leiber & Stoller.

New York, March 1963

ZTSP 85856 IT AIN'T AS EASY AS THAT (Bert Russell)-1   United Artists 594
ZTSP 85857 ALL I WANT TO DO IS RUN (Bert Russell,Carl Spencer)   United Artists 594

THE FOUR PENNIES (The Chiffons): Sylvia Peterson (lead vo), Judy Craig, Barbara Lee Jones, Patricia Bennett (vo) with orch. arr-cond. by Sammy Lowe: fl, g, el-b, dm, castanets, timpani, strings. A Bright Tunes Production (=The Tokens: Mitch Margo, Phil Margo, Hank Medress, Jay Siegel).

New York, March 1963

P4KM-7061 MY BLOCK (Bert Russell,Jimmy Radcliffe,Carl Spencer)   Rust 5071

THE ISLEY BROTHERS: Ronnie Isley (lead vo), Rudolph and O'Kelly Isley (vo) with orch. arr. by Alan Lorber or Garry Sherman: ts, bs, 2g, el-b, dm, strings. Omit strings-1. Prod. by Bert Berns.

Bell Sound Studios, New York, April 29, 1963

ZTSP 85878 TANGO (Isley,Isley,Isley)-1	United Artists 603, LP6313
ZTSP 85879 SHE'S GONE (Isley,Isley,Isley)	United Artists 603, LP6313

GARNET MIMMS & THE ENCHANTERS: Garnet Mimms (vo) with orch. arr-cond. by Garry Sherman: tb; as; ts; Paul Griffin (p); 2g; el-b; Gary Chester (dm); strings; Dionne Warwick, Dee Dee Warwick, Cissy Houston (bkd-vo). Prod. by Jerry Ragovoy. A Bert Berns Prod.

Bell Sound Studios, New York, May 1963

5044 CRY BABY (Bert Russell,Norman Meade)   U.A. 629, LP3305

THE KNIGHT BROTHERS: Richard Dunbar and Jimmy Diggs (vo) with tp, ts, bs, p, 2g, el-b, dm. Add handclaps-1. Dir. by Bert Berns. Prod. by Herb Cohen.

New York, May 23, 1963

12456 LOVE (CAN'T YOU HEAR ME) (Jimmy Diggs,Richard Dunbar)-1	Checker 1049
12457 MARGARET (Jimmy Diggs,Richard Dunbar)	Checker 1049

MARV JOHNSON (vo) with Garnet Mimms (2nd vo); 2tp; ts; bs; p; 2g; el-b; dm; prob. Cissy Houston, Dee Dee Warwick, Sylvia Shemwell, Estelle Brown (bkd-vo). Add handclaps-1; org, timbales-2. Prod. by Bert Berns.

Bell Sound Studios, New York, June 7 & 12, 1963

ZTSP 85902 COME ON AND STOP (Bert Russell)-1	United Artists 617
ZTSP 85903 NOT AVAILABLE (Mark Barkan,Ben Raleigh)	United Artists 617
ZTSP 87412 CRYING ON MY PILLOW (Phil Johnson,Carl Spencer)-2	United Artists 643
ZTSP 87413 CONGRATULATIONS, YOU'VE HURT ME AGAIN (Joy Byers)	United Artists 643

JIMMY RADCLIFFE (vo) with fl; 2ac-g; el-b; dm; marimba; prob. Dee Dee Warwick (vo duet-2/bkd-vo), Cissy Houston, Sylvia Shemwell, Estelle Brown (bkd-vo). Omit dm add cga-1. Prod. by Bert Berns.

New York, June 12, 1963

ZTSP 66065 THROUGH A LONG AND SLEEPLESS NIGHT (Mack Gordon,Alfred Newman)	Musicor 1033
ZTSP 66066 MOMENT OF WEAKNESS (Jimmy Radcliffe,Oramay Diamond)	Musicor 1033
R5KM-7188 WHAT I WANT I CAN NEVER HAVE (Gloria Shayne)-1	Musicor 1042
DEEP IN THE HEART OF HARLEM (Jimmy Radcliffe,Carl Spencer)-2	Musicor unissued

ART SMALLY (vo) with Prod. by Bert Berns.

New York, June 1963

DONNA LEE (Bert Russell,Phil Medley)	United Artists 619
YOU'RE A BETTER MAN THAN ME	United Artists 619

DANTE (Don Drowty) (vo) with p; Vinnie Bell (g): g; el-b; dm; Jeff Barry, Ellie Greenwich (bkd-vo). Add chimes-1, triangle-2. Prod. by Bert Berns.

New York, June 1963

SPECIAL KIND OF LOVE (Herb Alpert,Don Drowty)-1	unissued
STARBRIGHT (Don Drowty)-2	unissued
CRACKIN' UP (Ellas "Bo Diddley" McDaniel)	unissued

JUNIOR LEWIS (Clarence Lewis) (vo) with orch. arr. by Horace Ott (org,p): tp, ts, bs, g, el-b, dm, mixed-cho. Omit org add tamb, handclaps, crowd noise-1. Prod. by Stanley Kahan and Mal Williams.

New York, June 1963

50039	RAISE YOUR HAND (Bob Elgin,Bert Russell)	Scepter 1257
50040	(TELL ME) WHERE DO I GO FROM HERE (Bob Elgin,Horace Ott)	Scepter 1257, 1268
50138	HI-DEE YOU ALL (HOOTENANNY SOUL) (Willie Denson,Stanley Kahan,Wes Farrell)-1	Scepter 1268

THE WANDERERS: Ray Pollard (lead tenor), Frank Joyner (second tenor), Robert Yarborough (baritone), Sheppard Grant (bass) with tp; p; 12 string g; Jimmy Spruill (g); el-b; dm; Cissy Houston, Dee Dee Warwick, Sylvia Shemwell, Estelle Brown (bkd-vo). Prod. by Bert Berns. A Roy Rifkind Enterprise.

New York, July 3, 1963

ZTSP 87422	I'LL KNOW (Frank Loesser)	United Artists 648
ZTSP 87423	YOU CAN'T RUN AWAY FROM ME (Bert Russell)	United Artists 648
	GIVING UP ON LOVE (Bob Feldman,Jerry Goldstein,Richard Gottehrer)	unissued

THE FOUR COINS: George Mahramas (lead tenor vo); Jack Mahramas, George Mantalis (tenor vo); Jim Gregorakis (baritone vo) with 2tp, p, g, ac-g, b, dm, triangle. Add marimba-1; ts, claves-2. A Leiber & Stoller Prod.

New York, July 1963

63-3272	NINA (Bert Russell,Teddy Vann)-1	Vee Jay 551
63-3273	(LITTLE DARLIN') TAKE A BOW (Arnold "Brooks Arthur" Brodsky,Jack Keller)-2	Vee Jay 551

BETTY HARRIS (vo) with orch. arr-cond. by Garry Sherman: tp; tb; ts; bs; p; 2g; el-b; dm; strings; Cissy Houston, Dee Dee Warwick, Sylvia Shemwell, Estelle Brown, 3 males (bkd-vo). Dir. by Bert Berns. A Leiber & Stoller Prod.

Bell Sound Studios, New York, July 1963

JB-12029	I'LL BE A LIAR (Bert Russell)	Jubilee 5456
JB-12030	CRY TO ME (Bert Russell)	Jubilee 5456

THE ISLEY BROTHERS: Ronnie Isley (lead vo), Rudolph and O'Kelly Isley (vo) with King Curtis (ts); p; 2g; el-b; dm; prob. Cissy Houston, Dee Dee Warwick, Sylvia Shemwell, Estelle Brown (bkd-vo). Add 2tp-1; org omit p-2; 12 string g omit ts, p, 2g –3; strings omit bkd-vo -4. Arr-cond. by Alan Lorber and Garry Sherman. Prod. by Bert Berns.

Bell Sound Studios, New York, August 15, 1963

ZTSP 87402	SURF AND SHOUT (Bert Russell,Ruth Batchelor)-1	United Artists 638, LP6313
ZTSP 87403	WHAT'CHA GONNA DO (Isley,Isley,Isley)-2	United Artists 638, LP6313
ZTSP 87444	YOU'LL NEVER LEAVE HIM (Bert Russell,Mike Stoller)-3	United Artists 659, LP6313
ZTSP 87445	PLEASE, PLEASE, PLEASE (James Brown,Johnny Terry)	United Artists 659, LP6313
U026541	STAGGER LEE (Lloyd Price,Harold Logan)	U.A. LP6313
U026544	LET'S GO, LET'S GO, LET'S GO (Hank Ballard)	U.A. LP6313
U026545	SHAKE IT WITH ME BABY (Isley,Isley,Isley)	U.A. LP6313
U026547	SHE'S THE ONE (Isley,Isley,Isley)-4	U.A. LP6313
U026549	LONG TALL SALLY (Enotris Johnson)-2	U.A. LP6313
	DO THE TWIST (Dale Hawkins)	U.A. LP6313

SOLOMON BURKE (vo,bkd-vo) with orch. arr-cond. by Garry Sherman: Irvin Markowitz, Robert Scott (tp); Ben Smith, Sam Taylor (ts); Haywood Henry (bs); Artie Butler (p); Billy Butler, George Barnes, Bob Bushnell (g,12 string g); Russ Saunders (el-b); Bobby Donaldson (dm,triangle,tamb); prob. Cissy Houston, Dee Dee Warwick, Sylvia Shemwell, Estelle Brown (bkd-vo).Omit horns-1. A Bert Berns Prod.

New York, August 16, 1963

A-7146 WON'T YOU GIVE HIM (ONE MORE CHANCE)	
(Angela Martin,Bobby Scott)-1	Atlantic 2254, LP8096
A-7147 BEAUTIFUL BROWN EYES (Bert Russell,Solomon Burke)	Atlantic 2205, LP8096
A-7147 BEAUTIFUL BROWN EYES (Bert Russell,Solomon Burke) (stereo alt.tk)	Atlantic SD8096
A-7148 YOU'RE GOOD FOR ME (Horace Ott,Don Covay)	Atlantic 2205, LP8096

TAMMY MONTGOMERY (vo) with orch. arr-cond. by Garry Sherman: tp; as; org/p; 2g; el-b; dm; prob. Cissy Houston, Dee Dee Warwick, Sylvia Shemwell, Estelle Brown (bkd-vo). Add Jimmy Radcliffe (duet vo -1). A Bert Berns Production.

New York, August 1963

12595 I CAN'T HOLD IT IN ANYMORE (Jimmy Radcliffe,Phil Stern)	Checker unissued
12596 IF I WOULD MARRY YOU (Bert Russell,Tammy Montgomery)	Checker 1072
12597 THIS TIME TOMORROW (Jimmy Radcliffe,Carl Spencer)	Checker 1072
I'VE GOT NOTHING TO SAY BUT GOODBYE	
(Jimmy Radcliffe,Phil Stern,Wally Gold)	Checker unissued

GARNET MIMMS & THE ENCHANTERS: Garnet Mimms (vo) with orch. arr-cond. by Garry Sherman: tb; as; ts; p; 2g; el-b; dm; strings; prob. Cissy Houston, Dee Dee Warwick, Sylvia Shemwell, Estelle Brown (bkd-vo). Omit strings-1. Prod. by Jerry Ragovoy. A Bert Berns Production-2.

New York, September 6, 1963

UNTIL YOU WERE GONE (Joy Byers)	U.A. LP3305
I KEEP WANTING YOU (Buddy Kaye,Phil Springer)	U.A. LP3305
ZTSP 87442 FOR YOUR PRECIOUS LOVE (Brooks,Brooks,Butler)-2	U.A. 658, LP3305
ZTSP 87443 BABY DON'T YOU WEEP (Bert Russell,Norman Meade)-1-2	U.A. 658, LP3305
ZTSP 91080 ANYTIME YOU WANT ME (Norman Meade,Garnet Mimms)-1	U.A. LP3305, 694
ZTSP 122860 THE TRUTH HURTS (Oramay Diamond,Jimmy Radcliffe)-1	U.A. LP3305, Veep 1252

RUSSELL BYRD (Bert Berns) (vo,prod) with

New York, September 16, 1963

7507 THAT'S WHERE I HURT (Jerry Wexler,Bert Berns)	Atlantic/Keetch unissued
7508 CHICO & MARIA	Atlantic/Keetch unissued

BILLY ADAMS (vo) with orch. arr. by Horace Ott (org-1,p): tp; ts; bs; g; el-b; dm; triangle; prob. Cissy Houston, Dee Dee Warwick, Sylvia Shemwell, Estelle Brown (bkd-vo). Prod. by Stanley Kahan and Mal Williams.

New York, September 1963

6081 GO (GO ON, GET OUT OF HERE) (Bert Russell,Ruth Batchelor)-1	Amy 893
6082 YOU AND ME (Van McCoy)	Amy 893

GERRY LEVENE (Michael John Gibbs) (vo) with 2tp; Harry Stoneham (org); Big Jim Sullivan, Jimmy Page (g); Alan Weighell (el-b); Bobby Graham or Clem Cattini (dm); mixed-cho. Music Director: Mike Leander. Production: Bert Berns.

Decca Studio 2, London, October 1963

DR.31912 IT'S DRIVING ME WILD (Bert Russell,Ethel Haft)	Decca(E)11815

JOHNNY B. GREAT (Johnny Goodison) (vo) with Big Jim Sullivan (12 string g), Jimmy Page (g), Alan Weighell (el-b); Bobby Graham or Clem Cattini (dm), mixed-cho. Music Director: Mike Leander. Production: Bert Berns.

Decca Studio 2, London, October 1963

DR.31913 YOU'LL NEVER LEAVE HIM (Bert Russell,Mike Stoller)   Decca(E)11804

THE ORCHIDS: Georgina Oliver (lead vo), Pamela Jarman, Valerie Jones (vo) with Harry Stoneham (p); Big Jim Sullivan, Jimmy Page (g); Alan Weighell (el-b); Bobby Graham or Clem Cattini (dm); Stan Barrett (chimes,perc). Music Director: Mike Leander. Production: Bert Berns.

Decca Studio 2, London, October 1963

DR.31914 JUST LIKE MINE (Bert Russell)   Decca(E)unissued

THE REDCAPS: Dave Walker (vo,handclaps), Mac Broadhurst (ts), Roy Brown (g), Mike Walker (el-b), Alan Morley (dm). Additional/replacement session musicians probably include Big Jim Sullivan, Jimmy Page (g) Alan Weighell (el-b); Bobby Graham or Clem Cattini (dm). Music Director: Mike Leander. Production: Bert Berns.

Decca Studio 2, London, October 1963

DR.31915 COME ON GIRL (Bob Elgin,Bert Russell,Kay Rogers)   Decca(E)11789

BRENDA AND JOHNNY (Brenda Boswell and Johnny B. Great (Johnny Goodison)) (vo) with Harry Stoneham (org,p); Big Jim Sullivan, Jimmy Page (g); Alan Weighell (el-b); Bobby Graham or Clem Cattini (dm). Music Director: Mike Leander. Production: Bert Berns.

Decca Studio 2, London, October 1963

DR.31916 THIS CAN'T BE LOVE (Rodgers,Hart)   Decca(E)11837

THE KNIGHT BROS.: Richard Dunbar and Jimmy Diggs (vo) with 2tb; bs; p; 2g; el-b; dm; prob. Cissy Houston, Dee Dee Warwick, Sylvia Shemwell, Estelle Brown (bkd-vo). Dir. by Bert Berns. Prod. by Herb Cohen.

New York, October 24, 1963

12795 I REALLY LOVE YOU (Jimmy Diggs)   Checker 1064
12796 COME ON GIRL (Bob Elgin,Bert Russell,Kay Rogers)   Checker 1076
12797 SECOND HAND LOVER (Jimmy Diggs,Richard Dunbar)   Checker 1064
12798 CITY LIFE (Jimmy Diggs)   Checker 1076

BETTY HARRIS (vo) with orch. arr-cond. by Garry Sherman: Eddie Bert (tb); p; Carl Lynch, Billy Butler (g); el-b; Gary Chester (dm); strings; Cissy Houston, Dee Dee Warwick, Sylvia Shemwell, Estelle Brown (bkd-vo). Prod. by Bert Berns. A Leiber & Stoller Production.

Bell Sound Studio A, New York, November 13, 1963

HIS KISS   Jubilee unissued
tk.36 WHY DON'T YOU TELL HIM (Bert Russell,Garry Sherman,Ed Silvers)   Jubilee unissued
tk.37 WHY DON'T YOU TELL HIM (Bert Russell,Garry Sherman,Ed Silvers)   Jubilee unissued
IT'S DARK OUTSIDE   Jubilee unissued

BETTY HARRIS (vo) with orch. arr-cond. by Garry Sherman: tp; tb; ts; bs; p; Trade Martin, another (g); el-b; Gary Chester (dm); Cissy Houston, Dee Dee Warwick, Sylvia Shemwell, Estelle Brown (bkd-vo). Dir. by Bert Berns. A Leiber-Stoller Production.

Bell Sound Studio A, New York, November 13, 1963

JB-12105 tk.3 MO JO HANNAH (Andre Williams,Clarence Paul,Barbara Paul)   Jubilee 5480
JB-12106 tk.4 NOW IS THE HOUR (Clement Scott,Dorothy Stewart,Maewa Kaihau)   Jubilee 5480
tk.8 EVERYBODY'S LOVE aka JUST LIKE MINE (Bert Russell)   Jubilee unissued

BETTY HARRIS (vo). Overdub/edit session: vocals corrected on tracks recorded 11/13/63. Prod. by Bert Berns. A Leiber & Stoller Production.

Bell Sound Studio A, New York, November 26, 1963

MO JO HANNAH	Jubilee unissued
JB-12060 tk.2/overdub tk.11 HIS KISS (Bert Russell,Mike Stoller)	Jubilee 5465
JB-12059 tk.12 IT'S DARK OUTSIDE (Edith Neary,Wes Farrell)	Jubilee 5465

HOAGY LANDS (Victor Hoagland) (vo) with tp; tb; ts; bs; p; g; Mike Leander (12 string g); el-b; dm; Dee Dee Warwick, Cissy Houston, Sylvia Shemwell, Estelle Brown (bkd-vo). A Bert Berns Production.

New York, December 5, 1963

A-7428 BABY COME ON HOME (Bert Russell)	Atlantic 2217
A-7429 BABY LET ME HOLD YOUR HAND (Bert Russell,Wes Farrell)	Atlantic 2217
7430 BETTER NOT BELIEVE HIM (Bert Russell,Ruth Batchelor)	unissued

THE DRIFTERS: Rudy Lewis (lead tenor-1/tenor vo), Johnny Moore (lead tenor-2/tenor vo), Charles Thomas (tenor vo), Eugene Pearson (baritone vo), Johnny Terry (bass vo) with orch. arr-cond. by Garry Sherman: Joe Wilder, Irving Markowitz (tp); Seldon Powell (ts); Haywood Henry (bs); Paul Griffin (p); Bill Suyker, Alvin Shackman (g); Milt Hinton (b); Gary Chester (dm); Arthur Marotti (maracas,perc); Dee Dee Warwick, Cissy Houston, Sylvia Shemwell, Estelle Brown (bkd-vo). A Bert Berns Production.

New York, December 12, 1963

A-7466 BEAUTIFUL MUSIC(Barry Mann,Cynthia Weil,Jerry Leiber,Mike Stoller)-1	unissued
A-7467 ONE WAY LOVE (Bert Russell,Jerry Ragovoy)-2	Atlantic 2225, LP8093
A-7468 VAYA CON DIOS (Larry Russell,Inez James,Buddy Pepper)-1	Atlantic 2216, LP8093

SOLOMON BURKE (vo) with orch. arr-cond. by Garry Sherman: Lamar Wright (tp); Tony Studd (b-tb); Charles De Angelis (ts); Haywood Henry (bs); Paul Griffin (p); Bill Suyker, Al Shackman, Bob Bushnell (g); Russ Saunders (el-b); Gary Chester (dm); Dee Dee Warwick, Cissy Houston, Sylvia Shemwell, Estelle Brown (bkd-vo). Add strings-1. A Bert Berns Production.

New York, December 12, 1963

A-7470 HE'LL HAVE TO GO (Joe Allison,Audrey Allison)-1	Atlantic 2218, LP8096
A-7471 SOMEONE TO LOVE ME (Solomon Burke)	Atlantic 2226, LP8096
A-7472 GOODBYE BABY (BABY GOODBYE) (Bert Russell,Wes Farrell)	Atlantic 2226, LP8096
A-7472 GOODBYE BABY (BABY GOODBYE) (Russell,Farrell) (stereo alt.take)	Atlantic LP8096

GARNET MIMMS (vo) with orch. arr-cond. by Jerry Ragovoy-1 or Garry Sherman: tp; tb; ts; bs; p; 2g; el-b; dm; prob. Dee Dee Warwick, Cissy Houston, Sylvia Shemwell, Estelle Brown (bkd-vo). Add strings-2. A Jerry Ragovoy Production.

New York, December 18, 1963

ZTSP 91079 TELL ME BABY (Carl Spencer,Bob Halley)	U.A. 694, LP3396
ZTSP 91121 ONE GIRL (Norman Meade,Bert Russell)-2	U.A. LP3396, 715
ZTSP 94991 LOOK AWAY (Norman Meade,Bert Russell)	U.A. LP3396, 773
ZTSP 98544 EVERY TIME (Ben Raleigh,Norman Meade)-1	U.A. LP3396, 868, 887

LARRY HALE (Larry Capel) (vo) with orch. arr-cond. by Horace Ott: 2tp; p; 2g; el-b; dm; handclaps; Dee Dee Warwick, Cissy Houston; Sylvia Shemwell; Estelle Brown (bkd-vo). Omit 2tp, handclaps add cow-bell -1. A Bert Berns Production.

New York, December 1963

ZTSP 91093 IN FRONT OF HER HOUSE (Bert Russell,Stanley J.Kahan)-1	United Artists 701
ZTSP 91094 SOMETIMES (Larry Capel,Earline Phillips)	United Artists 701

THE VIBRATIONS: Carl Fisher (lead tenor vo); James Johnson, Ricky Owens (tenor vo); Dave Govan (baritone vo); Don Bradley (bass vo) with orch. arr.-cond. by Teacho Wiltshire: Bill Berry, Leo Ball (tp); Joe D. Thomas (ts); Leroy Glover (org); Paul Griffin, Frank Anderson (p); Robert Rodriguez (b); David Griffin, Julian Cabrera, Carlos Vidal (cga); Efraim Pineiro (timbales). Add crowd noise effects-1. Dir. by Bert Berns. An Award Music Production (Gregory Carroll).

New York, January 7, 1964

A-7527 MY GIRL SLOOPY (Bert Russell,Wes Farrell)-1		Atlantic 2221
A-7528 DADDY WOO-WOO (Gregory Carroll,Sammie Armstrong,Carlton Fisher)		Atlantic 2221

LOU CHRISTIE (Lugee Sacco) (vo) with bs; org; p; 2g; el-b; dm; vb; Jeff Barry, Ellie Greenwich, The Tammys: Cathy Owens, Linda Jones, Gretchen Owens (bkd-vo). Omit bkd-vo, add mixed-cho -2; omit bs, vb-3. Arr.-cond. by Garry Sherman-1 or Teacho Wiltshire. Prod. by Bert Berns & Nick Cenci.

Bell Sound Studios, New York, January 8, 1964

17912 THERE THEY GO (Jimmie Crane)	Roulette 4545, LP25332
17913 MAYBE YOU'LL BE THERE (Rube Bloom,Sammy Gallop)-2	Roulette 4554, LP25332
17914 OUTSIDE THE GATES OF HEAVEN (Twyla Herbert,Lou Christie)-1	Roulette LP25332
17915 YOU MAY BE HOLDING MY BABY (Bert Russell,Paul Colby)-3	Roulette LP25332

WES FARRELL (vo) with orch. arr.-cond. by Garry Sherman: 2tp, tb, org, 2ac-g, el-b, dm, male-cho. Omit horns, org-1. Prod. by Si Rady.

New York, January 10, 1964

24805 YOU DON'T DO WHAT I SAY (Wes Farrell,Chip Taylor)-1	Capitol 5179
24806 THE LETTER (Wes Farrell,Bert Berns)	Capitol 5179
24807 DON'T GO BREAKING SANDY'S HEART (Jeff Chase)	unissued

THE ISLEY BROTHERS: Ronnie Isley (lead vo), Rudolph and O'Kelly Isley (vo) with tp; King Curtis (ts); bs; org; Jimi Hendrix (g); el-b; dm; prob. Cissy Houston, Dee Dee Warwick, Sylvia Shemwell, Estelle Brown (bkd-vo). Omit bkd-vo -1; all vo-2. Prod. by Bert Berns.

Bell Sound Studios, New York, January 14, 1964

ZTSP 91119 WHO'S THAT LADY (Isley,Isley,Isley)-1	United Artists 714
ZTSP 91120 MY LITTLE GIRL (Isley,Isley,Isley)	United Artists 714
ZTSP 104926 LOVE IS A WONDERFUL THING (Isley,Isley,Isley)	Veep 1230
ZTSP 104927 OPEN UP HER EYES (Isley,Isley,Isley)	Veep 1230
FOOTPRINTS IN THE SNOW (Isley,Isley,Isley)	United Artists/Veep unissued
THE BASEMENT (Isley,Isley,Isley)-2	United Artists/Veep unissued
CONCH (Isley,Isley,Isley)-2	United Artists/Veep unissued

BEN E. KING (vo,bkd-vo) with orch. arr.-cond. by Seymour Barab: Tony Studd (b-tb); Stan Free (p); Everett Barksdale, Al Gorgoni, Bill Suyker (g); Russ Saunders (el-b); Gary Chester (dm,tamb,timpani); strings; Dee Dee Warwick, Cissy Houston, Sylvia Shemwell, Estelle Brown (bkd-vo). A Bert Berns Production.

New York, January 15, 1964

64C-7530 THAT'S WHEN IT HURTS (Jerry Wexler,Bert Berns)	Atco 6288, LP165
64C-7531 AROUND THE CORNER (Ezio Leoni,Carl Sigman)	Atco 6288, LP165

LITTLE ESTHER PHILLIPS (with **Jimmy Ricks** (A-7607)) (vo) with orch. arr.-cond. by Garry Sherman: Lamar Wright (tp); Tony Studd (tb); Charles De Angelis (ts); Haywood Henry (bs); Leroy Glover (org); Paul Griffin (p); Cornell Dupree, Bill Suyker (g); Jimmy Lewis (el-b); Ray Lucas (dm); Dee Dee Warwick, Cissy Houston, Sylvia Shemwell, Estelle Brown (bkd-vo). Add strings-1. A Bert Berns Production.

New York, February 6 and 7, 1964

A-7604 HELLO WALLS (Willie Nelson)-1	Atlantic 2223
A-7605 MO JO HANNAH (Andre Williams,Clarence Paul,Barbara Paul)	Atlantic 2229
A-7606 I SAW ME (Eva June Davis,George Jones)	Atlantic 2304
A-7607 DOUBLE CROSSING BLUES (Jessie Mae Robinson)	Atlantic 2223

LINDA LAURIE (Linda Gertz) (vo) and Bert Berns (whistling-1,vo) with orch. arr-cond. by Garry Sherman: Ernie Royal, Irving Markowitz (tp); Ernie Hayes (p); Bucky Pizzarelli, Bill Suyker (g); Milt Hinton (b); Gary Chester (dm); Julian Cabrera (cga); Willie Bobo (cow-bell). Add Dee Dee Warwick, Cissy Houston, Sylvia Shemwell, Estelle Brown (bkd-vo)-1. A Bert Berns Production.

New York, February 18 or 28, 1964

K-7650 JOSE HE SAY (Bert Russell)-1	Keetch 6001
K-7651 CHICO (Bert Russell,Linda Laurie)	Keetch 6001

LAVERN BAKER (vo) with orch. arr-cond. by Garry Sherman: Paul Griffin (p); Bill Suyker, Vinnie Bell (g); Jimmy Tyrell (el-b); Milt Hinton (b); Gary Chester (dm,tamb); 8 strings; Dee Dee Warwick, Cissy Houston, Sylvia Shemwell, Estelle Brown (bkd-vo). Add hca-1, omit strings-2. A Bert Berns Production.

New York, April 2, 1964

A-7720 FLY ME TO THE MOON (Bart Howard)	Atlantic 2267
A-7721 GO AWAY (Bert Russell)	Atlantic 2234
A-7722 REMIND MY BABY OF ME (Gary Geld,Peter Udell)	unissued
A-7723 YOU BETTER FIND YOURSELF ANOTHER FOOL (Nugetre,Tom Dowd)-1-2	Atlantic 2234
A-7724 AIN'T GONNA CRY NO MORE (Barry Mann)-2	Atlantic 2267

BEN E. KING (vo) with orch. arr-cond. by Sammy Lowe: Ernie Royal, Wilbur "Dud" Bascomb, Leon Merian (tp); Haywood Henry (bs); James Bethea, Eric Gale (g); Alonzo Collins (el-b); Abie Baker (b); Panama Francis (dm,scraper,triangle); 5 strings; mixed-cho. Prod. by Jerry Wexler and/or Bert Berns.

New York, April 23, 1964

64C-7754 THIS IS MY DREAM (Rudy Clark)	Atco LP17464
C-7755 WHAT CAN A MAN DO	unissued

THE MUSTANGS: Bert Berns and Wes Farrell (vo) with ac-g, b, dm, claves or overdubbed-1 on part of track from HOAGY LANDS version of BABY LET ME HOLD YOUR HAND (see 12/5/63 session (master number 7428 (Keetch 6002 label) or 7429 (Atlantic 2217 label)). A Bert Berns Production.

New York, April 27, 1964

K-7428 BABY LET ME TAKE YOU HOME (Bert Russell,Wes Farrell)-1	Keetch 6002
K-7758 DAVIE WAS A BAD BOY (Wes Farrell,Bert Russell)	Keetch 6002

BEN E. KING (vo) with orch. arr-cond. by Phil Medley: Ernie Royal, Wilbur "Dud" Bascomb, Lamar Wright, Irving Markowitz (tp); Haywood Henry (bs); Paul Griffin (p,org); Jimmy Spruill, Bill Suyker (g); Jimmy Lewis (el-b); Gary Chester (dm); Ted Sommer, Joe Venuto, Artie Butler (timpani,marimba,shaker,handclaps); Dee Dee Warwick, Cissy Houston, Sylvia Shemwell, Estelle Brown, male bass (bkd-vo). A Bert Berns Production.

New York, May 14, 1964

64C-7874 WHAT CAN A MAN DO (Rudy Clark)	Atco 6303
64C-7875 LET THE WATER RUN DOWN (Bert Russell)	Atco 6315, LP174
64C-7876 IT'S ALL OVER (Bert Russell,Mike Leander)	Atco 6315, LP174
64C-7877 SI SENOR (arr.Jerry Wexler)	Atco 6303, LP174

THE MUSTANGS: Bert Berns and Wes Farrell (vo) with

New York, May 15, 1964

7880 SWEET TO ME	Keetch/Atlantic unissued
7881 I REMEMBER	Keetch/Atlantic unissued
7882 EVERYTHING IS ALL RIGHT	Keetch/Atlantic unissued

THE DRIFTERS: Johnny Moore (lead tenor vo-1/tenor vo), Charlie Thomas (lead tenor vo-2/tenor vo), Eugene Pearson (baritone vo), Johnny Terry (bass vo) with orch. arr-cond. by Teacho Wiltshire: Ernie Hayes (p); Everett Barksdale, Bill Suyker, Bob Bushnell (g); Milt Hinton (b); Gary Chester (dm); George Devens (scraper,triangle,castanets,vb); 9 strings. Prod. by Bert Berns and Mike Leander.

New York, May 21, 1964

A-7922 UNDER THE BOARDWALK (Artie Resnick,Kenny Young)-1	Atlantic 2237, LP8093
A-7922 UNDER THE BOARDWALK (Artie Resnick,Kenny Young)-1	
(stereo alt.take)	Atlantic LP SD8093
7923 PLAYBOY (key of E)-1	unissued
A-7924 HE'S JUST A PLAYBOY (Bert Russell)-1	Atlantic 2253, LP8113
A-7925 I DON'T WANT TO GO ON WITHOUT YOU	
(Bert Russell,Jerry Wexler)-2	Atlantic 2237, LP8113

BETTY HARRIS (vo). Overdub/edit session: vocals corrected on track recorded 11/13/63. Prod. by Bert Berns. A Leiber & Stoller Production.

Bell Sound Studio B, New York, May 25, 1964

WHY DON'T YOU TELL HIM	Jubilee unissued

SOLOMON BURKE (vo) with orch. arr-cond. by Phil Medley: Lamar Wright, Wilbur "Dud" Bascomb, William Berry (tp); Jimmy Cleveland (tb); Haywood Henry (bs); Leroy Glover (p,org); Jimmy Spruill, George Barnes, Al Shackman (g); Jimmy Lewis (el-b); Bobby Donaldson (dm); Elise Bretton, Lillian Clark, Lois Winter, Jerome Graff, Arne Markussen, Bill Sanford (bkd-vo -1); prob. Cissy Houston, Dee Dee Warwick, Sylvia Shemwell, Estelle Brown (bkd-vo,handcaps -2). A Bert Berns Production.

New York, May 28, 1964

7936 LILI MARLENE (Tommie Connor,Hans Leip,Norbert Schultze)-1	unissued
7937 YOU MAY BE HOLDING MY BABY (Bert Russell,Paul Colby)-2	unissued
A-7938 EVERYBODY NEEDS SOMEBODY TO LOVE	
(Bert Russell,Solomon Burke,Jerry Wexler)-2	Atlantic 2241, LP8109

JOHNNY THUNDER (Gil Hamilton) (vo) with orch. arr. by Teacho Wiltshire: 2tp; tb; ts; bs; p; Jimmy Spruill (g); g; el-b; dm; prob. Cissy Houston, Dee Dee Warwick, Sylvia Shemwell, Estelle Brown (bkd-vo). Add timbales-1; castanets omit tp, tb, ts, bs, bkd-vo -2. Prod. by Bert Berns.

New York, May 1964

D-169A MORE, MORE, MORE, LOVE, LOVE, LOVE (Bert Russell)-1	Diamond 169
D-169B SHOUT IT TO THE WORLD (Barry "Barry Richards" Winer)-1-2	Diamond 169
D-175A SEND HER TO ME (Bert Russell,Ruth Batchelor)	Diamond 175

DANTE (Don Drowty) (vo) with 2tp, p, g, el-b, dm, male-vo-gp. Omit 2tp, p add org, claves-1. Add scraper-2. Prod. by Bert Berns.

New York, May 1964

JO-JO (Bert Russell,Don Drowty)	unissued
BABY COME ON (Bert Russell,Don Drowty)-1-2	unissued
TELL ME BABY (Don Drowty)-1	unissued

KENNY HAMBER (vo) with 2tp, tb, ts, bs, g, ac-g, el-b, dm, prob. Dee Dee Warwick, Cissy Houston, Sylvia Shemwell, Estelle Brown (bkd-vo,handclaps). Add org-1. A Bert Berns Production.

Atlantic Sudios, New York, June 19, 1964

JAC-7993 SHOW ME YOUR MONKEY (Bert Russell,Mike Leander)	De Jac 1254
JAC-7994 TIME (Russell Dale Johnson)-1	De Jac 1254

HANS, CHRIS & ANDERSON (vo) with Charles De Angelis (fl,s); Buddy Lucas (hca,ts); Paul Griffin (p); Bill Suyker, Jimmy Spruill (g); Russ Saunders (el-b); Gary Chester (dm); Ted Sommer (triangle,perc). Arr-cond. by Phil Medley. A Bert Berns Production.

New York, July 22, 1964

64C-8046 THE PIED PIPER (Kathryn Reynolds)	Atco 6318
8047 EVERY NIGHT	unissued
64C-8048 DONNA (Ritchie Valens)	Atco 6318

THE PUSSYCATS (The Montells): Mary Parsons (lead vo-1,unison duet vo-2), Sheron Regular (unison duet vo-2,vo), Edythe Flemings, Charlotte Parsons (vo) with orch. arr-cond. by Teacho Wiltshire: Ernie Royal (tp); Ernie Hayes (p); Everett Barksdale, Bill Suyker (g); Jimmy Lewis (el-b); Milt Hinton (b); Gary Chester (dm); Ted Sommer (tamb,scraper,castanets,timpani); 10 strings. Omit strings-3, tp-4. A Bert Berns Production.

Atlantic Studios, New York, August 4, 1964

K-8055 COME ON AND SKA (Tom Dowd)-2-3	Keetch 6003
K-8056 YOU MAY BE HOLDING MY BABY (Bert Russell,Paul Colby)-1-4	Keetch 6003

THE DRIFTERS: Johnny Moore (lead tenor vo), Charlie Thomas (tenor vo), Eugene Pearson (baritone vo), Johnny Terry (bass vo) with orch. arr-cond. by Teacho Wiltshire: same band/session as above. A Bert Berns Production.

Atlantic Studios, New York, August 4, 1964

A-8057 I'VE GOT SAND IN MY SHOES (Artie Resnick,Kenny Young)-4	Atlantic 2253, LP8113
A-8058 SATURDAY NIGHT AT THE MOVIES (Barry Mann,Cynthia Weil)	Atlantic 2260, LP8103

SOLOMON BURKE (vo) with orch. arr-cond. by Ray Ellis: Ernie Royal, Irving Markowitz (tp); Buddy Lucas (ts); Haywood Henry (bs); Ernie Hayes (p); Billy Butler, Bill Suyker, Bert Berns (g); Russ Saunders (el-b); Gary Chester (dm); Joe Venuto, Paul Falise (perc,xyl); 6 strings; Dee Dee Warwick, Cissy Houston, Sylvia Shemwell, Estelle Brown (bkd-vo). Omit horns-1, strings-2. A Bert Berns Prod.

New York, August 23 or 28, 1964

A-8151 YES I DO (Bert Russell)-1	Atlantic 2254
A-8152 THE PRICE (Solomon Burke Sr.,Solomon Burke Jr.,J.B.Moore)-2	Atlantic 2259, LP8109

THE VIBRATIONS: Carl Fisher (lead tenor vo); James Johnson, Ricky Owens (tenor vo); Dave Govan (baritone vo); Don Bradley (bass vo) with orch. arr. by Teacho Wiltshire and Johnny Pate: 2tp, tb, ts, bs, p, 2g, el-b, dm, scraper, cow-bell, fem-cho. (Horns possibly overdubbed in Chicago.) Prod. by Carl Davis and Curtis Mayfield.

New York, September 2, 1964

CO 83760-6 WATUSI TIME (James Johnson,Carlton "Dell Sharh" Fisher)	Okeh 7205, LP14111
CO 83761-4 SLOOP DANCE (Wes Farrell,Bert Russell)	Okeh 7205, LP14111
CO 83933-5 AIN'T LOVE THAT WAY (Carlton "Dell Sharh" Fisher)	Okeh 7220, LP14111

ROY HAMILTON (vo) with orch. arr-cond. by Teacho Wiltshire: 2tp; tb; fl; p; 2g; el-b; dm; scraper; maracas; prob. Cissy Houston, Dee Dee Warwick, Sylvia Shemwell, Estelle Brown (bkd-vo). Omit fl add bs-1. A Bert Berns Production.

New York, September 4, 1964

64-XY-693 YOU CAN COUNT ON ME (Roy Hamilton,Billy Barnes)	MGM 13291
64-XY-694 SWEET VIOLET (Bill Cook)-1	MGM 13315
64-XY-695 SHE MAKE ME WANNA DANCE (Bert Russell)-1	MGM 13291
64-XY-696 A THOUSAND TEARS AGO (Bert Berns)	MGM 13315

JIMMY RADCLIFFE (vo) overdubbed on backing track arr-cond. by Burt Bacharach: p, 2g, el-b, dm, timpani, shaker, harp, strings, mixed-cho. Jimmy Radcliffe vocals in Italian-1. Prod. by Bert Berns.

New York, September 1964

R5KM-7187 LONG AFTER TONIGHT IS ALL OVER (Burt Bacharach,Hal David)   Musicor 1042
6015/2/N STAVOLTA NO (LONG AFTER TONIGHT IS ALL OVER)
    (Burt Bacharach,Hal David,Guilio "Mogol" Rapetti)-1   Musicor(Italy)JBMR 6015

ELAINE & DEREK: Elaine Thompson (vo), Derek Thompson (ac-g) with Jimmy Page (g), Alan Weighell (el-b), Bobby Graham (dm). Add Stan Barrett (vb), hca-1; Bert Berns (speech, whistling)-2. Production: Bert Berns.

London, October 1964

DR.34213 TEDDY BEARS AND HOBBY HORSES (Nathan Schnapf)-1   Parrot 9718
DR.34214 JOSE HE SAY (Bert Russell)-2   Parrot 9718

LULU (Marie Lawrie) (vo) with Reg Guest (p), Jimmy Page (12 string g-5/g), Big Jim Sullivan (g), Alan Weighell (el-b), Bobby Graham (dm), Stan Barrett (tamb), strings, mixed-cho. Add timpani-1, org-2, Bert Berns (vo)-3, handclaps-4, chimes-5, 2tp-6. Omit tamb, strings-2; mixed-cho -3. Music Director: Mike Leander. Production: Bert Berns.

London, October 1964

DR.34290 HERE COMES THE NIGHT (Bert Russell)-1   Parrot 9714
DR.34292 THAT'S REALLY SOME GOOD (Rufus Thomas)-2-3   Decca(E)12017, Decca(E)LP SPA94
DR.34293 I'LL COME RUNNING OVER (Bert Russell,Ilene Stuart)-2-4   Parrot 9714
         YOU'LL NEVER LEAVE HER (Bert Russell,Mike Stoller)-5-6   Decca(E)LP4719
         SHE WILL BREAK YOUR HEART
            (Jerry Butler,Curtis Mayfield,   Calvin Carter)-6 Decca(E)LP4719

THEM: Van Morrison (hca-1,vo), Pat McCauley (org), Billy Harrison (g), Alan Henderson (el-b), Ronnie Millings (dm,tamb). Additional/replacement session musicians include Phil Coulter (org); Jimmy Page (g); Alan Weighell (el-b); Bobby Graham or Andy White (dm); Perry Ford, Tommy Scott (bkd-vo -2). Production: Bert Berns.

Decca Studio 2, London, October 1964

DR.34355 BABY PLEASE DON'T GO (Big Joe Williams)-1   Parrot 9727
XDR.34960 HERE COMES THE NIGHT (Bert Berns)-2   Parrot 9749

TAMI LYNN (Gloria Brown) (vo) with orch. arr. by Ray Ellis: Melvin Lastie, Wilbur "Dud" Bascomb (tp); Tony Studd (tb); Chuck De Angelis (ts); Haywood Henry (bs); Ernie Hayes (p); Billy Butler, George Barnes (g); Jimmy Lewis (b); Ted Sommer (dm); Herb Wasserman (tamb,handclaps,perc); 13 strings; male-cho. Omit strings-1, male-cho -2. Prod. by Bert Berns.

A&R Recording Studios, New York, October 30, 1964

64C-8304 I'M GONNA RUN AWAY FROM YOU (Bert Berns)   Atco 6342
8305 YOU MY LOVE (Martin "Marty Sanders" Kupersmith,Wes Farrell)-1   unissued
8306 AT THE PARTY (Bert Berns)-1   unissued
64C-8307 THE BOY NEXT DOOR (Melvin Lastie,Gloria Brown)-1-2   Atco 6342

Note: A stereo version of I'M GONNA RUN AWAY FROM YOU was issued in 1972 on Cotillion LP9052 LOVE IS HERE AND NOW YOU'RE GONE. Tami Lynn's second vocal and the male background vocal group are missing on the stereo version. These elements may have been recorded at the time of mono mixdown on the original version. Also the stereo version has female background vocals by three of THE ANGELS: Barbara Allbut, Peggy Farina aka Peggy Santiglia, Bernadette Dalia aka Bernadette Carroll overdubbed in New York on February 10, 1965.

THE DRIFTERS: Charlie Thomas (lead tenor vo), Johnny Moore (tenor vo), Eugene Pearson (baritone vo), Johnny Terry (bass vo) with p, 2g, el-b, dm. A Bert Berns Production.

New York, November 2, 1964

8297 NIGHT SHIFT   Atlantic unissued

THE DRIFTERS: Johnny Moore (lead tenor vo), Charlie Thomas (tenor vo), Eugene Pearson (baritone vo), Johnny Terry (bass vo) with orch. arr-cond. by Teacho Wiltshire: Lamar Wright, Irving Markowitz (tp); Jack Jennings (tb); Leroy Glover (org); Artie Butler (p); Bill Suyker (g); Russ Saunders (b); Gary Chester (dm); tamb; scraper; cow-bell; strings. No org audible, Leroy Glover may play p and Artie Butler play perc. Jack Jennings usually plays perc rather than tb, or the tb player may be Jack Jeffers. Johnny Moore (solo vo)-1. A Bert Berns Production.

New York, November 12, 1964

8323 IN THE PARK (Barry Mann,Cynthia Weil)-1		Atlantic unissued
A-8324 AT THE CLUB (Gerry Goffin,Carole King)		Atlantic 2268, LP8113

WILSON PICKETT (vo) and Cissy Houston (vo-1) with orch. arr-cond. by Teacho Wiltshire: Ernie Royal, Clark Terry, Jack Cortner, Joe Mitchell (tp); Tony Studd (bass tb); Joe Grimaldi (ts); Haywood Henry (bs); Paul Griffin (p); Wally Richardson, Cornell Dupree (g); Jimmy Lewis (el-b); Panama Francis (dm); Ted Sommer (tamb). A Bert Berns Production.

Atlantic Studios, New York, November 13, 1964

A-8325 TEARDROPS WILL FALL (Marion Smith,Gerry "Dickie Doo" Granahan)-1		Atlantic LP8114
A-8329 COME HOME BABY (Barry Mann,Cynthia Weil)-1		Atlantic 2271, LP8114
A-8330 TAKE A LITTLE LOVE (Wilson Pickett)		Atlantic 2271, LP8114

THE DRIFTERS: Johnny Moore (lead tenor vo), Charlie Thomas (tenor vo), Eugene Pearson (baritone vo), Johnny Terry (bass vo) and Abdul Samad (Billy Davis) (g) overdubbed on band-track from HE WILL BREAK YOUR HEART (61C-5862) by BEN E. KING (arr-cond. by Klaus Ogerman): Robert Mosely or Moe Wechsler (p); Don Arnone, John "Bucky" Pizzarelli (g); Wendell Marshall (b); Gary Chester (dm); Ted Sommer, Bob Rosengarden (triangle,perc); 10 strings. A Bert Berns Production.

New York, December 31, 1964

A-8447 ANSWER THE PHONE (Jerry Wexler,Johnny Moore)		Atlantic 2268, LP8113

BARBARA LEWIS (vo) with orch. arr-cond. by Teacho Wiltshire: Clark Terry, Wilbur "Dud" Bascomb (tp); Jimmy Cleveland (tb); Tony Studd (bass tb); Charles Brown (ts); Haywood Henry (bs); Paul Griffin (p); Bill Suyker (g); Jimmy Lewis (el-b); Gary Chester (dm); Artie Butler (perc,handclaps). Overdub 1/65: Van McCoy, Kendra Spottswood (bkd-vo). Overdub 1/14/65: strings. Dir. by Bert Berns. An Ollie McLaughlin Production.

New York, January 8, 1965

A-8468 BABY I'M YOURS (Van McCoy)		Atlantic 2283, LP8110
A-8469 STOP THAT GIRL (Jackie DeShannon,Jimmy Page)		Atlantic LP8110
A-8470 MAMA MAMA PLEASE (Bill Carr,Connie St. John)		unissued

BEN E. KING (vo) with orch. arr-cond. by Bert Keyes: Joe Newman, Bill Berry (tp); Art Kaplan (ts); Patti Bown (p); Carl Lynch, Bill Suyker (g); Leonard Gaskin (b); Herb Lovelle (dm); Phil Kraus (tamb,vb); fem-cho. A Bert Berns Production.

New York, February 18, 1965

65C-8648 THE WAY YOU SHAKE IT (Bert Berns,Ahmet Ertegun,Ben E. King)		Atco 6343
65C-8649 THE RECORD (BABY, I LOVE YOU) (Artie Resnick,Kenny Young)		Atco 6343
65C-8650 NOT NOW (I'LL TELL YOU WHEN) (Ben E. King,James Albert Bethea)		Atco 6357
8651 ON MY WORD (Chip Taylor)		unissued

BEN E. KING (vo) with orch. arr-cond. by Bert Keyes: Billy Berry (tp); Patti Bown (p); Eric Gale, Everett Barksdale (g); Leonard Gaskin (b); Herb Lovelle (dm); Phil Kraus (timpani,triangle); strings; fem-cho. A Bert Berns Production.

New York, February 18, 1965

65C-8652 CRY NO MORE (Bert Berns,Jerry Ragovoy)		Atco 6371
65C-8653 SHE'S GONE AGAIN (Ben E. King)		Atco 6357
65C-8654 (THERE'S) NO PLACE TO HIDE (Roger Atkins,Helen Miller)		Atco 6371

RAY ELLIS (arr-cond) with Ernie Royal, Irving Markowitz (tp); Phil Bodner (as,fl,cl); Paul Griffin (p); Bill Suyker, Everett Barksdale (g); Russ Saunders, Bob Bushnell (el-b); Gary Chester (dm); Ed Shaughnessy (timpani,chimes); 11 strings; Lois Winter, Elise Bretton, Lillian Clark, Peggy Powers, Jerome Graff, Dave Vogel (bkd-vo). Prod. by Nesuhi Ertegun.

New York, February 22, 1965

65C-8655 PORTRAIT OF JAN (Ray Ellis)	Atco LP187
65C-8656 FLIGHT TO MEXICO (Ray Ellis,Bert Berns)	Atco LP187
8657 NO. 3 (GUAJIRA)	unissued

SAL MINEO (vo) with g, el-b, dm, tamb, handclaps, crowd noise. An Award Movie Production by Bert Berns.

New York, February 1965

YW1-34921 TAKE ME BACK (Bert Russell,Tom Dowd)	Fontana 1504
YW1-34922 SAVE THE LAST DANCE FOR ME (Doc Pomus,Mort Shuman)	Fontana 1504

GARNET MIMMS (vo) with orch. arr-cond. by Garry Sherman: tp; tb; ts; p; 2g; el-b; dm; tamb; timpani; strings; prob. Cissy Houston, Sylvia Shemwell, Estelle Brown, Myrna Smith (bkd-vo). Prod. by Jerry Ragovoy.

New York, March 3, 1965

ZTSP 98503 IT WAS EASIER TO HURT HER (Jerry Ragovoy,Bert Russell)	U.A. 848, LP3498
ZTSP 98543 WELCOME HOME (Chip Taylor)	U.A. 868, LP3498

THE DRIFTERS: Johnny Moore (lead tenor vo except -1/tenor vo), Charlie Thomas (lead tenor vo-1/ tenor vo), Eugene Pearson (baritone vo), Johnny Terry (bass vo) with orch. arr-cond. by Bert Keyes: Jimmy Nottingham, Irving Markowitz (tp); Bob Asher (tb); Seldon Powell (ts); Haywood Henry (bs); Patti Bown (p); Eric Gale, Everett Barksdale (g); Leonard Gaskin (b); Herb Lovelle (dm); Jack Jennings (perc). Omit horns add handclaps-2. A Bert Berns Production.

New York, March 17, 1965

8745 LOOKING THROUGH THE EYES OF LOVE (Barry Mann,Cynthia Weil)	Atlantic unissued
A-8746 FOLLOW ME (Mort Shuman,Kenny Lynch)	Atlantic 2292, LP8113
A-8746 FOLLOW ME (stereo alt.take)	Atlantic SD8113
A-8747 CHAINS OF LOVE (Jimmy Bishop,Kenny Gamble)-1	Atlantic 2285, LP8113
A-8748 FAR FROM THE MADDENING CROWD (Marlin Greene,Dan Penn)	Atlantic 2298, LP8113
A-8749 COME ON OVER TO MY PLACE (Cynthia Weil,Barry Mann)-2	Atlantic 2285, LP8113

THE EXCITERS: Brenda Reid (lead vo), Carol Johnson, Lillian Walker, Herb Rooney (vo) with orch. cond. by Teacho Wiltshire: tp, 2tb, ts, bs, p, 2g, el-b, dm, triangle, scraper, strings. Add handclaps omit tp, 2tb, ts, strings-1. Prod. by Bert Berns.

Mirasound Studios, New York, March 24, 1965

18528 THERE THEY GO (Bert Berns)	Roulette 4632, LP25326
18529 RUN MASCARA (Bert Berns)	Roulette 4614, LP25326
18530 MY FATHER (Herb Rooney,Andrew Pope)	Roulette 4614, LP25326
18531 I KNEW YOU WOULD (Bert Berns)-1	Roulette 4632, LP25326

TONY ORLANDO (vo) with orch. arr-cond. by Bert Keyes: Wilbur "Dud" Bascomb, Myron D. Shain (tp); Haywood Henry (bs); Patti Bown (p); Bill Suyker, George Barnes (g); Russ Saunders (b); Herb Lovelle (dm); Ted Sommer (dm,perc); George Ockner, Max Cohn (v); George Ricci (cello). Prod. by Bert Berns.

New York, March 31, 1965

8810 TURN AROUND (Bert Russell,Audrey Saxon)	Atco unissued
8811 IT WON'T HURT (HALF AS MUCH) (Bert Berns)	Atco unissued

THE STRANGELOVES: Bob Feldman, Jerry Goldstein, Richard Gottehrer (vo) with ts, bs, p, Everett Barksdale (g), g, el-b, dm, timpani. Omit saxes add handclaps-1. Arr. by Bassett Hand (=FGG). A Feldman, Goldstein, Gottehrer Production.

Bell Sound Studios, New York, April 1965

W-1003	I WANT CANDY (Feldman,Goldstein,Gottehrer,Bert Berns)	Bang 501, LP211
W-1004	IT'S ABOUT MY BABY(Feldman,Goldstein,Gottehrer)-1	Bang 501, LP211

THEM: Van Morrison (hca-1,vo), Peter Bardens (org), Billy Harrison (g), Alan Henderson (el-b), Patrick McAuley (dm,tamb). Additional/replacement session musicians probably include Jimmy Page (g). Add male bkd-vo -2, maracas-3. Production: Bert Berns.

Regent Sound Studios, London, May 3-5, 1965

XDR.36257	(IT WON'T HURT) HALF AS MUCH (Bert Berns)-2	Parrot 9784
	LITTLE GIRL (Van Morrison)-3	Decca(E)LP4700
	GO ON HOME BABY (Bert Berns)-1-2	Decca(E)LP4700
	MY LITTLE BABY (Bert Berns,Wes Farrell)-2	Decca(E)LP4700
	I GAVE MY LOVE A DIAMOND (Bert Berns)	Decca(E)LP4700

MOSES K AND THE PROPHETS: Kenny McDowell (double-tracked vo) with Phil Coulter (p), g, ac-g, el-b, Andy White (dm), tamb, Tommy Scott (handclaps-1). Production: Bert Berns.

Regent Sound Studios, London, May 1965

XDR.36628	I WENT OUT WITH MY BABY TONIGHT (Bert Berns)-1	Decca(E)12244
	ANSWER YOUR PHONE (Jerry Wexler,Johnny Moore)	Decca (E) unissued

TROY SEALS & THE LOSERS: Troy Seals (vo,g); The Losers: Joe Parrino (g), Russell Warmolts (el-b), Brian Keenan (dm). Prod. by Bert Berns.

New York, May 23, 1965

8967	THERE GOES MY BABY (Ben Nelson,Lover Patterson,GeorgeTreadwell)	Atlantic/Atco unissued
8968	SEE SEE RIDER (trad.)	Atlantic/Atco unissued
8969	WATCH YOUR STEP (Bobby Parker)	Atlantic/Atco unissued
8970	IF YOU LOVE ME LIKE YOU SAY (Little Johnny Taylor)	Atlantic/Atco unissued
8971	DON'T CRY NO MORE (Don "Deadric Malone" Robey)	Atlantic/Atco unissued

THE DRIFTERS: Johnny Moore (lead tenor vo), Charlie Thomas (tenor vo), Eugene Pearson (baritone vo), Johnny Terry (bass vo) with orch. arr-cond. by Gene Page: Joe Newman, Irving Markowitz (tp); Tony Studd (tb); Seldon Powell (ts); Haywood Henry (bs); Paul Griffin (p); Eric Gale, Carl Lynch, Everett Barksdale (g); Russ Saunders (el-b); Herb Lovelle (dm); George Devens (vb); Jack Jennings, Emil Richards (tamb-1,cymbals-2,marimba-3); 10 strings. Omit strings-4. Prod. by Bert Berns & Jeff Barry-2 or A Bert Berns Production.

New York, June 30, 1965

A-9078	I'LL TAKE YOU WHERE THE MUSIC'S PLAYING	
	(Jeff Barry,Ellie Greenwich)-1-2	Atlantic 2298, LP8113
A-9079	NYLON STOCKINGS (Tony Bruno,Victor Millrose)-3	Atlantic 2310
A-9080	WE GOTTA SING (Barry Mann,Cynthia Weil)-1-4	Atlantic 2310

THE WITCHES (The Montells): Mary Parsons (lead vo-1,unison duet vo-2), Sheron Regular (unison duet vo-2,vo), Edythe Flemings, Charlotte Parsons (vo) with orch. arr-cond. by Artie Butler: tp, tb, ts, bs, p, Eric Gale (g), g, el-b, dm, tamb, vb. Omit horns, vb-2. Prod. by Bert Berns, A Web IV Music Inc. Production.

Mirasound Studios, New York, June 1965

W-10011	MY LITTLE BABY (Bert Berns,Wes Farrell)-2	Bang 505
W-10012	SHE'S GOT YOU NOW (Buddy Smith)-1	Bang 505

BARBARA LEWIS (vo) with orch. arr. by Artie Butler: Patti Bown (p); Vinnie Bell, Al Gorgoni, Trade Martin (g); Bob Bushnell (el-b); Gary Chester (dm); Ted Sommer, Alvin Rogers (tamb,chimes); 10 strings; fem-cho. Omit perc, strings, fem-cho -1. Dir. by Bert Berns. An Ollie McLaughlin Production.

New York, July 1, 1965

A-9083 MAKE ME YOUR BABY (Helen Miller,Roger Atkins)	Atlantic 2300, LP8173
A-9084 I'M SO AFRAID (Curtis Mayfield)	unissued
A-9085 LOVE TO BE LOVED (David Parker)-1	Atlantic 2300

THE LOSERS: Brian Keenan (vo,hca,dm,tamb), Joe Parrino (g,bkd-vo), Russell Warmolts (el-b,bkd-vo). Prod. by Bert Berns.

New York, July 1, 1965

65C-9086 MERSEY-SSIPPI (Brian Keenan)	Atco 6373
9087 THIS GIRL OF MINE	unissued

THE LOSERS: Brian Keenan (vo,dm,tamb), Joe Parrino (g,bkd-vo), Russell Warmolts (el-b,bkd-vo). Prod. by Bert Berns.

New York, July 26, 1965

9211 SHE BELONGS TO ME	unissued
65C-9212 LOVE ME LIKE THE RAIN (Brian Keenan)	Atco 6373

THE LOST SOULS: four males (lead vo,2g,el-b,dm,tamb,bkd-vo). Prod. by Bert Berns, A Web IV Production.

New York, August 1965

W-10027 THE GIRL I LOVE (Bert Berns)	Bang 509
W-10028 SIMPLE TO SAY (Joseph Shefsky)	Bang 509
W-10047 I GAVE MY LOVE A DIAMOND (Bert Berns)	Bang 513 (unissued)
W-10048 I WONDER IF SHE REMEMBERS ME (Bert Berns)	Bang 513 (unissued)

THE DEBS (vo) with p, 2g, el-b, dm. A (Dennis) Lambert- (Lou) Courtney Production.

New York, September 23, 1965

YW1-36929 SLOOPY'S GONNA HANG ON (Wes Farrell,Bert Russell)	Mercury 72494

JOHNNY THUNDER (Gil Hamilton) (vo) with org, 2g, el-b, dm, tamb, mixed-cho. Arr. By Artie Butler. Prod. by Bert Berns. A Web IV Production.

New York, September 1965

D-192A EVERYBODY DO THE SLOOPY (Bert Berns,Wes Farrell)	Diamond 192

PATTI LABELLE & THE BLUEBELLES: Patricia "Patti LaBelle" Holte (lead vo), Wynona "Nona" Hendryx, Cynthia "Cindy" Birdsong, Sarah Dash (vo) with orch. arr-cond. by Artie Butler: Ernie Royal (tp); Benny Powell (tb); Joe Grimaldi (ts); Richard DiCicco aka Richie Rome, Leroy Glover (p,org); Billy Butler, Bill Suyker, Al Gorgoni (g); Russ Saunders (el-b); Gary Chester (dm); Jack Jennings, Joe Venuto (tamb,vb,chimes); 8 strings. A Bert Berns Production.

New York, October 7, 1965

A-9372 PATTI'S PRAYER (Bob Finiz)	Atlantic 2333, LP8119
A-9373 GROOVY KIND OF LOVE (Toni Wine,Carole Bayer)	Atlantic 2318, LP8119
A-9374 ALL OR NOTIIING (Pam Sawyer,Lori Burton)	Atlantic 2311, LP8119
A-9375 WHO CAN I TURN TO (WHEN NOBODY NEEDS ME) (Leslie Bricusse,Anthony Newley)	Atlantic LP8119

PATTI LABELLE & THE BLUEBELLES: Patricia "Patti LaBelle" Holte (lead vo), Wynona "Nona" Hendryx, Cynthia "Cindy" Birdsong, Sarah Dash (vo) with Leroy Glover (org,p); Wally Richardson, Walter Raim (g,ac-g); Richard Romoff (el-b); Alvin Rogers (dm); Jack Jennings (tamb). Arr-cond. by Artie Butler. A Bert Berns Production.

New York, October 20, 1965

9448 DON'T NEED TRUE LOVE		unissued
A-9449 YOU FORGOT HOW TO LOVE (Bert Berns,Ilene Stewart)		Atlantic 2311

NANCY AMES (vo) with p, 2g, el-b, dm, tamb, fem-cho. Arr-cond. by Teacho Wiltshire. Prod. by Manny Kellem and Billy Sherrill.

New York, October 1965

ZSP 112281 I'VE GOT A LOT OF LOVE (LEFT IN ME) (Ronnie Wilkins,John Hurley)	Epic 9874
ZSP 112282 FRIENDS AND LOVERS FOREVER (Bert Berns,Wes Farrell)	Epic 9874

SOLOMON BURKE (vo) with orch. arr-cond. by Leroy Glover: Joe Newman, Ernie Royal (tp); Benny Powell (tb); Seldon Powell, Art Kaplan (ts); Haywood Henry (bs); Felix Cavaliere (org); Paul Griffin (p); Eric Gale, Trade Martin, Charlie Brown (g); Jimmy Lewis (el-b); Herb Lovelle (dm); George Devens (tamb); 4 females (bkd-vo). Prod. by Bert Berns.

New York, November 5, 1965

A-9483 I DON'T WANT YOU NO MORE (Solomon Burke)	Atlantic 2349
A-9484 (NO, NO, NO) CAN'T STOP LOVIN' YOU NOW (Solomon Burke)	Atlantic 2314
A-9485 BABY COME ON HOME (Bert Berns)	Atlantic 2314, LP8158

BARBARA LEWIS (vo) with orch. arr-cond. by Artie Butler: Joe Newman, Melvin Davis (tp); Benny Powell (tb); Paul Winter (saxes); Phil Bodner (fl); Leroy Glover (p); Bill Suyker, Al Gorgoni, Vinnie Bell (g); Dick Romoff (el-b); Gary Chester (dm); Jack Jennings (timpani,chimes), strings, fem-cho. Prod. by Bert Berns.

New York, November 15, 1965

A-9649 DON'T FORGET ABOUT ME (Gerry Goffin,Carole King)	Atlantic 2316, LP8118
A-9650 BETTER NOT BELIEVE HIM (Bert Russell,Ruth Batchelor)	Atlantic LP8118
A-9651 HE'S SO BAD (Bert Berns,Wes Farrell)	Atlantic LP8118

THE EXCITERS: Brenda Reid (lead vo), Carol Johnson, Lillian Walker, Herb Rooney (vo) with orch. arr-cond. by Artie Butler: Irvin Markowitz, Burt Collins (tp); Eddie Bert (tb); Joe Grimaldi (ts); Art Kaplan (bs); Leroy Glover (p); Trade Martin, Charles Massey, Al Gorgoni (g); Al Lucas (b); Herb Lovelle (dm); Willie Correa (cga); George Devens (tamb,vb). Prod. by Bert Berns, Web IV Productions.

New York, November 29, 1965

S-20029 YOU KNOW IT AIN'T RIGHT (Bert Berns,Wes Farrell)	Shout 214
W-10057 YOU BETTER COME HOME (Bert Russell)	Bang 518

THE EXCITERS: Brenda Reid (lead vo), Carol Johnson, Lillian Walker, Herb Rooney (vo) with orch. arr-cond. by Artie Butler: Leroy Glover (p); Vinnie Bell, Bill Suyker, Al Gorgoni (g); Dick Romoff (el-b); Gary Chester (dm); Ted Sommer (timpani); George Devens (vb); 4 strings. Prod. by Bert Berns, Web IV Productions.

New York, December 6, 1965

W-10051 A LITTLE BIT OF SOAP (Bert Russell)	Bang 515
W-10052 I'M GONNA GET HIM SOMEDAY (Herb Rooney,Andrew Pope)	Bang 515
W-10058 WEDDINGS MAKE ME CRY (Herb Rooney,Andrew Pope)	Bang 518

PATTI LABELLE & THE BLUEBELLES: Patricia "Patti LaBelle" Holte (lead vo), Wynona "Nona" Hendryx, Cynthia "Cindy" Birdsong, Sarah Dash (vo) with Art Kaplan (fl); Leroy Glover (p); Eric Gale, Bill Suyker (g,ac-g); Richard Romoff (el-b); Gary Chester (dm); Ted Sommer, George Devens (timpani,chimes,vb); Gene Bianco-1 or Margaret Ross-2 (harp); strings. Arr-cond. by Artie Butler-1 or Jimmy Wisner-2. Prod. by Bert Berns.

New York, December 21, 1965

A-9691 UNCHAINED MELODY (Hy Zaret,Alex North)-1	Atlantic 2408, LP8119
A-9692 EBB TIDE (Robert Maxwell)-1 (BB5/28/66)	Atlantic 2333, LP8119
A-9693 HE (Jack Richards,Richard Mullan)-1 (BB5/14/66)	Atlantic LP8119
A-9694 TRY TO REMEMBER (Harvey Schmidt,Tom Jones)-1	Atlantic LP8119
A-9695 PEOPLE (Bob Merrill,Jule Styne)-2	Atlantic LP8119
A-9696 YESTERDAY (John Lennon,Paul McCartney)-2	Atlantic LP8119
A-9697 MORE (Riz Ortolani,Nino Oliviero,Norman Newell)-2	Atlantic LP8119
A-9698 OVER THE RAINBOW (Harold Arlen,Yip Harburg)-2	Atlantic 2318
A-9698 OVER THE RAINBOW (Harold Arlen,Yip Harburg)-2 (stereo alt.take)	Atlantic LP8119

LANCE FOX & THE BLOODHOUNDS: Richard "Ritchie Adams" Ziegler (lead vo) with org, g, el-b, dm, tamb, 2 males (bkd-vo). A Jerry Ragovoy Production.

New York, December 1965

W-10065 YOU GOT LOVE (Jerry Ragovoy,Bert Berns)	Bang 523
W-10066 THAT'S YOUR PROBLEM (IT AIN'T MINE) (Ritchie Adams,Jerry Ragovoy)	Bang 523

GARNET MIMMS (vo) with orch. arr-cond. by Garry Sherman: tp; tb; ts; bs; p; 2g; el-b; dm; prob. Cissy Houston, Sylvia Shemwell, Estelle Brown, Myrna Smith (bkd-vo). Prod. by Jerry Ragovoy.

New York, January 26, 1966

ZTSP 106647 I'LL TAKE GOOD CARE OF YOU (Jerry Ragovoy,Bert Berns)	United Artists 995, LP3498
OOH BABY	unissued

THE DRIFTERS: Johnny Moore (lead tenor vo-1/tenor vo), Charlie Thomas (lead tenor vo-2/tenor vo), Eugene Pearson (baritone vo), Johnny Terry (bass vo) with orch. arr-cond. by Artie Butler: Ernie Royal, Irving Markowitz (tp); Eddie Bert, Jimmy Cleveland (tb); Joe Grimes (Joe Grimaldi) (ts); Art Kaplan (bs); Paul Griffin (p); Al Gorgoni, Bill Suyker, Trade Martin (g); Dick Romoff (b); Herb Lovelle (dm); George Devens (vb-1,castanets-2,triangle-3, chimes-4). A Bert Berns Production.

New York, January 27, 1966

A-9880 UP IN THE STREETS OF HARLEM (Bert Berns)-1-3	Atlantic 2336
A-9881 MEMORIES ARE MADE OF THIS	
(Richard Dehr,Terry Gilkyson,Frank Miller)-1-4	Atlantic 2325
A-9882 YOU CAN'T LOVE 'EM ALL (Berns,Leiber,Stoller,Nugetre)-2	Atlantic 2336

THE DRIFTERS: Johnny Moore (lead tenor vo), Charlie Thomas (tenor vo), Eugene Pearson (baritone vo), Johnny Terry (bass vo) with Leroy Glover (p); Al Gorgoni, Bill Suyker (g,ac-g); Dick Romoff (b); Buddy Saltzman (dm); Jack Jennings (marimba); Arif Mardin (perc). Arr-cond. by Artie Butler. A Bert Berns Production.

New York, February 8, 1966

A-9912 MY ISLANDS IN THE SUN (Abdul Samad,Johnny Moore)	Atlantic 2325

THE BUSHMEN: four or five males (lead vo,org-1,p,g,el-b,dm,bkd-vo). Prod. by Shelby S. Singleton Jr.

New York, July 22, 1966

YW1-38193 FRIENDS AND LOVERS FOREVER (Wes Farrell,Bert Berns)-1	Smash 2054
YW1-38194 YOU'VE BEEN WITH HIM (Wes Farrell,Bert Berns)	Smash 2054

THE DRIFTERS: Johnny Moore (lead tenor vo-1/tenor vo), Charlie Thomas (lead tenor vo-2/tenor vo), Eugene Pearson (baritone vo), Johnny Terry (bass vo) with orch. arr.-cond. by Leroy Glover: Wilbur "Dud" Bascomb, Clark Terry (tp); Seldon Powell, Buddy Lucas (ts); Haywood Henry (bs); Ernie Hayes (p); Al Gorgoni, Eric Gale, Hugh McCracken (g); Jimmy Tyrell (el-b); Herb Lovelle (dm); Jack Jennings, Ted Sommer (tamb,perc). A Bert Berns Production.

A&R Recording Studios, New York, July 26, 1966

A-10544 TAKES A GOOD WOMAN (Max Barnes)-2		Atlantic unissued
A-10545 ARETHA (Bert Berns,Jeff Barry)-1		Atlantic 2366

BOBBY HARRIS (vo) with tp; ts; bs; p; 2g; el-b; dm; prob. The Sweet Inspirations: Cissy Houston, Sylvia Shemwell, Myrna Smith, Estelle Brown (bkd-vo). Add cga-1, org-2. A Bert Berns Production.

New York, July 1966

S-20008 STICKY, STICKY (Bert Berns)-1		Shout 203
S-20009 MR. SUCCESS (Bert Berns)-2		Shout 203

ARSENIO (Arsenio Rodriguez) (lead vo except -1/bkd-vo,g) with female (lead vo-1/bkd-vo); ac-g; b; dm; bgo; cga; scraper; cow-bell; 1 female, 2 males (bkd-vo). Add 2tp, tb, ts, bs-2. Arr. by Artie Butler. Prod. by Bert Berns.

A&R Recording Studios, New York, August 1966

W-10101 HANG ON SLOOPY (Bert Berns,Wes Farrell)-2		Bang 533, LP216
W-10102 VAYA P'AL MONTE (Arsenio Rodriguez)-1		Bang 533, LP216
LA YUCA (Arsenio Rodriguez)-2		Bang LP216
BAILA CON MIGO (Arsenio Rodriguez)-1-2		Bang LP216
MANISERO Y MARTA (Moises Simons)		Bang LP216
QUE NO LLEGUE LA NOCHE Y LA PARED(Arsenio Rodriguez, Roberto Anglero)-1-2		Bang LP216
LA BAMBA (arr.Arsenio Rodriguez)-1		Bang LP216
TRES MARIAS (Arsenio Rodriguez)		Bang LP216
CIELITO LINDO (arr.Arsenio Rodriguez)		Bang LP216
PARA BAILAR EL MONTUNO (Arsenio Rodriguez)		Bang LP216
RANDY (Arsenio Rodriguez)-1		Bang LP216
EL ELEMENTO DEL BRONX (Arsenio Rodriguez)		Bang LP216

FREDDIE SCOTT (vo) with orch. arr. by Garry Sherman: tp; ts; bs; p; 2g; el-b; dm; tamb; prob. The Sweet Inspirations: Cissy Houston, Sylvia Shemwell, Myrna Smith, Estelle Brown (bkd-vo). Omit p, tamb, bkd-vo; add org-1. Prod. by Bert Berns.

A&R Recording Studios, New York, September 9, 1966

S-20014 ARE YOU LONELY FOR ME (Bert Berns)		Shout 207, LP501
S-20015 WHERE WERE YOU (Freddie Scott)-1		Shout 207, LP501

THE EXCITERS: Brenda Reid (lead vo), Carol Johnson, Lillian Walker, Herb Rooney (vo) with 2tp, tb, ts, bs, p, 2g, el-b, dm. A Bert Berns Production.

New York, September 1966

W-10103 NUMBER ONE (Herb Rooney,Andrew Pope)		Shout 205
W-10104 YOU GOT LOVE (Jerry Ragovoy,Bert Berns)		Shout 205

JACK ELY & THE COURTMEN: Jack Ely (lead vo) with org, g, el-b, dm. Add The Sweet Inspirations, Neil Diamond (bkd-vo); crowd noise-1. A Bert Berns Production.

Bell Sound Studios, New York, September 1966

W-10105 RIDE RIDE BABY (Bert Berns,Jeff Barry)-1		Bang 534
W-10106 LOUIE GO HOME (Mark Lindsay,Paul Revere)		Bang 534

FREDDIE SCOTT (vo) with orch. arr-cond. by Garry Sherman: tp; ts; bs; p; 2g; el-b; dm; tamb; strings; prob. The Sweet Inspirations: Cissy Houston, Sylvia Shemwell, Myrna Smith, Estelle Brown (bkd-vo). Prod. by Bert Berns.

A&R Recording Studios, New York, October 7, 1966

S-20023 NO ONE COULD EVER LOVE YOU (Bert Berns,Jerry Ragovoy)   Shout 211, LP501

ROY C (Roy Charles Hammond) (vo) with orch. arr. by Artie Butler: 2tp; tb; ts; bs; p; Eric Gale (g); g; el-b; dm; prob. The Sweet Inspirations: Cissy Houston, Sylvia Shemwell, Myrna Smith, Estelle Brown (bkd-vo). Add vb-1, Bert Berns (bkd-vo)-2. Prod. by Bert Berns.

Bell Sound Studios, New York, October 1966

S-20012 STOP WHAT YOUR DOIN' (Gregory Carroll,Helena Walquer,Roy C.Hammond)-1   Shout 206
S-20013 GONE GONE (Bert Berns)-2   Shout 206

THE McCOYS: Rick Zehringer (lead vo,g), Bobby Peterson (el-p -1,org-2,bkd-vo), Randy Hobbs (el-b,bkd-vo), Randy Zehringer (dm). Add hca-2. A Berns and Barry Production-1 or Prod. by Bert Berns-2..

Century Sound Studios, New York, November 1966

W-10113 I GOT TO GO BACK (AND WATCH THAT LITTLE GIRL DANCE)
        (Bert Berns,Jeff Barry)-1   Bang 538
W-10136 I WONDER IF SHE REMEMBERS ME (Bert Berns)-2   Bang 549

FREDDIE SCOTT (vo) with orch. arr-cond. by Garry Sherman: tp; ts; bs; p; 2g; el-b; dm; tamb; prob. The Sweet Inspirations: Cissy Houston, Sylvia Shemwell, Myrna Smith, Estelle Brown (bkd-vo). Add vb-1, org-2. Omit tamb-1. Prod. by Bert Berns.

Century Sound Studios, New York, January 11 and 13, 1967

S-20022 CRY TO ME (Berns)   Shout 211, LP501
        LET IT BE ME (Curtis,Becaud,Delanoe)-1   Shout LP501
        OPEN THE DOOR TO YOUR HEART (Darrell Eubanks,Lawrence Murphy) Shout LP501
        SHAKE A HAND (Joe Morris)-2   Shout LP501
        FOR YOUR LOVE (Ed Townsend)   Shout LP501
        THE LOVE OF MY WOMAN (Ed Townsend)-1   Shout LP501
        BRING IT ON HOME TO ME (Sam Cooke)   Shout LP501
S-20032 HE WILL BREAK YOUR HEART (Butler,Mayfield,Carter)-2   Shout 216, LP501
S-20055 SPANISH HARLEM (Leiber,Spector)-1   Shout 227, LP501

FREDDIE SCOTT (vo) with orch. arr-cond. by Garry Sherman: tp; ts; bs; p; 2g; el-b; dm; tamb; prob. The Sweet Inspirations: Cissy Houston, Sylvia Shemwell, Myrna Smith, Estelle Brown (bkd-vo). Prod. by Bert Berns.

A&R Recording Studios, New York, January 17, 1967

S-20024 AM I GROOVING YOU (Berns,Jeff Barry)   Shout 212
        YOU'LL NEVER LEAVE HIM (Bert Russell,Mike Stoller)   Shout unissued

BOBBY HARRIS (vo) with tp; ts; bs; org; p; Eric Gale (g); g; el-b; dm; prob. The Sweet Inspirations: Cissy Houston, Sylvia Shemwell, Myrna Smith, Estelle Brown (bkd-vo). Prod. by Bert Berns.

New York, January 1967

S-20020 THE LOVE OF MY WOMAN (Ed Townsend)   Shout 210
S-20021 BABY COME BACK TO ME (Johnny Northern,Ralph Bailey)   Shout 210

HOAGY LANDS (vo) with Prod. by Bert Berns.

New York, January 1967

32 MILES OUT OF WAYCROSS (MOJO MAMMA) (Bert Berns,Jerry Wexler)   Bang unissued

WILSON PICKETT (vo) with Gene "Bowlegs" Miller (tp); Charlie Chalmers, Jimmy Mitchell (ts); Floyd Newman (bs); Spooner Oldham (org,el-p); Chips Moman, Jimmy Johnson (g); Tommy Cogbill (el-b); Roger Hawkins (dm). Add fem-cho (overdubbed in New York)-1. Prod. by Jerry Wexler.

Fame Studios, Muscle Shoals, February 1, 1967

A-11647 FUNKY BROADWAY (Christian)	Atlantic 2430, LP8145
11648 MOJO MAMMA (Bert Berns,Jerry Wexler)-1	Atlantic LP8145

VAN MORRISON (hca-1,vo) with Garry Sherman (org), Al Gorgoni (g), Hugh McCracken or Donald Thomas (g), Bob Bushnell or Russell Savakus (el-b), Herbie Lovelle or Gary Chester (dm), Jeff Barry (bkd-vo -2,tamb). Add Cissy Houston, Dee Dee Warwick, Myrna Smith (bkd-vo)-3; Bert Berns, Brooks Arthur (bkd-vo)-4. Arr. by Garry Sherman. Prod. by Bert Berns.

A&R Recording Studio A, New York, March 28, 1967

tk.4 RO RO ROSEY (Van Morrison)-1 (3.04)	Bang LP218
W-10141 (tk.4 edit) RO RO ROSEY (Van Morrison)-1-3 (2.58)	Bang 552
tk.22 BROWN EYED GIRL (Van Morrison)-2-3 (3.06)	Bang 545, LP218
W-10207 (tk.9) MIDNIGHT SPECIAL (arr.Bert Berns)-1-3 (2.51)	Bang 585, LP218
W-10128 (tk.13) GOODBYE BABY (BABY GOODBYE) (Bert Berns,Wes Farrell)-3 (2.57)	Bang 545, LP218

VAN MORRISON (hca-1,vo) with Artie Butler or Paul Griffin (org-2,p-3), Eric Gale (g), Hugh McCracken or Donald Thomas (g,ac-g), Bob Bushnell or Russell Savakus (el-b), Herbie Lovelle or Gary Chester (dm), George Devens or Jeff Barry (tamb). Arr. by Garry Sherman. Prod. by Bert Berns.

A&R Recording Studio A, New York, March 29, 1967

tk.4 T.B. SHEETS (Van Morrison)-1-2 (9.44)	Bang LP218
W-10208 (tk.14 edit) SPANISH ROSE (Van Morrison) (3.09)	Bang 585, LP218
tk.6 (edit) WHO DROVE THE RED SPORTS CAR (Van Morrison)-3 (5.35)	Bang LP218
tk.8 HE AIN'T GIVE YOU NONE (Van Morrison)-2-3 (5.13)	Bang LP218

THE EXCITERS: Brenda Reid (lead vo), Carol Johnson, Lillian Walker, Herb Rooney (vo) with orch. arr. by Garry Sherman: tp; ts; bs; p; Eric Gale (g); g; el-b; dm; tamb; prob. The Sweet Inspirations: Cissy Houston, Sylvia Shemwell, Myrna Smith, Estelle Brown (bkd-vo). Prod. by Bert Berns.

New York, April 1967

S-20028 SOUL MOTION (Bert Berns,Jeff Barry)	Shout 214

GARY (U.S.) BONDS (Gary Anderson) (vo) with band (+ org) and bkd-vo as above (split session). A (Frank) Guida-(Doug) Morris-(Eliot) Greenberg Production. (Bert Berns present).

New York, April 1967

U4KM-0967 SEND HER TO ME (Bert Russell,Ruth Batchelor)	Legrand 1043

FREDDIE SCOTT (vo) with orch. arr-cond. by Garry Sherman: tp, ts, bs, p, 2g, el-b, dm, tamb. Add prob. The Sweet Inspirations: Cissy Houston, Sylvia Shemwell, Myrna Smith, Estelle Brown (bkd-vo)-1. Prod. by Bert Berns.

A&R Recording Studios, New York, May 24, 1967

S-20033 I'LL BE GONE (Rose Marie McCoy,Scott)	Shout 216
S-20040 RUN JOE (Louis Jordan,Joe Willoughby,Dr.Walt Merrick)-1	Shout 220
S-20041 HE AIN'T GIVE YOU NONE (Van Morrison)-1	Shout 220

ERMA FRANKLIN (vo) with p; 2g; el-b; dm; prob.The Sweet Inspirations: Cissy Houston, Sylvia Shemwell, Myrna Smith, Estelle Brown (bkd-vo). Add org omit bkd-vo -2. Arr-cond. by Garry Sherman-1. Prod. by Bert Berns.

New York, June 1967

S-20036 BIG BOSS MAN (Al Smith,Luther Dixon)-1	Shout 218
S-20037 DON'T CATCH THE DOG'S BONE (Carolyn Franklin)-2	Shout 218

LORRAINE ELLISON (vo) with orch. arr. by Garry Sherman: tp; tb; ts; bs; org; p; 2g; el-b; dm; strings; prob. The Sweet Inspirations: Cissy Houston, Sylvia Shemwell, Myrna Smith, Estelle Brown (bkd-vo). Prod. by Jerry Ragovoy.

A&R Recording Studios, New York, June 1967

K51322 I WANT TO BE LOVED (Samuel Bell)	Loma 2083, Warner Bros. LP1821
K51323 HEART BE STILL (Jerry Ragovoy,Bert Berns)	Loma 2074, Warner Bros. LP1821

ERMA FRANKLIN (vo) with orch. arr-cond. By Garry Sherman: tp; ts; p; 2g; Eric Gale (el-b); dm; prob. The Sweet Inspirations: Cissy Houston, Sylvia Shemwell, Myrna Smith, Estelle Brown (bkd-vo). Prod. by Bert Berns.

New York, August 1967

S-20042 PIECE OF MY HEART (Bert Berns,Jerry Ragovoy)	Shout 221
S-20043 BABY, WHAT YOU WANT ME TO DO (Jimmy Reed)	Shout 221

DONALD HEIGHT (vo) with orch. arr-cond. by Garry Sherman: tp; tb; ts; bs; org; p; 2g; el-b; dm; prob. The Sweet Inspirations: Cissy Houston, Sylvia Shemwell, Myrna Smith, Estelle Brown (bkd-vo). Prod. by Bert Berns.

Century Sound Studios, New York, August 1967

S-20046 GOOD TO ME (Otis Redding,Julius Green)	Shout 223

VAN MORRISON (vo) with Artie Butler or Paul Griffin (org-1,p-2); Al Gorgoni or Hugh McCracken or Donald Thomas (2g); Bob Bushnell or Russell Savakus (el-b); Herbie Lovelle or Gary Chester (dm); George Devens (tamb,cga,triangle); Cissy Houston, Dee Dee Warwick, Myrna Smith (bkd-vo). Arr. by Garry Sherman. Prod. by Bert Berns.

Century Sound Studios, New York, September, 1967

THE SMILE YOU SMILE (Van Morrison)-1 (2.55)	Bang LP222
IT'S ALL RIGHT (Van Morrison)-1 (5.04)	Bang LP222
W-10142 CHICK-A-BOOM (Van Morrison,Bert Berns)-2 (3.12)	Bang 552

VAN MORRISON (vo) with Artie Butler or Paul Griffin (org-1,p-2); Al Gorgoni or Hugh McCracken or Donald Thomas (g,ac-g); Bob Bushnell or Russell Savakus (el-b); Herbie Lovelle or Gary Chester (dm); George Devens (cga,tamb); Cissy Houston, Dee Dee Warwick, Myrna Smith (bkd-vo -3). Arr. by Garry Sherman. Prod. by Bert Berns.

Incredible Sounds Studios, New York, November, 1967

BESIDE YOU (Van Morrison)-1 (6.07)	Bang LP400
THE BACK ROOM (Van Morrison)-1-2-3 (5.30)	Bang LP222
MADAME GEORGE (Van Morrison)-2-3 (5.17)	Bang LP400
SEND YOUR MIND (Van Morrison)-1-3 (2.54)	Bang LP222

FREDDIE SCOTT (vo) with as, org, 2g, el-b, dm, fem-cho. Omit as, org-1. Prod. by Bert Berns & Freddie Scott.

New York, November 1967

S-20054 JUST LIKE A FLOWER (Freddie Scott,Sal Trimachi)	Shout 227
OUR LOVE GROWS (Freddie Scott)-1	Shout unissued

ERMA FRANKLIN (vo) with tp; tb; ts; bs; p; 2g; el-b; dm; tamb; prob. The Sweet Inspirations: Cissy Houston, Sylvia Shemwell, Myrna Smith, Estelle Brown (bkd-vo). Omit horns-1. Arr-cond. by Garry Sherman. Prod. by Bert Berns.

Bell Sound Studios, New York, November 1967

S-20060 OPEN UP YOUR SOUL (Bert Berns,Jerry Ragovoy)	Shout 230
S-20069 THE RIGHT TO CRY (Gerry Goffin,Carole King)-1	Shout 234

VAN MORRISON (vo) with Al Gorgoni or Hugh McCracken or Donald Thomas (2g); Bob Bushnell or Russell Savakus (el-b); Herbie Lovelle or Gary Chester (dm). Prod. by Bert Berns.

Incredible Sounds Studios, New York, December 11, 1967

(edit) JOE HARPER SATURDAY MORNING (Van Morrison) (2.53)   Bang LP222

ABBREVIATIONS

ac-g = acoustic guitar, arr = arranged, as = alto saxophone, b = upright bass, BBadmo/dy/yr = Billboard advertisement date, BBmo/dy/yr = Billboard review date, bgo = bongos, bjo = banjo, bkd-vo = background vocal, bs = baritone saxophone, CBadmo/dy/yr = Cash Box advertisement date, CBmo/dy/yr = Cash Box review date, cga = congas, cl = clarinet, cond = conducted, COPmo/dy/yr = U.S. Copyright registration date, dir = directed, (E) = English/U.K. issue, el-b = electric bass, el-p = electric piano, (F) = French issue, f-h = french horn, fem-cho = female chorus, fl = flute, (G) = German issue, g = electric guitar, hca = harmonica, (J) = Japanese issue, LOCmo/dy/yr = Library of Congress registration date, mixed-cho = male and female chorus, orch = orchestra, org = organ, p = piano, perc = percussion, prob = probably, prod = produced, rel = released, s = saxophone, ss = soprano saxophone, tamb = tambourine, tb = trombone, tp = trumpet, ts = tenor saxophone, tu = tuba, v = violin, vb = vibes, vo = vocal, xyl = xylophone.

ACKNOWLEDGMENTS

THE NAME BERT Berns first stood out to me reading Charlie Gillett's landmark history of rock music, *The Sound of the City*, where I immediately recognized a common ingredient to the records Berns made that Gillett cited. I spent years looking for his name in the small print on 45 RPM records. Some of his best records were never hits. His music became a subject of fascination for me. I wrote an article in the *San Francisco Chronicle* in 1975 about Berns that attracted the attention of both Jerry Wexler, his mentor, and Ilene Berns, his widow.

Occasionally I would run into people who knew him and ask them about the man. Tony Orlando was one—I was following him around for another *Chronicle* article on the day of his return to performing after a year recovering from a dramatic breakdown, a big day in his life to be sure—and he introduced me to his friend, Brooks Arthur, who came to the Bay Area to spend the day with Tony. Brooks engineered many of Berns's greatest records.

I met Cassandra Berns, his grown daughter, at a performance by Big Brother and the Holding Company in San Francisco in 1994 when Melissa Etheridge was going to sit in with the band and sing three songs as a kind of audition for a film under preproduction at the time on the life of Janis Joplin. The producers had paid a lot of money for the rights to the Berns song "Piece of My Heart" and were probably even going to use the song's title for the movie. Cassandra's brother Brett Berns was sick that night at his hotel room, but when we did finally meet some weeks later, the idea for the book was born in a memorable night playing those old 45s and staying up way too late talking.

Most of the interviews for this book were conducted in New York, Nashville, and Los Angeles between May and November 1998. The actuarial tables have been cruel to this generation since then. Among the losses—Ellie Greenwich, Gene Pitney, Phil Ramone, Red Schwartz, Ray Passman, Solomon Burke, Wilson Pickett, Jimmy Jones, Jerry Leiber, Jerry Ragovoy, Tom Dowd, Hal David, Herbie Wasserman, Paul Griffin, Erma Franklin, Paul Marshall, Sid Bernstein, Linda Laurie, Berns's niece Robin Levine, all these and more.

Many people went above and beyond in assisting. Richard Gottehrer conducted a memorable tour of the hallways of 1650 Broadway and the neighborhood. Jerry Leiber kept inviting me back, took me to dinner at Lawry's, and was his magnificent self on all occasions. Wassel (Carmine DeNoia) was a gracious host at many dinners and always an entertaining, congenial companion. Solomon Burke met me at his "office," Jerry's Deli in the Valley, and Jeff Barry spent all afternoon sitting around the pool at the Sunset Marquis. Doug Morris cleared his schedule to talk Berns and fondle old 45s. Phil Ramone canceled his interview midsession to schedule another, longer interview. Ellie Greenwich spent months avoiding a meeting, but when she finally invited me over, she spent the rest of the day reliving events and revisiting feelings she would have rather not. Berns's old pals Ray Passman and Paul Colby made major contributions. Ilene Berns gave me six hours of passion, fury, and offense taken at forty-year-old insults as fresh as if they had been delivered only the week before.

Neil Zusman served as investigator, administrative assistant, driver, and confidant during the New York stage of the project. "Moist" Paula Henderson, the world's sexiest baritone sax player, transcribed the interviews and already had Betty Harris records in her collection. The late, great Pat Baird at BMI provided a lot of encouragement, support, and photos. John Ingrassia at Sony Music took time to help.

Interviews included Solomon Burke, Betty Harris, Garnet Mimms, Charles Thomas, Ben E. King, Barbara Lewis, Sarah Dash, Wilson Pickett, Freddie Scott, Rick Derringer, Erma Franklin, Jerry Leiber, Mike Stoller, Jeff Barry, Ellie Greenwich, Tom Dowd, Brooks Arthur, Phil Ramone, Artie Butler, Garry Sherman, Jerry Ragovoy, Ray Passman, Paul Colby, Ilene Berns, Ersel Hickey, Mickey Lee Lane, Dion DiMucci, Don Drowty, Cornelia Medley, Sylvia and Al Levine, Robin Levine, Carmine DeNoia, Burt Gordon, Bob Feldman, Richard Gottehrer, Juggy Murray, Cissy Houston, Peter Sullivan, Julie Rifkind, Roy Rifkind, Bob Rolontz, Bob Altschuler, Miriam Bienstock, Juggy Gayles, Sammy Vargas, Janet Minto, Paul Marshall, Felix Cavaliere, Jimmy Jones, Carole King, Bob Crewe, Seymour Strauss, Irv Hertzog, Hy Weiss, Marcy Burke, Peter Anders, Ritchie Cordell, Richie Barrett, Johnny Otis, James Johnson, Marv Schlacter, Gil Hamilton, Wally Roker, Hal David, Doug Morris, Jack Hooke, Bertha Morris, Howard Storm, Rita Brookshire, Artie Resnick, Red Schwartz, Ed Silvers, Lennie Bleecher, Tony Powers, Gene Pitney, Grelun Landon, Herb Cox, Ray Smith, Linda Laurie, Bob Johnston, Beverly Warren, Brenda Reid, Kenny Hamber, Artie Wayne, Tami Lynn, Andrew Loog Oldham, Ren Gravatt, Billy Fields, Herb Wasserman, Joan Wile, Nik Cohn, Seymour Stein, Joshie Jo Armstead, Joseph Shefsky, Paul Griffin, Morty Craft, David Kapralik, Kenny Rankin, Sid Bernstein, Patricia Mellin, Fred Gershon, Chris Huston, Beverly Lee, Valerie Simpson, Eric Burdon, and Burt Bacharach.

The British Berns Bureau, Rob Hughes and Mick Patrick, blazed many trails, conducted a number of interviews, and were key conspirators. Their Ace Records collections (*The Bert Berns Story*, Vols. 1 & 2) remain the definitive set. The Rob Hughes sessionography is the single greatest work of Berns scholarship.

Many fellow journalists generously shared information. Jerry Capeci gave me a Gangster 101 tutorial over lunch in Brooklyn. Tony Scherman had done a lot of spadework on the Brill Building; his files were invaluable. The late, great Alan Betrock was a huge supporter; his papers led to the discovery of the Berns demo tapes. Ned Sublette, Cuban music's greatest historian, has cheered the project along from those first days in New York. Many others helped: Fred Dannen, John Jackson, John Broven, William Knoedelseder, Dan Moldea, Richard Ben-Veniste. Bill Bastone showed me the FBI files on Tommy Eboli. Some old-hand FBI agents remembered the record business: John Pritchard, Joe Spinelli, Victor Guerrero.

Records by Val Shively, John Tefteller, Craig Moerer. Also Ray Passman, Alan Betrock (by way of Andy Schwartz). Robert Christgau loaned the use of his stereo and apartment to record a stack of borrowed 45s. Alan Warner managed to locate the Bert Berns demo tape from Mellin publishing in the vast EMI Music publishing archives. Ilene Berns started it off all those years ago sending me those Freddie Scott and Arsenio Rodriguez albums.

Thanks also to the San Francisco Public Library, the Performing Arts Library at Lincoln Center, New York, the Rock and Roll Hall of Fame Library and Archive, Cleveland, Ohio, and the *San Francisco Chronicle* library.

Frank Weimann of the Literary Group has put up with this venture for many moons. Editor Charlie Winton of Counterpoint Press is the real hero of the book, a swashbuckling publisher, brilliant editor, and friend for life. Dennis McNally gave the draft the first read. Thanks to the whole Counterpoint team, especially production coordinator Kelly Winton, copyeditor Mikayla Butchart, publicist Megan Fishmann and cover designer Tim Green.

In my personal life, so many people have been so supportive for so long, it would be a big mistake to try to single them out, but I would be highly remiss were I not to mention both my dear ex-wife, Keta Bill, and my great pal and wise counsel, Mark Schickman. And, as always, I am deeply grateful for the love of my darling daughter, Carla Selvin.

BIBLIOGRAPHY

BOOKS

Abadinsky, Howard. *Organized Crime*, 6th ed. Belmont, CA: Wadsworth, 2000.

Bach, Steven. *Marlene Dietrich: Life and Legend*. Cambridge: Da Capo, 1992.

Bacharach, Burt, with Robert Greenfield. *Anyone Who Had a Heart: My Life and Music*. New York: Harper Collins, 2013.

Bego, Mark. *I Fall to Pieces: The Music and the Life of Patsy Cline*. New York: Adams Media, 1995.

Bernstein, Sid, as told to Arthur Aaron. *"It's Sid Bernstein Calling . . . ": The Promoter Who Brought the Beatles to America*. New York: Jonathan David, 2002.

Betrock, Alan. *Girl Groups: The Story of a Sound*. New York: Delilah Books, 1982.

Bleiel, Jeff. *That's All: Bobby Darin on Record, Stage & Screen*. Ann Arbor, MI: Popular Culture Ink, 1993.

Bono, Sonny. *And the Beat Goes On*. New York: Pocket Books, 1991.

Bowman, Rob. *Soulsville U.S.A.: The Story of Stax Records*. New York: Schirmer Trade Books, 1997.

Brocken, Michael: *Bacharach: Maestro! The Life of a Pop Genius*. London: Chrome Dreams, 2003.

Bronson, Fred: *The Billboard Book of Number 1 Hits*. New York: Billboard Books, 1992.

Broven, John. *Record Makers and Breakers: Voices of the Independent Rock 'N' Roll Pioneers*. Champaign: University of Illinois, 2009.

———. *Walking to New Orleans: The Story of New Orleans Rhythm & Blues*. Sussex: Blues Unlimited, 1974.

Brown, Ruth, with Andrew Yule. *Miss Rhythm: The Autobiography of Ruth Brown, Rhythm and Blues Legend*. New York: Donald I. Fine Books, 1996.

Bruck, Connie. *Master of the Game: Steve Ross and the Creation of Time Warner*. New York: Simon & Schuster, 1994.

Bushkin, Richard. *Inside Tracks: A First-Hand History of Popular Music from the World's Greatest Record Producers and Engineers*. New York: Avon Books, 1999.

Charles, Ray, and David Ritz. *Brother Ray: Ray Charles' Own Story*. New York: Dial, 1978.

Clarke, Donald. *The Rise and Fall of Popular Music*. New York: St. Martin's Griffin, 1995.

Cohen, Mitchell S. *Carole King: A Biography in Words & Pictures*. New York: Chappell Music, 1976.

Cohn, Nik. *Rock from the Beginning*. New York: Stein and Day, 1969.

Cohodas, Nadine. *Queen: The Life and Music of Dinah Washington*. New York: Pantheon Books, 2004.

Colby, Paul, with Martin Fitzpatrick. *The Bitter End Years: Hanging Out at America's Nightclub.* New York: Cooper Square, 2002.

Coleman, Ray. *The Man Who Made the Beatles: An Intimate Biography of Brian Epstein.* New York: McGraw-Hill, 1989.

Cornyn, Stan, with Paul Scanlon. *Exploding: The Highs, Hits, Hype, Heroes, and Hustlers of the Warner Music Group.* New York: HarperEntertainment, 2002.

Cotten, Lee. *Shake Rattle & Roll: The Golden Age of American Rock 'n Roll.* Vol. 1, *1952–1955.* Ypsilanti, MI: Pierian, 1989.

Cross, Colin, with Paul Kendall and Mick Farren. *Encyclopedia of British Beat Groups & Solo Artists of the Sixties.* London: Omnibus, 1980.

Cunningham, Mark. *Good Vibrations: A History of Record Production.* London: Sanctuary, 1996.

Dachs, David. *Anything Goes: The World of Popular Music.* Indianapolis: Bobbs-Merrill, 1964.

Dannen, Frederic. *Hit Men: Power Brokers and Fast Money inside the Music Business.* New York: Vintage Books, 1990.

Darden, Robert. *People Get Ready!: A New History of Black Gospel Music.* New York: Continuum, 2004.

Darin, Dodd. *Dream Lovers: The Magnificent Shattered Lives of Bobby Darin and Sandra Dee.* New York: Warner Books, 1994.

Davis, John H. *Mafia Dynasty: The Rise and Fall of the Gambino Crime Family.* New York: HarperTorch, 1993.

Dawson, Jim, and Steve Propes. *What Was the First Rock 'n' Roll Record.* London: Faber & Faber, 1992.

———. *The Twist: The Story of the Dance That Changed the World.* London: Faber & Faber, 1995.

DiMucci, Dion, with Davin Seay. *The Wanderer: Dion's Story.* Sag Harbor, NY: Beech Tree Books, 1988.

Dobkin, Matt. *I Never Loved a Man the Way I Love You: Aretha Franklin, Respect, and the Making of a Soul Music Masterpiece.* New York: St. Martin's, 2004.

Dominic, Serene. *Burt Bacharach: Song By Song.* New York: Schirmer Trade Books, 2003.

Doncaster, Patrick, and Tony Jasper with Cliff Richard. *Cliff.* London: Sidgwick & Jackson, 1981.

Douglas, Tony. *Lonely Teardrops: The Jackie Wilson Story.* London: Sanctuary, 1997.

Einarson, John, and Richie Furay. *For What It's Worth: The Story of Buffalo Springfield.* London: Rogan House, 1997.

Elliott, Martin. *The Rolling Stones: Complete Recording Sessions, from the Early Chart-Toppers to the Infamous Rarities—January 1963 to November 1989.* London: Blandford, 1990.

Emerson, Ken. *Always Magic in the Air: The Bomp and Brilliance of the Brill Building Era.* New York: Viking Penguin, 2005.

Ertegun, Ahmet, et al. *What'd I Say: The Atlantic Story; 50 Years of Music.* New York: Welcome Rain, 2001.

Evanier, David. *Roman Candle: The Life of Bobby Darin.* Stuttgart, Germany: Holtzbrinck, 2004.

Ewen, David. *All the Years of American Popular Music: A Comprehensive History.* Upper Saddle River, NJ: Prentice Hall, 1977.

Fisher, Eddie. *Eddie: My Life, My Loves.* New York: Harper & Row, 1981.

Fitzpatrick, John J., and James E. Fogerty. *Collecting Phil Spector: The Man, the Legend, and the Music.* Saint Paul, MN: Spectacle Press, 1991.

Fletcher, Tony. *All Hopped Up And Ready to Go: Music from the Streets of New York 1927–77*. New York: W. W. Norton, 2009.

Floyd, Samuel A. Jr. *The Power of Black Music: Interpreting Its History from Africa to the United States*. Oxford: Oxford University, 1995.

Fong-Torres, Ben. *The Hits Just Keep on Coming; The History of Top 40 Radio*. San Francisco: Miller Freeman Books, 1998.

———. *Not Fade Away: A Backstage Pass to 20 Years of Rock & Roll*. San Francisco: Miller Freeman Books, 1999.

Foster, Mo. *Play like Elvis: How British Musicians Bought the American Dream*. London: Sanctuary, 2000.

Fox, Ted. *In the Groove: The People behind the Music*. New York: St. Martin's, 1986.

Frame, Pete. *The Restless Generation: How Rock Music Changed the Face of 1950s Britain*. London: Rogan House, 2007.

Francis, Connie. *Who's Sorry Now?* New York: St. Martin's, 1984.

Franzese, Michael, and Dary Matera. *Quitting the Mob: How the "Yuppie Don" Left the Mafia and Lived to Tell His Story*. New York: HarperCollins, 1992.

Friedman, Josh Alan. *Tell the Truth until They Bleed: Coming Clean in the Dirty World of Blues and Rock 'n' Roll*. New York: Backbeat Books, 2008.

Friedwald, Will. *Sinatra! The Song Is You, A Singer's Art*. New York: Scribner, 1995.

Garland, Phyl. *The Sound of Soul*. Chicago: Henry Regnery, 1969.

George, Nelson. *Where Did Our Love Go?: The Rise and Fall of the Motown Sound*. New York: St. Martin's, 1985.

Gillett, Charlie. *The Sound of the City: The Rise of Rock and Roll*. New York: Outerbridge & Dienstfrey, 1970.

———. *Making Tracks: Atlantic Records and the Growth of a Multi-Billion-Dollar Industry*. New York: E. P. Dutton, 1974.

Goldman, Albert. *Elvis*. New York: McGraw-Hill, 1981.

Gould, Jonathan. *Can't Buy Me Love: The Beatles, Britain, and America*. New York: Three Rivers, 2007.

Gourse, Leslie. *Sassy: The Life of Sarah Vaughan*. New York: Charles Scribner's Sons, 1993.

Graham, Bobby, and Patrick Harrington. *The Session Man: The Story of Bobby Graham*. Raglan, UK: Broom House, 2004.

Greenfield, Robert. *The Last Sultan: The Life and Times of Ahmet Ertegun*. New York: Simon & Schuster, 2012.

Groia, Phillip. *They All Sang on the Corner: A Second Look at New York City's Rhythm and Blues Vocal Groups*. Port Jefferson, NY: Phillie Dee Enterprises, 1983.

Guralnick, Peter. *Sweet Soul Music: Rhythm and Blues and the Southern Dream of Freedom*. New York: Harper & Row, 1986.

Halberstadt, Alex. *Lonely Avenue: The Unlikely Life & Times of Doc Pomus*. Cambridge: Da Capo, 2007.

Hamm, Charles. *Yesterdays: Popular Song in America*. New York: W. W. Norton, 1979.

Heilbut, Anthony. *The Gospel Sound: Good News and Bad Times*. New York: Simon & Schuster, 1971.

Heylin, Clinton. *Bob Dylan: A Life in Stolen Moments, Day by Day; 1941–1995*. New York: Schirmer Trade Books, 1996.

———. *Van Morrison: Can You Feel the Silence?* New York: Viking, 2002.

Hildebrand, Lee. *Stars of Soul and Rhythm & Blues: Top Recording Artists and Showstopping Performers, from Memphis and Motown to Now*. New York: Billboard Books, 1994.

Holz, Charlie. *MegaGuide to Singles.* N.p.: PSG-HomeCraft Software, 1996.

Houston, Cissy, with Jonathan Singer. *How Sweet the Sound: My Life with God and Gospel.* New York: Doubleday, 1998.

Howlett, Kevin. *The Beatles at the Beeb: The Story of Their Radio Career, 1962–65.* Ypsilanti, MI: Pierian, 1983.

Hyland, William G. *The Song Is Ended: Songwriters and American Music, 1900–1950.* Oxford: Oxford University, 1995.

Jackson, Hal, with James Haskins. *The House That Jack Built: My Life as a Trailblazer in Broadcasting and Entertainment.* New York: Amistad, 2001.

Jackson, John A. *American Bandstand: Dick Clark and the Making of a Rock 'n' Roll Empire.* Oxford: Oxford University, 1997.

———. *Big Beat Heat: Alan Freed and the Early Years of Rock & Roll.* New York: Schirmer, 1991.

Jasen, David. *Tin Pan Alley: The Composers, the Songs, the Performers, and Their Times; The Golden Age of American Popular Music from 1886 to 1956.* New York: Donald I. Fine Books, 1988.

Jenkins, Stephen. *The Story of the Bronx from the Purchase Made by the Dutch from the Indians in 1639 to the Present Day.* New York: G. P. Putnam's Sons, 1912.

Jepsen, Jorgen Grunnet, ed. *Jazz Records 1942–1965.* Holte, Denmark: Karl Emil Knudsen, 1966.

Jorgensen, Ernst. *Elvis Presley: A Life in Music; The Complete Recording Sessions.* New York: St. Martin's, 1998.

King, Carole. *A Natural Woman: A Memoir.* New York: Grand Central Publishing, 2012.

Knoedelseder, William. *Stiffed: A True Story of MCA, the Music Business, and the Mafia.* New York: HarperCollins, 1993.

LaBelle, Patti, with Laura B. Randolph. *Don't Block the Blessings: Revelations of a Lifetime.* New York: Riverhead Books, 1996.

Lacey, Robert. *Little Man: Meyer Lansky and the Gangster Life.* New York: Little, Brown, 1991.

Larkin, Colin, ed. *The Guinness Encyclopedia of Popular Music.* London: Guinness, 1992.

Leiber, Jerry, and Mike Stoller with David Ritz. *Hound Dog: The Leiber & Stoller Autobiography.* New York: Simon & Schuster, 2009.

Leiber, Jerry, with Bob Spitz. "A Hound Dog's Life: Gospel, Half-Truths, Rumors, and Outrageous Lies." Unpublished manuscript, 1995.

Lewisohn, Mark. *The Beatles Recording Sessions: The Official Abbey Road Studio Session Notes 1962–1970.* New York: Harmony Books, 1988.

Liebling, A.J. *The Telephone Booth Indian.* New York: Doubleday, Doran, 1942.

Lucchese, John A. *Joey Dee and the Story of the Twist: The Star Who Brought the Crowds to New York's Peppermint Lounge.* New York: Macfadden Books, 1962.

Lydon, Michael. *Ray Charles: Man and Music.* New York: Riverhead Books, 1998.

Maas, Peter. *The Valachi Papers.* New York: G.P. Putnam's Sons, 1968.

MacDonald, Ian. *Revolution in the Head: The Beatles' Records and the Sixties.* New York: Henry Holt, 1994.

Macfarlane, Colin. *Tom Jones: The Boy from Nowhere.* New York: St. Martin's, 1988.

Marcus, Greil. *The Dustbin of History.* Cambridge: Harvard University, 1995.

Marks, Edward B., with Abbott J. Liebling. *They All Sang: From Tony Pastor to Rudy Vallee.* New York: Viking, 1934.

Marsh, Dave. *Before I Get Old: The Story of the Who.* New York: St. Martin's, 1983.

———. *Louie Louie: The History and Mythology of the World's Most Famous Rock 'n Roll Song.* Ann Arbor: University of Michigan, 1993.

Marx, Samuel, and Jan Clayton. *Rodgers & Hart: Bewitched, Bothered, and Bewildered.* New York: G.P. Putnam's Sons, 1976.

May, Chris, and Tim Phillips. *British Beat.* London: Socion Books, 1979.

McAleer, Dave. *The Fab British Rock 'n' Roll Invasion of 1964.* New York: St. Martin's, 1994.

Millar, Bill. *The Coasters.* London: Star Books, 1975.

———. *The Drifters: The Rise and Fall of the Black Vocal Group.* New York: Collier Books, 1971.

Morrow, Cousin Bruce, and Laura Baudo. *Cousin Brucie: My Life in Rock 'n' Roll Radio.* Sag Harbor, NY: Beech Tree Books, 1987.

Murray, Albert. *Good Morning Blues: The Autobiography of Count Basie.* New York: Random House, 1985.

Nash, Jay Robert. *World Encyclopedia of Organized Crime.* Cambridge: Da Capo, 1993.

Nassour, Ellis. *Honky Tonk Angel: The Intimate Story of Patsy Cline.* New York: St. Martin's, 1993.

Nolan, Frederick. *Lorenz Hart: A Poet on Broadway.* Oxford: Oxford University Press, 1994.

Norman, Philip. *Shout! The Beatles in Their Generation.* New York: Fireside, 2003.

———. *Symphony for the Devil: The Rolling Stones Story.* New York: Simon & Schuster, 1984.

O'Neil, Thomas. *The Grammys: For the Record.* New York: Penguin, 1993.

Oldham, Andrew Loog. *Stoned.* New York: Vintage Books, 2003.

Olsen, Dale A., and Daniel E. Sheehy. *South America, Mexico, Central America, and the Caribbean.* Vol. 2, *The Garland Encyclopedia of World Music.* New York: Garland, 1998.

Orlando, Tony, with Patsi Bale Cox. *Halfway to Paradise.* New York: St. Martin's, 2002.

Palmer, Robert. *Baby, That Was Rock & Roll: The Legendary Leiber & Stoller.* San Diego: Harvest/HBJ, 1979.

Passman, Arnold. *The Deejays.* London: Macmillan, 1971.

Podolsky, Rich. *Don Kirshner: The Man With the Golden Ear; How He Changed the Face of Rock and Roll.* Milwaukee: Hal Leonard Books, 2012.

Posner, Gerald. *Motown: Music, Money, Sex, and Power.* New York: Random House, 2002.

Powell, Josephine. *Tito Puente: When the Drums Are Dreaming.* Bloomington: AuthorHouse, 2007.

Reese, Della, with Franklin Lett and Mimi Eichler. *Angels along the Way: My Life with Help from Above.* New York: G.P. Putnam's Sons, 1997.

Reig, Teddy, and Edward Berger. *Reminiscing in Tempo: My Life as a Jazz Hustler.* Metuchen, NJ: Scarecrow Press and the Institute of Jazz Studies, Rutgers University, 1990.

Repsch, John. *The Legendary Joe Meek: The Telstar Man.* London: Woodford House, 1989.

Ribowski, Mark. *He's a Rebel: The Truth about Phil Spector—Rock and Roll's Legendary Madman.* New York: E.P. Dutton, 1989.

Rice, Jo, and Tim Rice, Paul Gambaccini, and Mike Read. *The Guinness Book of British Hit Singles.* London: Guinness, 1977.

Roberts, John Storm. *The Latin Tinge: The Impact of Latin American Music on the United States.* Oxford: Oxford University Press, 1979.

Rogan, Johnny. *Starmakers and Svengalis: The History of British Pop Management.* New York: Futura, 1988.

———. *Van Morrison: No Surrender.* London: Secker & Warburg, 2005.

Rohde, H. Kandy. *The Gold of Rock & Roll 1955–1967.* Westminister, MD: Arbor House, 1970.

Ruppli, Michel. *Atlantic Records: A Discography.* Westport, CT: Greenwood, 1979.

Salerno, Ralph, and John S. Tompkins. *The Crime Confederation.* Garden City, NY: Doubleday, 1969.

Secrest, Meryle. *Somewhere for Me: A Biography of Richard Rodgers.* New York: Knopf, 2001.

Sedaka, Neil. *Laughter in the Rain: My Own Story.* New York: G.P. Putnam's Sons, 1982.

Selvin, Joel. *Ricky Nelson: Idol for a Generation.* Chicago: Contemporary Books, 1990.

Shaw, Arnold. *Honkers and Shouters: The Golden Years of Rhythm & Blues.* London: Macmillan, 1978.

———. *The Rockin' 50s.* New York: Hawthorn, 1974.

———. *The Street That Never Slept.* Coward, McCann & Geoghegan, 1971.

———. *The World of Soul: Black America's Contribution to the Pop Music Scene.* New York: Cowles, 1970.

Simon, George T. *The Big Bands.* London: Macmillan, 1967.

Smith, Joe. *Off the Record: An Oral History of Popular Music.* New York: Warner Books, 1988.

Smith, Wes. *The Pied Pipers of Rock 'n' Roll: Radio Deejays of the 50s and 60s.* Atlanta: Longstreet, 1989.

Southall, Brian. *Abbey Road: The Story of the World's Most Famous Recording Studios.* Somerset, U.K.: Patrick Stephens, 1982.

Spitz, Bob. *The Beatles: The Biography.* New York: Little, Brown, 2005.

Starr, Michael Seth. *Bobby Darin: A Life.* Lanham, MD: Taylor Trade Publishing, 2004.

Tosches, Nick. *Unsung Heroes of Rock 'n' Roll.* New York: Charles Scribner's Sons, 1984.

Tremlett, George. *The Cliff Richard Story.* New York: Futura, 1975.

Turner, Steve. *Van Morrison: Too Late to Stop Now.* New York: Viking, 1993.

U.S. Treasury Department Bureau of Narcotics. *Mafia: The Government's Secret File on Organized Crime.* New York: Skyhorse, 2009.

Wade, Dorothy, and Justine Picardie. *Music Man: Ahmet Ertegun, Atlantic Records, and the Triumph of Rock 'n' Roll.* New York: W.W. Norton, 1990.

Warner, Jay. *The Billboard Book of American Singing Groups: A History, 1940–1990.* New York: Billboard Books, 1992.

Wasserman, Herb. *A Different Drummer: What Makes Me Tic, A Memoir.* Lincoln, NE: Writers Club, 2000.

Weller, Sheila. *Girls Like Us: Carole King, Joni Mitchell, Carly Simon—and the Journey of a Generation.* New York: Washington Square, 2008.

Werner, Craig. *A Change Is Gonna Come: Music, Race & the Soul of America.* New York: Plume, 1998.

———. *Higher Ground: Stevie Wonder, Aretha Franklin, Curtis Mayfield, and the Rise and Fall of American Soul.* New York: Crown Publishers, 2004.

Wexler, Jerry, and David Ritz. *Rhythm and the Blues: A Life in American Music.* New York: Knopf, 1993.

Whitburn, Joel. *Joel Whitburn's Top Pop Albums 1955–1992.* Menomonee Falls, WI: Record Research, 1993.

———. *Joel Whitburn's Top Pop Records 1940–1955.* Menomonee Falls, WI: Record Research, 1973.

————. *Joel Whitburn's Top Pop Singles 1955–1993*. Menomonee Falls, WI: Record Research, 1994.

————. *Joel Whitburn's Top Rhythm & Blues Records 1949–1971*. Menomonee Falls, WI: Record Research, 1973.

Wild, David. *He Is . . . I Say: How I Learned to Stop Worrying and Love Neil Diamond*. Cambridge: Da Capo, 2008.

Wiseman, Rich. *Neil Diamond: Solitary Star*. New York: Dodd, Mead, 1987.

Zmijewsky, Steven, and Boris Zmijewsky. *Elvis: The Films and Career of Elvis Presley*. New York: Citadel, 1976.

ARTICLES, LINER NOTES, INTERVIEWS, HEARINGS

"ABC-Para. Seeks Other Lines for New Gotham Operation." *Billboard* (November 9, 1963).

"ABC-Paramount Will Reactivate Apt Label." *Billboard* (January 9, 1965).

"America's Favorite Offshore Resorts." *House & Garden* (May 1956).

"Atl. Debuts Budget Line; 21 LP's Out." *Billboard* (June 19, 1965).

"Atl. Has Hot Sales Summer." *Billboard* (August 30, 1966).

"Atl. Sales Doubled in 1967—8 Singles Hit Gold; Albums Spurt." *Billboard* (January 6, 1968).

"Atl'ic, Atco Waxes Hot." *Billboard* (August 1, 1964).

"Atlantic Back on 'Hot 100.'" *Billboard* (May 9, 1964).

"Atlantic Ends Strong Year." *Billboard* (December 11, 1961).

"Atlantic Getting into the Swing-Frug, Etc." *Billboard* (March 6, 1965).

"Atlantic Has Sales Burst." *Billboard* (May 1, 1965).

"Atlantic Hits $7 Million for Firm's Biggest Score." *Billboard* (December 29, 1962).

"Atlantic Making UK Take Notice with Five Hot-Selling Records." *Billboard* (September 17, 1966).

"Atlantic Says Company Is Not for Sale." *Billboard* (June 5, 1965).

"Atlantic, New Orleans Disk Producer in Singles Pact." *Billboard* (May 29, 1965).

"Atlantic's Ahmet Ertegun Says the Public Will Keep Twistin'." *Billboard* (February 24, 1962).

"Berns Solos Bang; Maps New Horizons." *Billboard* (July 23, 1966).

"Bert Berns Is Dead at 38." *Billboard* (January 13, 1968).

"Big 7 Making Drive to Get New Writers." *Billboard* (March 27, 1965).

"Bossa Nova Wave Loses Nothing in Translation." *Billboard* (September 1, 1962).

"Burns [sic] Forms Keetch; Dist. Is Atlantic." *Billboard* (March 21, 1964).

"Dee, Edsels, Jones & Jazz Sell in N.Y.C." *Billboard* (February 24, 1962).

"Goldner Quits Roulette to Go on Own." *Billboard* (June 22, 1963).

"Goldner Runs Tiger & Daisy." *Billboard* (March 7, 1964).

"Has the Twist Had It Trade Sees Fad Fading Fast." *Billboard* (May 26, 1962).

"Is Bossa Nova the new Twist?" *Billboard* (September 1, 1962).

"Leiber, Stoller Form Own Production Co.; Serving All." *Billboard* (January 30, 1961).

"Leiber, Stoller Team Join UA." *Billboard* (August 14, 1961).

"Mike Off Again." *Melody Maker* (October 10, 1964).

"N.Y. Becomes Twistin' Town U.S.A. as Dance Fad Grows." *Billboard* (November 13, 1961).

"Nevins-Kirshner Score With Artists, Cleffers." *Billboard* (November 27, 1961).

"News of the World." *Billboard* (October 24, 1964).

"Phil Kahl Sells Interests in Pubs, Roulette Diskery" *Billboard* (January 20, 1962).

"Planetary Buys Kolsky Interest in Roulette." *Billboard* (August 21, 1961).

"Rifkind Named Manager of Bang Records." *Billboard* (May 29, 1965).

"Roulette Acquires 'Hanky Panky' Disk." *Billboard* (May 21, 1966).

"Roulette Wheels Turn Again." *Billboard* (September 12, 1964).

"Signing of Bobby Darin Start of Capitol Beef-Up." *Billboard* (July 21, 1962).

"Singles Get N.Y.C. Boro Action; Crystals on Philles Break out." *Billboard* (November 6, 1961).

"Solomons Set Brisk Pace for U.K. Music Business." *Billboard* (February 6, 1965).

"Talmadge Resigns from UA: Picker in." *Billboard* (February 15, 1964).

"United Artists Records Hits Top Mark of $7 Million in 1962." *Billboard* (January 8, 1963).

"US A&R Man on Decca Talent Search." *Melody Maker* (October 5, 1963).

"Webb [*sic*] IV Formed by Berns, Atl. Officers." *Billboard* (March 6, 1965).

"Weintraub Whirling into World of Folk." *Billboard* (May 25, 1963).

"Wexler Bats Down a Rumor." *Billboard* (October 26, 1963).

Ackerman, Paul, and June Bundy. "20-Year Shift in Music Patterns." *Billboard* (November 5, 1959).

Arfin, Richard. "The 'Shadow' Reappears." *Goldmine* (July 12, 1991).

Ball, Susan. "50s Doo-Wop Group Renews Harmony." *The New York Times* (August 13, 1995).

Bemelmans, Ludwig. "The Best Way to See Cuba." *Holiday* (December 1957).

Bennetts, Leslie. "Devil in a Bespoke Suit." *Vanity Fair* (January 1998).

Berns, Bert. *Blowin' Your Mind!* LP liner notes. Bang Records (1967).

———. *Give 'Em Soul* LP liner notes. Capitol Records (1963).

Charles, Don. "The Hit Sound of Jeff Barry." *Goldmine* (April 2, 1993).

Chavetz, Zev. "Leiber and Stoller." *Los Angeles Times West Magazine* (March 19, 2006).

Clark, Sue. "Wexler: A Man of Dedication." *Rolling Stone* (September 28, 1968).

Colbert, Haines. "For Deejays: Babes, Booze and Bribes." *Miami News* (May 31, 1959).

Cole, David. "Ladies and gentleman, the next in line . . . Hoagy Lands." *In the Basement* (August/October 2001).

Dannen, Fredric. "The Godfather of Rock & Roll." *Rolling Stone* (November 17, 1988).

Fileti, Donn. *The Best of the Flamingos* CD booklet liner notes. Rhino Records (1990).

Fine, Marshall. "Tin Pan Alley's Myth." *Gannett Westchester Newspapers* (May 14, 1989).

Finkle, Dave. "Bert Berns: Soul Sauce." *Record World* (February 5, 1966).

Firestone, David. "Sure-Footed in the Slippery World of Rock." *The New York Times* (January 22, 1998).

Fish, Scott K. "Gary Chester: Taking a Stand." *Modern Drummer* (April 1983).

Flanagan, Bill. *Bang Masters* CD booklet liner notes. Legacy/Epic Records (1991).

Fricke, David. "Leiber and Stoller." *Rolling Stone* (April 19, 1990).

Garvey, Dennis. *The Exciters/Soul Motion: The Complete Bang, Shout and RCA Recordings 1966–1969* CD booklet. Ace Records (2009).

Geller, Harvey. "Broadway's Brill Building: The House the Hit Parade Built." *Rolling Stone* (February 14, 1974).

Gilliland, John. "Pop Chronicles." Unpublished transcripts of radio interviews with Mitch Miller, Leiber and Stoller, Burt Bacharach, Ahmet Ertegun, Jerry Wexler, Phil Spector. (1968).

Greene, Bob. "The Hood in Our Neighborhood." *Newsday* (December 24, 1965).

Grendysa, Peter. *Frankie Lymon and the Teenagers: The Complete Recordings* CD box set liner notes. Bear Family Records (1994).

Guralnick, Peter. "The Further Adventures of Doc Pomus: Call the Doctor." *Village Voice Rock & Roll Quarterly* (Summer 1988).

———. "They Wrote the Songs: Words, Music, and Irony by Leiber and Stoller." *Boston Phoenix* (March 20, 1979).

Halberstadt, Alex. "Jerry Wexler—The Great Atlantic Records Producer Gave Us Rhythm and Blues." *Salon.com* (September 6, 2000).

Hall, Claude. "Chappell Sells Back Rights to Roulette." *Billboard* (September 10, 1966).

Hilburn, Robert. "The Flip Side of Phil Spector." *Los Angeles Times* (February 13, 1977).

———. "Spector on Spector: 10 Golden Memories." *Los Angeles Times* (November 10, 1991).

Hirshey, Gerri. *Home in Your Heart: The Best of Solomon Burke* CD booklet liner notes. Rhino Records (1992).

Hoskyns, Barney. "The Soul Man with a Huckster's Soul." *Mojo* (September 1998).

Hughes, Rob. *Betty Harris: Soul Perfection Plus* CD booklet liner notes. Westside Records (1998).

Kamp, David. "The Hit Factory." *Vanity Fair* (November 2001).

Kaye, Lenny. "The Shadow Morton Story." *Melody Maker* (March 9, 1974).

Knoedelseder, William K. Jr. "Morris Levy: Big Clout in Record Business." *Los Angeles Times* (July 20, 1986).

Kolanjian, Steve. *The Best of Little Anthony and the Imperials* CD booklet liner notes. Rhino Records (1989).

———. *The Exciters: "Tell Him"* CD booklet liner notes. United Artists Records (1991).

Laredo, Joseph F. *Great Gentlemen of Song: Spotlight on Bob Manning* CD booklet liner notes. Capitol Records (1994).

Ledgerwood, Michael. Leiber and Stoller record company press biography. A&M Records (1975).

Lisheron, Mark. "Rhythm-and-Jews." *Common Quest* (Summer 1997).

Maher, Jack. "When Business Turns Soft, Just Work Harder—Atlantic." *Billboard* (June 6, 1963).

March, Michael. "Jerry Leiber: Talking Back." *Fusion* (1972).

Marsh, Dave. "The Paranoia of Romance: Welcome to Phil Spector's Nightmare." *Boston Phoenix* (March 29, 1977).

McFadden, Robert. "A Building with a History, from Bootleggers to Beatles." *The New York Times* (February 22, 1993).

Nathan, David. *Ben E. King Anthology* CD booklet liner notes. Rhino Records (1993).

Newman, Ralph. "The George Goldner Story as Told by Sam Goldner," parts 1–2. *Goldmine* (1974).

O'Haire, Patrick. "'September Song' for Tin Pan Alley." *New York Daily News* (September 15, 1974).

Patrick, Mick, and Rob Hughes. *The Bert Berns Story, Vol 1: Twist and Shout 1960–1964* CD booklet liner notes. Ace Records (2008).

Patrick, Mick. *The Bert Berns Story, Vol. 2: Mr. Success 1964–1967* CD booklet liner notes. Ace Records (2010).

Perez-Pena, Richard. "Here's Who First Asked Rock's Big Question." *The New York Times* (September 19, 1992).

Quaglieri, Al. *Hang On Sloopy: The Best of the McCoys* CD booklet liner notes. Legacy/Epic Records (1995).

———. *I Want Candy: The Best of the Strangeloves* CD booklet liner notes. Legacy/Epic Records (1995).

Redmond, Michael, and Steven West. *The Best of the Chantels* CD booklet liner notes. Rhino Records (1990).

———. *The Best of the Cleftones* CD booklet liner notes. Rhino Records (1990).

Reif, Rita. "Tin Pan Alley in Distress." *The New York Times* (April 11, 1976).

Rolontz, Bob. "Atlantic Records: Home of the Blues." *Music Business* (October 17, 1964).

———. "Double in Brass: Indie Promo Men Get New Status." *Billboard* (January 12, 1963).

———. "The Drifters: 10 Years at the Top." *Music Business* (February 13, 1965).

Rudman, Kal. "David & Bacharach Profile" part 1. *Billboard* (August 8, 1964).

———. "David & Bacharach Profile" part 2. *Billboard* (August 15, 1964).

Rutledge, Jeff. Unpublished transcript of interview with Morris Levy (n.d.).

Scherman, Tony. "Paul Griffin and the Musicians of Brill Building Pop." *Goldmine* (September 3, 1993).

———. "The Record Man." *Goldmine* (September 3, 1993).

Tosches, Nick. "Hipsters and Hoodlums." *Vanity Fair* (December 2000).

Traum, Happy. "Van Morrison: The Interview." *Rolling Stone* (July 9, 1970).

Trillin, Calvin. "You Don't Ask, You Don't Get." *The New Yorker* (February 25, 1991).

Trow, George W. S., Jr. "Eclectic, Reminiscent, Amused, Fickle, Perverse" part 1. *The New Yorker* (May 29, 1978), and June 5, 1978.

———. "Eclectic, Reminiscent, Amused, Fickle, Perverse" part 2. *The New Yorker* (June 5, 1978).

U.S. House of Representatives, Special Subcommittee on Legislature Oversight of the Committee on Interstate and Foreign Commerce. Testimony of George Goldner, Alan Freed. (1960).

Velie, Lester. "Suckers in Paradise." *Saturday Evening Post* (March 28, 1953).

Vera, Billy, and Randy Poe, et al. *Rockin' & Driftin'—The Drifters Box* CD box set liner notes. Rhino Records (1996).

Wenner, Jann. "Phil Spector: The *Rolling Stone* Interview." *Rolling Stone* (November 1, 1969).

Wexler, Jerry. "Personal Recollection: Clyde McPhatter & the Drifters Years." *Rolling Stone* (July 20, 1972).

Wexler, Mark S. "Phil Spector, Freaky Genius of Rock, Is Alive If Not Well and Searching for Gold Once More." *People* (September 22, 1975).

Williams, Richard. "In Pop, the Nearest Equivalent to Hitchcock Might Be Phil Spector." *Melody Maker* (November 27, 1976).

———. "Phil Spector." *Let It Rock* (October 1972).

Wilson, Earl. "Alan Freed Telling All." *New York Post* (November 25, 1959).

———. "They Work for a Song." *Liberty* (October 16, 1943).

INDEX